URBAN DYNAMICS

The use of computer models to simulate urban systems has developed rapidly in recent years. There have been two significant traditions: the first relates to the building of integrated models following the seminal research of Lowry first published in 1964, but with relatively simple submodels; the second has been intensive research on particular submodels with a variety of techniques. The companion volume to this book explored fully the range of possible techniques. In this volume, the most effective are selected for a model-building exercise which integrates the two traditions: the construction of an integrated model (in a modular form with alternative components) using the most advanced submodels. The book concludes with a presentation of an example of an operational model of this type.

The editors are among the most distinguished contributors to the subject. C.S. Bertuglia is a Professor at the Politechnico di Torino and the Universita di Udine. Dr Leonardi, until his untimely death in 1987, had had a distinguished research career, mainly at the International Institute for Applied Systems Analysis in Vienna. Both Professor Bertuglia and Dr Leonardi had a long association with the Istituto Ricerce Regionale Economic Sociale (IRES) in Turin. A.G. Wilson has been Professor of Urban and Regional Geography in the University of Leeds since 1970. The editors assembled an international team of distinguished authors to work with them: Alex Anas from Northwestern University in the United States, Gunther Haag from the University of Stuttgart and, particularly in the development of the integrated operational model, Sylvia Ocelli, Giovani Rabino and Roberto Tadei from IRES in Turin.

The authors, working as a team on the project on which the book is based, have created a unique synthesis which will prove essential reading for students and practitioners – indeed, all those in planning-related disciplines who need to be informed about the research front-line on the modelling of urban change.

URBAN DYNAMICS

Designing an integrated model

Edited by
C.S. Bertuglia, G. Leonardi and A.G. Wilson

ROUTLEDGE
London and New York

First published 1990
by Routledge
11 New Fetter Lane, London EC4P 4EE

Simultaneously published in the USA and Canada
by Routledge
a division of Routledge, Chapman and Hall, Inc.
29 West 35th Street, New York, NY 10001

© 1990 C.S. Bertuglia, G. Leonardi, and A.G. Wilson

Printed and bound in Great Britain by
Billings & Sons Limited, Worcester

British Library Cataloguing in Publication Data

Urban dynamics: designing an integrated model
  1. Urban regions. Social planning. Mathematical
models
  I. Bertuglia, C.S. (Cristo Sergio) II. Leonardi, G.
III. Wilson, A.G.
307′.12′0724
ISBN 0-415-00466-7

Library of Congress Cataloging in Publication Data

Urban dynamics: designing an integrated model / edited by C.S.
  Bertuglia, G. Leonardi, and A.G. Wilson.
     p. cm.
  Bibliography: p.
  Includes index.
  ISBN 0-415-00466-7
  1. Urban economics – Mathematical models. I. Bertuglia,
Cristoforo Sergio. II. Leonardi, Giorgio. III. Wilson, A.G. (Alan
Geoffrey), 1939–
HT321.U2914 1989
330.9173′2–dc19   89-5924
                                    CIP

CONTENTS

TABLES AND FIGURES

Tables

Figures

Contributors

A Anas
Department of Civil Engineering and Economics,
Northwestern University, Evanston, Ill.

C S Bertuglia
Istituto Ricerche Economico Sociale, Turin

G Haag
Institut für Theoretische Physik der
Universität Stuttgart

G Leonardi

S Occelli
Istituto Ricerche Economico Sociale, Turin

G Rabino
Istituto Ricerche Economico Sociale, Turin

R Tadei
Istituto Ricerche Economico Sociale, Turin

A G Wilson
School of Geography, University of Leeds

ACKNOWLEDGEMENTS

The research reported in this book is a continuation of a major transport project sponsored by the Italian Consiglio Nazionale delle Richerche (CNR) and we are very grateful for their support. The study was carried out under contract number CNR-IRES 82.000450.93. The meetings of the various contributing authors took place mostly in the Istituto Ricerche Economic-Sociale (IRES) in Turin and we are grateful for their hospitality. The book conforms with the research diffusion policies of the CNR.

We would particularly like to thank Mandy Smith for the effort and skills involved in producing the final typescript.

The Editors

Chapter 1

INTRODUCTION

C.S. Bertuglia and A.G. Wilson

1.1 Origins and Objectives of the Study

In order to fully understand the contents and aims of this book
we need to refer to a previous book, which in a sense represents
the first stage of a long-term project and has determined the
subsequent research policy followed here. The previous book is
Urban Systems: contemporary approaches to modelling, edited by
C S Bertuglia, G Leonardi, S Occelli, G A Rabino, R Tadei and
A G Wilson, published in 1987 by Croom Helm.

The task of designing an integrated dynamic urban model
required as a preliminary step an overall review of the current
approaches which appeared both promising and amenable to a consistent integration. The broad review of the first volume
covered such diverse approaches as economics, both classic (as
in the contribution of Beckmann) and Marxian (as in the contribution of Sheppard), stochastic choice theory (as in the
contribution of Leonardi), spatial interaction and dynamic
systems theory (as in the contributions of Wilson, Smith and
de Palma and Lefèvre), and so on.

However, since the work for the first volume was completed,
it became evident that relatively few paths of promising
research were emerging and that only few choices were sensible
within the seemingly endless list of different assemblies of
submodels. First, it was clear that the introduction and

treatment of dynamics had a prominent role as a theme for further exploration, being at the same time the main missing part in most existing urban models and the field in which more theoretical progress could be made, taking advantage of the recent achievements of nonlinear systems theory. 'Dynamics' is a very used, and often abused, term nowadays, and tends to be too generic without further qualifications. However, in the review, three distinct and well-defined types of dynamic approaches were identified as useful for urban modelling.

(a) The dynamics of the general accounting framework for changes of state of countable units (eg people), as in the compartmental models described by de Palma and Lefèvre in the first volume and in the master equations described by Haag in this volume. This type of dynamic model has a wide range of applications. Originated in physics, it has been shown to be well suited to cope with population mobility as well as such topics as housing and labour mobility.

(b) The dynamics of changes in physical stocks, that is the buildings required by urban activities. This type of dynamics is introduced and extended by Wilson in both volumes. Wilson shows how relatively simple models, combining spatial interaction theory with nonlinear differential equations, can produce non-trivial behaviour such as structural instability and bifurcations. Although the work of Wilson was originally designed to study the dynamics of retail activities, in both volumes it is shown how the approach can be extended to deal with many other types of urban stocks and infrastructures, including the transport network.

(c) The dynamics of choice behaviour, dealing with the way urban actors confronted with a choice situation (eg looking for a new dwelling) collect information about alternatives, evaluate them and select the preferred one. Of course the study of rational choice behaviour is not an entirely new subject, being a leading theme both in classic microeconomics and more recently in random utility theory. However, these approaches pay little attention to the dynamic aspects and focus on equilibrium. The contributions of Leonardi in both volumes introduce and develop the theory of stochastic extremal processes, which are proposed as an ideal tool to analyse the way in which choice behaviour unfolds over time.

An important theme emerging from the review in the first volume was the problem of reconciling urban modelling with economic theory. The rather abstract framework of urban economics has developed powerful tools of analysis, and provided all of us with a deeper understanding of urban phenomena. However, nobody would use an urban economic model for real applications, including the urban economists themselves. On the other hand, many more empirically-oriented urban models, like those based on spatial interaction, have proved to be operational and very amenable to the introduction of realistic features; but they seem to ignore, or at least not to be aware of, the ingredients an urban economist would consider as essential, such as endogenous price formation. A second major goal of our study, hopefully reflected in this volume, has been to look for an integration of the desirable features of both modelling traditions.

While in the first volume the field is broadly reviewed, in this volume the approach is much more oriented towards an explicit development of operational urban economic models. The main contributor to this field, Anas, shows in his work how much of the classic economic theory can be consistently combined with the more recently developed behavioural choice models and also with other apparently 'non-economic' principles, like entropy maximizing.

1.2 The Scope of the Model

In this section we set out the principles on which the design
of an integrated comprehensive urban model can be based, and
the way in which these principles determine our approach to
the book. As we said already in the previous section, although
there is virtually some role for many approaches, in designing
an integrated model system (albeit with some alternative ways
of selecting sub-models) it is necessary to establish an overall framework of a coherent kind. We try to set out the
skeleton of that here.

Implicit in all the sub-models is the need to allocate
and match 'demand' to 'supply'; 'needs' to 'facilities'. Much
of the previous book can be seen as an account of different
approaches to this issue. Here, in Part I, we review the main
broad approaches in terms which allow us to assemble larger
components of an integrated model. Two 'dimensions' underpin
this approach. The first identifies the major market or
allocation systems, and particularly the housing and labour
markets, but also land, services and transport. There is a
distinction between the two groups to which we will return
shortly. The second classifies the major components into three
groups: as 'population', 'stocks' or 'facilities', and 'prices'.
The task of dynamic modelling can then be seen as one of finding suitable approaches for modelling the major sub-systems,
in each example of which there are suitable procedures for
modelling change in the corresponding components - population,
stocks and prices.

The suitable broad approaches for this task are reviewed
in Part I below. We consider in turn the economic approach
which in some sense lays the foundations for other approaches
by discussing mechanisms for adjustment of both quantities and
prices (Chapter Two). We discuss separately a particular set
of spatial-interaction based adjustment methods for stocks and

4

prices in Chapter Three. The integrated system has to be
knitted together by a suitable set of probabilistic accounts
and the broadest framework for this is offered by the master
equations approach to which we devote Chapter Four. With
suitable additional assumptions, the master equation approach
also becomes a model system, and at appropriate points below
we show how it can be applied in this way. Finally, we pursue
probabilistic models further by discussing stochastic extremal
processes in Chapter Five.

The most general population transitions can be represented
within the master equations framework with additional assumptions being drawn from the economic and stochastic extremal
processes chapters. We judged this to be the appropriate
approach for the housing and labour markets – and this is what
distinguishes these systems from the other two. There are two
broad sub-divisions in each case. It is possible to take an
economic approach (in which the master equation accounts can be
considered to be implicit) and, in part – certainly with respect
to prices – there are strong assumptions about equilibrium. Or
we take the master equations approach directly and add alternative mechanisms for the probabilities.

In the case of the service and transport sectors, we assume
that if there is a supply-side change, then the users of the
system move to the new equilibrium very rapidly, and in effect
instantaneously. In this case, it is possible to focus on the
problem of modelling stock dynamics and the techniques of
Chapter Three become dominant – though we relax this assumption
for the service sector later. In the case of the transport
sector, explicit supply modelling is more difficult. With the
present state-of-the-art, the land market also presents a
difficult problem. We focus on an economic approach with an
emphasis on 'rents' as the mechanism of adjustment. Again,
however, we have shown in Chapter Three that stock models can
have an economic component, particularly in relation to price

adjustment, and we pursue this in Chapter Ten below.

This argument is expanded in Chapter Six. This, and the rest of Part II, then constitutes a description of the major sub-system models, including the alternatives we have decided to pursue as the principal elements of an integrated model. In Part III we draw some conclusions on the task of assembling an integrated model from these elements.

Chapter 2

GENERAL ECONOMIC PRINCIPLES FOR BUILDING COMPREHENSIVE URBAN
MODELS

A. Anas

2.1 Introduction

The early urban models of Lowry (1964), Hill (1965) and
Forrester (1969) did not rely on economic theory. They have
been criticized and essentially ignored by economists. See,
for example, Mills (1972-B, page 80) for a critique of
Forrester's model. This separation from economics makes these
models inadequate from many practical points of view such as
doing cost-benefit analysis or predicting the response of real
estate prices to public investments.

   Urban economics which emerged with the contributions of
Alonso (1964), Muth (1969), and Mills (1967) is now a well-
established subdiscipline of the social sciences and has begun
yielding applied results such as the Urban Institute model of
housing markets (de Leeuw and Struyk, 1975), The National
Bureau of Economic Research model of housing markets (Kain and
Apgar, 1976 and 1977), and the Chicago Area Transportation Land
Use Analysis System (Anas, 1983).

   Elsewhere, we have provided an extensive survey of the
literature on urban and regional simulation models (Anas, 1985).
The purpose of this Chapter is to identify and explain the
basic principles of economic theory which must be considered
in building urban models. The question of "what is an economic
urban model?" is not easy to answer and specific urban models

7

can deviate greatly from economic principles. Although an
economic model is generally understood to include prices, this
feature is necessary but not sufficient for economic modelling,
since economics explains a great deal about the behaviour of
prices in relation to each other. The principles of utility
and profit maximization may be more characteristic of "what is
economics?" but even these concepts are not applied uniformly.
It is important to recall that famous economists such as
Leontief (1953) developed peculiar economic models such as
input-output. Also important is the fact that econometric
models, for example the well-known regional econometric models
(Glickmann, 1979), have only the vaguest connection with microeconomic theory. This Chapter, therefore, will not attempt to
lay down minimal requirements for what an economic model is.
Our concern is primarily one of theoretical methodology. We
introduce key textbook concepts from microeconomic theory and
consider the applicability of these to building urban models.
We pay particular attention to how these concepts can be
treated (or mistreated) in discrete choice modelling which
emerged as a branch of econometrics and has had some appeal in
urban modelling.

2.2 General Equilibrium (The Competitive Case)

2.2.1 Introduction

The case of general competitive equilibrium assumes the presence
of a large number of consumers ($i = 1 \ldots I$) and a finite number
of commodities ($j = 1 \ldots J$) produced by constant-returns-to-
scale firms with different production functions for each commodity (or in each industry). Each firm is small relative to
total output in its industry and thus cannot affect output
prices, or the quantity of the commodities (factors of production) which it uses as inputs in production. Similarly because

consumers are many they cannot individually affect prices.
Firms being competitive, and with constant returns to scale,
they make zero profit. Consumers have an income budget which
may be defined as the value of an initial basket of commodities
which they hold. Liquidating this basket they can then purchase a basket of commodities which maximizes their utility.
Utility functions are generally assumed to be strictly concave
in the commodities and thus in this typical case, each consumer
buys some positive amount of each commodity. General equilibrium in this model is concerned with finding those prices for
each commodity that clear all of the markets.

2.2.2 Excess demand functions

In formulating general equilibrium as a mathematical system,
the construction of Walrasian excess demand functions plays a
key role. These are constructed by considering the response
of each consumer and firm to an arbitrary (non-equilibrium)
commodity price vector $\overline{p} = [p_1, p_2, \ldots, p_J]$. Given this
price vector we compute the utility maximizing demand of each
firm (in each industry) for each commodity j. We sum all of
these demands (over all consumers and firms) and subtract the
summed output of all firms in the jth industry. This is the
excess demand function for commodity j as a function of all
the commodity prices. Because the economy is out of equilibrium, firms make nonzero profits (or losses) and these must
be allocated among the consumers in determining their incomes.
In short run equilibrium, the number of firms,
$N_1, N_2, \ldots, N_J$ in each industry is given and the aggregate
excess demand functions are written as

$$E_j(p_1, \ldots, p_J; N_1, \ldots, N_J) = 0; \quad j = 1 \ldots J \qquad (2.1)$$

Industries and firms make positive profits or losses. In long run equilibrium, it is assumed that the number of firms can change by entry and exit until profits in every industry become zero. Thus

$$E_j(p_1, \ldots, p_J; N_1, \ldots, N_J) = 0; \quad j = 1 \ldots J \qquad (2.2)$$

$$\pi_j(p_1, \ldots, p_J) = 0; \quad j = 1 \ldots J \qquad (2.3)$$

where π_j is the profit function of a representative firm in industry j. A more stylized way of expressing equilibrium is to focus on the prices as the unknowns and write the equations as

$$E_j(\bar{p}) \triangleq D_j(\bar{p}) - S_j(\bar{p}) = 0; \quad j = 1 \ldots J \qquad (2.4)$$

with $\bar{p} = \bar{p}^*$ the equilibrium price vector that solves the above system. The most important property of a well-behaved aggregate excess demand system which includes all prices (ie a general equilibrium system) is that each excess demand function is linearly homogeneous of degree zero. Thus

$$E_j(\bar{p}) = E_j(\lambda\bar{p}) \qquad (2.5)$$

for each j, and where λ is an arbitrary constant. A second property is that all prices are nonnegative at equilibrium $\bar{p}^* \geq 0$. A third property (which holds for the standard model of the firm and household) is that each commodity acts as a substitute for all the others.

Thus

$$\partial E_j(\bar{p})/\partial p_j \leq 0 \qquad (2.6)$$

and

$$\partial E_j(\bar{p})/\partial p_k \geq 0 \text{ for } k \neq j \qquad (2.7)$$

2.2.3 Walras's law

This law is a result which follows from the summation of all the consumers' budget constraints. It is stated as

$$\sum_j p_j E_j(\bar{p}) = 0 \text{ for any } \bar{p} \tag{2.8}$$

It says that when the excess demand for each commodity is multiplied by that commodity's price and these products are added over all the commodities, one gets zero no matter what price vector $\bar{p}$ is used. While this law obviously holds at equilibrium, since each $E_j(\bar{p}^*) = 0$, it is less obvious that it holds for any $\bar{p}$, out of equilibrium. Walras's law is important because it introduces a functional dependence among the excess demand functions. This makes one of the prices arbitrary and the corresponding excess demand equation is redundant. Thus, economics can only determine relative prices. The equilibrium system can now be written as follows

$$E_j(1, \frac{p_2}{p_1}, \ldots, \frac{p_J}{p_1}) = 0; \; j = 2 \ldots J \tag{2.9}$$

where the price of commodity one is chosen to be the numeraire price. The system may be solved for the other prices relative to p_1. Thus if $\bar{p}^*$ is an equilibrium relative price vector, then so is $k\bar{p}^*$ where k is any constant.

2.2.4 A general theorem for the existence of a unique
        equilibrium

We will now prove a theorem which can be applied directly to the excess demand functions to determine whether the equilibrium is unique.

Theorem 2.2.4.1

Suppose that the J excess demand functions satisfy the following conditions:

(a) $E_j(\overline{p}) = E_j(\lambda\overline{p})$ for each j and any $\lambda > 0$

(b) $\sum_j p_j E_j(\overline{p}) = 0$

(c) $\partial E_j(\overline{p})/\partial p_j < 0$

 $\partial E_j(\overline{p})/\partial p_k > 0$, k ≠ j

(d) each excess demand function is continuously differentiable

(e) when $p_j = 0$ and other prices are positive then $E_j(\overline{p}) > 0$.

Then a unique equilibrium relative price vector $\overline{p}*$ exists.

Proof: Conditions (a), (b), (d) and (e) are sufficient to prove that at least one equilibrium exists. See, for example, Varian (1978, pages 142 - 3). By definition of linear homogeneity, it follows from (a) that

$$\sum_i p_i \frac{\partial E_j(\overline{p})}{\partial p_i} = 0 \text{ for each i}$$

or

$$p_j\left(\frac{\partial E_j(\overline{p})}{\partial p_j}\right) + \sum_{i \neq j} p_i\left(\frac{\partial E_j(\overline{p})}{\partial p_i}\right) = 0$$

Multiplying by minus one

12

$$p_j \left(- \frac{\partial E_j(\overline{p})}{\partial p_j}\right) - \sum_{i \neq j} p_i \frac{\partial E_j(\overline{p})}{\partial p_i} = 0$$

Since from (c) each $\partial E_j(\overline{p})/\partial p_i > 0$ we replace it by $|\partial E_j(\overline{p})/\partial p_i|$. Also we replace $-\partial E_j(\overline{p})/\partial p_j$, which from (c) is positive, with $|\partial E_j(\overline{p})/\partial p_j|$. This gives

$$p_j \left| \frac{\partial E_j(\overline{p})}{\partial p_j} \right| - \sum_{i \neq j} p_i \left| \frac{\partial E_j(\overline{p})}{\partial p_i} \right| = 0, \text{ each } j$$

The above condition applied to all of the $j = 1 \ldots J$ equations. But from (b), which is Walras's law, we know that one equation is redundant since (b) is always satisfied as an identity. Thus, dropping the jth equation and fixing p_j arbitrarily in the remaining equations, we may write

$$p_j \left| \frac{\partial E_j(\overline{p})}{\partial p_j} \right| - \sum_{i \neq j} p_i \left| \frac{\partial E_j(\overline{p})}{\partial p_i} \right| > 0, \text{ each } j$$

These are now J-1 conditions. More precisely, these conditions state that the Jacobian of the excess demand system (with one excess demand equation dropped) has a dominant diagonal, since $\overline{p}$ is a vector of positive elements. Moreover, from (c) this is a negative diagonal. We may now refer to a well-known result from mathematical economics due to McKenzie (1960) (also see Gale and Nikaido, 1965) that an equation system with a negative dominant diagonal has a unique solution (ie given that a solution exists), because it can be shown through some lemmas that

$$(-1)^n |j| > 0$$

where N (in our case N = J - 1) is the order of the Jacobian, J. Q.E.D.

In proving the existence of a unique equilibrium each of the conditions (a) - (d) above is used. Removing one or more

of these is necessary to create a system of excess demands
which does not produce a unique equilibrium or has no equilibrium. Therefore, these conditions are very important in
economic model building. We should also recall that these
conditions are sufficient but not necessary for a unique
equilibrium to exist. Especially important is condition (c)
which states that all commodities are strict gross substitutes.

2.2.5 Stability of equilibrium

There is nothing in Walrasian general equilibrium theory that
says how prices may adjust when they are out of equilibrium.
This makes it difficult to examine the question of the
stability of the unique equilibrium since stability analysis
requires a disequilibrium price adjustment procedure. In the
literature, stability (local and global) is examined by post-
ulating a dynamic system of price adjustment of the form

$$dp_j/dt = f_j(p_1, p_2, \ldots, p_J) \tag{2.10}$$

where t is time and $f_j(.)$ is the price adjustment mechanism
prevailing out of equilibrium.

The most important articles in this literature are Arrow
and Hurwicz (1958), Hahn (1958), Arrow, Block and Hurwicz
(1959), Quirk and Ruppert (1965), Uzawa (1961) and Negishi
(1962). The last one is a survey article. The strongest
result regarding stability is proven by Arrow and Hurwicz
(1958) for the case where the function $f_j(.)$ is defined as

$$f_j(.) = a_j E_j(\overline{p}) \tag{2.11}$$

where a_j is an arbitrary constant and $E_j(.)$ the excess demand
function in the jth market. They prove that when commodities
are strict gross substitutes and the conditions of Theorem

2.2.4.1 hold then the unique equilibrium is globally stable.
Little or nothing is known for more general adjustment processes. Scarf (1960) provides several examples of the
instability of competitive equilibrium in the global sense.

The price adjustment process (2.10) or (2.11) is a
tâtonnement process. This means that it is assumed that there
is no trade when the system is out of equilibrium. This is
clearly not how real markets adjust. Namely this is a totally
unsatisfactory dynamic mechanism. What is needed is a non-
tâtonnement process which allows transactions to occur out of
equilibrium by means of credit or by means of barter exchange.
The strongest result under these assumptions is due to Negishi
(1962) who examines the non-tâtonnement process

$$\frac{dP_j}{dt} = X_j(\overline{P},\overline{X}) - \overline{X}_j, \text{ each } j \tag{2.12}$$

$$\frac{\overline{X}_{ij}}{dt} = F_{ij}(\overline{P},\overline{X}), \text{ each } j \text{ and } i \tag{2.13}$$

when $X_j(\overline{P},\overline{X})$ is the aggregate demand for commodity j as a
function of the price vector $\overline{p}$ and the total stock of each
commodity $\overline{X}_j$. Equation (2.13) expresses the adjustment of the
quantity of commodity j held by consumer i as a function
$F_{ij}(.)$ of the prices and total stocks $\overline{X}$. In barter exchange
to get a certain quantity of a commodity one must offer something else of the same value in return and such an exchange
does not alter the value of the commodity stocks held by an
individual in disequilibrium. Negishi assumes the following
conditions to express this:

$$\sum_j p_j \dot{\overline{X}}_{ij} = \sum_j p_j F_{ij}(\overline{P},\overline{X}) = 0 \tag{2.14}$$

He then proves that any non-tâtonnement process of the form
(2.12), (2.13) satisfies (2.14) gross-substitutability and
Walras's law is stable but not globally stable.

15

2.2.6 Optimality of equilibrium

It is a well-known result (see, for example, Quirk and
Saposnik, 1960) that the unique competitive equilibrium of
Theorem 2.2.4.1 is a Pareto optimum. The converse also holds:
any Pareto optimum in a general equilibrium economy can be
decentralized into a competitive equilibrium. Pareto
optimality here has the usual meaning: namely it is not possible to shift the allocation of commodities from one market
agent (household, firm) to another, and improve the welfare
(utility or profit) of one without reducing the welfare of at
least one other market agent. A government can decentralize
any Pareto optimum by instituting transfer payments among
individuals such that their incomes correspond to the value of
their commodity stocks at the particular optimum. The cor-
respondence between Pareto optima and equilibria holds for the
competitive case but breaks down when we have externalities or
monopolistic competition. These cases of market failure will
be discussed in Sections 2.3 and 2.4.

2.2.7 Urban general equilibrium

There are two important differences between a spatially disaggregated urban economy and the general aspatial economy of
general equilibrium analysis. The first difference is that
an urban area is not a closed economy. No urban area locally
produces all commodities and has to trade with other cities
and agricultural areas for important commodities such as food,
labour, capital, etc. Many other commodities and services
such as haircuts, urban transportation, housing, are local in
character. While the local markets are closed at the urban
level the interurban markets clear at the regional, national
and international levels. Therefore, the prices of these goods
are determined exogenously to the urban area. The values of

16

the endogenous prices must be determined conditional on the
values of the exogenous prices. If the exogenous markets are
not in equilibrium, then the exogenous prices will change
inducing further adjustments within the urban area, namely in
the endogenous prices. On the other hand, it is usually
assumed that a metropolitan area is "small" relative to the
larger regional system within which it trades and that, therefore, changes in the prices which are endogenous to the metropolitan area cannot alter the prices which are exogenous to it.
This assumption is clearly not always true. In some cases
primate cities are a very large part of a national economy and
even smaller cities may produce a very large share of the
national output of a locally utilized commodity (such as
building materials).

Within the above assumption urban general equilibrium at
the aggregate level requires that:

$$E_j(p_1, p_2, \ldots, p_N, \overline{p}_{N+1}, \ldots, \overline{p}_J) = 0 \qquad (2.15)$$

for each $j = 1, 2, \ldots, N$, where the first N are the locally
traded commodities and the remaining J-N are the exogenous
markets with the corresponding prices fixed exogenously. The
solution has the form

$$p_j = F_j(p_1, p_2, \ldots, p_{j-1}, p_{j+1}, \ldots, p_N, \overline{p}_{N+1}, \ldots, \overline{p}_J)$$

$$(2.16)$$

for $j = 1, 2, \ldots, N$ but $\overline{p}_{N+1}, \ldots, \overline{p}_J$ are assumed not to be
influenced by the endogenous prices. Obviously, Walras's law
does not hold at the level of the urban economy.

The second difference between an urban and an aspatial
general equilibrium model is the locational factor. In
addition to the continuous choice of each commodity, each

17

market agent must choose a (usually) single location where consumption or production activity is to occur. This introduces several complexities at once. One is that income, wealth and all prices faced by each agent become indexed by location and are affected by transportation cost. A second complexity is that the discrete choice of a single location (or even of several) introduces a nonconvexity in utility and profit maximization. Despite this complexity, the standard general equilibrium model has been applied to the urban case with success, establishing the existence and uniqueness of equilibrium. See, for example, Schweizer, Varaiya and Hartwick (1976) for a statement of how location and space introduce differences into traditional-aspatial-treatments of general equilibrium such as Arrow and Hahn (1971) and Debreu (1959).

2.2.8 The case of discrete choice

In recent years discrete choice models have been applied to urban equilibrium problems (see Anas, 1982). These are appealing for a number of reasons: (i) they deal naturally with the discrete problem of location choice; (ii) they do not require a strictly concave utility function but can still generate general realistic results; (iii) they treat with great success the problem of heterogeneous preferences. Despite their appeal, these models originate from econometrics and are thus not fully reconciled with classical microeconomic theory. In particular budget constraints are not always explicitly treated in these models and excess demand functions constructed from these models are not always homogeneous of degree zero. The purpose of this Section is to give a simple exposition of a general equilibrium model constructed from discrete choice models.

Consider $j = 1 \ldots J$ discrete substitute submarkets such that each market agent chooses only one of these and pays the price P_j to locate in the jth (chosen) submarket. Then $Z_i = (Y - P_i)/P_o$ is the quantity of the composite commodity demanded by the consumer choosing the ith discrete submarket, P_o being the price of the composite commodity, and Y being the income. Let $S_o(P_o)$ be the supply of the composite commodity and let $S_i(P_i)$ be the supply of the discrete commodity at location i. Finally let $D_i(P_o,\overline{P})$ be the number of market agents who choose location i (ie the demand). Furthermore, let the number of total market agents be given as N. Then,

$$\sum_i D_i(P_o, \overline{P}) - N = 0 \qquad (2.17)$$

is an identity. The excess demand function for the ith discrete location is

$$E_i(P_o, \overline{P}) \triangleq D_i(P_o, \overline{P}) - S_i(P_i); \text{ all } i = 1 \ldots J \quad (2.18)$$

and the excess demand function for the composite commodity is

$$E_o(P_o, \overline{P}) = \frac{1}{P_o}\sum_i (Y - P_i)(D_i(P_o, \overline{P})) - S_o(P_o) \qquad (2.19)$$

To apply Theorem 2.2.4.1 to the existence and uniqueness of this system of equations we must be able to assume realistically that conditions (a) - (d) are satisfied. Of these (c) and (d) are usually satisfied by discrete choice models. Condition (a) can be satisfied by appropriately specifying the models but is not always satisfied because some prices and incomes may be exogenously specified in an urban model. For the same reason Walras's law may not always be satisfied. To see this we can construct Walras's law:

$$\sum_i (Y - P_i)D_i(P_o, \overline{P}) - P_o S_o(P_o)$$

$$+ \sum_i P_i D_i(P_o, \overline{P}) - \sum_i P_i S_i(P_i) \stackrel{?}{=} 0$$

$$Y\sum_i D_i(P_o, \overline{P}) - \sum_i P_i S_i(P_i) - P_o S_o(P_o) \stackrel{?}{=} 0$$

$$YN - \sum_i P_i S_i(P_i) - P_o S_o(P_o) \stackrel{?}{=} 0$$

We can see from the last line that Walras's law holds only if the system is closed in income such that average income Y is indeed the average revenue from all the commodities in the system. Namely,

$$Y = \frac{\sum_i P_i S_i(P_i) - P_o S_o(P_o)}{N} \qquad (2.20)$$

With discrete choice models, there is the special case of short run equilibrium. In this case each S_i is fixed (corresponding to, for example, durable structures). Then

$$\sum_i D_i(P_o, \overline{P}) - \sum_i S_i = 0 \qquad (2.21)$$

as long as $\sum_i S_i = N$ and one of the equations in (2.19) is redundant. This dependency condition replaces Walras's law and if homogeneity of degree zero also holds then the mathematics of Theorem 2.2.4.1 still apply. It should be recalled, however, that even if Theorem 2.2.4.1 does not apply, the condition $(-1)^N|J| > 0$ may still hold. Indeed, Anas (1982) is able to prove this for special cases involving multinomial and nested multinomial logit models.

2.3   General Equilibrium (Monopolistic Competition)

2.3.1   Introduction

The case of a perfectly competitive economy may be regarded as myth and therefore the results of Section 2.2 may be generalized to less than perfectly competitive cases. In particular the case of monopolistic competition is both more realistic and more interesting. It is also more relevant to the urban case, since because of scale economies monopolies are formed and may dominate the economies of cities.

2.3.2   Monopolistic competition

When the production of a commodity is subject to economies of scale, then the industry for that good may consist of a small number of firms. When this happens each firm has some control over the price of its output. It is no longer a price taker but a price maker. Similarly, if the firm is a major buyer of some of its inputs it can influence the input price also. Thus, a firm may have monopoly power, monopsony power or both. It maximizes profit with respect to the prices which it controls as well as with respect to the input quantities which it purchases. In such an environment, the firm needs to know the market demand function for its output and the market supply functions for each input over which it has monopsony power. Furthermore, the behaviour of the firm depends crucially on what it assumes about the behaviour of its monopolistic competitors. Although the behaviour of a single monopoly has found a place in every microeconomics textbook, economists have done little to examine the properties of monopolistic competition for an entire economic system. Cases of duopoly and oligopoly examined derive only very special results under very restrictive assumptions about functional forms.

2.3.3 Reaction functions and Nash equilibria

Let the profit function of the jth oligopolist be

$$\Pi_j(p_1, \ldots, p_J; X_{j1}, X_{j2}, \ldots, X_{jM}) \tag{2.22}$$

where $\bar{x}$ is the vector of commodity inputs in the production process and $\bar{p}$ is the vector of prices of the competing oligopolists. Then this oligopolist maximizes profit as follows:

$$\max_{(p_j, \ \bar{x}_j | \forall p_i, \ i \neq j)} \Pi_j(p_1, \ldots, p_J; x_{j1}, x_{j2}, \ldots, x_{jM}) \tag{2.23}$$

If each oligopolist behaves in this way, then a Nash equilibrium may occur at the price vector $\bar{p}^*$ and input demand $\bar{x}_j^*$. Such an equilibrium is given by:

$$\max_{(p_1, \ \bar{x}_1)} \Pi_1(p_1, p_2^*, \ldots, p_J^*; \bar{x}_1)$$

$$\max_{(p_2, \ \bar{x}_2)} \Pi_2(p_1^*, p_2, \ldots, p_J^*; \bar{x}_2)$$

$$\vdots$$

$$\max_{(p_j, \ \bar{x}_j)} \Pi_j(p_1^*, p_2^*, \ldots, p_j, \ldots p_J^*; \bar{x}_j)$$

$$\vdots$$

$$\max_{(p_J, \ \bar{x}_J)} \Pi_J(p_1^*, p_2^*, \ldots, p_j^*, \ldots, P_J; \bar{x}_J) \tag{2.24}$$

The jth maximization yields p_j^*, $\bar{x}_j^*$ which are the equilibrium price and input quantities entering the profit functions.

Assuming such an equilibrium exists and is established, it determines prices of the oligopolists. It is not necessary that the market(s) for the J oligopolists' output(s) will be cleared at these prices. Demands may exceed produced output

because it may be profitable to produce less than the demanded
quantity and thus create a scarcity. Whether this occurs or
not depends on the nature of the monopolist-monopsonist's cost
function. Thus, it is not always possible to require that the
price vector which satisfies a Nash equilibrium be consistent
with Walrasian equilibrium. An application of the above
observation may be the case of unemployment. This can occur
because large monopolist-monopsonists may find it profitable
not to employ all of the labour force which wishes to be
employed thus creating involuntary unemployment.

2.3.4 Existence, uniqueness, stability and optimality of
       Nash equilibria

There are no general results on the existence, uniqueness and
stability of Nash equilibria. It is easy to construct examples
where such equilibria do not exist or are not unique. The
basic reason for this is that the profit maximization problem
is not a convex problem in general. The presence of monopolistic competition means that if a Nash equilibrium exists,
such an equilibrium need not be a Pareto optimum. This means
that monopolistic behaviour can be regulated by means of taxes
and/or price controls in order to improve the welfare levels
of consumers until a Pareto optimal situation emerges.

2.3.5 The urban case and discrete choice models

Urban areas are concentrations of economic activity. A very
important factor which creates such concentration is scale
economies in production. Therefore, one or more (probably
more) of the private goods within an urban area are produced
by monopolistically competitive behaviour. Ultimately, each
urban producer, no matter how small a market he may control,
is relatively isolated in space and has local monopoly power

within his market area. Thus the model of monopolistic competition is extremely well suited to the urban case. However,
as we saw, the lack of any interesting general results makes
the application of this model very difficult. The owners of
discrete urban sites such as land areas, large apartment
buildings, single family homes, etc can be viewed as monopolistic competitors. They have price setting powers which
derive from the locational or attribute-related heterogeneity
of their holdings. Since the demands for locations, housing
units and buildings can be expressed as a discrete choice
process, it is reasonable to attempt to develop models of supply-
side monopolistic behaviour given a demand-side model of discrete choice. The only such model is that of Anas (1980) for
the housing market. This model formulates housing demand as a
discrete choice process. Then each landlord is a rent-setter
who seeks to maximize his expected return given the known
probability that a vacancy might occur at the rent the landlord quotes. Unpublished work by the author (Anas, 1981) shows
that a unique Nash equilibrium exists under certain restrictive
conditions: (a) in the short run, (b) assuming there are no
dwelling maintenance costs, (c) the demand for dwellings is a
multinomial logit model, and (d) the utility function is linear
in rent or loglinear in the disposable income after rent. It
is also shown that when utility is linear in the natural
logarithm of rent, then an equilibrium does not exist and the
system exhibits divergent oscillations.

2.4 General Equilibrium (With Externalities)

2.4.1 Externalities

The presence of externalities of consumption and production is
one of the most interesting problems in economic model building. These are especially important in urban contexts.

Pollution, noise, traffic congestion, adjacent but incompatible
land uses are major kinds of urban externalities. Consumption
and production activities can both generate "goods" and "bads"
which, however, are not commodities which can be exchanged or
transacted in markets. If the pollution emitted from a nearby
factory poses health hazards for me, I cannot protect myself
against it by buying more clean air in the "clean air market".
There is no such market and while clean air has value it does
not have a market price. What I may do to protect myself is
to relocate away from the source of pollution to a cleaner
area. What I have done is to obtain more clean air by buying
and selling housing (a market commodity). Pollution in this
example is an externality. Its harmful effects are external to
the markets of priceable commodities. It is also a production
externality because it is a by-product of the production process but its effect falls on consumers.

There are beneficial externalities also, such as natural
amenities, proximity to a park or open space or the planting
of trees by a homeowner which also beautifies the home of his
neighbour. Traffic congestion is a major example of a negative
externality. Adding an extra car to a road increases the
travel times of other cars on the road.

2.4.2 Equilibrium with externalities

Suppose that the Walrasian general economy creates $k = 1 \ldots K$
externalities. The values of these will be denoted as e_k,
$k = 1 \ldots K$. The equilibrium conditions can now be written as
follows using D_j and S_j to denote the supply and demand of the
jth commodity:

$$E_j(\overline{p}, \overline{e}) \overset{\Delta}{=} D_j(\overline{p}, \overline{e}) - S_j(\overline{p}, \overline{e}) = 0; \quad j = 1 \ldots J \quad (2.25)$$

and

$$e_k = f_k[D_j(\overline{p}, \overline{e}), \ S_j(\overline{p}, \overline{e}); \ j = 1 \ \dots \ J]; \ k = 1 \ \dots \ K$$
$$(2.26)$$

The first J equations are the usual excess demand functions
where both demand and supply depend not only on the market
prices $\overline{p}$ but also on the level of the externalities $\overline{e}$. Given
fixed externality levels, equations (2.25) can be solved for a
conditional equilibrium price vector $\overline{p}$. To get the complete
solution we must include the K equations (2.26) which given a
$\overline{p}$ can be solved for the externality levels $\overline{e}$. Each function
$f_g[.]$ is a technological or physical relationship describing
the creation of the kth externality. Equations (2.25) and
(2.26) together are solved for the equilibrium prices and
externality levels, $\overline{p}*$, $\overline{e}*$.

2.4.3 Existence, uniqueness, stability and optimality of equilibria

No general results have been established about the existence,
uniqueness and stability of systems such as (2.25), (2.26).
Such results depend on how $\overline{e}$ enter the externality functions
f[.]. The sufficient conditions $(-1)^{J+K}|J| > 0$, where J is
the Jacobian matrix of (2.25) and (2.26) may be used to
establish existence and uniqueness. However, this approach is
sure to fail in the general case. In general, if an equili-
brium position $\overline{p}*$, $\overline{e}*$ exists it is not a Pareto optimum,
because the presence of externalities distorts the efficiency
of markets. This is one form of market failure recognized in
economics. In some cases there is a way to levy taxes τ_k on
each externality such that if the appropriate consumers or
producers causing the externality pay the tax then the resulting equilibrium will be a Pareto optimum if the tax is computed in such a way that it is equal to the marginal cost
created by this externality. The equation system should be

modified as:

$$D_j(\overline{p},\ \overline{e},\ \overline{\tau}) - S_j(\overline{p},\ \overline{e},\ \overline{\tau}) = 0;\ j = 1\ \dots\ J \qquad (2.27)$$

$$e_k = f_k[D_j(\overline{p},\ \overline{e},\ \overline{\tau}),\ S_j(\overline{p},\ \overline{e},\ \overline{\tau});\ j = 1\ \dots\ J];\ k = 1\ \dots\ K$$
$$(2.28)$$

$$\tau_k = g_k[\overline{p},\ \overline{e},\ D_j(\overline{p},\ \overline{e},\ \overline{\tau}),\ S_j(\overline{p},\ \overline{e},\ \overline{\tau});\ j = 1\ \dots\ J];$$

$$k = 1\ \dots\ K \qquad (2.29)$$

where (2.29) are equations which compute the correct tax level
such that the equilibrium is a Pareto optimum, if such an
equilibrium $\overline{p}^*$, $\overline{e}^*$, $\overline{\tau}^*$ exists. Corrective taxation is a
"pricing" oriented approach to achieve Pareto optimality.
There are other methods such as physically restricting an
activity to achieve Pareto optimality. For example, a polluter
may be taxed or prohibited from polluting. Both methods may
succeed in achieving Pareto optimality.

2.4.4 Urban externalities

Urban economists have paid extensive attention to the study of
traffic congestion in monocentric cities. See Mills (1972-B).
For a recent survey see Anas (1985). In the case of this
problem the existence and uniqueness of an equilibrium has
been demonstrated for specially specified models and the correct levels of congestion tolls have been shown to establish
Pareto efficiency. Other urban externalities have not been
studied carefully by urban economists. Discrete choice models
of route choice in congested networks have been examined (see,
for example, Daganzo and Sheffi, 1977). The aim of this type
of research has been to formulate computational techniques and
not to compute the correction tolls on the different links of

a road network.

2.5 General Equilibrium (With Public Goods)

2.5.1 Public goods

Many goods and services, in urban areas especially, are produced by local governments. These fall in the category of
public goods and are the source of major market failure and
distortion. They represent a high level of expenditure and
their correct treatment within economic models is indispens-
able. A public good is defined as a commodity, facility or
service such that if it is provided to at least one market
agent then other market agents cannot be excluded from consuming it through any market mechanism. Economists distinguish
pure public goods from congestible public goods. A pure public good is one the enjoyment of which by some market agent
does not diminish (or change) the enjoyment of it by other
market agents. A congestible public good is one where the
enjoyment of it by some definitely changes the enjoyment of it
by others through an externality which depends, usually, on
the intensity with which the public good is used or consumed.
An example of a pure public good is an urban sculpture in a
central square. People can derive enjoyment from it by know-
ing it is there and by viewing it as they pass it regardless
of the presence of others (unless they obstruct the view).
An example of a congestible public good is a road or an urban
park used at a high enough intensity to discourage others by
reducing their enjoyment because of high travel times in one
case or too much crowding in the other.

2.5.2 The demand revelation problem

A big theoretical problem with a public good is that since no

28

one can be excluded from consuming it no one is obliged (or would be wise) to reveal his or her demand for the public good. Suppose the government provides y acres of urban parkland and charges each citizen x dollars a year to maintain this land. Suppose, further, that my demand for urban parkland at x dollars a year is not y but less than y. Then I am getting more than I want and I would be a foolish economic man to tell the government the truth.

The question, then, is the following: since it is not possible to organize a market for a public good because of the nonexclusivity mechanism, how is the government to know the correct quantity (and quality) of a public good to be supplied? This is an unsolved problem in economics, known as the "demand revelation" problem. For a review of this problem and the key literature see Feldman (1981). Several economists have proposed various non-market mechanisms that may be used by the government to find the correct demand function for a public good. These try to construct a number of economic incentives to make it rational for individuals to tell the truth and reveal their demand functions. However, none of these proposed techniques is successful. Each fails in some way and leads to inconsistent results. Thus, the demand revelation problem remains unsolved.

2.5.3 Equilibrium with public goods

The presence of $j = J + 1 \ldots K$ pure public goods in addition to the $j = 1 \ldots J$ private goods leads to the following Walrasian equilibrium formulation:

$$E_j(\overline{p}, \overline{\theta}) = D_j(\overline{p}, \overline{\theta}) - S_j(\overline{p}, \overline{\theta}) = 0; \quad j = 1 \ldots J \quad (2.30)$$

$$E_j(\overline{p}, \overline{\theta}) = D_j(p, \theta) - S_j(p, \theta) = 0; \quad j = J + 1 \ldots K$$
$$(2.31)$$

Here $\bar{\theta}$ is the tax-price charged by the government for each "unit" of the public good supplied. An equilibrium $(\bar{p}^*, \bar{\theta})$ may exist (and could be unique) but cannot be attained because the demand functions $D_j(\bar{p}, \bar{\theta})$ for the public goods cannot be known by the government. Note that the private good demand functions need not be known by anybody since there are markets (for each private good) and the demand levels are properly revealed in these markets by the action of competitive pricing. The equilibrium formulation (2.30), (2.31) which is generally unattainable is known as a first best which means that if it could be attained it would be a Pareto optimum.

2.5.4 The theory of second best

Since the tax-prices $\bar{\theta}^*$ cannot be correctly computed and thus the first best cannot be attained, economists have developed the theory of the second best. The logic of the theory of the second best is as follows. Since $\bar{\theta}^*$ cannot be computed there is market failure, ie a distortion of the first best allocation occurs. To correct this distortion the government may want to introduce another compensating distortion. Such a compensating distortion is known as second best because it does not fully compensate for the lack of a first best solution but comes close to the Pareto efficient first best case.

In the first best equilibrium formulation (2.30), (2.31) one possible second best strategy is to set $\bar{\theta} = 0$ and thus drop equations (2.31) replacing them with, for example, one other equation which states that total taxes collected by a uniform head (per person) tax ϕ are sufficient to pay for some quantity of the public goods. This second best equilibrium can be written as follows:

$$E_j(\bar{p}, 0, \bar{g}, \phi) = D_j(\bar{p}, 0, \bar{g}, \phi) - S_j(\bar{p}, 0, \bar{g}, \phi) = 0;$$
$$j = 1 \ldots J \qquad (2.32)$$

Here $\overline{g} = [g_{J+1}, g_{J+2}, \ldots, g_K]$ is the vector of the levels of the public good predetermined by the government, $\overline{\theta}$ has been set equal to zero and ϕ is the uniform tax rate. More equations may be imposed to find the levels g_K of each public good and the tax rate ϕ. For example, let $F_K(.)$ be an equation describing some rule of thumb for deciding the allocation of g_K and let $B(.)$ be the equation for the government excess budget. Then,

$$F_k(\overline{p}, 0, \phi, \overline{g}) = 0; \; k = J + 1 \ldots K \qquad (2.33)$$

and

$$B(\overline{p}, 0, \phi, \overline{g}) = 0. \qquad (2.34)$$

Clearly the functions $F_k(.)$ are not unique. Many different rules for deciding the levels $\overline{g}$ can be proposed. Also the idea of a uniform head tax ϕ is not the only available taxing strategy. One can levy taxes in relation to income and other consumer characteristics. This would be a different second best. Obviously, then, there is no unique second best strategy in general, but many different second bests exist.

An example of the first best/second best problem is that of urban traffic congestion. It is known that the first best strategy is to force each traveller to pay a congestion toll. But such tolls are impossible to levy in the practical sense. Therefore, since travellers don't pay these tolls, they create more congestion than is optimal (in the first best case). One second best strategy is to subsidize transit fares (introducing, thus, the compensating distortion) and reducing congestion. Another second best strategy is to put a tax on car ownership (thus achieving another reduction in traffic). A third strategy is to put a tax on gasoline (per gallon purchased), thus achieving a different reduction in traffic. A fourth strategy is a tax on parking etc. Each of these strategies is a different second best and it is very difficult to calculate which of the many possible second best strategies comes the closest to the first best case. This is difficult because it requires that the government knows the preferences of market agents. But if the government knows these preferences it could solve (2.30), (2.31) directly and there would be no need for a second best strategy. Second best strategies can only be compared by means of simple theoretical models (which may be too removed from reality) or by means of complex simulation models which may be too difficult to implement due to data limitations.

2.6 Dynamics and Disequilibrium

2.6.1 Introduction

All of the above sections deal with static general equilibrium analysis, but obviously dynamics is of much deeper interest. Economists have made interesting contributions to dynamics but this area of economics is in its infancy particularly because it is tied in with the presence of disequilibria.

There are many styles of dynamic modelling in economics based on different, but equally plausible, assumptions. It is unlikely that synthesis of these diverse styles into one will emerge in the near future. Therefore, it is useful to examine the logic of each style.

2.6.2 Temporary equilibrium models

One way to model the dynamics of an economic system is to take any of the Walrasian based formulations in Sections 2.2 to 2.5 and add a time dimension. A short run or temporary equilibrium approach then assumes that equilibria can be attained instantaneously at every point in time along any dynamic path. Obviously these models exaggerate the force and rapidity of economic adjustments such as price adjustment or the readjustment of durable good stocks (like housing). Going back to the "pure" competitive market Walrasian model described by equations (2.4) we may express the temporary equilibrium path as follows:

$$E_j[\overline{p}(t), \overline{Y}(t)] = 0; \quad j = 1 \ldots J \qquad (2.35)$$

Here, $\overline{Y}(t)$ is the path of the exogenous variables $\overline{Y}$ which in (2.4) were constant over time since (2.4) is a static model. On the other hand, $\overline{p}(t)$ is now the time path of the Walrasian equilibrium prices. These $\overline{p}*(t)$ may be obtained by solving (2.4) repeatedly at each t. This model assumes instantaneous adjustments in prices and implicitly in the quantities of all goods as well. It is, therefore, unrealistic if some goods adjust slowly because time passes during their adjustment.

2.6.3 Lags in adjustment

There are many ways of making temporary equilibrium models more realistic by including lags in adjustment. Again, there are many rather arbitrary ways of doing so and it is not clear which way is the most realistic. This is best left to empirical research. The simplest kind of lag in adjustment is a lag in the exogenous variables. Using discrete notation, (2.35) becomes

$$E_{jt}[\overline{p}_t, \overline{Y}_{t-n}] = 0; \quad j = 1 \ldots J \text{ and } t = 1 \ldots T \qquad (2.36)$$

where the value of $\overline{Y}$ relevant to the price adjustment at time t is lagged by n periods. This is best explained as an information lag. More recent values of $\overline{Y}$ are simply not known to the market participants.

More serious adjustment problems can occur when the supply

of some commodity is fixed as a durable good accumulated in the past. The competitive excess demand system can now be modified as follows:

$$E_j[\overline{p}(t), \overline{Y}(t), \overline{S}(t)] = D_j[\overline{p}(t), \overline{Y}(t), \overline{S}(t)]$$

$$- S_j[\overline{p}(t), \overline{Y}(t), \overline{S}(t)] - S_j(t); \; j = 1 \ldots J \qquad (2.37)$$

Here, $S_j(t)$ is the stock of the jth commodity accumulated in the past and available for consumption at time t, $D_j[.]$ and $S_j[.]$ are the demand for a supply of the jth commodity at time t and $\overline{Y}(t)$ is the usual vector of exogenous variables driving the system. Demand and supply are functions of $\overline{p}(t)$, $\overline{Y}(t)$ as before but also depend on the commodity stocks $\overline{S}(t)$. The above formulation assumes that all of the stock (new plus inherited) is utilized at each time period. This can be assured if $S_j[.]$ can obtain a negative value corresponding to stock removal, $S_j[.] + S_j(t)$ being positive. Note, however, that stock removal can be costly, therefore some vacancies or unutilized stock may result and may be modified as follows:

$$E_j[.] = D_j[\overline{p}(t), Y(t), \overline{S}(t)] - (S_j[\overline{p}(t), Y(t), \overline{S}(t)] + S_j(t))$$

$$\times \; \pi_j[\overline{p}(t), Y(t), \overline{S}(t)]; \; j = 1 \ldots J \qquad (2.38)$$

Here $\pi_j(.)$ is the proportion of the total stock which is utilized in the market at time t. Once again it is possible to lag the dependence of demand and supply on Y if information lags are significant.

2.6.4 Expectations: adaptive and rational

The dynamic formulations in 2.6.2 and 2.6.3 represent behaviour as myopic. The future does not enter into the current state and the dynamics are not influenced by the future or expectations of it. Adaptive expectation models assume that future values are estimated from current and past values by extrapolation. Thus (2.35) may be restated as:

$$E_j[\overline{p}(t), (\overline{Y}(s)_{-\infty}^t), \dot{\overline{Y}}(t), \ddot{\overline{Y}}(t), \ldots] = 0; \; j = 1 \ldots J$$

$$(2.39)$$

which states that excess demands depend on all past values of the exogenous variables $\overline{Y}(t)$ (stream from $s = -\infty$ to current t ($s = t$)) and also on the most recent derivatives (past derivatives might also be relevant). More precisely we may write

$$E_j[\overline{p}(t), (\hat{\overline{Y}}(s)|_t^\infty)] = 0; \; j = 1 \ldots J$$

$$(2.40)$$

where

$$\{\hat{\overline{Y}}(s)|_t^\infty\} = f[\{\overline{Y}(s)\rfloor_{-\infty}^t\}, \dot{\overline{Y}}(t), \ddot{\overline{Y}}(t), \ldots]$$

$$(2.41)$$

Equations (2.40) state that the expected future path of $\overline{Y}(t)$ (denoted as $\hat{\overline{Y}}(s)$) influences excess demands. This future path is estimated via the adaptive expectations function, (2.41). Rational expectation models assume that future values are known precisely. This is probably the most untenable assumption (and the most peculiar one) in economics. Stochastic versions of these models assume that future states are known up to a probability distribution.

Rational and adaptive expectation models can be built not only around the vector of exogenous variables but also around the endogenous prices. If market agents can estimate future prices and exogenous variables, then they can engage in multiperiod optimization or speculative behaviour. Therefore, the excess demand for a commodity at time t will be determined by the current endogenous price but will depend also on the estimated future path of the prices. Thus

$$E_j[\overline{p}(t),\ (\hat{\overline{p}}(s)|_t^\infty),\ \overline{Y}(t),\ (\hat{\overline{Y}}(s)|_t^\infty)] = 0;\ j = 1\ \ldots\ J \tag{2.42}$$

where $\hat{\overline{Y}}(s)$ is given by (2.41) and

$$(\hat{\overline{p}}(s)|_t^\infty) = g[(\overline{p}(s)\ _{-\infty}^t),\ \dot{\overline{p}}(t),\ \ddot{\overline{p}}(t),\ \ldots] \tag{2.43}$$

is the price expectation function. Solving (2.42) we find the temporal equilibrium price vector $\overline{p}^*(t)$ as a function of the future expected prices

$$\overline{p}^*(t) = F[\overline{Y}(t),\ (\hat{\overline{p}}(s)|_t^\infty),\ (\hat{\overline{Y}}(s)|_t^\infty) \tag{2.44}$$

It may appear strange to the non-economist that current prices should be a function of expected future prices, but this is in fact the essence of speculation. Indeed substituting (2.41) and (2.43) into (2.44) we find the result that $\overline{p}^*(t)$ is implicitly a function of past information.

The assumption of dependence of current prices on the future ones becomes more difficult to maintain when we move from adaptive to rational expectations. In this case

$$\overline{p}^*(t) = F[(\overline{Y}(t)|_t^\infty),\ (\overline{p}^*(t)|_t^\infty)] \tag{2.45}$$

which holds for all t. How is the price path function $\overline{p}^*(t)$ to be solved? Actually, a rational expectations model is the limiting form of an adaptive expectations model. Suppose that we use equation (2.44) recursively to generate $_1\overline{p}^*(t)$, a first-trial future price path. We may plug this into the right side of (2.45) to compute $_2\overline{p}^*(t)$ from the left side of (2.45), plug this new path back into (2.45) and so on until the path obtained from the left side is arbitrarily close to the path plugged into the right. If this process is convergent, then a rational expectations equilibrium exists, and the resulting prices are said to be rational.

2.6.5 Price adjustment in disequilibrium and quantity rationing

So far in this Section we discussed dynamic equilibrium concepts. The economy does not deviate from a dynamic path. The more interesting type of dynamics, however, is disequilibrium dynamics or adjustment processes which take place when the economy is out of equilibrium. Disequilibrium analysis in economics (especially in microeconomics) is in its infancy. Even the most advanced treatments of disequilibrium are an evidence of this (see Benassy, 1982).

The only serious investigation of price and quantity adjustments in disequilibrium has been done in connection with the stability analysis of general Walrasian equilibrium. This work was discussed in Section 2.2.5. To repeat only the main points a differential equation such as (2.10) is a tâtonnement process. It assumes that there is no trade when the system is out of equilibrium. This, of course, is impossible because it means that there will never be any exchange if the system never achieves equilibrium due to exogenous shocks. What is needed, therefore, is a theory of commodity exchange when the general equilibrium system is out of equilibrium such as Negishi's (1962) non-tâtonnement process (2.12), (2.13). Such a theory, however, needs to be developed rigorously within microeconomics before it can make a contribution to multimarket disequilibrium theory.

2.6.6 Short-side models

A rather macroeconomic and therefore somewhat unsatisfactory
treatment of disequilibrium is the short-side or Fair–Jaffee
(1972) type model. Such a model consists of two relationships:
a price adjustment equation and a transaction rule at the
aggregate level. Thus

$$\dot{\overline{p}}(t) = f[\overline{D}(\overline{p}(t)) - \overline{S}(\overline{p}(t))] \tag{2.46}$$

and

$$\overline{Q}(t) = \min[\overline{D}(\overline{p}(t)), \ \overline{S}(\overline{p}(t))] \tag{2.47}$$

where $\overline{Q}(t)$ is the vector of transacted quantities at time t.
Note, however, that this model says nothing about how excess
demands (or supplies) may be subject to rationing within time t.
Recently, Anas and Eum (1984, 1986) have applied this type of
model to the urban housing market.

2.6.7 Structural dynamics and stability

In recent years there has been an outpouring of mathematical
literature from non-economists calling for the application of
structural dynamics models to urban modelling. The well-known
literature is beyond the scope of this Chapter. What we wish
to do here is to view these developments from the side of
economics. Within economics, and especially microeconomics,
there has been only a sprinkling of interest in questions of
structural dynamics. An example is the paper by Benhabib
and Day (1981) which introduces time dependent preferences
into a simple model of consumer utility maximization and
derives chaotic adjustment patterns. What I will do here is
to provide the basic clues as to what may be gained, and how,
from applying structural dynamic models within economics.
        First of all, all models of structural change dynamics

have the following fundamental characteristic: as one or more exogenous variables change smoothly and continuously over time, one or more endogenous variables show sudden jumps and discontinuities in their time paths. A little thought shows that this behaviour can occur when the underlying temporary equilibrium system has multiple equilibria. If the system is at any one locally optimal equilibrium point, it will show a tendency to jump to another local equilibrium point when this other point becomes more approachable due to the smooth exogenous changes. For example, if the system always finds the globally optimal equilibrium point, and smooth exogenous variables serve to "line up" one or more locally optimal equilibrium points to make them simultaneously global, then suddenly the system can shift to a new globally optimal equilibrium. This observation means that structural change dynamics can be generated only from economic models of temporary equilibrium paths which display multiple equilibrium possibilities. As we saw, the standard competitive case does not qualify (Section 2.2), but the monopolistic competition, externality and public goods cases (Sections 2.3, 2.4 and 2.5 respectively) can all generate multiple equilibria. It is therefore in these areas that we must look for interesting and economically meaningful structural dynamics models of the future.

2.7 The Dynamic Comprehensive Urban Model

2.7.1 Introduction

At present there is no dynamic comprehensive urban model which incorporates all of the scope and detail discussed in the previous Section. This, however, is not a problem in urban modelling alone but other branches of economics such as regional modelling, transportation, labour markets, public finance, international economics etc also lack complete and

comprehensive operational models. In this Section we discuss
the relevance of each of the previous Sections to the possible
development of a comprehensive and dynamic urban model. We
try to sketch the nature, scope, detail and methodological
character of such a model and we point out some difficulties
in its development.

2.7.2 The sectors and their interrelationships

The comprehensive urban model would consist of three sector
groupings: (a) Employment/Industry, (b) Labour/Households,
(c) Public Sector.

(a) Employment/Industry: There ought to be a distinction
between basic (export-oriented) industries and local (population serving) industries. The firms in the basic sector are
more likely to be subject to increasing returns to scale and a
form of oligopolistic competition (as in Section 2.3) may be
used to model their behaviour. Other basic sectors and some
of the local sector may be treated as competitive industries,
subject to constant returns to scale (homogeneous of degree
one production functions). A major industry is housing and
industrial building production. This can be treated as a
competitive industry. Finally, there is a need to treat the
production of transportation services by modelling the
behaviour of private firms in this sector. In an economic
model the behaviour of a firm ought to be complete. Thus, the
typical firm in an industry decides where to locate its
plant(s), how much to produce in each plant, how much of each
input factor (labour, capital commodities) to use in the
production process, from where and by what travel mode and
route to obtain the input factors and, if monopoly/monopsony
power exists, how much to price each output and input. The
type of building in which a firm operates is particularly

important in an urban model.

(b) Labour/Households: Households may be classified into classes by income, age, education, family size, etc. They decide where and in what type of housing unit to live, where and in what industry to seek employment, by what mode and route to travel, where to shop and what quantity of each commodity to purchase etc.

(c) Public Sector: The public sector may consist of local governments (in the Chicago area there are over 300) and higher level public agencies and state governments. Each public sector has to balance a budget and can do so by setting taxes, tolls or fees for various public goods and services. They also decide, using whatever second best strategy is appropriate, the quantity of each public good to be supplied and the level of maintenance and reinvestment for each public good.

The interrelationships of these three sector groups is assured by means of competition and mobility within the metropolitan area by both households and firms. The urban area is divided into zones among which such mobility is explicitly described. The sectors are linked together by means of supply and demand computations. The demand by firms, households and the public sector(s) for each commodity can be summed together at each location and the supply can be determined in a similar way. In an equilibrium model demand and supply are equated and one obtains as many equations as commodities (including labour, capital, etc) and solves these simultaneously for the prices. In a temporary equilibrium model this can be done for each point in time. There will be additional equations for price setting, externalities, and public goods as shown in Sections 2.3, 2.4 and 2.5.

2.7.3 State dependence and transitions

In a dynamic urban model firms and households must be identified not only with their usual socioeconomic classification
but also by their current choices (location etc) in the beginning of the time period. During the time period households
make transitions to another state by means of Markovian or
semi-Markovian transition rules which take the form of probabilities or could be deterministic. This kind of state
dependence greatly expands the dimensions of the problem and
can be very costly in building detailed and large urban models.

2.7.4 Integration versus unification

A unified comprehensive model has the characteristic that it
can be stated as one consistent simultaneous equation system.
In some cases it may be naturally decomposable into subsystems
which may be solvable recursively, but normally this should
not be possible. It is, however, possible to force an urban
model into a more compartmental form by making assumptions
that certain subsystems interact with one another in a limited
way or are arranged in recursive hierarchies. Such a comprehensive model is integrated but not unified. Integrated
models, though less elegant, are more practical and easier to
formulate and solve.

2.7.5 Specific examples of economic urban models

The literature on economic and non-economic urban simulation
models is reviewed in Anas (1985). None of those models
qualify as the "comprehensive dynamic economic model". It is
beyond our scope to review all of these models. Instead we
will focus on three examples which represent steps towards
the comprehensive urban model and which have been published

in the literature or appear elsewhere in this volume.

1. The Chicago Area Transportation Land Use Analysis System
(CATLAS). This model, discussed in detail in Anas (1983) and
also in Anas and Duann (1984), is a unified treatment of the
housing and travel sectors of an urban area. A temporary
equilibrium is assumed to occur in the housing market and the
housing stock adjusts recursively with a one year lag. The
location and level of employment is given and the service
sector is not modelled. The model has been estimated econom-
etrically and has been applied to long run dynamic simulations.
The model utilizes logit and nested logit equations throughout.

2. The Swedish Prototype of the Regulated Housing Market.
This model is presented in detail (with all the equations) in
Chapter 7 of this volume. It is, like CATLAS, based on logit
equations but is formulated to take into account the complex
institutional structure of the partially regulated Swedish
housing market which serves as the prototype of most European
housing markets.

3. Lowry Type General Equilibrium Model of Employment,
Housing and Travel Networks. Described in Anas (1984-A), this
static model is a unified treatment of employment, housing and
travel networks as in the original Lowry model but with added
economic content.

2.8 Concluding Comment

We believe that the job of building the comprehensive urban
model will take several decades. What we have attempted to do
in this Chapter is to scan the field of economics highlighting
those concepts which are, in one way or another, vital
ingredients of the ultimate comprehensive urban model. We

have made no effort to provide a literature review for this was not the mission of this Chapter. The Chapter can be useful to the model builder as an "organizing framework" for understanding the relevant concepts from economics and for recognizing the mathematical essentials of the treatment of competition, oligopoly, externalities, public goods and dynamic theory.

Chapter 3

APPROACHES TO STOCK DYNAMICS BASED ON SPATIAL INTERACTION
MODELS

A.G. Wilson

3.1 Introduction

Since the publication of the paper by Harris and Wilson (1978),
a set of principles has been established for the dynamic
modelling of urban and regional subsystems with particular
emphasis being placed on supply-side structures and the way
these patterns evolve and change. The methods involve a focus
on the scale of supply-side facilities at each possible location for such facilities and in particular an emphasis on
input and output flows at each such location. Thus spatial
interaction models underpin this approach to dynamics and the
balancing factors which appear in these models provide a
mechanism for representing competition between facilities at
different locations and hence a representation of spatial
interdependence. The relationships specified in particular
cases are typically nonlinear. These properties of interdependence and nonlinearity combine to generate bifurcations -
fundamental structural change - at critical values of parameters or "external" variables and this offers new and important insights into the nature of urban and regional change.

    In this introductory chapter, we outline these methods in
broad terms (Section 3.2) and the present range of application
(Section 3.3). We then discuss both short run (Section 3.4)
and longer run (Section 3.5) research and development problems

associated with the variety of subsystems for which these
methods are relevant. We review the implications of the
analytical insights gained in relation to the use of these
models in planning (Section 3.6). In Section 3.7 we pick up
the major short-term research issues and show how these ideas
can be embedded in a more explicit dynamic and extended
economic framework. There are brief concluding comments in
Section 3.8.

3.2 The Methods

We first recall the principles for a sectorally-aggregated
abstractly-specified subsystem. Let O_i be a set of fixed and
given demands or "needs" and let Z_j be the scale of facilities
at j which can contribute to meeting these. Let T_{ij} be the
amount of O_i which is met at j, and let c_{ij} be a measure of
impedance between i and j (such as travel time or a generalized
cost). For many situations, a production-constrained spatial
interaction model will describe this subsystem:

$$T_{ij} = A_i O_i Z_j^{\alpha} e^{-\beta c_{ij}} \qquad (3.1)$$

α is a parameter which is usually interpreted as a measure of
consumer scale economies and β is a parameter which measures
the importance of travel impedance. Further

$$A_i = 1/\sum_k Z_k^{\alpha} e^{-\beta c_{ij}} \qquad (3.2)$$

to ensure that

$$\sum_j T_{ij} = O_i \qquad (3.3)$$

Then the Harris and Wilson (1978) hypothesis is that

$$\frac{\partial Z_j}{\partial t} = \varepsilon(D_j - C_j)f(Z_j) \tag{3.4}$$

where

$$D_j = \sum_i T_{ij} \tag{3.5}$$

is the amount of revenue attracted to j (assuming O_i is measured in suitable units) and

$$C_j = C_j(Z_j) \tag{3.6}$$

is a function which represents the cost of providing Z_j at j. The function $f(Z_j)$ in (3.4) determines the way Z_j changes for small Z_j. It is usually convenient to take this as a constant or as Z_j, an issue we return to later; and, for convenience of initial exploration, $C_j(Z_j)$ has often been taken as the linear function $k_j Z_j$ for a suitable set of constants, k_j, taken as unit costs of provision, varying for each zone j. Then (3.4) becomes

$$\frac{\partial Z_j}{\partial t} = \varepsilon(D_j - k_j Z_j)Z_j \tag{3.7}$$

and the model is specified by (3.1), (3.2), (3.5) and (3.7). (3.7) is usually taken in difference equation form.

It is also useful to note the following point which can be seen from a scrutiny of (3.4) and (3.7). In the general case, the system is in equilibrium if

$$D_j = C_j(Z_j) \tag{3.8}$$

and in the specific case of (3.7), this takes the form

$$D_j = k_j Z_j \tag{3.9}$$

47

If we substitute for D_j from (3.5) and for T_{ij} from (3.1) and (3.2), we can write the simultaneous equations (3.9) explicitly as

$$\sum_i \frac{O_j Z_j^\alpha e^{-\beta c_{ij}}}{\sum_k Z_k^\alpha e^{-\beta c_{ik}}} = k_j Z_j \tag{3.10}$$

This formulation demonstrates the high degree of inter-dependence - all the Z_ks appear in each j equation - and the nature of the nonlinearities.

Much experience has been gained in running the model in this form - see, for example, Wilson and Clarke (1979) and Clarke and Wilson (1983-B). It is understood that high α and low β generate spatial configurations with a small number of large Z_j and all the possible Z_js zero; low α and high β produce a more even spread of Z_js; if $\alpha < 1$, $Z_j > 0$ for all j. The spatial patterns which are generated in particular cases, however, are obviously also determined by the sets of "external" variables $\{O_i\}$ and $\{c_{ij}\}$ which are, in effect, parameters for the $\{Z_j\}$-model. There are critical values of α, β, $\{O_i\}$ (or $\{c_{ij}\}$ even) at which there are discrete changes in a number of Z_j variables and hence structural changes in pattern.

It has also been demonstrated that it is possible to build on the ideas of May (1976) - cf Wilson (1981-A, 1981-B) - and show that if ε in equation (3.7) exceeds some critical value, there are different kinds of bifurcations as time elapses, even when the system never reaches equilibrium.

3.3 The Range of Application

The following list shows the current range of application of the ideas outlined in Section 3.2 above:

*	agriculture	Wilson and Birkin (1985)
*	industry	Wilson and Birkin (1983)
		Birkin and Wilson (1984-A, 1984-B)
*	retailing	Wilson and Clarke (1979)
		Clarke and Wilson (1983-B)
		G P Clarke (1984)
		M Clarke (1984)
*	education	Wilson and Crouchley (1984)
		Irwin and Wilson (1985)
*	residential location and housing	Clarke and Wilson (1983-A)
*	comprehensive	Birkin, Clarke and Wilson (1984)

What has to be done in each case is to take the general model of Section 3.2, establish an appropriate level of resolution by distinguishing sectors in relation to both demand and supply and then articulate the two principal functions which lie at the heart of the theory which the model represents: the attractiveness function in the spatial model and the cost function, $C_j(Z_j)$. The first of these is shown in equation (3.1) as Z_j^{α} but it could be written more generally as $F(Z_j, \alpha, \ldots)$ and may itself be a function of other variables and parameters. The cost function also needs to be more fully articulated: in effect it requires specifications of the production functions of the various supply-side processes.

Eventually it is important to stitch the submodels together into a comprehensive model and this demands an appropriate accounting framework. There is a long tradition of comprehensive model building going back to Lowry (1964). The ideas of Section 3.2 and the range of application sketched here offer two main lines of advance on the original Lowry model. First, when the Z_js represent retail supply and housing

supply respectively, more realistic mechanisms are offered for
the determination of these variables. Secondly, the range of
submodels is extended to include agriculture - which for
present purposes can be thought of as a land use model particularly in relation to the rural-urban fringe - and industry
as endogenous sectors.

The central argument for linking the submodels in a
comprehensive framework turns on the notion of interdependence.
The O_is of one model are the Z_js of another; and vice versa.
In the industrial subsystem, in the case of flows of intermediate goods and services, the feedbacks are even stronger:
the O_is of the system are mostly made up of the Z_ks of the
same system.

3.4 Short-run Research and Development Issues

We discuss a series of inter-related topics which are important
for a short-run R and D programme.

(i) Information system design

The various submodels (cf Chapters 10 and 16), and
the comprehensive model (cf Chapters 6 and 7), each need a
variety of data-arrays as inputs and can generate a similar
variety of outputs. The running of models, and their useful-
ness in planning, will be facilitated if - probably in connection with the task of designing an accounting system for
the comprehensive model - a suitable information system could
be designed to contain this information in such a way that it
is easily accessible.

(ii) Empirical research

Most of the models desperately need testing with real
data, and this will inevitably lead to further theoretical
refinement. To date, these efforts have been largely confined

to the retail system (M Clarke, 1984 and G P Clarke, 1984) and
a coarse representation of the old Lowry system (Birkin, Clarke
and Wilson, 1984, Lombardo and Rabino, 1983). This involves
the collection of time series data within the kind of information system described above.

(iii) Sensitivity testing

For reasons which will be elaborated in Section 3.5
below, we need to use sensitivity testing to gain a better
understanding of the stability of structures in relation to
variations of parameters and, particularly - because these
have not been the subject of numerical experiment (except, for
a very simple case, in Harris, Choukroun and Wilson, 1982) -
in relation to "external" variables.

(iv) Revised detailed model mechanisms

In the models developed and explored to date, we have
usually employed only the most obvious choices for the crucial
functions in the various submodels. New possibilities need to
be explored and related to ongoing empirical work. Topics
include the representation of supply-side externalities and
scale (dis)economies in the supply side (in relation to the
C_js); the adequate representation of inertia in the representation of change; the specification of different speeds of change
and the time structures of the various processes - refinements
of the ideas simply embodied in ε parameters; the adequate
representation of hierarchical structures.

(v) The incorporation of prices and price dynamics

In the agricultural case (Wilson and Birkin, 1985)
it has been necessary to make land prices and the prices of
products explicit in order to represent the original von Thünen
theory within this representation. This has led to the
development of spatial "cobweb" models. These ideas could now

be extended into other subsystems and could be tested
empirically.

(vi) Economic interpretation
    There is also a more general issue of economic
interpretation. The models represented here can be seen as
"imperfect market" versions of some neo-classical models.
This needs to be articulated so that improved economic evaluation outputs can be derived from the models; and possibly to
allow alternative economic mechanisms to be incorporated.

(vii) Further extension of range of submodels
    There are a number of areas where it may be approp-
riate to re-package the subsystem definitions to emphasise
contemporary problems. Two examples are the articulation of
a labour market model with particular reference to unemployment
and to changing labour skill patterns on both supply and demand
sides. A second example is the more explicit treatment of
facility and household structure.

3.5 Notes of Caution: longer run research issues

The insights which have been gained in the advent of this
style of dynamic modelling are matched by a number of
problems; and so results should be interpreted with caution -
though some of the "problems" can also be considered to offer
further insights into the nature of real geographical structures.
We consider a number of these issues in turn.

(i) The backcloth problem
    Our intuitive understanding of spatial bifurcation
phenomena is based on the analysis of the functions $D_j(Z_j)$ and
$C_j(Z_j)$ and the way they intersect - intersections representing
equilibrium points, the form of the intersection determining

stability. But to carry out this analysis in the neighbourhood of a critical parameter value, we have to assume we know
$\{W_k\}$, $k \neq j$ - which we have called the "backcloth" (cf Wilson
and Clarke, 1979). But we could, of course, repeat the
analysis for any such k and have to make a similar assumption.
There is no easy way out of this difficulty except to say that
it is an important topic for further research. And to make
two further points: first, we have now carried out a large
number of numerical experiments and associated bifurcation
analyses of sample zones; secondly, in practical applications,
we have a known starting point - the state of the system at
the current time. This helps to reduce the order of combinatorial issues associated with the backcloth problem.
However, research is worthwhile, because it is this difficulty
which is at the basis of a particularly hard research task:
to be able to compute values of parameters like α and β (or
0_i or c_{ij}) at which bifurcations take place. At present, we
can interpret bifurcations we find - in reality or in numerical
experiments - but we do not have a systematic calculation
procedure. We return to this issue again in a broader context
below.

(ii)   The nature of bifurcation
        A further complicating feature is that there are
different possible causes for bifurcations which are observed
or anticipated. We have concentrated here on the Harris-
Wilson (1978) mechanism. An alternative is that proposed by
Poston and Wilson (1977). This involves an assumption about
the shape of the utility function of consumers with respect
to facility size. With some difficulty, this assumption can
be built into the attractiveness function of the spatial interaction model and the consequences of doing this are explored
in Clarke, Clarke and Wilson (1985). The general point to
make, however, is that there is a range of possible mechanisms,

and in reality a mix of these are likely to be at work. The
representation and disentangling of these, therefore, constitutes another research task.

(iii) Multiple equilibrium solutions

A feature of nonlinear systems is that the sets of
simultaneous equations whose relations represent equilibria
have multiple solutions. Under suitable conditions of con-
vexity, it may be possible to identify the equilibrium solution which is the global optimum of the corresponding mathematical programming problem. Even that possibility does not
necessarily help, however: there is no reason to think that a
real system, even if it is in equilibrium, is in the global
optimum state. What is needed, ideally, is a knowledge of the
set of possible equilibria, the differences between them, the
probabilities of transition and their possible underlying
influences on the trajectories of real systems which are not
in equilibrium anyway.

(iv) Representations of dynamical systems

Suppose we can characterise a system of interest by
state variables, parameters and, as a special kind of third
variable, time. Then it is possible in principle to exhibit
the behaviours of such a system by various geometric plots:
(i) trajectories in state space; (ii) "regions" of typical
structure or behaviour in parameter space; (iii) particular
state variables against time (with corresponding plots of the
parameter variation with time which is generating the state
variable behaviour); and (iv) trajectories in a combined state-
parameter space. We are accustomed to seeing many such plots
in the dynamical systems literature, but only for simple
systems (necessarily because of the limitations of three dimensions for representation). We need to explore further ways of
representing this kind of knowledge for real complicated urban

systems with large numbers of variables and parameters - taking
due account of the issue of multiplicity of equilibrium solutions mentioned earlier. This involves either taking "slices"
of the various spaces involved or being inventive about identifying and labelling structures and modes of behaviour which can
be characterised in relation to the values of a small number of
parameters. This identifies a range of research problems, one
of which we take up under the next sub-heading as it is worth
selecting for special attention.

(v) "Types" of pattern and modes of behaviour
        At the present time, we are restricted to descrip-
tions of pattern as "concentrated" or "dispersed" and modes of
behaviour in relation to progress towards or away from such
concepts. If we can find ways of refining these concepts,
then we would have a better chance of making progress with (iv)
above.

(vi) Criticality
        We made the point in (i) above that while we could
interpret bifurcations - historical or discovered during
numerical experiments - we could not systematically predict
them. We then remarked in (iv) above that a possible
representation of dynamical behaviour involved the subdivision
of parameter space into "regions", the boundaries of which
represented bifurcation points at which structural change
takes place. We can now see that this provides a more precise
specification of the first problem; but its solution remains
a major research task.

3.6 Implications for Planning

The next step is to review the implications of the above
analysis for the use of models in planning. The first point

to emphasise is a negative one but is very important. Because of the existence of multiple equilibria for realistic systems, and because of the existence of a great variety of bifurcations, an enormous combinatorial problem is exposed: any particular system has a great variety of possible trajectories open to it. The models can be used to interpret a historical trajectory or to predict at least some of the possible states - good or bad - which may be reached in the future. What they cannot be used for is simple conditional forecasting of a traditional type: change some parameters and predict the most likely equilibrium state. There are too many possible future states.

But the knowledge and insights which have been acquired can be used positively. The stability of possible desired future states can be investigated (usually involving sensitivity testing); and the feasibility of finding one path (or preferably more, alternative paths) to achieve such states can be investigated. The resilience of the system, when on such a trajectory, against perturbation can be investigated. And when a global equilibrium state can be calculated, then especially if it is much "better" than the alternatives, the model which generates and articulates such a state at least functions as a design tool.

One clear implication of this analysis is that we need measures of "goodness" and "badness" of system states. It seems best then to go beyond measures of mere economic performance to include anything which is considered relevant to the associated political and social processes. This involves the development of whole batteries of performance indicators which can be calculated from model-generated outputs which are recorded (along with the pi's themselves, and the raw data) in a suitably-defined information system.

The planner can then become a user of this system: changing projections and parameters, running models, calculating performance indicators, investigating stability and feasibility of trajectories. Optimisation models can be run to generate ideas for alternative designs - continually experimenting with the system. Perhaps, now, being a satisficer rather than an optimiser. In the longer run, an information system of this type can be used for monitoring as new data measurements are added which can be compared to plan targets within the information system.

3.7 An Extended "Economic" Model

In this Section we take the model presented in Section 3.2 and tackle two of the short-run research questions of Section 3.4: mainly relating to prices and price dynamics, but also to economic interpretation. We noted in the latter respect that the model of Section 3.2 was an "imperfect market" version of a neo-classical economic model. In fact, we will show that, properly interpreted with prices and land rents incorporated, it is more like a perfect market model; and so we complete the story by investigating the possibility of an imperfect market model, with interesting consequences. The argument follows that first presented in Wilson (1985).

It is important to be more explicit about the mechanism which is at the heart of the model represented in Section 3.2: the $D_j - C_j = 0$ mechanism. Retailers are responding to demand for goods or services which sum to a total D_j, and they are supplying these at a cost to them of C_j. They have to achieve the $D_j = C_j$ balance. But this is not like market clearing. It is a combination of a clearing mechanism for a market in the goods at a more aggregate level with the outcome of spatial competition among retailers. To clarify this, it is useful to distinguish four kinds of agents in the system: consumers, retailers, land owners or developers, and the suppliers of goods to retailers. There are four markets or similar "balancing" operations which relate these agents as indicated on Figure 3.1. The same diagram is shown in Figure 3.2 with corresponding algebraic variables defined. p^G is now the unit price of goods to retailers from what is assumed to be a · regional or national market. Z_j is still taken as a measure of the scale of retail activity at j - say floorspace - and λ is taken as the unit cost of inputs other than goods and land. Land rent is shown as r_j. p_j is the price of goods as supplied by the retailer (or other supplier of a service) at j. $\hat{p}_i$ is the perceived price at i.

Then the following processes can be assumed to fix the various quantities and prices:

(i) E_i and p^G will be determined by an aggregate supply-demand relationship. This is mediated by the perceived price at i, $\hat{p}_i$.

(ii) The retailer at j will have to determine Z_j and p_j to make himself or herself maximally "attractive" to consumers. This will be done so as to balance total costs, C_j, against revenue, D_j.

(iii) Land owners are assumed to be able to extract a unit rent r_j, measured in relation to Z_j, on the basis of a bid rent mechanism.

An appropriate model to represent these processes can now be written down as follows.

The first task is to deal with $\hat{p}_i$. Economic theory would usually take it as $p_j + c_{ij}$ when purchases are made at j. However, this immediately implies the need for a knowledge of destination choice, and although that may be the basis of a possible model, for present purposes we make an alternative assumption:

$$\hat{p}_i = \frac{\sum_j p_j e^{-\beta c_{ij}}}{\sum_j e^{-\beta c_{ij}}} \tag{3.11}$$

Stock Dynamics

That is, it is an average of j-prices, with weightings via the cost impedance term from the interaction model. This seems intuitively reasonable. We can then take

$$E_i = E_i^o(\hat{p}_i)^{-\gamma_1} \tag{3.12}$$

with total demand given by

$$E^D = \sum_i E_i = \sum_i E_i^o(\hat{p}_i)^{-\gamma_1} \tag{3.13}$$

We assume now that E_i^o, and hence E_i, are measured in suitable "quantity units". Let

$$E^S = E_o^S(p^G)^{\gamma_2} \tag{3.14}$$

be the total amount which can be supplied at price p^a, and then equating supply and demand implies

$$E^D = E^S \tag{3.15}$$

or

$$\sum_i E_i^o(\hat{p}_i)^{-\gamma_1} = E_o^S(p^G)^{\gamma_2} \tag{3.16}$$

For the present, assume the array $\{p_j\}$ is known, and then (3.16) can be used to determine p^G. In effect, we have an aggregate market mediated by the retailers' price, p_j.

Then assume the attractiveness of the establishment at j is given by

$$W_j = Z_j^{\alpha_1}(p_j)^{-\alpha_2} \tag{3.17}$$

for $\alpha_1 > 0$, $\alpha_2 > 0$. The spatial interaction model is then

$$S_{ij} = A_i E_i W_j e^{-\beta c_{ij}} \tag{3.18}$$

59

with

$$A_i = 1/\sum_k W_k e^{-\beta c_{ik}} \qquad (3.19)$$

to ensure that

$$\sum_j S_{ij} = E_i \qquad (3.20)$$

For the retailers at j, revenues are given by

$$D_j = p_j \sum_i S_{ij} \qquad (3.21)$$

and costs by

$$C_j = (p^G + \lambda + r_j)Z_j \qquad (3.22)$$

Finally, we need to add mechanisms to the model which will determine Z_j, p_j and r_j. It is easiest to do this if we assume (realistically) that initial values of Z_j, p_j and r_j are always available at time t, say, so that we can concentrate on specifying the adjustment process which gives these quantities at time t + 1. We can then use a 3-D cobweb mechanism similar in principle to that used by Wilson and Birkin (1985) in the context of agricultural location:

$$\Delta Z_j = \varepsilon_1 F_1(D_j - C_j)(f_1(Z_j) \qquad (3.23)$$

$$\Delta p_j = \pm\varepsilon_2 F_2(D_j - C_j)f_2(p_j) \qquad (3.24)$$

$$\Delta r_j = \varepsilon_3 F_3(D_j - C_j)f_3(r_j) \qquad (3.25)$$

The functions f_1, f_2 and f_3 represent the form of the variables near Z_j, p_j or $r_j = 0$. For the purposes of illustration, we take them to be 1, p_j and r_j respectively. The functions F_1,

F_2 and F_3 are normally taken as $D_j - C_j$ at the present state-of-the-art; though ultimately, alternatives should be explored. Thus, specifically, we can take (with time labels now explicit)

$$\Delta Z_j(t, \; t+1) = \varepsilon_1(D_j^t - C_j^t) \tag{3.26}$$

$$\Delta p_j(t, \; t+1) = \pm\varepsilon_2(D_j^t - D_j^t)p_j^t \tag{3.27}$$

$$\Delta r_j(t, \; t+1) = \varepsilon_3(D_j^t - C_j^t)r_j^t \tag{3.28}$$

Then

$$Z_j^{t+1} = Z_j^t + \Delta Z_j(t, \; t+1) \tag{3.29}$$

$$p_j^{t+1} = p_j^t + \Delta p_j(t, \; t+1) \tag{3.30}$$

$$r_j^{t+1} = r_j^t + \Delta r_j(t, \; t+1) \tag{3.31}$$

Equations (3.26) and (3.29) thus essentially represent the adjustment process used to produce equilibrium in the model of Section 3.2. Indeed, if ε_1 is taken as 1 and $\varepsilon_2 = \varepsilon_3 = 0$, then the outcome of an iteration of the model (interpreting $t \rightarrow t+1 \rightarrow t+2 \ldots$ as steps towards equilibrium rather than as increments in time) is precisely that of the method (cf Clarke and Clarke, 1984) usually used to obtain equilibrium for the Section 3.2 model.

Equations (3.27) and (3.30) represent the price adjustment. Assuming $\varepsilon_2 > 0$, the $\pm$ in equation (3.27) represents different kinds of services. For large-scale retailers, owners of superstores, if an "excess" profit is being made ("normal" profits being part of λ), then the strategy will be to reduce p_j. This will have the effect both of increasing custom through a change in the attractiveness term W_j in (3.17) and will increase demand through a decrease in $\hat{p}_i$ in (3.11).

If, however, the service is some kind of "superior" good, like a high-quality restaurant, the appropriate strategy faced with $D_j - C_j > 0$ might be to increase p_j.

The parameters ε_1, ε_2 and ε_3 can be taken as representing the relative strengths of the adjustment processes and clearly this raises substantial questions for empirical work. These will be taken up in Section 3.8 below.

Consider now the model as a whole as given by (3.11) - (3.31). It can be interpreted either as an extended equilibrium model or as a dynamic model the behaviour of which will be influenced from step to step by underlying equilibrium even if an equilibrium is never achieved. The next step in understanding the range of possible system behaviours is to resort to numerical experiments. Some results of this are presented in Wilson (1985).

We now return to the equation of perfect and imperfect markets. The model presented above is "imperfect" in that consumers behave according to a spatial interaction model rather than going to the nearest possible destination. All this can be rationalised by the use of discrete choice theory if appropriate. However, the retailer's behaviour and the $D_j - C_j = 0$ mechanism still imply a kind of perfection. It is useful, and it turns out to be interesting, to explore ways of relaxing this condition.

The model at present is analogous to the transportation problem of linear programming relative to an entropy maximising model - cf Evans (1973), Senior and Wilson (1974), Wilson and Senior (1974). The route to an alternative model therefore lies in the same direction. First, to take the model in mathematical programming form; secondly, to incorporate an entropy term in the variables which are to be relaxed, $-\Sigma_j Z_j (\log Z_j - 1)$ say; and thirdly to relax the constraint $D_j - C_j = 0$. Only the third of these tasks presents any problem. In the transportation problem of linear programming, the relaxed constraint, in our present notation, is

$$\sum_{ij} S_{ij} c_{ij} = C \qquad (3.32)$$

where C takes a value which exceeds the linear programming minimum (and this corresponds to a finite value of β in the spatial interaction model). This argument would suggest imposing a constraint of the form

$$\sum_j (C_j - D_j) = B \qquad (3.33)$$

for some B > 0 which represents the excess "costs" which can be incurred because of market imperfection. However, it turns out that the resulting model, as we will see later, does not have suitable limiting properties. A better condition is

$$\sum_j (C_j - D_j)^2 = B \qquad (3.34)$$

which forces $C_j \to D_j$ as B → 0. (This is not the case with (3.33) since as B → 0, we can have $C_j > D_j$ for some j and $C_j < D_j$ for other j's and still satisfy the constraint.) We now explore the model which can be achieved with these ideas. It does tend to have the two supreme advantages which the entropy-maximising spatial interaction model has over the transportation problem of linear programming: first, it is conceivably more realistic; secondly, there is an explicit formula for Z_j (or S_{ij}). And as a corollary, the restricted programming model is a special case of the more general one. We conduct the argument in terms of the Section 3.2 model. The "economic" embellishments of this section can be added without inherent difficulty.

The mathematical programme which generates the Section 3.2 model can be written (cf Coelho and Wilson, 1976, Coelho,

Williams and Wilson, 1978)

$$\underset{\{S_{ij}, Z_j\}}{\text{Max}} \quad M = -\sum_{ij} S_{ij}(\log S_{ij} - 1)$$

$$+ \sum_i a_i (E_i - \sum_j S_{ij})$$

$$+ \sum_j \lambda_j (C_j - \sum_i S_{ij})$$

$$+ \alpha (\sum_{ij} S_{ij} \log Z_j - H)$$

$$+ \beta (C - \sum_{ij} S_{ij} c_{ij}) \tag{3.35}$$

The constraints are incorporated into the objective function with Lagrangian multipliers. We have written C_j explicitly instead of $k_j W_j$ to facilitate the derivation of more general results later.

In the light of the earlier argument, we now want to add an entropy term in Z_j and modify the constraint $C_j = \sum_i S_{ij}$. The new mathematical programme is then:

$$\underset{\{S_{ij}, Z_j\}}{\text{Max}} \quad M = -\sum_j Z_j(\log Z_j - 1) - \sum_{ij} S_{ij}(\log S_{ij} - 1)$$

$$+ \sum_i a_i (E_i - \sum_j S_{ij})$$

$$+ \lambda \sum_j [(C_j - \sum_i S_{ij})^2 - B]$$

$$+ \alpha (\sum_{ij} S_{ij} \log Z_j - H)$$

$$+ \beta (C - \sum_{ij} S_{ij} c_{ij}) \tag{3.36}$$

We now have to solve

$$\frac{\partial M}{\partial S_{ij}} = 0 \tag{3.37}$$

for $\{S_{ij}\}$ and, more interestingly,

$$\frac{\partial M}{\partial Z_j} = 0 \qquad (3.38)$$

for $\{Z_j\}$ - although it does turn out that the spatial inter-action model is modified too.

$$\frac{\partial M}{\partial S_{ij}} = -\log S_{ij} - a_i - 2\lambda(C_j - \sum_i S_{ij}) + \alpha \log Z_j - \beta c_{ij} = 0$$

$$(3.39)$$

So, replacing -2λ by λ for convenience

$$S_{ij} = e^{-a_i} e^{-\lambda(D_j - C_j)} Z_j^\alpha e^{-\beta c_{ij}} \qquad (3.40)$$

where we have put $D_j = \sum_i S_{ij}$ also for convenience. Put

$$e^{-a_i} = A_i E_i \qquad (3.41)$$

in the usual way and solve the relevant constraint for A_i. Then

$$S_{ij} = A_i E_i e^{-\lambda(D_j - C_j)} Z_j^\alpha e^{-\beta c_{ij}} \qquad (3.42)$$

with

$$A_i = 1/\sum_i e^{-\lambda(D_k - C_k)} F_k^\alpha e^{-\beta c_{ik}} \qquad (3.43)$$

$$\frac{\partial M}{\partial Z_j} = -\log Z_j + 2\lambda(C_j - \sum_i S_{ij})\frac{\partial C_j}{\partial Z_j} + \alpha(\sum_i S_{ij})/Z_j = 0$$

$$(3.44)$$

Again, putting $-2\lambda = \lambda$,

$$Z_j = e^{\lambda(D_j - C_j)\frac{\partial C_j}{\partial Z_j}} e^{\alpha D_j/Z_j} \qquad (3.45)$$

This is the formula we have been seeking for a "dispersed" $\{Z_j\}$ pattern. A reasonable conjection is that Z_j tends to the Harris and Wilson (1978) Z_j as $\lambda \to \infty$ (and when $C_j = kZ_j$, taking k as a constant to be absorbed into the λ). If k_j varies, it should be left explicitly:

$$Z_j = e^{\lambda k_j(D_j - k_j Z_j)} e^{\alpha D_j/Z_j} \qquad (3.46)$$

There is, of course, one snag: Z_j appears on both sides of (3.45) and (3.46) - and indeed it is implied in D_j and C_j. The equations for $\{Z_j\}$, say (3.46) to be explicit, therefore, have to be solved iteratively. If we again take t as the basis of either a dynamic model or an iteration count in a sequential progression to equilibrium,

$$Z_j^{t+1} = e^{\lambda k_j(D_j^t - k_j Z_j^t)} e^{\alpha D_j^t/Z_j^t} \qquad (3.47)$$

The equations have some sensible properties: when $D_j^t > k_j Z_j^t$, Z_j grows; and vice versa. However, experience to date suggests that this is a delicately-balanced iterative procedure. This experience is reported in Wilson (1985).

There are alternative ways of relaxing the $D_j = C_j$ constraints, but none seem, as yet, to be as satisfactory or interesting as the one used above. The known alternatives are sketched in Wilson (1985).

We end this section with the remark that it is relatively easy in principle to merge the ideas of the "economic" extension with those of $\{Z_j\}$ - entropy-maximising dispersion. Suppose t, t+1 in (3.47) are times. Then we can get an increment and probably more realistic alternative as follows:

$$Z_j^{t+1} - Z_j^t = e^{\lambda k_j (D_j^t - k_j Z_j^t)} e^{\alpha D_j^t / Z_j^t} - Z_j^t \qquad (3.48)$$

The obvious modification, therefore,

$$\Delta Z_j(t,\ t+1) = \varepsilon_1 \left[e^{\lambda k_j (D_j^t - k_j Z_j^t)} e^{\alpha D_j^t / Z_j^t} - Z_j^t \right] \qquad (3.49)$$

and

$$Z_j^{t+1} = Z_j^t + \Delta Z_j^t \qquad (3.50)$$

Equations (3.49) and (3.50) could then be substituted for (3.26) and (3.29) in the earlier model.

3.8 Concluding Comments: problems of implementation

A constructive introduction to this section is to compare the position which has now been reached to that of the Lowry (1964) model and its closely related variants. The service part of that model was based on a set of spatial interaction models, say $\{S_{ij}^g\}$, for $g = 1, 2, 3$ representing local, intermediate and metropolitan services (corresponding to high, medium and low β values respectively). The quantities $D_j^g = \sum_i S_{ij}^g$ were then calculated and retail employment taken as proportional to these. In the original Lowry model, attractiveness terms did not appear in the service equations. In later variants they did, but it was not until about 1976 onwards that there was any systematic attempt to achieve the "balancing" of the stock dynamics of this chapter. However, there is a snag: the new model is likely to be much more effective, but it does demand detail, parti- cularly on the form of cost functions. It is not clear without much experimentation, therefore, what the appropriate sectoral level of resolution should be. We return to this issue in Chapter 8. It is also now clear that there are many choices about the particular form of model to be used - especially in relation to the "economic" and "dispersion" extensions presented

67

in Section 3.7. Nonetheless, what is clear is that a powerful "kit" of model building methods has been assembled and
we argued in 3.3 that this could be widely applied. However,
we have already discussed the difficulty of applying these
ideas for any short-run model-building project in the service
sector. It is more difficult for other sectors. We therefore
restrict the application in this book to services in Chapter 8
below. This also has the advantage that the merits of alternative models can be explored in relation to other sectors.

Chapter 4

MASTER EQUATIONS

G. Haag

4.1 Deterministic and Probabilistic Description of the Evolutions of Systems

The master equation provides a fairly general mathematical method for describing the time development of any complex system (Weidlich and Haag, 1983). Before going into details of its structure, some examples will be given that illustrate the scope of its applications which range from physics, chemistry and biology, to economics (Haken, 1977), sociology and psychology. We shall also remark on the relation between deterministic and probabilistic descriptions of systems.

Consider a system which can pass through different states in the course of time. For simplicity, we will assume that the number of different states $\underset{\sim}{i}$ is finite, so that the index $\underset{\sim}{i}$ characterizing each state is a discrete number of a set $\underset{\sim}{i} = \{i_1, i_2, \ldots, i_L\}$ of discrete numbers. Let us assume now that at an initial time t_o the system is in state $\underset{\sim}{i}_o = \underset{\sim}{i}(t_o)$. Two possible descriptions of the evolution over time are then feasible:

(a) The information about the dynamics of the system can be complete. For this case the description is fully deterministic and leads to the unique determination of the states $\underset{\sim}{i}(t)$ at later times $t > t_o$. Any computer can be taken as an example

for such a deterministic system with a finite - though very
large - number of states $\underset{\sim}{i}$. Beginning with an initial state
$\underset{\sim o}{i}$ set by the program, the central processor, the memory units
and the peripheral devices of the computer traverse a sequence
of states, $\underset{\sim 1}{i}$, $\underset{\sim 2}{i}$, ..., $\underset{\sim N}{i}$, which are fully predetermined by
the prescribed program. Finally, the unique result of the
calculation represents the final state of the system.

(b) The information about the dynamics of the system can be
incomplete. In this case the description of the time evolution is probabilistic only. That means an exact prediction
of the state $\underset{\sim}{i}(t)$ reached by the system is not possible.
Instead, the members of an ensemble of identical systems -
each of them prepared in the same initial state $\underset{\sim}{i}(t_o)$ - will
develop into different states $\underset{\sim}{i}(t)$ at time t. The best
information available in this situation is the probability
with which a system reaches the state i at time t, given that
it was prepared in state $\underset{\sim o}{i}$ at time t_o. This special prob-
ability $p(\underset{\sim}{i}, t \,|\, \underset{\sim o}{i}, t_o)$ is denoted as "conditional probability".
The master equation will turn out to be the tool for determin-
ing this quantity.

Let us now compare the deterministic and the probabilistic
approach as sketched for cases (a) and (b). In describing the
evolution of systems the latter obviously is the more general
one, since the case of "incomplete knowledge" about the systems
comprises "complete knowledge" as a limiting case whereas the
converse is not true. This fact is revealed by the shape of
the probability distribution $P(\underset{\sim}{i}; t)$ itself: for many cases
the master equation leads to an evolution of the distribution
such that it develops one outstanding mode which is peaked
sharply around the most likely state. This means that the
system assumes the state $\underset{\sim}{i} = \underset{\sim Max}{i}(t)$ with overwhelming probability at time t, whereas all other alternative states

$i \neq i_{\mathrm{Max}}(t)$ are highly improbable at the same time. Usually, this case is denoted by a quasi-deterministic evolution of the system along the path $i(t) \simeq i_{\mathrm{Max}}(t)$.

4.2 Some General Concepts of Probability Theory

Before deriving the master equation it is useful to introduce some fundamental concepts of probability theory that especially apply to systems whose evolution are described in probabilistic terms (Stratonovich, 1967). As before, it is assumed that the system can be in one of the mutually exclusive different states which are characterized by a vector i consisting of one or several discrete numbers. In the course of time, transitions between different states can take place.

Since in general one does not know with certainty in which state the system is, the probability distribution function

$$P(i; t) \tag{4.1}$$

is introduced. By definition, $P(i; t)$ is the probability of finding the system in state i at time t. This probability has to be interpreted as follows. In an ensemble of a large number of equally prepared systems, so that each of them belongs to the same probability distribution, one would find systems in state i at time t with approximately the relative frequency $P(i; t)$. In the limiting case of an infinite number of systems, those found in state i are found there with exactly the relative frequency $P(i; t)$. Since the system is with certainty in one of the states i at any time t, the distribution function has to satisfy the condition

$$\sum_{i} P(i; t) = 1 \tag{4.2}$$

where the sum extends over all states i.

Furthermore, we now introduce the most important quantity for the time evolution of the system, the conditional probability

$$p(i_2, t_2|i_1, t_1) \qquad (4.3)$$

By definition it is the probability to find the system in the state i_2 at time t_2, given that it was with certainty in the state i_1 at time t_1. The conditional probability is fundamental for the dynamics of the system, since it describes how the probability spreads out in the time interval $(t_2 - t_1)$, given that it was concentrated on the state i_1 at time t_1. The conditional probability may also depend on the previous history of the system, that is on states traversed before arriving at state i_1 at time t_1. In this general case the probability evolution process may become very complicated.

Fortunately, in many cases the so-called Markov assumption holds, at least as a good approximation. This postulates that the evolution within time of the conditional probability $p(i_2, t_2|i_1, t_1)$ only depends on the initial state i_1 at time t_1 and the state i_2 at t_2 but not on states of the system prior to t_1. In other words, after arriving at state i_1, the system has lost its historic memory and previous states do not matter in the process of further evolution. Since in many cases systems can be defined such that the Markov assumption is satisfied, this assumption will be assumed below.

Let us now draw some conclusions about the properties of the conditional probability. From the definition, the following equations must be satisfied:

$$p(i_2, t_1|i_1, t_1) = \delta_{i_2, i_1} \qquad (4.4)$$

where

$$\delta_{i_2, \, i_1} = \begin{cases} 1 & \text{for} \quad i_2 = i_1 \\ 0 & \text{for} \quad i_2 \neq i_1 \end{cases}$$

and

$$\sum_{i_2} p(i_2, \, t_2 | i_1, \, t_1) = 1 \qquad (4.5)$$

Equation (4.4) follows because at time $t_2 = t_1$ the state is i_1 with probability 1. Equation (4.5) holds, since the system at any time t_2 must be in one of the states i_2 of the system.

From (4.3), (4.4) and (4.5) it becomes clear that the conditional probability is the special probability distribution which evolves from the initial distribution $P(i; \, t_1) = \delta_{i, \, i_1}$. Further, we recall the so-called joint probability:

$$p(i_n, \, t_n; \, i_{n-1}, \, t_{n-1}; \, \cdots; \, i_2, \, t_2; \, i_1, \, t_1) \qquad (4.6)$$

By definition, this n-fold function is the joint probability to find the system in state i_1 at t_1, in state i_2 at t_2 and $\cdots$ in state i_n at t_n. From this definition, it follows that the lower order joint probabilities can be obtained from the higher ones by the following reduction formula:

$$p(i_3, \, t_3; \, i_1, \, t_1) = \sum_{i_2} p(i_3, \, t_3; \, i_2, \, t_2; \, i_1, \, t_1) \qquad (4.7)$$

or, in the general case, by

$$p(i_n, \, t_n; \, \cdots; \, i_{k+1}, \, t_{k+1}; \, i_{k-1}, \, t_{k-1}; \, \cdots; \, i_1, \, t_1)$$

$$= \sum_{i_k} p(i_n, \, t_n; \, \cdots; \, i_{k+1}, \, t_{k+1}; \, i_k, \, t_k; \, i_{k-1}, \, t_{k-1}; \, \cdots; \, i_1, \, t_1)$$

$$(4.8)$$

Clearly, the summation in (4.7) of $p(\underset{\sim}{i}_3, t_3; \underset{\sim}{i}_2, t_2; \underset{\sim}{i}_1, t_1)$
over all possible states at t_2 leads to the probability of
being in state $\underset{\sim}{i}_1$ at t_1 and in state $\underset{\sim}{i}_3$ at t_3 irrespective of
the state at time t_2. That means it leads to $p(\underset{\sim}{i}_3, t_3; \underset{\sim}{i}_1, t_1)$.

If we introduce the Markov assumption, all joint probabilities can be expressed in terms of the probability (4.1)
and the conditional probability (4.3). In particular, the
two-fold joint probability has clearly the form

$$p(\underset{\sim}{i}_2, t_2; \underset{\sim}{i}_1, t_1) = p(\underset{\sim}{i}_2, t_2|\underset{\sim}{i}_1, t_1)P(\underset{\sim}{i}_1; t_1) \qquad (4.9)$$

This result can be generalised taking into account that the
conditional probability does not, by Markov assumption, depend
on the previous history. Then

$$p(\underset{\sim}{i}_n, t_n; \underset{\sim}{i}_{n-1}, t_{n-1}; \cdots; \underset{\sim}{i}_2, t_2; \underset{\sim}{i}_1, t_1)$$

$$= p(\underset{\sim}{i}_n, t_n|\underset{\sim}{i}_{n-1}, t_{n-1}) \cdots p(\underset{\sim}{i}_2, t_2|\underset{\sim}{i}_1, t_1)P(\underset{\sim}{i}_1; t_1)$$

$$(4.10)$$

The composition formulae (4.9) and (4.10) may now be combined
with the reduction formulae like (4.7) and (4.8), in order to
derive the Chapman-Kolmogorov equation. Taking the sum over
$\underset{\sim}{i}_1$ in (4.9) and using the reduction formula (4.8) yields

$$P(\underset{\sim}{i}_2; t_2) = \sum_{\underset{\sim}{i}_1} p(\underset{\sim}{i}_2, t_2; \underset{\sim}{i}_1, t_1)$$

$$= \sum_{\underset{\sim}{i}_1} p(\underset{\sim}{i}_2, t_2|\underset{\sim}{i}_1, t_1)P(\underset{\sim}{i}_1; t_1) \qquad (4.11)$$

Equation (4.11) shows how the probability distribution $P(\underset{\sim}{i}; t)$
is propagated in the course of time by means of the conditional
probability $p(\underset{\sim}{i}_2, t_2|\underset{\sim}{i}_1, t_1)$. Therefore, the latter is also
referred to as the propagator. By inserting (4.9), (4.10) in

(4.7) we obtain

$$p(\underset{\sim}{i}_3,\ t_3|\underset{\sim}{i}_1,\ t_1)P(\underset{\sim}{i}_1;\ t_1)$$

$$= \sum_{\underset{\sim}{i}_2} p(\underset{\sim}{i}_3,\ t_3|\underset{\sim}{i}_2,\ t_2)p(\underset{\sim}{i}_2,\ t_2|\underset{\sim}{i}_1,\ t_1)P(\underset{\sim}{i}_1;\ t_1) \qquad (4.12)$$

Since this equation must hold for an arbitrary initial distribution $P(\underset{\sim}{i}_1;\ t_1)$, we can also conclude that

$$p(\underset{\sim}{i}_3,\ t_3|\underset{\sim}{i}_1,\ t_1) = \sum_{\underset{\sim}{i}_2} p(\underset{\sim}{i}_3,\ t_3|\underset{\sim}{i}_2,\ t_2)p(\underset{\sim}{i}_2,\ t_2|\underset{\sim}{i}_1,\ t_1)$$

$$\qquad (4.13)$$

Equation (4.13) is the well-known Chapman-Kolmogorov equation. It shows how the propagator from t_1 to t_3 can be decomposed into propagators from t_1 to t_2 and from t_2 to t_3.

4.3 The Master Equation: equation of motion for mean values and variances

In Section 4.2 we saw that the propagator, the conditional probability is the crucial quantity determining the evolution of any probability distribution $P(\underset{\sim}{i};\ t)$ over time (see in particular (4.11)). The master equation is nothing but a differential equation in time for the propagator: or for the probability distribution itself. It can be derived by considering equation (4.11) for times $t_1 = t$, $t_2 = t{+}\tau$, where τ is an (infinitesimally) short time interval. Proceeding in this way, we obtain the short-time evolution.

$$P(\underset{\sim}{i}_2;\ t{+}\tau) = \sum_{\underset{\sim}{i}_1} p(\underset{\sim}{i}_2,\ t{+}\tau|\underset{\sim}{i}_1,\ t)P(\underset{\sim}{i}_1;\ t) \qquad (4.14)$$

The short-term propagator is now being expanded in a Taylor series around t with respect to the variable $t_2 = t{+}\tau$, yielding

75

$$p(i_2, t+\tau | i_1, t) = p(i_2, t | i_1, t) + \tau \frac{\partial p(i_2, t_2 | i_1, t)}{\partial t_2}\bigg|_{t_2=t}$$

$$+ \text{ higher powers in } \tau \quad (4.15)$$

Making use of (4.4) and (4.5) in (4.15) we obtain

$$p(i_2, t | i_1, t) = \delta_{i_2, i_1}$$

$$\sum_{i} \frac{\partial p(i, t_2 | i_1, t)}{\partial t_2}\bigg|_{t_2=t} = 0 \quad (4.16)$$

where the sum extends over all states i of the system. Re-inserting (4.16) in (4.15) gives us

$$p(i_2, t+\tau | i_1, t) = \tau w(i_2; i_1) \qquad \text{for } i_1 \neq i_2 \quad (4.17)$$

$$p(i_2, t+\tau | i_1, t) = 1 - \tau \sum_{i \neq i_2} w(i; i_2) \quad \text{for } i_1 = i_2$$

where the abbreviation

$$w(i_2; i_1) = \frac{\partial p(i_2, t_2 | i_1, t)}{\partial t_2}\bigg|_{t_2=t} \quad (4.18)$$

has been introduced and where the higher powers in τ have been omitted since these contributions can be neglected in the limit $\tau \to 0$. What is the interpretation of (4.17)? Given that the system was in state i_1, the probability that it reaches state i_2 in the infinitesimally short-time interval is proportional to that interval and to the transition rate* $w(i_2; i_1)$ from i_1 to i_2. On the other hand, the probability

---

* There exists no normalization condition like (4.5) for the transition rates.

to remain in the same state during the interval τ is one minus
the probability transferred to all other states within the
time interval.

The master equation is established if (4.17) is inserted
in (4.14). Dividing (4.14) by τ, then after trivial rearrangement and taking the limit $\tau \to 0$ with

$$\lim_{\tau \to 0} \frac{p(\underset{\sim}{n};\ t+\tau) - p(\underset{\sim}{n};\ t)}{\tau} = \frac{\partial p(\underset{\sim}{n};\ t)}{\partial t}$$

we obtain

$$\frac{\partial P(\underset{\sim}{n};\ t)}{\partial t} = \sum_{\underset{\sim}{m}} w(\underset{\sim}{n};\ \underset{\sim}{m})P(\underset{\sim}{m};\ t) - \sum_{\underset{\sim}{m}} w(\underset{\sim}{m};\ \underset{\sim}{n})P(\underset{\sim}{n};\ t) \qquad (4.19)$$

which is the master equation. The sum extends over all states
$\underset{\sim}{m}$. (To avoid subscripted indices, we now use $\underset{\sim}{n}$ and $\underset{\sim}{m}$ instead
of $\underset{\sim}{i}_1$ and $\underset{\sim}{i}_2$ respectively.) This is a system of first-order
differential equations for the evolution with time of the
distribution function $P(\underset{\sim}{n};\ t)$. The master equation is valid
for any probability distribution $P(\underset{\sim}{n};\ t)$, in particular for
the conditional probability $p(\underset{\sim}{n};\ t|\underset{\sim}{n}_0;\ t_0)$ itself. Therefore,
it is very wide in scope.

The master equation can be interpreted in an illustrative
way as follows. The quantities $w(\underset{\sim}{m};\ \underset{\sim}{n})$ are transition probabilities per time unit (or transition rates) in the following
sense: $w(\underset{\sim}{m};\ \underset{\sim}{n})P(\underset{\sim}{n};\ t)$ is the probability transferred from
state $\underset{\sim}{n}$ to the state $\underset{\sim}{m}$ per unit of time, which is also referred
to as the probability flux from $\underset{\sim}{n}$ to $\underset{\sim}{m}$. Then (4.19) can also
be read as a rate equation for probabilities.

The change per unit of time of the probability of state
$\underset{\sim}{n}$ (that is the left-hand side of (4.19) is the sum of two terms
with opposite effects). Firstly, there is a probability flux
from all other states $\underset{\sim}{m}$ into state $\underset{\sim}{n}$. This is the first term
of the right-hand side of (4.19). Secondly, there is the
probability flux out of state $\underset{\sim}{n}$ into all other states $\underset{\sim}{m}$, the

second term of the right-hand side of (4.19). The change per time unit of the probability $P(\underset{\sim}{n}; t)$ is caused by the difference of the probability fluxes.

One solves the master equation by summing up all probability fluxes to and from each state, that is, by calculating the corresponding rise or decay in the course of time of the probabilities of each state $\underset{\sim}{n}$. Since the approach generates a complex system of equations for the probability distribution, both exact and approximate methods of solution are valuable. A variety of such methods, involving more or less restrictive assumptions, are available in Haken (1977), Weidlich and Haag (1983), Haag, Weidlich and Alber (1977), Haag (1978), Haag and Hänggi (1979), Hänggi and Haag (1980).

The master equation gives the most detailed knowledge about the evolution of a system under conditions of uncertainty or restricted information. The quantities representing this restricted information are the transition rates, namely, the transition probabilities per unit of time $w(\underset{\sim}{m}; \underset{\sim}{n})$, to reach $\underset{\sim}{m}$ from $\underset{\sim}{n}$. These transition rates can often be inferred from phenomenological and substantive considerations (see Sections 7.2 and 10.2 in Chapters 7 and 10 below). If the transition probabilities $w(\underset{\sim}{m}; \underset{\sim}{n})$ do not explicitly depend on time t, the master equation thus describes a probability equilibration process starting with an arbitrary initial distribution $P(\underset{\sim}{n}; t_0)$ and ending up with a unique final distribution $P(\underset{\sim}{n}; \infty) = P_{st}(\underset{\sim}{n})$. The latter is the probability distribution obeying the stationary master equation

$$0 = \sum_{\underset{\sim}{m}} \{ w(\underset{\sim}{n}; \underset{\sim}{m}) P_{st}(\underset{\sim}{m}) - w(\underset{\sim}{m}; \underset{\sim}{n}) P_{st}(\underset{\sim}{n}) \} \quad \text{for all } \underset{\sim}{n} \quad (4.20)$$

In general, it is not easy to obtain an analytical form for $P_{st}(\underset{\sim}{n})$. In special cases, however, the condition of "detailed balance" is fulfilled:

$$w(\underset{\sim}{n};\ \underset{\sim}{m})P_{st}(\underset{\sim}{m}) = w(\underset{\sim}{m};\ \underset{\sim}{n})P_{st}(\underset{\sim}{n}) \tag{4.21}$$

This means that not only the global balance of all probability
fluxes (4.20) holds, but that a probability flux balance between
each pair of states holds separately. If (4.21) holds, the
stationary solution can easily be constructed (Haken, 1977).
Take any chain ζ of states $\underset{\sim}{n}_o = \underset{\sim}{0}$, $\underset{\sim}{n}_1 = \underset{\sim}{1}$, ... $\underset{\sim}{n}_{n-1} = (\underset{\sim}{n}-1)$,
$\underset{\sim}{n}_n = \underset{\sim}{n}$ from a reference state $\underset{\sim}{0}$ to an arbitrary state $\underset{\sim}{n}$, so
that all transition probabilities $w(\underset{\sim}{\gamma};\ \underset{\sim}{\gamma}-1)$, $w(\underset{\sim}{\gamma}-1;\ \underset{\sim}{\gamma})$ are
nonvanishing. The repeated application of (4.21) then yields

$$P_{st}(\underset{\sim}{n}) = P_{st}(\underset{\sim}{0}) \prod_{\underset{\sim}{\gamma}=\underset{\sim}{0}}^{\underset{\sim}{n}-1} \frac{w(\underset{\sim}{\gamma}+1;\ \underset{\sim}{\gamma})}{w(\underset{\sim}{\gamma};\ \underset{\sim}{\gamma}+1)} \tag{4.22}$$

For many cases of application, however, it is sufficient
to consider the time evolution of certain mean values over
the states. For those purposes, equations of motion for mean
values and variances will now be derived. In most cases,
however, the full information contained in the probability
distribution cannot be exploited because of lack of sufficiently
comprehensive empiric data. Therefore, it is convenient to
make a transition to a less exhaustive description in terms of
equations of motion for the mean values $\overline{\underset{\sim}{n}}$ only.
The mean value of a function $f(\underset{\sim}{n})$ of $\underset{\sim}{n}$ is defined by

$$\overline{f(\underset{\sim}{n})} = \sum_{\underset{\sim}{n}} f(\underset{\sim}{n})P(\underset{\sim}{n};\ t) \tag{4.23}$$

In particular the mean occupation numbers of a state are given
by

$$\overline{\underset{\sim}{n}}(t) = \sum_{\underset{\sim}{n}} \underset{\sim}{n}P(\underset{\sim}{n};\ t) \tag{4.24}$$

The variance $\sigma^2(t)$ is obtained from

$$\sigma^2(t) = (\overline{n^2}(t) - \overline{n}(t)^2) \tag{4.25}$$

79

The equations of motion for the mean values and the variances are obtained by multiplying the left-hand side and the right-hand side of the master equation accordingly and taking the sum over all configurations. This leads in general not to a closed set of mean value equations but to a hierarchical system. To solve the equation for the first moment $\overline{\underset{\sim}{n}}(t)$ the change with time of the second moment $\overline{\underset{\sim}{n}^2}(t)$ has to be known; and for solving the equations of motion for the second moment the third moment $\overline{\underset{\sim}{n}^3}(t)$ is needed, and so on. But, if it is justified to assume that the probability distribution $P(\underset{\sim}{n};\ t)$ has only one highly peaked maximum, a closed set of approximate mean value equations can be obtained. The general form of these approximate mean value equations is:

$$\frac{d(\overline{\underset{\sim}{n}})t}{dt} = \underset{\overline{\underset{\sim}{m}}}{\Sigma}\ w(\overline{\underset{\sim}{n}}(t);\ \overline{\underset{\sim}{m}}(t))\overline{\underset{\sim}{m}}(t)\ -\ \underset{\overline{\underset{\sim}{m}}}{\Sigma}\ w(\overline{\underset{\sim}{m}}(t),\ \overline{\underset{\sim}{n}}(t))\overline{\underset{\sim}{n}}(t)$$

$$(4.26)$$

or formally this can be written as

$$\frac{d\overline{n}_i(t)}{dt} = F_i(\overline{n}_1(t),\ \overline{n}_2(t),\ \ldots,\ \overline{n}_L(t))\quad i = 1 \ldots L$$

$$(4.27)$$

The equations (4.26) and (4.27) are an autonomous closed non-linear set of differential equations*. Hence in this case the

---

* The master equation (4.19) is always linear in the probability distribution function $P(\underset{\sim}{m},\ t)$, even if the transition rates $w(\underset{\sim}{m};\ \underset{\sim}{n})$ are nonlinear in the state variables $\underset{\sim}{m};\ \underset{\sim}{n}$. The mean value equations are only linear if the transition rates $w(\overline{\underset{\sim}{m}}(t),\ \overline{\underset{\sim}{n}}(t))$ are constant (independent of $\overline{\underset{\sim}{m}}(t),\ \overline{\underset{\sim}{n}}(t)$).

macrovariables $\overline{n}_i(t)$ obey a quasi-closed self-contained sub-
dynamic. The intuitive reason for this behaviour is that the
rapidly-fluctuating random forces exerted by microvariables
(such as the decision behaviour of a single individual) only
lead to small fluctuations of the macrovariable around this
smoothly developing ensemble average.

The stationary solution of (4.26) and (4.27), $\hat{n}$, can be
written formally as

$$F_i(\hat{n}_1, \hat{n}_2, \ldots, \hat{n}_L; \alpha c) = 0; \quad i = 1 \ldots L \qquad (4.28)$$

and we note that

$$\lim_{t\to\infty} \overline{n}(t) = \hat{n} \qquad (4.29)$$

then correspond to the maxima of the stationary probability
distribution function $P_{st}(n)$ and $\overline{n}(t)$ correspond to the maxima
of the moving probability distribution $P(n; t)$.

But, the solutions may be more complicated if (4.26) and
(4.27) exhibit "bifurcation behaviour" (see Haken, 1975,
Sattinger, 1973, Marsden and McCracken, 1976). In this case
the solutions of (4.26), (4.27) obtained with slightly different initial values $\overline{n}(0)$ in the vicinity of a "critical
value" n_c (say an unstable critical point) have completely
different paths $n^\alpha(t)$ from the members α of the ensemble. The
individual paths then can deviate significantly from their
mean value $n(t)$. In other words, infinitesimally small
differences of certain "causes" such as the random forces,
may lead to very large differences of the "effects", ie the
paths of the macrovariables. The non-uniqueness of stationary
points (the solutions of (4.28)) is a necessary condition for
the appearance of bifurcation phenomena. In this sense those
critical or stationary points which are related to maxima (or
minima) of the probability distribution function are stable

(or unstable).

It must be emphasised that one of the most important advantages of the master equation approach is that it provides the link between the micro-economic transition rates $w(\underset{\sim}{m}; \underset{\sim}{n})$ which depend on the individual decision behaviour of members of the population and the meso- or macro-economic mean value equations of the form (4.26), (4.27).

All that we have to do if we want to model a socio-economic system by means of a master equation approach is to specify the so-called transition rates between different states, $w(\underset{\sim}{m}; \underset{\sim}{n})$.

In physics the transition rates may often be derived from first principles. In social science, however, it is often necessary to resort to a phenomeno-logical approach starting from appropriate but flexible choices of the socio-configuration and the transition rates. In social science, two procedures to obtain the transition rates appear to be possible:

(a) The transition rates could be determined empirically for an ensemble of members (actors) of the society under certain socio-economic conditions.

(b) A plausible theoretical form for $w(\underset{\sim}{m}; \underset{\sim}{n})$ could be established. This form should be flexible enough to describe a variety of possibilities; that is, it must contain one or more open parameters. Inserting the hypothesis into the equations of the model results in certain structures for the socio-configuration. These could then be compared with reality in order to verify or not the plausibility of the chosen transitional rates.

How this works will become explicit in the discussion of the master equation approach to the housing market (Chapter 9), the service sector (Chapter 11) and the labour market

(Chapter 14). Also, some further mathematical tools will be introduced in these Chapters.

Chapter 5

STOCHASTIC EXTREMAL PROCESSES

G. Leonardi

5.1 Introduction

The purpose of this chapter is to introduce the theory of
stochastic extremal processes and its applications to urban
economic problems. Such a process can be broadly defined as
a special type of secondary stochastic process, that is, a
point process, generating a sequence of random events over
time, coupled with a sequence of random variables, each
element in the sequence being associated with each instant
of occurrence of the events in the point process. Such
secondary stochastic processes are well studied in probability
theory and statistics, mainly with regard to the behaviour of
the sum of the random variables in the sequence associated
with the random events. The peculiarity of a stochastic
extremal process is that not the sum, but the maximum in the
sequence is studied.

From this general description the relevance of the theory
to economic analysis should become apparent: the economic
agents under study can be assumed to have a maximizing
behaviour. For example, in discrete demand analysis the
stochastic point process might describe the flow of information about alternatives received by a demand unit - at each
random event the demand unit becomes aware of a specific
alternative available. The random variable associated with

each random event might be the utility associated with that specific alternative. If demand is utility maximizing, at any given time record will be kept of the highest-utility alternative known so far. Thus, the unfolding over time of utility-maximizing behaviour is precisely a stochastic extremal process. Moreover, this formulation allows in a natural way the introduction of some realistic features usually not considered in static deterministic models, like imperfect information, progressive learning and forgetting, heterogeneity in individual preferences.

Another example is provided by the other side of the market, the supply behaviour. Assume a supplier is selling a discrete supply unit and trying to maximize the revenue, that is selling at the highest possible price. In this case, the point process might be the flow of information about potential consumers; at each random event the supplier becomes aware of a specific consumer interested in buying. The random variable associated with each random event might be the bid price offered by that specific consumer, that is the maximum price he is willing to pay. Since the supplier is revenue-maximizing, at any given time in the bidding process, he will keep record of the highest bid price offered so far. Thus, the unfolding over time of bid-price maximizing behaviour can be cast in the terminology of stochastic extremal processes.

Although the two examples above refer to demand and supply behaviour separately, one is usually interested in the interactions between them. This coupling usually gives rise to an assignment process, where demand units are matched against supply units according to rules determined by the signals (utilities and prices) they exchange with each other. The dynamic unfolding of an assignment process is therefore the main application of stochastic extremal processes proposed in this chapter, and this determines its structure, which is outlined here.

Although the emphasis of the whole chapter is on dynamics, the first two sections, 5.2 and 5.3, briefly review the static, or equilibrium, assignment problem, both in its deterministic and in its stochastic version. This will, hopefully, make the economic-orientated reader feel more comfortable, by using tools of analysis and formulations which should be familiar to him, like mathematical programming. At the same time, the start from the equilibrium assignment problem will provide the point of departure for the dynamic generalizations which are developed in subsequent sections. 5.4 and 5.5 constitute the bulk of the chapter, and they contain the definitions and main results on general stochastic extremal processes. The level of generality adopted here is not the highest possible, but it is tailored to the kinds of applications proposed in the rest of the chapter, as well as those in Chapters Nine and Fifteen.

In the final section, 5.7, we go back to the assignment problem, which is now treated in dynamic stochastic terms, by applying the results of Sections 5.4 to 5.6. The model developed in this section constitutes the main theoretical result of this chapter as far as urban economic applications are concerned. Its applications to the housing market and the labour market are discussed in detail in Chapters Nine and Fifteen.

It is worth emphasizing that the chapter ends, as it starts, with a statement about a mathematical programming embedding property. It is shown that the dynamic assignment problem has a unique equilibrium, which is the same as the one used as a starting point in Sections 5.2 and 5.3, and that a concave mathematical program embedding it exists. Embedding market equilibria into mathematical programming formulations is not new in economics. It is a classic approach to derive market clearing conditions by maximizing total benefit (sum of consumers' and producers' surplus). Here it will be shown that the equilibrium stochastic assignment can be interpreted

in precisely the same terms, and is therefore perfectly consistent with classic economic theory, although it has been
derived with an approach rooted in mathematical statistics.

5.2 A Static Deterministic Assignment Problem

Before any stochastic and dynamic generalization is developed,
it is worth reviewing the static deterministic assignment
problem in its simplest form, together with its main properties,
most of which carry over to more complex models. The simplest
and neatest formulation of the assignment problem is the
linear programming one first proposed by Hitchcock (1941) and
Koopmans (1949), and developed in algorithmic terms by
Dantzig (1951) and Ford and Fulkerson (1956). Define:

Γ	the set of demand units
Ω	the set of supply units
$P = \lvert\Gamma\rvert$	the cardinality (number of elements) of Γ
$Q = \lvert\Omega\rvert$	the cardinality of Ω
$u{:}\Gamma{\times}\Omega{\to}R$	a real-valued function on the cartesian product of Γ and Ω, called the utility function.

For a specific pair (h,z) $h\epsilon\Gamma$, $z\epsilon\Omega$, the value of u will be
denoted by

u_{hz}	the utility of assigning a demand unit $h\epsilon\Gamma$ to a supply unit $z\epsilon\Omega$.

Here it will also be assumed

$$P < Q$$

that is, we insist on every demand unit being assigned, while
some supply units will remain vacant.

Define also for each $(h,z)\epsilon\Gamma{\times}\Omega$, the boolean variables

$$x_{hz} = \begin{cases} 1, \text{ is h is assigned to z} \\ \\ 0, \text{ otherwise} \end{cases}$$

and assume utilities are additive and the goal of the assignment is to maximize total utility. This leads to the following linear program:

$$\max \sum_{h\epsilon\Gamma} \sum_{z\epsilon\Omega} x_{hz} u_{hz} \qquad (5.1)$$

subject to

$$\sum_{z\epsilon\Omega} x_{hz} = 1, \ h\epsilon\Gamma \qquad (5.2)$$

$$\sum_{h\epsilon\Gamma} x_{hz} \leq 1, \ z\epsilon\Omega \qquad (5.3)$$

$$x_{hz} \geq 0, \ h\epsilon\Gamma, \ z\epsilon\Omega \qquad (5.4)$$

Constraint (5.2) is a strict equality, since we want every demand unit to be assigned to some supply unit. Constraint (5.3) is an inequality, since a supply unit might remain vacant. Constraint (5.4) is simply a non-negativity condition. Note that the condition of x_{hz} taking only $(0,1)$ values has not been introduced explicitly in program (5.1) - (5.4). It is a well-known property of assignment problems that this condition will be automatically satisfied by the optimal solution (see Gass, 1958, for the proof).

Program (5.1) - (5.4) looks like a model appropriate for a normative assignment, planned by a single central decision-maker, rather than a behavioural model, reflecting the bargaining among individual demand and supply units. It will be shown that its optimal solution can be given a behavioural interpretation in terms of market equilibrium, ie a behavioural model is embedded in the mathematical programming formulation

$(5.1) - (5.4)$.

In order to show this, consider the dual of problem $(5.1) - (5.4)$. From the theory of linear programming, the dual is the following problem:

$$\min_{h\varepsilon\Gamma} \Sigma\ u_h + \Sigma_{z\varepsilon\Omega}\ r_z \tag{5.5}$$

subject to

$$u_h + r_z \geq u_{hz}, \quad h\varepsilon\Gamma,\ z\varepsilon\Omega \tag{5.6}$$

$$r_z \geq 0, \quad z\varepsilon\Omega \tag{5.7}$$

where u_h and r_z are the dual variables corresponding to constraints (5.2) and (5.3) respectively. Note that the variables u_h can take any real value, while the variables r_z can take only non-negative values. This is because constraint (5.2) is a strict equality, while constraint (5.3) is an inequality. Besides this purely mathematical reason, this fact will also be shown to have a precise economic meaning.

After some rearrangements, inequalities (5.6) can be summarized in a single inequality, for r_z given:

$$u_h \geq \max_{z\varepsilon\Omega}\ (u_{hz} - r_z), \quad h\varepsilon\Gamma \tag{5.8}$$

and since from the structure of the objective function (5.5) the variables u_h must take their minimum feasible value at optimality, (5.8) becomes a strict equality:

$$u_h = \max_{z\varepsilon\Omega}\ (u_{hz} - r_z), \quad h\varepsilon\Omega \tag{5.9}$$

Similar arguments applied to inequalities (5.6) and (5.7) yield the following equation, for u_h given:

$$r_z = \max[0, \max_{h \in \Omega} (u_{hz} - u_h)], \quad z \in \Omega \qquad (5.10)$$

Equations (5.9) and (5.10) can now be reinterpreted in micro-economic terms. If each demand unit is assumed to maximize his own utility and r_z is interpreted as the market price of alternative z, then the net utility of an alternative z for a demand unit h is

$$u_{hz} - r_z$$

(assuming u_{hz} and r_z are measured in common money units), and u_h as given by (5.9) is the maximum utility for h, that is the utility corresponding to the best alternative in Ω.

Similarly, each supply unit is assumed to maximize his own revenue, and therefore to set the price equal to the maximum bid he receives from the demand units.

The bid price of a demand unit h for an alternative (corresponding to a supplier) z is the maximum price he would be willing to pay for z without diminishing his maximum utility level. We also assume that the supplier is not willing to pay subsidies, in other words to accept negative bids: that is, we assume that prices are non-negative. Therefore two cases can be distinguished:

(a) $u_{hz} > u_h$, or $u_{hz} - u_h > 0$, that is alternative z, without the price charged on it, has for the demand unit h a higher utility than the maximum utility he can get from the rest of the market. In this case the maximum price h would be willing to pay for z is

$$u_{hz} - u_h$$

and the supplier of z will consider h as an alternative buyer;

(b) $u_{hz} \leq u_h$, that is alternative z, even without any price charged, is not better than what the rest of the market can offer. In this case the difference

$$u_{hz} - u_h$$

would be negative, and the supplier of z will not consider h as an alternative buyer.

In short, the supplier of z will consider the maximum bid:

$$\max_{h \in \Gamma} (u_{hz} - u_h)$$

and set the market price r_z equal to this quantity, if it is non-negative; otherwise, the price will remain undefined and conventionally set to zero since no transaction has occurred and z will remain vacant, having received no offer. This is precisely what is stated in equation (5.10).

To summarize, equation (5.9) can be considered as a model of demand utility-maximizing behaviour, while equation (5.10) can be considered as a model of supply bid-price maximizing behaviour. The simultaneous solution of (5.9) and (5.10) provides the equilibrium configuration of utilities and prices. Such a solution exists and is unique, since (5.9) and (5.10) are equivalent to the linear programs (5.5) - (5.7) and (5.1) - (5.4). Equations (5.9) and (5.10) constitute the starting point for all subsequent generalizations, and the linear program (5.1) - (5.4), or its dual (5.5) - (5.7), constitute the simplest example of a mathematical program embedding behavioural models for demand and supply and market equilibrium conditions.

We close this section with a remark on a simple, but very important general property of an assignment model, which will be extensively used in subsequent sections. If an arbitrary constant A is added to the utilities u_{hz}, this leaves the solution of the primal problem (5.1) - (5.4) unchanged; as for the dual problem (5.5) - (5.7), it shifts the origin of the utility scale, but leaves the prices unaltered.

To show the first part of this statement, replace u_{hz} by

$$u_{hz} + A$$

in the objective function (5.1).

Then, remembering constraint (5.2)

$$\sum_{h\epsilon\Gamma} \sum_{z\epsilon\Omega} x_{hz} (u_{hz} + A) = \sum_{h\epsilon\Gamma} \sum_{z\epsilon\Omega} x_{hz}u_{hz} + A \sum_{h\epsilon\Gamma} \sum_{z\epsilon\Omega} x_{hz}$$

$$= \sum_{h\epsilon\Gamma} \sum_{z\epsilon\Omega} x_{hz}u_{hz} + AP$$

That is, the objective function is the same as (5.1), except for the additive constant AP, which does not affect maximization and can be neglected.

To show the second part of the statement, replace u_{hz} by

$$u_{hz} + A$$

in constraint (5.6). Then one obtains the new program:

$$\min \sum_{h\epsilon\Gamma} u_h + \sum_{z\epsilon\Omega} r_z$$

subject to

$$u_h + r_z \geq u_{hz} + A$$

$$r_z \geq 0$$

and since adding (or subtracting) a constant leaves the minimization unaffected, we can subtract the constant AP from the objective function and obtain with some rearrangements:

$$\min \sum_{h\epsilon\Gamma} (u_h - A) + \sum_{z\epsilon\Omega} r_z$$

subject to

$$(u_h - A) + r_z \geq u_{hz}$$

$$r_z \geq 0$$

Defining the new variable

$$\bar{u}_h = u_h - A$$

this program becomes:

$$\min_{h \in \Gamma} \Sigma \; \bar{u}_h + \Sigma_{z \in \Omega} r_z \qquad (5.11)$$

subject to

$$\bar{u}_h + r_z \geq u_{hz} \qquad (5.12)$$

$$r_z \geq 0 \qquad (5.13)$$

Program (5.11) – (5.13) is identical to program (5.5) – (5.7), and therefore it has the same optimal solution, that is, the variables $\bar{u}_h$ have the same optimal value as the variables u_h in program (5.5) – (5.7), and the variables r_z are the same in both problems.

This property is important for theoretical and practical reasons. From the theoretical point of view, the fact that shifting utilities does not affect prices means that utilities are defined on an ordinal scale whose origin is arbitrary, while prices are not: they have a well-defined origin, the zero, and must be non-negative. In any event, a shift in the utility scale will leave both the demand behaviour (ie the assignment x_{hz}) and the supply behaviour (ie the prices r_z) unaltered. From the practical point of view, we have complete

freedom of adding suitable constants to the utilities whenever needed. This property will turn out to be very useful
later on in working out the results on asymptotic approximations.

5.3 A Static Stochastic Assignment Problem

The assignment model discussed in Section 5.2 assumes our
ability to give a very disaggregate description of the problem, like being able to specify a detailed list of each
individual demand and supply unit and the value of the utility
function for each demand-supply unit pair. However, when both
P and Q are very large, such a detailed description is impossible, and one is led to look for some form of aggregation and
structure to economize the description.

The first step towards this direction is to assume that
both demand and supply units can be subdivided into a smaller
set of classes with some degree of internal homogeneity. More
precisely, assume there are partitions

$$\{\Gamma_1, \ldots, \Gamma_m\} \text{ and } \{\Omega_1, \ldots, \Omega_n\} \text{ such that}$$

$$\Gamma = \bigcup_{i=1}^{m} \Gamma_i, \quad \Gamma_i \cap \Gamma_k = \emptyset \quad \text{for } i \neq k$$

$$\Omega = \bigcup_{j=1}^{n} \Omega_j, \quad \Omega_j \cap \Omega_k = \emptyset \quad \text{for } j \neq k$$

and define

$$P_i = |\Gamma_i| \quad i = 1, \ldots, m$$

$$Q_j = |\Omega_j| \quad j = 1, \ldots, n$$

Of course,

$$\sum_{i=1}^{m} P_i = P, \quad \sum_{j=1}^{n} Q_j = Q$$

As a second step, assume the utility function has the following structure:

$$u_{hz} = v_{ij} + \varepsilon_{hz} \quad \text{for} \quad h\varepsilon\Gamma_i, \; z\varepsilon\Omega_j \tag{5.14}$$

Thus we have split the utility into two parts: the term v_{ij}, which is common to all $(h,z)\varepsilon\Gamma_i \times \Omega_j$, and the term ε_{hz}, which is specific to each (h,z) and does not depend on i and j. Equation (5.14) can be read like this: all individuals $h\varepsilon\Gamma_i$ have a basic common evaluation of any alternative $z\varepsilon\Omega_j$, which is measured by v_{ij}, but each individual adds to the common evaluation his own term, ε_{hz}, which reflects the heterogeneity of preferences among all $h\varepsilon\Gamma$ for all $z\varepsilon\Omega$. Substituting the definition (5.14) into equations (5.9) and (5.10) we obtain with some rearrangements the following new equations for maximum utilities and prices:

$$u_h = \max_{1 \le j \le n} [v_{ij} + \max_{z\varepsilon\Omega_j} (\varepsilon_{hz} - r_z)] \quad \text{for} \; h\varepsilon\Gamma_i, \; i = 1, \, \ldots, \, m \tag{5.15}$$

$$r_z = \max \{0, \max_{1 \le i \le m} [v_{ij} + \max_{h\varepsilon\Gamma_i} (\varepsilon_{hz} - u_h)]\} \quad \text{for} \; z\varepsilon\Omega_j,$$

$$j = 1, \, \ldots, \, n \tag{5.16}$$

As a third step, assume that, while the terms v_{ij} are known deterministically, and related to the common attributes of all $(h,z)\varepsilon\Gamma_i \times \Omega_j$, the terms ε_{hz} are independent identically distributed (i.i.d.) random variables with common distribution function

$$F(x) = \Pr\{\varepsilon_{hz} \le x\} \quad \text{for all} \; (h,z)\varepsilon\Gamma \times \Omega \tag{5.17}$$

95

That is, we are not able to observe the specific value ε_{hz} for each (h,z) pair, but we know that for a randomly drawn (h,z) the inequality $\varepsilon_{hz} \le x$ holds with probability $F(x)$. We are actually using the formalism of probability to treat a deterministic description: out of any large sample drawn from $\Gamma \times \Omega$, we know that a fraction $F(x)$ will have a value of ε_{hz} less than, or equal to, x.

The models and assumptions introduced so far are closely related to those of classic random utility theory. Indeed equation (5.15), together with assumption (5.17) and for prices r_z fixed, specifies a standard random utility demand model, of the type discussed in Domencich and McFadden (1975) and Williams (1977). Equation (5.16), together with assumption (5.17) and for utilities u_h fixed, specifies a random bidding model, of the type discussed in Ellickson (1981) and Lerman and Kern (1983). However, here the two models are not treated independently: they are simultaneous equations modelling the demand-supply interactions in a market, and utilities and prices are not given exogenously, but determined endogenously.

Since the terms ε_{hz} are now treated as random variables, also u_h and r_z become random variables, or, in deterministic terms, their detailed list is replaced by a frequency distribution. Define:

$$H_i(x) = \Pr\{u_h \le x | h\varepsilon\Gamma_i\}, \quad i = 1, \ldots, m \qquad (5.18)$$

$$R_j(x) = \Pr\{r_z \le x | z\varepsilon\Omega_j\}, \quad j = 1, \ldots, n \qquad (5.19)$$

Then it is shown in Leonardi (1985-A) that:

$$H_i(x) = \left\{ \prod_{j=1}^{n} [D_j(x - v_{ij})]^{Q_j} \right., \quad i = 1, \ldots, m \qquad (5.20)$$

Stochastic Processes

$$R_j(x) = \begin{cases} \prod_{i=1}^{m} [G(x - v_{ij})]^{P_i}, & x \geq 0 \\ 0, & x < 0 \end{cases} \qquad j = 1, \ldots, n \quad (5.21)$$

where

$$D_j(x) = Pr\{\varepsilon_{hz} - r_z \leq x | z\varepsilon\Omega_j\} = \int_{-\infty}^{\infty} F(x + y)dR_j(y)$$

$$j = 1, \ldots, n \qquad (5.22)$$

$$G_i(x) = Pr\{\varepsilon_{hz} - u_h \leq x | h\varepsilon\Gamma_i\} = \int_{-\infty}^{\infty} F(x + y)dH_i(x)$$

$$i = 1, \ldots, m \qquad (5.23)$$

Equations (5.20) and (5.21) are the stochastic counterparts of equations (5.15) and (5.16). They are functional equations, the unknown functions being the distributions (5.18), for utilities, and (5.19), for prices. In principle, they can be solved once the specific form of $F(x)$ is known, although a closed-form solution is unlikely to be found in general. But, more important than this, the specific form of $F(x)$ is in general not known, since the ε_{hz} terms are not observable, and any tight assumption about it would be arbitrary.

To circumvent this problem we use the method of the asymptotic approximations based on the statistical theory of extremes. This method, whose application to random utility models was first proposed in Leonardi (1983-B, 1984), is based on the following observation: if under mild assumptions on $F(x)$ the functions (5.18) and (5.19) tend to a specific functional form as the system becomes large (that is, when P and Q become large), then further specific knowledge on $F(x)$ is not needed. Such asymptotic results are well-known in statistics, the central limit theorem being the most celebrated one, although of no use in our case. The asymptotic theory of extremes, on the other hand, seems specially tailored for the kind of problems we are dealing with (see Galambos, 1978, for a recent account). It deals with the asymptotic behaviour of maxima and minima of sequences of random variables. In our models (5.15) and (5.16), both the utilities u_h and the prices r_z are maxima of sequences of random variables, and some simple results from the theory can be used.

In order to do this, some new definitions are needed. Let

$$N = Q$$

and assume there are constants w_i and θ_i such that

$$Q_j = Nw_j, \quad j = 1, \ldots, n \tag{5.24}$$

$$P_i = N\theta_i, \quad i = 1, \ldots, m \tag{5.25}$$

As it was shown in (5.2), a constant can be added or sub-tracted to utilities without affecting the solution. As a specific choice, define the constant a_N as the root of the equation

$$1 - F(a_N) = \frac{1}{N} \tag{5.26}$$

Replacing v_{ij} by $v_{ij} - a_N$ in equations (5.20) and (5.21) and substituting from (5.24) and (5.25) one obtains:

$$H_i(x|H) = \prod_{j=1}^{n} [D_j(x + a_N - v_{ij}|N)]^{Nw_j}, \quad i = 1, \ldots, m$$

$$\tag{5.27}$$

$$R_j(x|N) = \begin{cases} \prod_{i=1}^{m} [G_i(x + a_N - v_{ij}|N)]^{N\theta_j}, & x \leq 0 \\ 0 & , x < 0 \end{cases} \quad j = 1, \ldots, n$$

$$(5.28)$$

where the dependence of the distributions on N is made explicit. Definitions (5.22) and (5.23) are also modified as follows:

$$D_j(x|N) = \int_{-\infty}^{\infty} F(x + y)dR_j(y|N), \quad j = 1, \ldots, n \quad (5.29)$$

$$G_i(x|N) = \int_{-\infty}^{\infty} F(x + y)dH_i(x|N), \quad i = 1, \ldots, m \quad (5.30)$$

Then the following result is proved in Leonardi (1985-A).

Theorem 5.3.1

Assume there is a $\beta > 0$ such that

$$\lim_{y \to \infty} \frac{1-F(x+y)}{1-F(y)} = e^{-\beta x} \quad (5.31)$$

then

$$\lim_{N \to \infty} H_i(x|N) = \exp(-\phi_i e^{-\beta x}), \quad i = 1, \ldots, m \quad (5.32)$$

$$\lim_{N \to \infty} R_j(x|N) = \begin{cases} \exp(-\psi_j e^{-\beta x}), & x \geq 0 \\ 0 & , x < 0 \end{cases} \quad j = 1, \ldots, n \quad (5.33)$$

where

$$\phi_i = \sum_j w_j e^{\beta(v_{ij}-r_j)}, \quad i = 1, \ldots, m \quad (5.34)$$

$$\psi_j = \sum_i \theta_i e^{\beta(v_{ij}-u_i)}, \quad j = 1, \ldots, n \quad (5.35)$$

The quantities u_i and r_j are defined as

$$u_i = \lim_{N \to \infty} \{-\frac{1}{\beta} \log \int_{-\infty}^{\infty} e^{-\beta x} dH_i(x|N)\}, \quad i = 1, \ldots, m \quad (5.36)$$

$$r_j = \lim_{N \to \infty} \{-\frac{1}{\beta} \log \int_{-\infty}^{\infty} e^{-\beta x} dR_j(x|N)\}, \quad j = 1, \ldots, n \quad (5.37)$$

and satisfy the equations:

$$e^{-\beta r_j} = \frac{1 - e^{-\psi_j}}{\psi_j}, \quad j = 1, \ldots, n \quad (5.38)$$

$$e^{-\beta u_i} = \frac{1}{\phi_i}, \quad i = 1, \ldots, m \quad (5.39)$$

A few words of comment on theorem 5.3.1 are needed. The main assumption is property (5.31), which loosely speaking says that $F(x)$ is asymptotically exponential in the right tail. This property is widely used in extreme value theory, and it defines the so-called "domain of attraction" of the double exponential distribution (see Galambos, 1978). Indeed the limits (5.32) and (5.33) are of the double exponential form. The double exponential distribution **also plays** an important role in random utility theory, where it is used as a functional specification for $F(x)$ in order to derive the so-called "logit" model. Note, however, that theorem 5.3.1 provides a more general result than ordinary random utility theory: property (5.31) does not impose a specific fucntional form on $F(x)$, it simply requires it to belong to a wide family of distributions. The second important assumption is that N is large enough to use limits (5.32) and (5.33) as approximations. But this assumption is surely justified in most applications of our concern. For instance, in a typical urban housing market N would be the total number of dwellings, which is usually very large.

The quantities u_i and r_j are the only parameters needed to determine the utility and price distributions. From their definitions (5.36) and (5.37) it is seen that they are average utilities and prices, respectively, although they are not arithmetic means. They can be computed by solving equations (5.38) and (5.39), which are simple algebraic equations, much easier than the functional equations (5.20) and (5.21). In a sense, the quantities u_i and r_i contain all the information we need on the stochastic assignment problem. It should not be forgotten, however, that they are just averages of probability distributions, and should not be confused with deterministic utilities and prices.

Theorem 5.3.1 provides a closed form solution for the dual variables in the assignment problem. A result is available also for the primal variables, that is the x_{hz}. Since we introduced an aggregation into subsets, we will replace x_{hz} by:

$$p_{ij}(N) = \frac{1}{P_i} \sum_{h \in \Gamma_i} \sum_{z \in \Omega_j} x_{hz}, \quad \begin{array}{l} i = 1, \ldots, m \\ j = 1, \ldots, n \end{array} \qquad (5.40)$$

This is the probability that a demand unit $h \in \Gamma_i$ chooses a supply unit $z \in \Omega_j$, when $Q = N$. We can also look at the assignment from the supply point of view, and define:

$$q_{ji}(N) = \frac{1}{Q_j} \sum_{h \in \Gamma_j} \sum_{z \in \Omega_j} x_{hz}, \quad \begin{array}{l} i = 1, \ldots, m \\ j = 1, \ldots, n \end{array} \qquad (5.41)$$

This is the probability that a supply unit $z \in \Omega_j$ chooses a demand unit $h \in \Gamma_i$, when $Q = N$. In Leonardi (1985-A and 1985-B) the following result is proved as an easy consequence of theorem 5.3.1:

Stochastic Processes

Corollary 5.3.1
Under the same assumptions of theorem 5.3.1

$$p_{ij} = \lim_{N\to\infty} p_{ij}(N) = \frac{Q_j e^{\beta(v_{ij}-r_j)}}{\sum_j Q_j e^{\beta(v_{ij}-r_j)}} \qquad (5.42)$$

$$q_{ji} = \lim_{N\to\infty} q_{ji}(N) = (1-e^{-\psi_j}) \frac{P_i e^{\beta(v_{ij}-u_i)}}{\sum_i P_i e^{\beta(v_{ij}-u_i)}}$$

$$i = 1, \ldots, m, \quad j = 1, \ldots, n \qquad (5.43)$$

Thus for large N both the demand and the supply choice models are of the logit type. Equation (5.42) is a standard logit model. Equation (5.43) has a multiplicative factor $(1-e^{-\psi_j})$ whose meaning is seen by summing over i:

$$\sum_i q_{ji} = 1 - e^{-\psi_j}, \quad j = 1, \ldots, n \qquad (5.44)$$

$1-e^{-\psi_j}$ is therefore the probability that a supply unit in Ω_j is assigned, and, conversely, $e^{-\psi_j}$ is the probability that it remains vacant.

Equations (5.38) and (5.39) can now be given a simple economic interpretation. Using equation (5.39) and definitions (5.24), (5.25) and (5.34) one obtains from equation (5.35):

$$\psi_j = \sum_{i=1}^{m} P_i \frac{e^{\beta v_{ij}}}{\sum_{j=1}^{n} Q_j e^{\beta(v_{ij}-r_j)}}, \quad j = 1, \ldots, n \qquad (5.45)$$

a function of the prices r_i only. Substitution of (5.45) into (5.38) and some rearrangements yield:

$$\sum_{i=1}^{m} P_i \frac{Q_j e^{\beta(v_{ij}-r_j)}}{\sum_{j=1}^{n} Q_j e^{\beta(v_{ij}-r_j)}} = Q_j(1-e^{-\psi_j}), \quad j = 1, \ldots, n \tag{5.46}$$

The left-hand side of (5.46) is from (5.42):

$\sum_i P_i p_{ij}$, the total demand in j, j = 1, ..., n

The right-hand side is from (5.43):

$Q_j \sum_i q_{ji}$, the total supply in j, j = 1, ..., n

Equations (5.46) are therefore market clearing conditions, equating total demand and total supply for each j.

So far it has not been proved that the solution of equations (5.38) and (5.39), or equivalently of equations (5.46), exists and is unique. This is implied by the following result, also proved in Leonardi (1985-A) which shows that equation (5.46) is embedded in a concave programming problem.

Theorem 5.3.2

The mathematical program

$$\max_{\{p_{ij}\}} \sum_{i=1}^{m} P_i \sum_{j=1}^{n} p_{ij}\left(v_{ij} - \frac{1}{\beta} \log \frac{p_{ij}}{Q_j}\right)$$

$$- \frac{1}{\beta} \sum_{j=1}^{n} Q_j \int_0^{A_j(p)/Q_j} \log \left[\frac{-\log(1-x)}{x}\right] dx \tag{5.47}$$

subject to

$$\sum_{j=1}^{n} p_{ij} = 1, \quad i = 1, \ldots, m \tag{5.48}$$

where

$$A_j(p) = \sum_{i=1}^{m} p_i p_{ij}, \quad j = 1, \ldots, m$$

is concave. Its solution is given by

$$p_{ij} = \frac{Q_j e^{\beta(v_{ij} - r_j)}}{\sum_{j=1}^{} Q_j e^{\beta(v_{ij} - r_j)}} \tag{5.49}$$

where r_j is the solution of equations (5.44).

Program (5.47) - (5.48) is the stochastic counterpart of the assignment problem (5.1) - (5.4). It can be given a classic economic interpretation in terms of total benefit maximization. This is shown as follows. Substitution of (5.49) in the first term of (5.47) and some rearrangements yield:

$$\sum_{i=1}^{m} P_i \sum_{j=1}^{n} p_{ij}\left(v_{ij} - \frac{1}{\beta} \log \frac{p_{ij}}{Q_j}\right) - \sum_{j=1}^{n} A_j(p) r_j$$

$$= \frac{1}{\beta} \sum_{i=1}^{m} P_i \log \sum_{j=1}^{n} Q_j e^{\beta(v_{ij} - r_j)} \tag{5.50}$$

But the function:

$$V_i(r) = \frac{1}{\beta} \log \sum_{j=1}^{n} Q_j e^{\beta(v_{ij} - r_j)}, \quad i = 1, \ldots, m$$

is the consumers' surplus associated with the demand function (5.49) (see Neuburger, 1971, Williams, 1977, Coelho, 1979, Leonardi, 1983-A) that is, it is their general integral, since it has the easily checked property:

$$\frac{\partial V_i}{\partial r_j} = p_{ij}$$

The right-hand side of (5.50) is therefore the total consumers' surplus, aggregated over all demand units.

Rearranging now equation (5.38) one has:

$$r_j = \frac{1}{\beta} \log \frac{\psi_j}{1-e^{-\psi_j}} \tag{5.51}$$

It has been shown with (5.44) that $1-e^{-\psi_j}$ is the fraction of assigned supply units in Ω_j, ie

$$1 - e^{-\psi_j} = A_j/Q_j \tag{5.52}$$

and

$$\psi_j = - \log (1-A_j/Q_j) \tag{5.53}$$

Substituting results (5.52) and (5.53) in equation (5.51) we obtain

$$r_j = \frac{1}{\beta} \log [\frac{- \log (1-A_j/Q_j)}{A_j/Q_j}] \tag{5.54}$$

The function

$$r(x) = \frac{1}{\beta} \log [\frac{- \log (1-x)}{x}] \tag{5.55}$$

is therefore the supply price function for a single unit, x being the quantity supplied (in this case, x is the probability that a unit is supplied). Substitution of (5.55) in the second term of (5.47) and some rearrangements yield:

$$\sum_{j=1}^{n} A_j(p)r_j - \frac{1}{\beta} \sum_{j=1}^{n} Q_j \int_0^{A_j(p)/Q_j} \log [\frac{- \log (1-x)}{x}] \, dx$$

$$= \sum_{j=1}^{n} Q_j \{\frac{A_j(p)}{Q_j} r_j - \int_0^{A_j(p)/Q_j} r(x) \, dx\} \tag{5.56}$$

But the quantity:

$$\frac{A_j(p)}{Q_j} r_j - \int_0^{A_j(p)/Q_j} r(x)\ dx$$

is the producers' surplus for a single supply unit in Ω_j. The right-hand side of (5.56) is therefore the total producers' surplus, aggregated over all supply units. Summing term by term equations (5.50) and (5.56) one thus obtains that the objective function (5.47) is the sum of total consumers' and producers' surplus, ie it is by definition the total benefit.

Having shown the equivalence to a classic economic model, it can be mentioned briefly as a closing remark on static assignment problems, that the first term in function (5.47) is also related to entropy, in the sense considered by Wilson (1970, 1974). It has indeed been shown in Leonardi (1985-B) that if the assumption $P < Q$ is replaced by $P = Q$, then the second term in (5.47) disappears and a pure doubly-constrained entropy maximizing problem is obtained. Therefore problem (5.47) - (5.48) can also be considered as a generalization of the doubly-constrained entropy maximizing problem to the case of inequality constraints, related to, but different from, the approach proposed by Jefferson and Scott (1979).

5.4 Defining a Stochastic Extremal Process

The assignment problems considered so far provide static or equilibrium solutions, but they do not describe the demand and supply behaviour over time in order to reach the equilibrium. In this and the following sections, we shall develop the mathematical tools to study this time unfolding. Before doing so, a short verbal description of the class of phenomena we want to model is worthwhile. So far demand and supply decision processes have been depicted by an instant shot at equilibrium, when everyone seems to have perfect information about everything - alternatives, potential buyers, up-to-date prices and bids. We know, however, that before equilibrium is reached a real decision process is not that perfect. Typically information about alternatives is received once in a while and one at a time in a random way. This means that it is never perfect, since the whole choice set is never known and information received is always more or less dated. Moreover, a real decision-maker does not keep track of all the information he has received so far. Being aware that information is dated, he keeps it in memory only for a limited time, and forgets about it as it becomes too old to be useful. A mathematical abstraction of the above verbal description requires therefore the following three main ingredients:

(a) a random point process, generating the time-sequence of events conveying information about alternatives;

(b) a random signal associated with each random event, summarizing the information received about some alternative (typically a utility, a bid price, and so on);

(c) a random life-length (ie duration in the memory of the receiver) of each signal.

It is further assumed that the receiver keeps a record of the maximum signal still in memory (since he is interested in maximizing utility, bid price, and so on).

A process with the above features will be called a stochastic extremal process. This terminology is not quite new in the literature. The term extremal process was first introduced in the work of Dwass (1964) and Lamperti (1964), although it referred to stochastic processes rather different from the ones discussed here. Our concept of stochastic extremal process is closer to that used in the work of Gaver (1976), and Biondini and Siddiqui (1975), who study the records and record times of a sequence of random signals generated by a point process. The application of such processes to utility-maximizing choice behaviour appeared first in Leonardi (1983-B).

Some precise definitions will now be introduced. Let us consider a stochastic point process $\{\xi_s\}$, where ξ_s denotes the number of random events which occur in a time interval of length s. Let

$$P_n(s) = Pr\{\xi_s = n\}, \quad n \geq 0 \qquad (5.57)$$

To the occurrence of each random event there corresponds a real random variable, called the signal associated with that event. Let X_τ be the value of the signal corresponding to an event which occurred at time τ, and define

$$D(x,\tau) = Pr\{X_\tau \leq x\} \qquad (5.58)$$

The lifetime of a signal corresponding to an event which occurred at time τ is a random variable, denoted by η_τ. In what follows it will be assumed that the lifetime distribution is time-independent, and

$$F(x) = Pr\{\eta_\tau > x\} \qquad (5.59)$$

will denote the survival function of a generic signal. Let ν_s denote the number of random events which occurred in a time interval of length s and produced signals which are still alive at the end of that interval. Let $\mu_s(t)$ be the maximum among such signals, when the interval ends at time t, ie $\mu_s(t)$ is the maximum among the signals generated in $(t-s,t)$ and still alive at time t. In the following paragraphs we will study the stochastic processes $\{\nu_s\}$ and $\{\mu_s(t)\}$. In particular, the process $\{\mu_s(t)\}$ defined as above is called a stochastic extremal process.

An example will help in understanding how the above framework can be applied. Consider a household collecting information about dwellings which are possible to move to. Assume

information collection started at time t-s and look at the
state of information at time t. In the time interval (t-s,t),
the household has received information about ξ_s = n dwellings
with probability $P_n(s)$, at times τ_1, τ_2, ..., τ_n, say. Therefore, it is possible to evaluate the utilities $X_{\tau 1}, X_{\tau 2}, \ldots X_{\tau n}$
associated with each dwelling. But these evaluations reflect
the market conditions (eg the prices) at times $\tau_1, \tau_2, \ldots, \tau_n < t$
and therefore they would not be perfectly up-to-date if a
decision had to be taken at time t. It is likely that some of
them, for instance τ_1, and τ_2, are too old to be taken into
account, and are therefore forgotten; in general the information received at times τ_1, ..., τ_n are remembered at time t
with probabilities $F(t-\tau_1)$, ..., $F(t-\tau_n)$. As a result out of
the n dwellings only ν_s = k, k < n, will be remembered at time
t, with utilities X_1, ..., X_k. Since the householder is a
utility maximizer, he keeps a record of the alternative with
the highest utility, and therefore performs the computation:

$$\mu_s(t) = \max(X_1, \ldots, X_k)$$

The maximum utility $\mu_s(t)$ recorded in this way is a stochastic
extremal process.

In what follows it will always be assumed that $\{\xi_s\}$ is a
homogeneous Poisson process, that is:

$$P_n(s) = e^{-\gamma s} \frac{(\gamma s)^n}{n!}, \quad \gamma > 0 \tag{5.60}$$

Moreover, if $\{\tau_k\}$ is the sequence of the instants of occurrence
of the events in the process $\{\xi_s\}$, it will be assumed that the
corresponding signals $\{X_{\tau k}\}$ are a sequence of independent
random variables. In order to derive some specific results
the survival function $F(x)$ will sometimes be assumed of the
exponential form

$$F(x) = e^{-\alpha x}, \quad \alpha > 0$$

but this assumption will not be required for most general results.

5.5 Some General Results on Stochastic Extremal Processes

We shall now determine the probability distribution of ν_s, the number of surviving signals, and $\mu_s(t)$, the maximum of such signals. For the process $\{\nu_s\}$, define

$$Q_n(s) = \Pr\{\nu_s = n\} \tag{5.61}$$

Then the following result holds:

Theorem 5.5.1

$$Q_n(s) = e^{-\gamma h(s)} \frac{[\gamma h(s)]^n}{n!} \tag{5.62}$$

where

$$h(s) = \int_0^s F(\tau) d\tau \tag{5.63}$$

Proof   For an arbitrary time origin, consider the time interval $(0,s]$. We know from assumption (5.59) that a signal corresponding to an event which occurred at time $s-\tau$, $0 < \tau \leq s$, is still alive at time s with probability $F(\tau)$.

Since from assumption (5.60), $\{\xi_s\}$ is a homogeneous Poisson process, the events occur at instants uniformly distributed in $(0,s]$, ie with density $1/s$. On account of the total probability theorem, the probability that a signal generated at an instant uniformly distributed in $(0,s]$ will still be alive at time s is:

$$p_s = \frac{1}{s}\int_0^s F(\tau)d \tag{5.64}$$

Therefore the probability that n signals out of k generated in $(0,s]$ will still be alive at time s is a Bernoulli distribution with parameter p_s:

$$\Pr\{\nu_s = n | \xi_s = k\} = \frac{k!}{n!(k-n)!}\, p_s^n (1-p_s)^{k-n} \tag{5.65}$$

Using again the total probability theorem, one can write

$$\Pr\{\nu_s = n\} = \sum_{k=n}^{\infty} \Pr\{\nu_s = n | \xi_s = k\}\, \Pr\{\xi_s = k\}$$

or, substituting from (5.60), (5.61) and (5.65) and rearranging:

$$Q_n(s) = e^{-\gamma s p_s}\, \frac{(\gamma s p_s)^n}{n!}$$

Comparing (5.63) with (5.64), one has:

$$s p_s = h(s)$$

hence statement (5.42) follows. <u>Q.E.D.</u>

Result (5.62) means that the number of surviving signals is a non-homogeneous Poisson process, with intensity function given by $\gamma h(s)$. In many applications it is of interest to know the limiting behaviour of (5.62) as $s \to \infty$, that is when signals have been collected for a long time interval. Define $f(x)$ as the density function of the lifetime of a signal. $f(x)$ is related to the survival function $F(x)$ by the equation

$$f(x) = -F'(x) \tag{5.66}$$

Assume $f(x)$ has finite mean μ,

$$\mu = \int_0^\infty xf(x)dx < \infty \qquad (5.67)$$

Then it is easily shown that

$$\lim_{s\to\infty} h(s) = \mu$$

Indeed, using integration by parts, and equation (5.66), from definition (5.63) one has:

$$\lim_{s\to\infty} h(s) = \int_0^\infty F(\tau)d\tau = F(\tau)\tau\Big|_0^\infty - \int_0^\infty \tau F'(\tau)d\tau = \int_0^\infty \tau f(\tau)d\tau = \mu$$

Applying this result to (5.62) one has:

$$\lim_{s\to\infty} Q_n(s) = e^{-\gamma\mu} \frac{(\gamma\mu)^n}{n!} \qquad (5.68)$$

That is, the limiting distribution of the number of surviving signals is a Poisson distribution with mean $\gamma\mu$. $\gamma\mu$ is the average number of signals surviving after a long collection time, and it is the product of the average number of signals generated per unit time, γ, and the average lifetime of a signal, μ.

For the process $\{\mu_s(t)\}$, define

$$H(x,t,s) = \Pr\{\mu_s(t) \le x\} \qquad (5.69)$$

Then the following result holds:

Theorem 5.5.2

$$H(x,t,s) = \exp\{-\gamma\int_0^s F(\tau)[1-D(x,t-\tau)d\tau\} \qquad (5.70)$$

Proof   Let τ measure the length of the time interval between the occurrence of an event in $(t-s,t)$ and time t, $0 < \tau \le s$, and $g(\tau)$ be its density. Since $\{\xi_s\}$ is a homogeneous Poisson

112

process, we know that

$$g(\tau) = \frac{1}{s} \tag{5.71}$$

Now we want to find the density of the time-distance from t of the surviving events, ie those which generated signals still surviving at time t. Define the event E_t as "a signal is still surviving at time t" and the conditional density $g(\tau|E_t)$ as the density of the distance of an event from t, given that it is surviving at time t. Then from Bayes' theorem one has:

$$g(\tau|E_t) = \frac{\Pr\{E_t|\tau\}g(\tau)}{\int_0^s \Pr\{E_t|\tau\}g(\tau)d\tau} \tag{5.72}$$

where $\Pr\{E_t|\tau\}$ is the probability that a signal is surviving at time t, given that it has been produced by an event at distance τ from t, ie at time t-τ. But from the definition (5.59) we know that:

$$\Pr\{E_t|\tau\} = \Pr\{\eta_{t-\tau} > \tau\} = F(\tau) \tag{5.73}$$

Hence substitution of (5.71) and (5.73) in equation (5.72) yields:

$$g(\tau|E_t) = \frac{F(\tau)}{\int_0^s F(\tau)d\tau} \tag{5.74}$$

or, recalling definition (5.63)

$$g(\tau|E_t) = \frac{F(\tau)}{h(s)} \tag{5.75}$$

The distribution of a signal produced at time t-τ is, from definition (5.58), $D(x,t-\tau)$. Hence, on account of the total probability theorem, the distribution of a generic signal produced in (t−s,t] and surviving at time t is, from (5.75):

$$\overline{D}(x,t,s) = \int_0^s D(x,t-\tau)g(\tau|E_t)d\tau = \frac{1}{h(s)} \int_0^s F(\tau)D(x,t-\tau)d\tau$$

(5.76)

We shall now determine the conditional probability $\Pr\{\mu_s(t) \leq x | \nu_s = n\}$, the distribution of the maximum signal surviving at time t, when the total number of signals produced in (t−s,t] and surviving at time t is n. Let $\{X_1,\ldots,X_n\}$ be the sequence of such signals. From the independence assumption and from result (5.76), this is a sequence of i.i.d. random variables with common distribution $\overline{D}(x,t,s)$. By definition

$$\mu_s(t) = \max_{1 \leq j \leq n} X_j$$

Therefore

$$\Pr\{\mu_s(t) \leq x | \nu_s = n\} = \Pr\{\max_{1 \leq j \leq n} X_j \leq x\}$$

$$= \Pr\{X_1 \leq x, \ldots, X_n \leq x\} = \prod_{j=1}^{n} \Pr\{X_j \leq x\}$$

$$= [\overline{D}(x,t,s)]^n \qquad (5.77)$$

Using the total probability theorem one can write the equation as

$$\Pr\{\mu_s(t) \leq x\} = \sum_{n=0}^{\infty} \Pr\{\mu_s(t) \leq x | \nu_s = n\}\Pr\{\nu_s = n\}$$

which, after substitution from definition (5.69) and results (5.62) and (5.77), becomes with some calculations:

$$H(x,t,s) = \exp\{-h(s)[1-\overline{D}(x,t,s)]\}$$

Or, using definition (5.63) and result (5.76):

$$H(x,t,s) = \exp\{-\gamma\int_0^s F(\tau)[1-D(x,t-\tau)]d\tau\}. \quad \underline{Q.E.D.}$$

In applications one is often interested in a process with an unbounded past history of signal collection, that is with a very large s. Let

$$H(x,t) = \lim_{s\to\infty} H(x,t,s) \tag{5.78}$$

then from Theorem 5.4.2:

$$H(x,t) = \exp\{-\gamma\int_0^s F(\tau)[1-D(x,t-\tau)]d\tau\} \tag{5.79}$$

Note that $H(x,t)$ (as well as $H(x,t,s)$) has a concentration of probability in the left tail, ie

$$H(-\infty,t) = e^{-\gamma\mu} > 0 \tag{5.80}$$

This means there is a finite probability that the maximum signal surviving at time t is equal to $-\infty$. From result (5.68) it is easily seen that (5.80) gives the probability that no signal is surviving at time t. Clearly when there is no surviving signal, either because none has been produced or because all those produced have died out, the maximum is undefined and conventionally set equal to $-\infty$.

As for the limiting behaviour of the process as $t\to\infty$, assume the limit $D(x) = \lim_{t\to\infty} D(x,t)$ exists, so that

$\lim_{t\to\infty} D(x,t-\tau) = D(x)$ for almost all τ. Then from the dominated

convergence theorem:

115

$$\lim_{t \to \infty} \int_0^\infty F(\tau)[1-D(x,t-\tau)]d\tau = [1-D(x)]\int_0^\infty F(\tau)d\tau = \mu[1-D(x)]$$

Hence:

$$H(x) = \lim_{t \to \infty} H(x,t) = \exp\{-\gamma\mu[1-D(x)]\} \qquad (5.81)$$

5.6 Asymptotic Approximation for Large Systems

The subject of asymptotic approximations has been mentioned
already in Section 5.3, where some results based on asymptotic
extreme value theory have been given for static assignment
problems. These results are stated in Theorems 5.3.1 and
5.3.2 without proof. Here the asymptotic approximation will
be worked out with the detailed proof for the distribution of
the maximum surviving signal. With some loss in generality,
a few additional assumptions will be introduced, which tailor
the results we will obtain for the applications to be developed
in section 5.7 and in Chapters Nine and Fifteen.

We shall assume there are two real constants $\lambda > 0$ and
$0 \leq w \leq 1$ and an integer N such that

$$\gamma = \lambda w N \qquad (5.82)$$

N will be called the size of the system, and we say the system
is large when $N \to \infty$. The meaning of representation (5.82) is
clarified by an example. Suppose we are considering the
information about dwellings in a housing market, as received
by a household. In this case, N is the total number of
dwellings (usually very large), w is the fraction of such
dwellings in a specific subset (for instance, in a given
zone), so that Nw is the total number of dwellings in this
subset. The household receives information about each
dwelling according to a Poisson process of intensity λ, ie λ
is the average number of signals each dwelling sends to the

household per unit time. In reality this exchange of information uses many different channels, including direct contact
with the landlord, advertising through newspapers and other
media, real estate agencies, informal diffusion of information
through other people. We are not interested, however, in
disaggregating all these channels: they will be treated in an
aggregate way, summarized by a single intensity parameter λ.
The total average number of signals a household receives from
all the wN dwellings per unit time is therefore λwN as stated
in assumption (5.82).

We shall also assume that the distribution of signals
depends on the size of the system, and replace the notation
$D(x,\tau)$ by $D_N(x,\tau)$, the distribution of signals generated at
time τ in a system of size N. Moreover, $D_N(x,\tau)$ is assumed to
have the representation:

$$D_N(x,\tau) = \int_{-\infty}^{\infty} F(x+y+a_N) dR_N(x,\tau) \tag{5.83}$$

where $F(x)$ is a time-independent probability distribution; a_N
is the root of the equation

$$1 - F(a_N) = 1/\lambda\mu N \tag{5.84}$$

$R_N(x,\tau)$ is a sequence of time-varying distributions, and

$$R(x,\tau) = \lim_{N\to\infty} R_N(x,\tau) \tag{5.85}$$

is assumed to exist.

The meaning of representation (5.83) is again best clarified by an example. Consider again the housing market, and
assume that to each of the wN dwellings there correspond two
random variables: ε the utility, with distribution
$Pr\{\varepsilon \le x\} = F(x)$; r_τ the price (usually varying over time),
with distribution $Pr\{r_\tau \le x\} = R_N(x,\tau)$. Then the net utility

117

for a household is $\varepsilon - r_\tau$.

Since the utilities ε are defined on an ordinal scale, we can arbitrarily shift their origin. It has been shown in section 5.2 that this operation does not affect either demand or supply behaviour. Let us therefore replace ε by $\varepsilon - a_N$, where a_N is defined by (5.84). Then the net utility, after this rescaling, is

$$\varepsilon - a_N - r_\tau \qquad (5.86)$$

We shall now look for the distribution of (5.86). From the total probability theorem one has:

$$\Pr\{\varepsilon - a_N - r_\tau \leq x\} = \int_{-\infty}^{\infty} \Pr\{\varepsilon - a_N - r_\tau \leq x | r_\tau = y\} dR_N(y,\tau)$$

and since

$$\Pr\{\varepsilon - a_N - r_\tau \leq x | r_\tau = y\} = \Pr\{\varepsilon - a_N - y \leq x\}$$

$$= \Pr\{\varepsilon \leq x + y + a_N\} = F(x + y + a_N)$$

it follows that

$$\Pr\{\varepsilon - a_N - r_\tau \leq x\} = \int_{-\infty}^{\infty} F(x + y + a_N) dR_N(y,\tau)$$

which is precisely assumption (5.83).

Define the sequence of distributions $H_N(x,t)$ as the distribution of the maximum signal surviving at time t, for an unbounded past history of signal collection and a system of size N. From equation (5.79) this is given by:

$$H_N(x,t) = \exp\{-\lambda w N \int_0^{\infty} F(\tau) |1 - D_N(x, t-\tau)| d\tau\} \qquad (5.87)$$

We are now ready to prove the main result of this section.

Theorem 5.6.1

Assume there is a $\beta > 0$ such that

$$\lim_{y \to \infty} \frac{1-F(x+y)}{1-F(y)} = e^{-\beta x} \tag{5.88}$$

Then

$$\lim_{N \to \infty} H_N(x,t) = \exp\{-we^{-\beta[x+r(t)]}\} \tag{5.89}$$

where $r(t)$ is defined as

$$r(t) = -\frac{1}{\beta} \log \{\int_0^\infty \frac{F(\tau)}{\mu} [\int_{-\infty}^\infty e^{-\beta y} dR(y,t-\tau)]d\tau\} \tag{5.90}$$

and

$$R(y,t) = \lim_{N \to \infty} R_N(y,t)$$

Proof   Equation (5.84) implies

$$\lim_{N \to \infty} a_N = \infty$$

therefore from assumption (5.88) it follows that

$$\lim_{N \to \infty} \frac{1-F(x+y+a_N)}{1-F(a_N)} = e^{-\beta(x+y)}$$

or, substituting from (5.84) and rearranging

$$\lim_{N \to \infty} [1-F(x+y+a_N)] = \frac{e^{-\beta(x+y)}}{\lambda\mu} \lim_{N \to \infty} \frac{1}{N}$$

Replacing this result in (5.83) one obtains:

$$\lim_{N \to \infty} [1-D_N(x,t-\tau)] = (\lim_{N \to \infty} \frac{1}{N})\frac{e^{-\beta x}}{\lambda\mu} \int_{-\infty}^\infty e^{-\beta y} dR(y,t-\tau) \tag{5.91}$$

where

$$R(y,t) = \lim_{N \to \infty} R_N(y,t)$$

Replacing the limit (5.91) in equation (5.87) we have:

$$\lim_{N \to \infty} H_N(x,t) = \exp\{-we^{-\beta x \int_0^\infty \frac{F(\tau)}{\mu}} [\int_{-\infty}^\infty e^{-\beta y} dR(y,t-\tau)]\}$$

or, taking definition (5.90) into account:

$$\lim_{N \to \infty} H_N(x,t) = \exp\{-we^{-\beta[x+r(t)]}\}. \quad \underline{Q.E.D.}$$

Much of the discussion on the result of Theorem 5.6.1 would be similar to that on the results of Theorem 5.3.1, and will not be repeated here.

It is worth pointing out the similarity between definition (5.35) and definition (5.90). Both define an average, but while (5.35) has no time in it (being related to a static problem), (5.90) is also a weighted time average, the weighting factor being the function:

$$\frac{F(\tau)}{\mu}$$

This is a monotone decreasing function, usually S-shaped and remembering that

$$\mu = \int_0^\infty F(\tau) d\tau$$

it is easily seen that

$$\frac{F(0)}{\mu} = 1/\mu, \quad \frac{F(\infty)}{\mu} = 0 \quad \text{and} \quad \int_0^\infty \frac{F(\tau)}{\mu} d\tau = 1$$

that is, it is a probability density.

As a special simple case, useful in many applications,

one can assume

$$F(\tau) = e^{-\alpha\tau}$$

In this case

$$\mu = 1/\alpha$$

and the weighting function becomes

$$\frac{F(\tau)}{\mu} = \alpha e^{-\alpha\tau}$$

an exponential distribution.

A noteworthy property of the asymptotic form (5.89) is that the probability concentration at $-\infty$ has now disappeared, since (5.89) defines a well-behaved probability distribution (the double exponential), absolutely continuous from $-\infty$ to $+\infty$, S-shaped and such that

$$H(-\infty,t) = 0$$

$$H(\infty,t) = 1$$

for all t.

5.7 Dynamic Assignment Problems as Stochastic Extremal Processes

We shall now develop a dynamic version of the stochastic assignment model discussed in Section 5.3. The basic definitions and assumptions of that section will be kept, unless otherwise specified. The main difference will be in the maximizing behaviour assumed for demand and supply units. In section 5.3 this is specified by equations (5.15) and (5.16),

based on perfect knowledge of the choice set and static
maximizing. Here it will be assumed that both demand and
supply evaluate alternatives according to a stochastic extremal
process of the type described in Sections 5.5 and 5.6. Namely,
it is assumed that the intensity of exchange of information
between any demand-supply pair $(h,z)\varepsilon\Gamma x\Omega$ is λ. That is λdt is
the probability that such an exchange occurs in $(t,t+dt]$. This
means, using the definitions introduced in section 5.3, that
demand units receive information about supply units $z\varepsilon\Omega_j$
according to a Poisson process with intensity $\lambda w_j N$, while
supply units receive information about demand units $h\varepsilon\Gamma_i$
according to a Poisson process with intensity $\lambda\theta_i N$. Moreover,
it is assumed for simplicity that the signals received by both
demand and supply units have the same life-time distribution,
with survival function $F(x)$.

In the static process considered in Section 5.3 the relevant signals for the demand units are the net utilities:

$$v_{ij} + \varepsilon_{hz} - r_z, \quad h\varepsilon\Gamma_i, \ z\varepsilon\Omega_j, \quad \begin{array}{l} i = 1, \ \ldots, \ m \\ j = 1, \ \ldots, \ n \end{array}$$

while the relevant signals for the supply units are the bid
prices:

$$v_{ij} + \varepsilon_{hz} - u_h, \quad h\varepsilon\Gamma_i, \ z\varepsilon\Omega_j, \quad \begin{array}{l} i = 1, \ \ldots, \ m \\ j = 1, \ \ldots, \ n \end{array}$$

where u_h and r_z are maximum utilities and market prices,
respectively.

In order to be used in the dynamic setting, the definitions of the above quantities need some amendment. We shall
define $u_h(t,N)$ as the maximum utility for a demand unit
$h\varepsilon\Gamma$ at time t and for a system of size N; $r_z(t,N)$ as the
market price for a supply unit $z\varepsilon\Omega$ at time t and for a system

of size N and subtract from the random utility terms ε_{hz} the constant a_N, defined by equation (5.84) (as we know, this does not affect the assignment problem). The signals for the demand units thus become

$$v_{ij} + \varepsilon_{hz} - a_N - r_z(t,N) \quad h\varepsilon\Gamma_i, \ z\varepsilon\Omega_j \quad \begin{array}{l} i = 1, \ldots, m \\ j = 1, \ldots, n \end{array}$$

and those for the supply units become

$$v_{ij} + \varepsilon_{hz} - a_N - u_h(t,N) \quad h\varepsilon\Gamma_i, \ z\varepsilon\Omega_j \quad \begin{array}{l} i = 1, \ldots, m \\ j = 1, \ldots, n \end{array}$$

The constants v_{ij} are deterministic quantities which are not affected by the information diffusion process. We shall there-fore focus our attention on the remaining parts, that is $\varepsilon_{hz} - a_N - r_z(t,N)$ for demand and $\varepsilon_{hz} - a_N - u_h(t,N)$ for supply.

Let $H_i(x,t,N) = \Pr\{u_h(t,N) \leq x | h\varepsilon\Gamma_i\}$ be the distribution of the maximum utility at time t in a system of size N for demand units $h\varepsilon\Gamma_i$, $i = 1, \ldots, m$; $R_j(x,t,N) = \Pr\{r_z(t,N) \leq x | z\varepsilon\Omega_j\}$ be the distribution of the market price at time t in a system of size N for supply units $z\varepsilon\Omega_j$, $j = 1, \ldots, n$; $D_j(x,t,N) = \Pr\{\varepsilon_{hz} - a_N - r_z(t,N) \leq x | z\varepsilon\Omega_j\}$ be the distribution of the demand signal, $j = 1, \ldots, n$; and $G_i(x,t,N) = \Pr\{\varepsilon_{hz} - a_N - u_h(t,N) \leq x | h\varepsilon\Gamma_i\}$ be the distribution of the supply signal, $i = 1, \ldots, m$. Then, arguing as in the example discussed in relation to assumption (5.84), the following equations are shown to hold:

$$D_j(x,t,N) = \int_{-\infty}^{\infty} F(x+y+a_N) dR_j(x,t,N), \quad j = 1, \ldots n$$

(5.92)

$$G_i(x,t,N) = \int_{-\infty}^{\infty} F(x+y+a_N) dH_i(x,t,N), \quad i = 1, \ldots, m$$

(5.93)

We shall now find the distributions of the maximum surviving signals for demand and supply, under the assumption of an unbounded signal collection time interval. The following definitions will be introduced: $\overline{H}_j(x,t,N)$ is the distribution of the maximum demand signal from Ω_j at time t in a system of size N, $j = 1, \ldots, n$; $\overline{R}_i(x,t,N)$, the distribution of the maximum supply signal from Γ_i at time t in a system of size N, $i = 1, \ldots, m$. Straightforward application of Theorem 5.5.2, in the special case contemplated by assumption (5.78) and equation (5.79), yields:

$$\overline{H}_j(x,t,N) = \exp\{-\lambda w_j N \int_0^\infty F(\tau)[1-D_j(x,t-\tau,N)]d\tau\}$$

$$j = 1, \ldots, n \tag{5.94}$$

$$\overline{R}_i(x,t,N) = \exp\{-\lambda \theta_i N \int_0^\infty F(\tau)[1-G_i(x,t-\tau,N)d\tau\}$$

$$i = 1, \ldots, m \tag{5.95}$$

Equations (5.94) and (5.95) are in the format of equation (5.87), and Theorem 5.6.1 can be used to obtain asymptotic approximations.

The main results are summarized in the following theorem.

Theorem 5.7.1

Assume there is a $\beta > 0$ such that

$$\lim_{y \to \infty} \frac{1-F(x+y)}{1-F(y)} = e^{-\beta x} \tag{5.96}$$

and define

$$\overline{H}_j(x,t) = \lim_{N \to \infty} \overline{H}_j(x,t,N), \quad j = 1, \ldots, n$$

$$\overline{R}_i(x,t) = \lim_{N\to\infty} R_i(x,t,N), \quad i = 1, \ldots, m$$

$$H_i(x,t) = \lim_{N\to\infty} H_i(x,t,N), \quad i = 1, \ldots, m$$

$$R_j(x,t) = \lim_{N\to\infty} R_j(x,t,N), \quad j = 1, \ldots, n$$

Then:

$$\overline{H}_j(x,t) = \exp\{-w_j e^{-\beta[x+r_j(t)]}\} \tag{5.97}$$

$$\overline{R}_i(x,t) = \exp\{-\theta_i e^{-\beta[x+u_i(t)]}\} \tag{5.98}$$

$$H_i(x,t) = \exp[-\phi_i(t)e^{-\beta x}] \tag{5.99}$$

$$R_j(x,t) = \begin{cases} \exp[-\psi_j(t)e^{-\beta x}], & x \geq 0 \\ 0 & , x < 0 \end{cases} \tag{5.100}$$

where:

$$r_j(t) = -\frac{1}{\beta} \log\{\int_0^\infty \frac{F(\tau)}{\mu} [\int_{-\infty}^\infty e^{-\beta y} dR_j(y,t-\tau)]d\tau\} \tag{5.101}$$

$$u_i(t) = -\frac{1}{\beta} \log\{\int_0^\infty \frac{F(\tau)}{\mu} [\int_{-\infty}^\infty e^{-\beta y} dH_i(y,t-\tau)]d\tau\} \tag{5.102}$$

$$\phi_i(t) = \sum_{j=1}^{n} w_j e^{\beta[v_{ij}-r_j(t)]} \tag{5.103}$$

$$\psi_j(t) = \sum_{i=1}^{m} \theta_i e^{\beta[v_{ij}-u_i(t)]} \tag{5.104}$$

and

$$i = 1, \ldots, m; \quad j = 1, \ldots, n$$

The quantities $u_i(t)$ and $r_j(t)$ satisfy the set of integral equations:

$$e^{-\beta u_i(t)} = \int_0^\infty \frac{F(\tau)}{\mu} \frac{1}{\phi_i(t-\tau)} \, d\tau, \quad i = 1, \ldots, m \quad (5.105)$$

$$e^{-\beta r_j(t)} = \int_0^\infty \frac{F(\tau)}{\mu} \frac{1-e^{-\psi_j(t-\tau)}}{\psi_j(t-\tau)} \, d\tau, \quad j = 1, \ldots, n \quad (5.106)$$

Proof   Results (5.97) and (5.98), as well as (5.101) and (5.102), follow from straightforward application of Theorem 5.6.1 to equations (5.94) and (5.95).

In order to prove (5.99), (5.100), (5.103) and (5.104) let us call $\tilde{u}_j(t)$ the random variable with distribution (5.97) and $\tilde{r}_i(t)$ the random variable with distribution (5.98), ie:

$$\Pr\{\tilde{u}_j(t) \leq x\} = \overline{H}_j(x,t), \quad j = 1, \ldots, n$$

$$\Pr\{\tilde{r}_i(t) \leq x\} = \overline{R}_i(x,t), \quad i = 1, \ldots, m$$

Similarly, let us call $u_i^*(t)$ the random variable with distribution (5.99) and $r_j^*(t)$ the random variable with distribution (5.100). That is

$$\Pr\{u_i^*(t) \leq x\} = H_i(x,t), \quad i = 1, \ldots, m$$

$$\Pr\{r_j^*(t) \leq x\} = R_j(x,t), \quad j = 1, \ldots, n$$

Then by definition:

$$u_i^*(t) = \max_{1 \leq j \leq n} [v_{ij} + \tilde{u}_j(t)], \quad i = 1, \ldots, m$$

$$r_j^*(t) = \max\{0, \max_{1 \leq i \leq m} [v_{ij} + \tilde{r}_i(t)]\}, \quad j = 1, \ldots, n$$

Hence:

$$H_i(x,t) = \Pr\{v_{i1} + \tilde{u}_1(t) \leq x, \ldots, v_{in} - \tilde{u}_n(t) \leq x\}$$

$$= \prod_{j=1}^{n} \Pr\{v_{ij} + \tilde{u}_j(t) \leq x\} = \prod_{j=1}^{n} \Pr\{\tilde{u}_j(t) \leq x - v_{ij}\}$$

$$= \prod_{j=1}^{n} \overline{H}_j(x - v_{ij}, t), \quad i = 1, \ldots, m \tag{5.107}$$

and similarly

$$R_j(x,t) = \begin{cases} \prod_{j=1}^{n} \overline{R}_i(x - v_{ij}, t), & x \geq 0 \\ 0 & , x < 0 \end{cases} \quad j = 1, \ldots, n$$

$$\tag{5.108}$$

Substituting (5.97) and (5.98) into (5.107) and (5.108), results (5.99), (5.100), (5.103) and (5.104) follow.

In order to prove equations (5.105) and (5.106), one simply observes that from (5.99) and (5.100):

$$\int_{-\infty}^{\infty} e^{-\beta y} dH_i(y,t) = \frac{1}{\phi_i(t)}, \quad i = 1, \ldots, m \tag{5.109}$$

$$\int_{-\infty}^{\infty} e^{-\beta y} dR_j(y,t) = \frac{1 - e^{-\psi_j(t)}}{\psi_j(t)}, \quad j = 1, \ldots, n \tag{5.110}$$

and replaces these results in (5.101) and (5.109). <u>Q.E.D.</u>

The results of Theorem 5.7.1 are substantially analogous to those of Theorem 5.3.1. They basically state that all the relevant distributions are asymptotically the double exponential type. The only significant difference between Theorem 5.3.1 and Theorem 5.7.1 is in the definition of the parameters

Stochastic Processes

r_j and u_i, which in the dynamic case includes a weighted time-average component.

A dynamic counterpart of corollary 5.3.1 can also be provided. Let us define $p_{ij}(t,N)$ as the probability that the highest utility supply unit a demand unit belonging to Γ_i has found and kept in memory up to time t belongs to Ω_j, i=1,...,m, j=1,...,n; $q_{ji}(t,N)$, the probability that the highest bid price demand unit a supply unit belonging to Ω_j has found and kept in memory up to time t belongs to Γ_i, i=1,...,m, j=1,...,n, and

$$p_{ij}(t) = \lim_{N\to\infty} p_{ij}(t,N), \quad i = 1, \ldots, m$$

$$q_{ji}(t) = \lim_{N\to\infty} q_{ji}(t,N), \quad j = 1, \ldots, n$$

Then the following result holds:

Corollary 5.7.1   Under the same assumptions of Theorem 5.7.1:

$$p_{ij}(t) = \frac{w_j e^{\beta[v_{ij}-r_j(t)]}}{\sum_{j=1}^{n} w_j e^{\beta[v_{ij}-r_j(t)]}} \tag{5.111}$$

$$q_{ji}(t) = [1-e^{-\psi_j(t)}] \frac{\theta_i e^{\beta[v_{ij}-u_i(t)]}}{\sum_{i=1}^{m} \theta_i e^{\beta[v_{ij}-u_i(t)]}} \tag{5.112}$$

i = 1, ..., m, j = 1, ..., n

Proof   Using the terminology introduced in the proof of Theorem 5.7.1, the highest utility alternative a demand unit belonging to Γ_i has found and kept in memory up to time t belongs to Ω_j if

$$v_{ij} + \tilde{u}_j(t) > v_{ik} + \tilde{u}_k(t) \quad \text{for all } k \neq j$$

that is, if its utility is higher than that of the other alternatives. Similarly, the highest bid-price alternative a supply unit belonging to Ω_j has found and kept in memory up to time t belongs to Γ_i if:

$$v_{ij} + \tilde{r}_i(t) > v_{kj} + \tilde{r}_k(t) \quad \text{for all } k \neq j$$

and

$$v_{ij} + \tilde{r}_i(t) \geq 0$$

that is, if its bid price is higher than that of the other alternatives, provided it is non-negative. From result (5.97) of Theorem 5.7.1 we know that:

$$Pr\{v_{ij} + \tilde{u}_j(t) \leq x\} = Pr\{\tilde{u}_j(t) \leq x - v_{ij}\}$$

$$= \overline{H}_j(x - v_{ij}, t) = \exp\{-w_j e^{-\beta[x - v_{ij} + r_j(t)]}\}$$

and after some rearrangements this yields, using the total probability theorem and taking definition (5.103) result (5.99) and the rule of integration by parts into account:

$$P_{ij}(t) = Pr\{v_{ij} + \tilde{u}_j(t) > v_{ik} + \tilde{u}_k(t), \forall k \neq j\}$$

$$= \int_{-\infty}^{\infty} [\underset{k \neq j}{\pi} \overline{H}_k(x - v_{ik}, t)] d\overline{H}_j(x - v_{ij}, t)$$

$$= w_j e^{\beta[v_{ij} - r_j(t)]} \int_{-\infty}^{\infty} e^{-\beta x} dH_i(x, t)$$

Substitution from (5.109) yields:

$$p_{ij}(t) = \frac{w_j e^{\beta[v_{ij}-r_j(t)]}}{\phi_i(t)} = \frac{w_j e^{\beta[v_{ij}-r_j(t)]}}{\sum_{j=1}^{n} w_j e^{\beta[v_{ij}-r_j(t)]}}$$

and result (5.111) is established. Similar arguments applied to the bid prices yield:

$$q_{ji}(t) = \Pr\{v_{ij}+\tilde{r}_i(t) > v_{kj}+\tilde{r}_k(t), \; \forall \, k \neq j, \; v_{ij}+\tilde{r}_i(t) \geq 0\}$$

$$= \int_0^\infty [\prod_{k \neq i} \overline{R}_k(x - v_{kj},t)] d\overline{R}_i(x - v_{ij},t)$$

$$= \theta_i e^{\beta[v_{ij} - u_i(t)]} \int_{-\infty}^\infty e^{-\beta x} dR_j(x)$$

Substitution from (5.110) yields:

$$q_{ji}(t) = [1 - e^{-\psi_j(t)}] \frac{\theta_i e^{\beta[v_{ij}-u_i(t)]}}{\psi_j(t)}$$

$$= [1 - e^{-\psi_j(t)}] \frac{\theta_i e^{\beta[v_{ij}-u_i(t)]}}{\sum_{i=1}^{m} \theta_i e^{\beta[v_{ij}-u_i(t)]}}$$

and result (5.112) is established. <u>Q.E.D.</u>

Corollary 5.7.1 is quite similar to corollary 5.3.1 in its results, and this is not surprising. Equations (5.111) and (5.112) define two logit models, which had to be expected from the double-exponential form of the distributions of Theorem 5.7.1 [in particular, those given by (5.97) and (5.98)].

Note that, as in the static case, while:

$$\sum_{j=1}^{n} p_{ij}(t) = 1$$

we have

$$\sum_{i=1}^{m} q_{ji} = 1 - e^{-\psi_j(t)} \leq 1$$

and the term $[1-e^{-\psi_j(t)}]$ has the meaning of probability that a supply unit in Ω_j has received and kept in memory up to time t at least one non-negative offer (bid price). Note also that we are emphasizing the concept of information kept, rather than that of decision taken. This is the correct way to interpret results of corollary 5.7.1. They do not provide actual decisions, but rather potential decisions which could be taken at time t, ie equations (5.111) and (5.112) furnish information about potential demand and supply, respectively.

Corollary 5.7.1 allows an economic interpretation of integral equations (5.105) and (5.106). Let us define the quantity $\bar{r}_j(t)$ by means of the equation:

$$e^{-\beta \bar{r}_j(t)} = \int_{-\infty}^{\infty} e^{-\beta y} dR_j(y,t)$$

That is, $\bar{r}_j(t)$ is the average price at instant t (not to be confused with $r_j(t)$, which is a weighted time average up to time t). From equation (5.110) one has:

$$e^{-\beta \bar{r}_j(t)} = \frac{1-e^{-\psi_j(t)}}{\psi_j(t)}, \quad j = 1, \ldots, n \qquad (5.113)$$

an equation similar to equation (5.36) in Theorem 5.3.1, for the static case. Substituting from equation (5.105) and definition (5.103) in definition (5.104) one obtains:

$$\psi_j(t) = \int_0^{\infty} \frac{F(\tau)}{\mu} \sum_{i=1}^{m} \theta_i \frac{e^{\beta v_{ij}}}{\sum_{j=1}^{n} w_j e^{\beta[v_{ij}-r_j(t-\tau)]}} d\tau, \quad j = 1, \ldots, n$$

or, remembering that $\theta_i = P_i N$ and $w_j = Q_j N$

$$\psi_j(t) = \int_0^\infty \frac{F(\tau)}{\mu} \sum_{i=1}^m P_i \frac{e^{\beta v_{ij}}}{\sum_{j=1}^n Q_j e^{\beta[v_{ij}-r_j(t-\tau)]}} \, d\tau$$

$$j = 1, \ldots, n \qquad\qquad\qquad (5.114)$$

From corollary 5.7.1 one has:

$$p_{ij}(t) = \frac{w_j e^{\beta[v_{ij}-r_j(t)]}}{\sum_{j=1}^n w_j e^{\beta[v_{ij}-r_j(t)]}} = \frac{Q_j e^{\beta[v_{ij}-r_j(t)]}}{\sum_{j=1}^n Q_j e^{\beta[v_{ij}-r_j(t)]}}$$

$$i = 1, \ldots, m, \quad j = 1, \ldots, n$$

Therefore, the term

$$\frac{e^{\beta v_{ij}}}{\sum_{j=1}^n Q_j e^{\beta[v_{ij}-r_j(t)]}}, \quad i = 1, \ldots, m, \quad j = 1, \ldots, n$$

gives the probability that a supply unit in Ω_j is considered as the best one by a demand unit in Γ_i, neglecting its price. This is, by definition, the condition under which the demand unit is willing to make his highest non-negative bid. The term

$$T_j(t) = \sum_{i=1}^m P_i \frac{e^{\beta v_{ij}}}{\sum_{j=1}^n Q_j e^{\beta[v_{ij}-r_j(t)]}}, \quad j = 1, \ldots, n$$

$$\qquad\qquad\qquad (5.115)$$

is therefore the expected number of demand units bidding for each supply unit in Ω_j at time t, ie it is the total potential demand at time t for supply unit in Ω_j. Using definition (5.115), equation (5.114) becomes:

$$\psi_j(t) = \int_0^\infty \frac{F(\tau)}{\mu} T_j(t-\tau)d\tau, \quad j = 1, \ldots, n \qquad (5.116)$$

that is, $\psi_j(t)$ is a weighted time average of the time-series of potential demand for a unit in Ω_j. Let us call this the average potential demand in Ω_j, that is $\psi_j(t)$ is the average potential demand for a unit $z\varepsilon\Omega_j$, $j = 1, \ldots, n$.

From corollary 5.7.1 one also has that:

$$[1-e^{-\psi_j(t)}] = \sum_{i=1}^m q_{ji}(t), \quad j = 1, \ldots, n \qquad (5.117)$$

is the probability that a supply unit in Ω_j is assigned to some demand unit, ie it is the expected unit supply for a $z\varepsilon\Omega_j$. Let us define:

$$S_j(t) = [1-e^{-\psi_j(t)}] \qquad (5.118)$$

Substitution of (5.118) in equation (5.113) yields

$$e^{-\beta\bar{r}_j(t)} = \frac{S_j(t)}{\psi_j(t)} \qquad (5.119)$$

or

$$\bar{r}_j(t) = \frac{1}{\beta} \log \frac{\psi_j(t)}{S_j(t)}, \quad j = 1, \ldots, n$$

that is, the average price at time t is proportional to the logarithm of the ratio between average potential demand and supply. Equation (5.106) can now be rewritten using (5.113) as:

$$e^{-\beta r_j(t)} = \int_0^\infty \frac{F(\tau)}{\mu} e^{-\beta \overline{r}_j(t-\tau)} d\tau$$

or, taking (5.119) into account:

$$e^{-\beta r_j(t)} = \int_0^\infty \frac{F(\tau)}{\mu} \frac{S_j(t-\tau)}{\psi_j(t-\tau)} d\tau, \ j = 1, \ldots, n \qquad (5.120)$$

relating the time average of prices to the time average of supply–demand ratios.

When a dynamic version of a static model is developed, it is important to build the generalization in such a way that consistency in the limit is kept, ie a desirable property of the dynamic model is that it admits the static model as an equilibrium for $t \to \infty$. The following corollary shows that this property holds and, moreover, that the equilibrium solution satisfies the mathematical program (5.47) – (5.48).

Corollary 5.7.2 Define

$$u_i = \lim_{t \to \infty} u_i(t)$$

$$r_j = \lim_{t \to \infty} r_j(t)$$

$$\phi_i = \lim_{t \to \infty} \phi_i(t)$$

$$\psi_j = \lim_{t \to \infty} \psi_j(t)$$

$$p_{ij} = \lim_{t \to \infty} p_{ij}(t)$$

$$i = 1, \ldots, m, \quad j = 1, \ldots, n$$

Then $\{r_j\}$ and $\{p_{ij}\}$ satisfy Theorem 5.3.2.

Proof   From equation (5.111), as $t \to \infty$

$$P_{ij} = \frac{w_j e^{\beta(v_{ij}-r_i)}}{\sum_{j=1}^{n} w_j e^{\beta(v_{ij}-r_j)}} = \frac{Q_j e^{\beta(v_{ij}-r_j)}}{\sum_{j=1}^{n} Q_j e^{\beta(v_{ij}-r_i)}}, \quad \begin{array}{l} i = 1, \ldots, m \\ j = 1, \ldots, n \end{array}$$

which is identical to equation (5.49). By using the dominated convergence theorem equations (5.105) and (5.106) become, as $t \to \infty$:

$$e^{-\beta u_i} = \frac{1}{\phi_i} \int_0^\infty \frac{F(\tau)}{\mu} d\tau = \frac{1}{\phi_i}, \quad i = 1, \ldots, m \qquad (5.121)$$

$$e^{-\beta r_j} = \frac{1-e^{-\psi_j}}{\psi_j} \int_0^\infty \frac{F(\tau)}{\mu} d\tau = \frac{1-e^{-\psi_j}}{\psi_j}, \quad j = 1, \ldots, n \qquad (5.122)$$

(the property $\int_0^\infty \frac{F(\tau)}{\mu} d\tau = 1$ has been used).

Equations (5.121) and (5.122) are identical to equations (5.38) and (5.39) in Theorem 5.3.1. It has been shown in Section 5.3 that they are equivalent to the market clearing conditions defined by equations (5.46):

$$\sum_{i=1}^{m} P_i \frac{Q_j e^{\beta(v_{ij}-r_j)}}{\sum_{j=1}^{n} Q_j e^{\beta(v_{ij}-r_j)}} = Q_j(1-e^{-\psi_j}), \quad j = 1, \ldots, n$$

where ψ_j, from equation (5.45), can be expressed as:

$$\psi_j = \sum_{i=1}^{m} P_i \frac{e^{\beta v_{ij}}}{\sum_{j=1}^{n} Q_j e^{\beta(v_{ij}-r_j)}}, \quad j = 1, \ldots, n$$

The conditions of Theorem 5.3.2 are therefore satisfied.
<u>Q.E.D.</u>

We close this section considering a specific assumption which makes equations (5.105) and (5.106) somewhat easier for computation. Assume the lifetime of a signal is exponentially distributed, ie

$$F(\tau) = e^{-\alpha\tau}, \quad \alpha = 1/\mu \tag{5.123}$$

Substitution of assumption (5.123) into equations (5.105) and (5.106) and transformation on the variable of integration yield:

$$e^{-\beta u_i(t)} = \int_{-\infty}^{t} \alpha e^{-\alpha(t-\tau)} \frac{1}{\phi_i(\tau)} \, d\tau, \quad i = 1, \ldots, m \tag{5.124}$$

$$e^{-\beta r_j(t)} = \int_{-\infty}^{t} \alpha e^{-\alpha(t-\tau)} \frac{1-e^{-\psi_j(\tau)}}{\psi_j(\tau)} \, d\tau, \quad j = 1, \ldots, n \tag{5.125}$$

Let us introduce the notation

$$X_i(t) = e^{-\beta u_i(t)}, \quad i = 1, \ldots, m \tag{5.126}$$

$$Y_j(t) = e^{-\beta r_j(t)}, \quad j = 1, \ldots, n \tag{5.127}$$

Then equations (5.124) and (5.125) become

$$X_i(t) = \int_{-\infty}^{t} \alpha e^{-\alpha(t-\tau)} \frac{1}{\phi_i(\tau)} \, d\tau, \quad i = 1, \ldots, m \tag{5.128}$$

$$Y_j(t) = \int_{-\infty}^{t} \alpha e^{-\alpha(t-\tau)} \frac{1-e^{-\psi_j(\tau)}}{\psi_j(\tau)} \, d\tau, \quad j = 1, \ldots, n \tag{5.129}$$

Differentiating both sides of equations (5.128) and (5.129) with respect to time we obtain the following equivalent differential equations:

$$\dot{X}_i(t) = \alpha \frac{1}{\phi_i(t)} - \alpha X_i(t), \quad i = 1, \ldots, m \qquad (5.130)$$

$$\dot{Y}_i(t) = \alpha \frac{1 - e^{-\psi_j(t)}}{\psi_j(t)} - \alpha Y_j(t), \quad j = 1, \ldots, n \qquad (5.131)$$

Equation (5.131) for prices can be rearranged in order to make its economic interpretation easier. From (5.127) one has

$$\dot{Y}_j(t) = -\beta e^{-\beta r_j(t)} \dot{r}_j(t) \qquad (5.132)$$

Therefore substitution of (5.127) and (5.132) in equation (5.131) yields, after some calculations:

$$\dot{r}_j(t) = \frac{\alpha}{\beta} \left[1 - \frac{1 - e^{-\psi_j(t)}}{\psi_j(t) e^{-\beta r_j(t)}} \right], \quad j = 1, \ldots, n \qquad (5.133)$$

Using definition (5.118), equation (5.133) becomes

$$\dot{r}_j(t) = \frac{\alpha}{\beta} \frac{\psi_j(t) e^{-\beta r_j(t)} - S_j(t)}{\psi_j(t) e^{-\beta r_j(t)}}, \quad j = 1, \ldots, n \qquad (5.134)$$

The term $\psi_j(t) e^{-\beta r_j(t)}$ can be interpreted with the aid of equation (5.114):

$$\psi_j(t) e^{-\beta r_j(t)} = \int_0^\infty \frac{F(\tau)}{\mu} \sum_{i=1}^m P_i \frac{e^{\beta[v_{ij} - v_j(t)]}}{\sum_{j=1}^n Q_j e^{\beta[v_{ij} - r_j(t-\tau)]}} \, d\tau$$

$$j = 1, \ldots, n$$

or, using definition (5.115)

$$\psi_j(t)e^{-\beta r_j(t)} = \int_0^\infty \frac{F(\tau)}{\mu} T_j(t-\tau)e^{-\beta r_j(t)} d\tau, \quad j = 1, \ldots, n$$
(5.135)

Since $T_j(t-\tau)$ is the expected number of bidders for a supply unit $z\epsilon\Omega_j$ at time $t-\tau$, $T_j(t-\tau)e^{-\beta r_j(t)}$ is the expected number of such bidders who would still accept z under the market conditions (ie with the price distribution) at time t. Equation (5.135) therefore specifies a demand forecasting rule, for a supply unit $z\epsilon\Omega_j$, based on taking the weighted time average of the expected number of bidders who would accept the prices at time t. Let us call this quantity $D_j(t)$ which equals $\psi_j(t)e^{-\beta r_j(t)}$ and is the demand forecast for a supply unit in Ω_j at time t. Then the differential equation (5.134) can be written as:

$$\dot{r}_j(t) = \frac{\alpha}{\beta} \frac{D_j(t) - S_j(t)}{D_j(t)}, \quad j = 1, \ldots, n$$
(5.136)

Equation (5.136) is a Walras-type equation, relating the rate of change of average prices to the difference between demand and supply. Of course the equilibrium condition of (5.136), provided an equilibrium exists (and we know it does and it is unique, because of corollary 5.7.2), is

$$\lim_{t\to\infty} \dot{r}_j(t) = 0, \quad j = 1, \ldots, n$$

equivalent to

$$\lim_{t\to\infty} D_j(t) = \lim_{t\to\infty} S_j(t), \quad j = 1, \ldots, n$$

and this is easily shown to coincide with the market clearing conditions (5.46).

We remark that another interpretation of equation (5.133) is possible. Substituting from equation (5.113) we get:

138

$$\dot{r}_j(t) = \frac{\alpha}{\beta} \{1 - e^{-\beta[\overline{r}_j(t) - r_j(t)]}\}, \quad j = 1, \ldots, n$$

(5.137)

Remember that $\overline{r}_j(t)$ is the average price at time t, while $r_j(t)$ is the time average of prices up to time t. Equation (5.137) therefore states that the rate of change in the price time average is an increasing function of the difference between average price and price time average. When $\overline{r}_j(t)$ is greater than the time average, we have an increase, when $\overline{r}_j(t)$ is less than the average, we have a decrease. It should be recalled that the time average $r_j(t)$, and not the instant average price $\overline{r}_j(t)$, is the most important average signal from supply to demand. This is seen from equation (5.111), defining the demand model, which contains the $r_j(t)$, and not the $\overline{r}_j(t)$. The reason for this is clear: from the assumptions we have made on the way information is received and kept in memory, no demand or supply unit is ever perfectly informed about the present. They rather estimate the present from past incomplete data, namely, by taking time averages. Of course they do not do this consciously, but the behavioural model assumed so far turns out to be equivalent to a time averaging process.

The equilibrium condition for equation (5.137) is

$$\lim_{t \to \infty} \overline{r}_j(t) = \lim_{t \to \infty} r_j(t)$$

(5.138)

that is, in the limit, instant and time average prices should coincide. From equation (5.113) we know that equation (5.138) is equivalent to

$$e^{-\beta r_j} = \frac{1 - e^{-\psi_j}}{\psi_j}, \quad j = 1, \ldots, n$$

(5.139)

which is nothing but equation (5.39) of Theorem 5.3.1 and, as we know, is equivalent to the market clearing conditions.

This concludes the assembly of the basic machinery which will be applied further in Chapters Nine and Fifteen.

Chapter 6

THE ELEMENTS FOR AN INTEGRATED APPROACH

G. Leonardi and A.G. Wilson

6.1 Introduction

In Chapter One we outlined the main features which underpin the
integrated model we are specifying. These can be summarised as:

*   Main components : population
                        stocks
                        prices
*   Main sub-systems: housing market
                        labour market
                        services
                        land
                        transport

We also identified a number of approaches which can contribute to model building in each of these areas:

*   Main approaches : economic   : population movement
                                                stock adjustment
                                                price adjustment
                        spatial interaction-: stock adjustment
                            based dynamics   price adjustment
                        master equations   : accounting
                        stochastic dynamics : probabilistic
                                               formulations

In the case of the service and transport systems, we noted
the assumption that when there is a supply-side change, it can
be assumed that the consumer response is effectively instantaneous. This means that it is possible to focus on equilibrium
models of consumer use, together with models of stock dynamics
(and price adjustments) for service sectors and corresponding
'planning' adjustments in the case of transport supply. In the
case of population movement in relation to residential location
or jobs, this assumption of rapid return-to-equilibrium, while
often made, is less realistic; and so then, in order both to
provide a proper set of accounts and to offer a framework
within which a variety of transition models can be embedded, a
master equations approach is appropriate. However, it is also
appropriate to consider economic models within which these
structures are implicit.

The possible elements of an integrated model which is
generated by this approach are shown in Figure 6.1, together
with chapter numbers (which for specific sub-models form the
rest of Part II), thus indicating the chapter within which the
development of a model for a sub-system component type and
particular approach can be found.

In the rest of the chapter, we explore the structures of
an integrated model in more detail. In Section 6.2 we present,
mainly in diagrammatic form, a more detailed explanation of the
main components, sub-systems and inter-relationships. In
Section 6.3 we comment on the structures of sub-models which
could be constructed and explain the choices which generate
the chapters which follow.

6.2 The Main Elements of a Set of an Integrated Model System

The next step in the argument is to identify more explicitly
the components in each of the main sub-systems. Some of these
are common to two or more sub-systems and it is through these

	Population				Stocks				Prices (rents)			
	ec	si-d	me	sd	ec	si-d	me	sd	ec	si-d	me	sd
Housing Market	7	p	8	9	7	p	8	9	7	p	8	9
Services	p	10	11	p	p	10	11	p	p	10	p	p
Land	------------------				12	p	p	p	12	p	p	p
Labour Market	13	p	14	15	p	p*	p‡	p	13	p	14	15
Transport	p	16	14	15	*	*	*	*	p	*	*	*

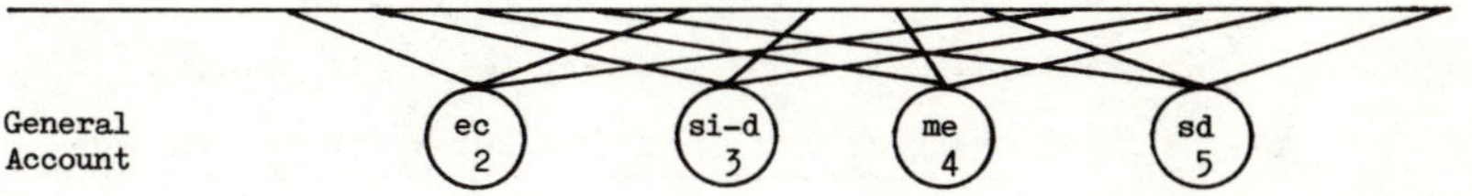

General Account: (ec 2) (si-d 3) (me 4) (sd 5)

Figure 6.1: Possible elements for an integrated model

KEY

Numbers	: 2,3,4,5,7,8,9,10,11,12,13,14,15,16: Chapter numbers where approach is used
ec	: economic
si-d	: spatial interaction - dynamics
me	: master equation
sd	: stochastic dynamics
P	: possible but not developed here
*	: difficult - exogenous
P*	: 'trial plans' used here - some jobs can be obtained from the services model, the rest of industry is exogenous

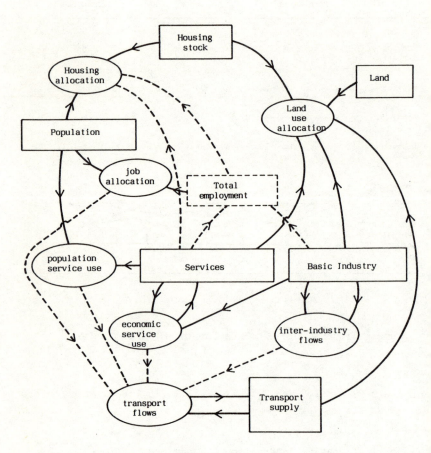

<u>Figure 6.2</u>: An integrated model: framework for the system state
at time t

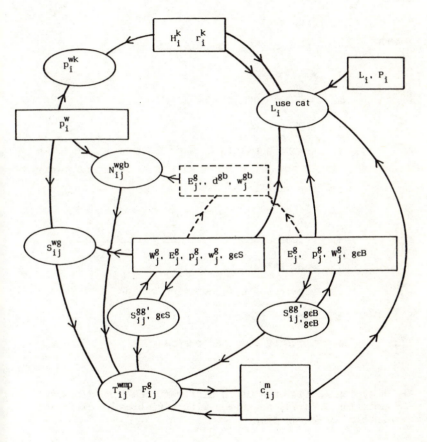

<u>Figure 6.3</u>: Main system arrays (illustrative notation): state at time t

145

KEY to Figure 6.3

H_i^k	:	houses by type k at i
r_i^k	:	rents
L_i	:	land supply
ρ_i	:	land rent
L_i^{usecat}	:	land at i by use cat
P_i^w	:	w-type pop in i
P_i^{wk}	:	ditto in house type k
F_{ij}^g	:	flows of goods
N_{ij}^{wgh}	:	w-type p res in i, wkg in sector g, in occ b in j
E_j^g	:	emp in g in j
W_j^g	:	$\left.\begin{matrix} attr \\ size \end{matrix}\right]$ of service sector
P_j^g	:	prices of goods
w_j^g	:	wage rates
w_j^{gb}	:	wage rates by occupation group
$S_{ij}^{wg}, S_{ij}^{gg'}$	:	service flows
T_{ij}^{wmp}	:	flows by mode and purpose

NB A typical notation, but in different chapters different notation is used, sometimes with variables at different levels of aggregation

relationships that there are accounting inter-dependencies
between such systems. The first step is shown in Figure 6.2.
The main components are shown in rectangular boxes; the circles
and elipses show the 'allocations' which relate these components.
The main types of components we identified in Section 6.1 appear
in the rectangles. As we will see below, these can be combined
with the 'allocations' to form sub-systems. It is important to
emphasise that we are concerned not simply with physical counts
of the elements of each sub-system, but also with their
characteristics. These include the various prices, like land
rents, costs of goods and services, wage rates and so on; and
also any aspects of quality, or whatever, needed to describe
(for example) different kinds of housing. We can begin to be
more explicit in this way by associating the main algebraic
variables which appear in our models with the various parts of
Figure 6.2 and this is done for an illustrative set in Figure
6.3. It is also useful to abstract from Figure 6.1 the groups
of components which make up the main sub-systems and this is
done in Figures 6.4 - 6.8. If these are imagined as superposed
on to Figure 6.2 then the 'overlaps' (through common components)
of the different sub-systems can be seen.

   The next major step in the argument is to be more explicit
about dynamics. Figures 6.2 - 6.8 all represent cross-sectional
portraits. Figure 6.9 indicates the general problem we now
face: how to specify mechanisms which carry the system from one
cross-section to another. In this case, the cross-sections are
each repetitions of the form of Figure 6.2. It would also be
possible to project a geographical cross-sectional 'map' and to
indicate the nature of the transitions, as shown in Figure 6.10.

   When we add the mechanisms of change to Figures 6.9 or
6.10, we can gain insights into the nature of the different
ways in which this can be done. The master equations format,
for instance, involves a detailed specification of all the
elements of transition - in effect, connecting each 'allocation',

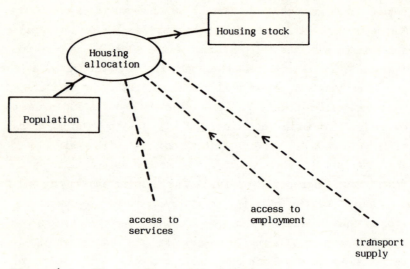

Figure 6.4: The housing market at time t

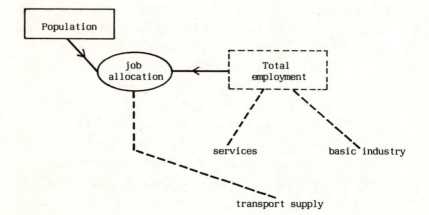

Figure 6.5: The labour market at time t

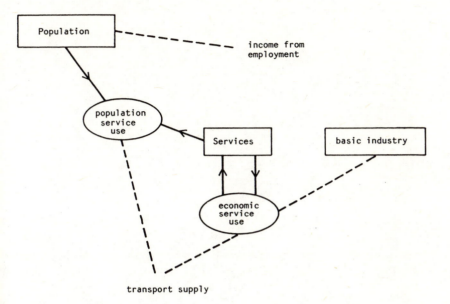

Figure 6.6:   Services

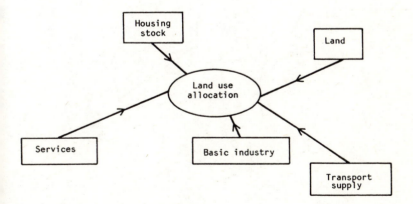

Figure 6.7:   The land market at time t

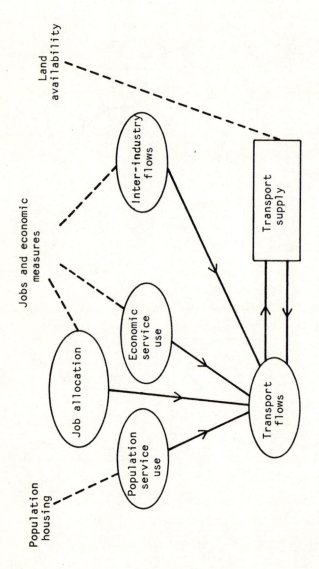

Figure 6.8: Transport at time t

that is (i,j) (or whatever) to (i',j') transitions (Figure
6.11). A more approximate, but often more manageable procedure
is to channel those who move into 'pools' and then to real-
locate from the pool (Figure 6.12).

The figures can also be used to illustrate another aspect
of dynamic specification: the extent to which the cross-sectional
elements are in equilibrium or not. A number of cases are shown
in Figure 6.13.

To fix ideas, we take the three kinds of components -
populations, stocks and prices - and subdivide the last category
into prices (of goods) and rents (of land), thus making four
kinds of components in all. We can then envisage that for each
type, the choice can be made either to build a cross-sectional
equilibrium model or to adjust incrementally during each period
(with the possibility of a tendency to equilibrium but typically
equilibrium not being achieved). The three cases shown in
Figure 6.13 are typical of the models presented in other chapters
of this book - but it is equally clear that other permutations
are possible. The three are:

(i)   Comparative statics: all components in equilibrium
at the cross-section;

(ii) Anas-type economic model in which the population
is assumed to be in equilibrium through discrete choice models;
the supply-demand balance is achieved at each cross-section by
price and rent adjustment; and stocks are adjusted during the
period;

(iii) A process which is typical of spatial-interaction-
based dynamics and the master equations approach where all
the adjustments are from period to period and equilibrium is
only achieved in the long term if there are no exogenous
changes.

Finally, it is also necessary to explore the possibility
of lags being involved in the change mechanism. This is shown
diagrammatically in Figure 6.14. More generally, a combination

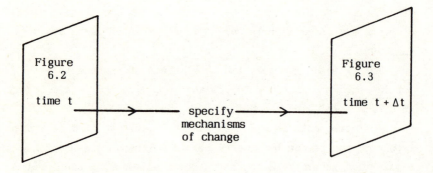

Figure
6.2

time t

specify
mechanisms
of change

Figure
6.3

time t + Δt

<u>Figure 6.9</u>   Transition from one cross-section to another

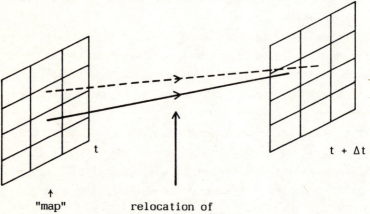

t

t + Δt

"map"

relocation of
different components

<u>Figure 6.10</u> As 6.9, with geographical zones added

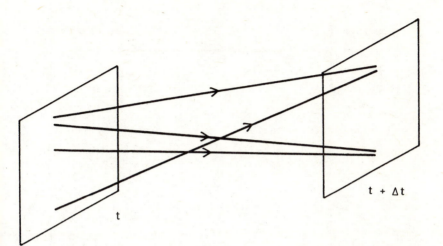

Figure 6.11: Master equations: individual transitions specified

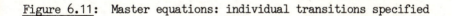

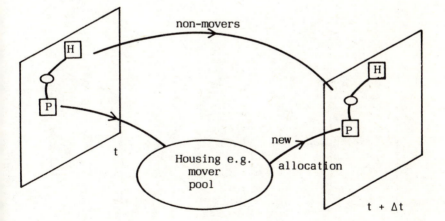

Figure 6.12 A mover pool

An Integrated Approach

cross-sectional
equilibrium (t)

inter period
adjustment
(t, t + Δt)

cross-sectional
equilibrium (t+ Δt)

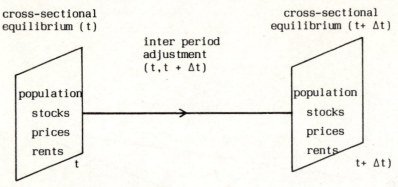

(i) Comparative statics

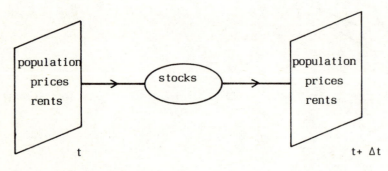

(ii) Typical economic model

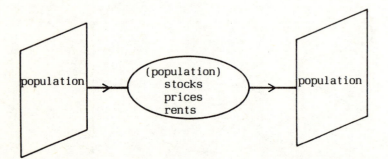

(iii) Spatial-interaction dynamics: (master equation)

Figure 6.13: Possible dynamic mechanisms

154

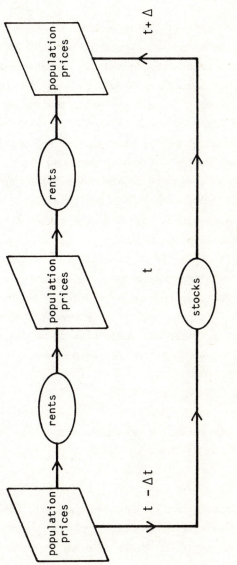

Figure 6.14: An example of lag structure

of decisions on lags and on different speeds of response
begins to create a framework for handling a great variety of
the dynamic interactions of processes.

6.3 The Approach Adopted in the Rest of Part II

In order to explain the structure of the rest of Part II, it
is useful to return to Figure 6.1 and to add a further commentary. A scan along rows shows the chapters within which
particular sub-models are constructed. The number of different
chapter numbers in a row indicates the number of alternative
submodels which we chose to explore in each case. In each row,
the number of times the same chapter appears is a measure of
'comprehensiveness': three appearances means that all three
types of component are treated within the submodel (except for
the 'land' row where the maximum possible is two).

A scan down columns shows the range of applications of
each of the main techniques.

In principle, it is possible to assemble an integrated
model by selecting any chapter referred to in a row and permut-
ing this choice with similar choices from other rows. (If a
'component' is not dealt with in one of these choices then the
corresponding variables would have to be dealt with exogenously.)
Possible 'ensembles' are, for example:

*   (7, 10, 12, 13, 16)

which is almost wholly economic, or:

*   (8, 11, 12, 14, 16)

which is almost wholly 'master equation', and so on. The task
is not quite as easy as this implies! One difficulty, for
example, is that the levels of disaggregation of variables in

different approaches are not always the same, and so for this and other reasons, some submodel modifications will usually be needed before an integrated model can be assembled. These and related issues are pursued in Part III, Chapter Seventeen.

Chapter 7

HOUSING 1: A DYNAMIC ECONOMIC MODEL OF THE REGULATED HOUSING
MARKET

A. Anas

7.1   Introduction and Background

Two ongoing modelling projects for Chicago and Stockholm by
the author have developed some basic mathematical ingredients
for building a generalized and transferable model of the
regulated housing market with price (or rent) controls. These
two projects are briefly described below. The remainder of
this Chapter explains the generalized form of the regulated
housing market model.

The results of the Chicago project are described and
documented in Anas (1982, 1983) and Anas and Duann (1984).
CATLAS (or The Chicago Area Transportation-Land Use Analysis
System) is a mathematical empirically implemented and policy
analytic model of the metropolitan housing market in Chicago.
The metropolitan area is divided into 1690 small geographic
zones which are treated as substitutable submarkets. The
American housing market is for the overwhelming part free of
price regulation. Thus, the model does not consider these
aspects which are much more dominant in the European cities
and generally absent in Chicago. CATLAS is dynamic and
operates with yearly periods. It simulated new construction,
demolitions and the occupancy-vacancy status of existing
dwellings. The construction and demolition equations are
recursive and are based on the assumption of a one year lag.

A form of adaptive expectations can be used subject to the
availability of appropriate data. CATLAS has been used to
simulate the effect of transportation investment on housing
and land values and thus perform an important part of the
cost-benefit analysis needed to evaluate such investments.
Since the results are published in the above-mentioned references, they will not be reviewed here.

The model of the Swedish housing market is based on two
months of interviews with public officials and experts in
Sweden. The paper by Anas et al (1985) describes the results
of these interviews and it is apparently the only comprehensive description of the Swedish housing market with due
attention to institutional structure.

The model is currently under development and its full
structure is described in Anas and Cho (1985).

The model explains market clearing in a Swedish metropolitan housing market such as Stockholm, Gothenburg or Malmo.
It differentiates owner-occupied and renter-occupied dwellings,
dwellings by age, by ownership (private landlords, non-profit
companies) and focusses on market transaction options. Households have the options of buying and selling homes in the free
market, in the black market, they can swap dwellings (a semi-
legal transaction method), they can rent in the rent-controlled
stock or they can enter a public queue which rations them to
a vacancy.

The current model does not pay attention to geographic
disaggregation but the Stockholm version to be implemented in
the future is likely to have separate representation of the
25 Swedish municipalities.

This Chapter draws from the Chicago and Swedish experience
to provide a prototypical description of the dynamic model of
a regulated housing market, focussing only on the essential
(key) elements and avoiding detail.

7.2 Dimensionality

7.2.1 Space

The metropolitan area can be divided into geographic zones which may be small neighbourhoods, legally defined municipalities, or large aggregations such as cities (the city of Chicago, or the city of Stockholm) versus suburban areas.

The Chicago model consists of 1690 zones. The Stockholm model will consist of 25 municipalities or, at the early stages, it will consist of city and suburbs.

7.2.2 Submarkets

Housing may be classified into submarkets by tenure (own versus rent), age, class, ownership by landlord type (private, public companies, public queue), size (by rooms or floor space) and by building type (single family versus multifamily).

7.2.3 Households

Households can be classified by wealth and income, race, stage in the life cycle, age of household head, newly formed or existing and current location (by submarket).

7.2.4 Time

Time is best treated in discrete periods t = 0, 1, 2, ... The model consists of relationships which represent market clearing during a period. These are equations which are solved simultaneously once for each period. There are also recursive relationships which represent adjustments in exogenous variables and in the stock of housing which occur during a period. These are generally lagged adjustments and do not affect the market until the next period begins. They occur independently of the simultaneous adjustments within each time period. In both the Chicago and Swedish models the time period is one year long. Figure 7.1 illustrates the behaviour of the simultaneous and recursive parts.

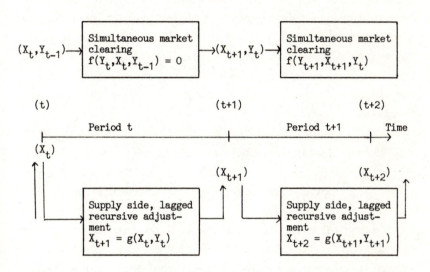

<u>Figure 7.1</u>: Recursive and simultaneous relationships in the dynamic housing market model

7.2.5 Origins and transitions

A basic feature of the dynamic model is that households have to be identified not only by the socioeconomic characteristics described in 7.2.3 but also by their current location (in the beginning of a period t) in space and submarkets. The market clearing model then focusses on the transition of households

during a period t from their current location (origin) to a
new location (effective at the beginning of t + 1). Possible
transitions for existing households are: (i) to stay in their
current origin; (ii) to move to another origin; (iii) to fail
to move to another origin and thus decide (unwillingly) to
stay in their current origin.

For new households (potentially new) the possible transitions are: (i) not to form a new household; (ii) to form a new
household and to move to another origin; (iii) to fail to move
to another origin and thus decide (unwillingly) to postpone
the effective date of household formation.

Thus, the model takes household formation into account
and includes feedbacks from the housing market into household
formation.

7.3 Market Clearing: a simple prototype

7.3.1 Free versus mixed markets with price regulation

The Chicago case is representative of a free market which
operates without price regulation. The decision tree of
Figure 7.2 describes the fundamental problem of choice facing
a representative household who has decided to relocate in this
market. For simplicity only two submarkets ($j = 1, 2$) are
considered and all households are assumed to be homogeneous
except for random differences. Thus, we do not consider a
classification of households by place of origin or socio-
economic characteristics.

The representative utility of a dwelling i in submarket
1 is $U_1 = U(R_1, \overline{X}_1)$ where R_1 is the rent of this dwelling and
$\overline{X}_1$ is the vector of its attributes. For submarket 2 we have
$U_2 = U(R_2, \overline{X}_2)$. Given N households, the proportion choosing j
is given by $P_1(U_1, U_2)$ and $P_2(U_1, U_2)$ respectively such that
$P_1(U_1, U_2) + P_2(U_1, U_2) = 1$. Properly defined, these choice

proportions satisfy $\partial P_i/\partial U_i > 0$ and $\partial P_i/\partial U_j < 0$ for $j \neq i$ and also $\partial P_i/\partial R_i < 0$ and $\partial P_i/\partial R_j > 0$ for $j \neq i$.

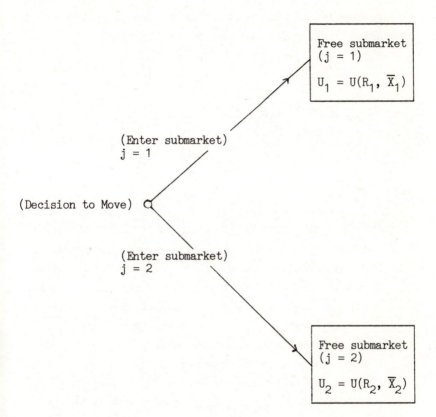

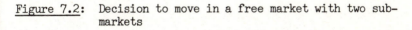

Figure 7.2: Decision to move in a free market with two sub-markets

On the supply side there is an available stock S_j of dwellings in each submarket. Each landlord must decide whether to offer a dwelling for rent or to keep it vacant given the going rent R_j. This is done by comparing the rent to the differential maintenance (or short-run occupancy) costs of a vacant versus an occupied dwelling. We denote the proportion of dwellings that will be offered for rent as $Q_j(R_j, \overline{Y}_j)$

163

where $\overline{Y}_j$ is a vector of supply side dwelling characteristics. We assume, of course, that $\partial Q_j/\partial R_j > 0$ and $\partial Q_j/\partial R_i = 0$ for $i = j$.

Now the equilibrium rent vector $\overline{R}^{t*}$ for time t can be obtained by solving the two simultaneous equations,

$$N^t P_1 [U(R_1^t, \overline{X}_1^t), U(R_2^t, \overline{X}_2^t)] - S_1^t Q_1(R_1^t, \overline{Y}_1^t) = 0$$

$$N^t P_2 [U(R_1^t, \overline{X}_1^t), U(R_2^t, \overline{X}_2^t)] - S_2^t Q_2(R_2^t, \overline{Y}_2^t) = 0 \qquad (7.1)$$

where

$$S_1^t + S_2^t \geq N^t$$

The above is essentially the structure of CATLAS (see Anas and Duann, 1984) and in that case it was generalized to many submarkets and two household groups. CATLAS was specified as a model in which the demand side choice probabilities $P(.)$ are nested logit models and the supply side probabilities $Q(.)$ are binary logit models. Anas (1982) proved that the solution $\overline{R}^{t*}$ is unique at each time period.

Now consider a mixed housing market. Submarket $j = 1$ is free of price regulation and the rent R_1 is determined in the market. Submarket $j = 2$ is controlled by the State and the rent R_2 is fixed according to various criteria of social justice. In Sweden the principle that is used is that developers of the controlled housing make no profit. This makes sense, from the Swedish point of view, since this housing is supplied by non-profit companies owned by the Swedish municipalities.

Figure 7.3 is the decision tree of the household in our hypothetical mixed market.

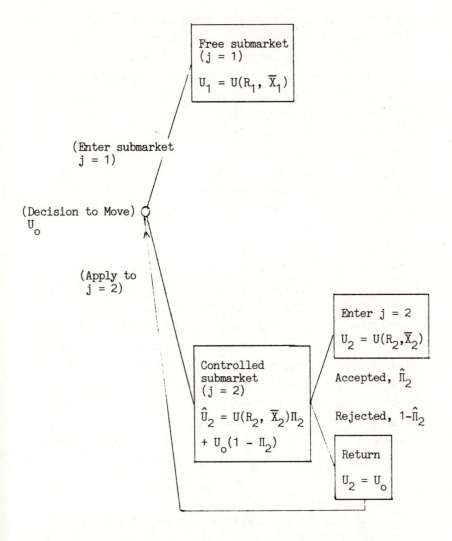

Figure 7.3: Decision tree of a household in a mixed market, facing a rationing decision in the controlled market with fixed rent, R_2 and acceptance probability $\hat{\Pi}_2$

165

Figure 7.3 is interpreted as follows. The household currently enjoys a representative utility U_o. This is the average utility over all N households. If the household decides to move, it has two choices. One is to enter the free submarket and pay rent R_1^*, deriving utility $U_1 = U(R_1^*, \overline{X}_1)$. Because this market equilibrates within a year freely, the household is certain to find a dwelling as long as it pays the equilibrium rent R_1^*. The second choice is to enter the controlled submarket. Because this submarket's rent is fixed, demand could exceed supply and there is no guarantee that all applicants will be successful in entering it. The landlords or a government housing agency have their own rules for deciding whether households will be given a dwelling or not. Since prices cannot rise to discourage excess demands a rationing decision must take place. The applicant household anticipates that it will be accepted with probability $\hat{\Pi}_2$ and rejected with probability $1 - \hat{\Pi}_2$. If it is rejected it returns to its current location where it obtains the utility U_o. It is assumed that the household makes one attempt to enter either market during the year. If this assumption seems unsatisfactory, then a time interval shorter than a year should be used.

If the household enters submarket 1, its utility is

$$U_1 = U(R_1, \overline{X}_1) \tag{7.2}$$

If it applies to submarket 2, its expected utility is,

$$\hat{U}_2 = \hat{U}(R_2, \overline{X}_2)\,\hat{\pi}_2 + (U_o)(1 - \hat{\pi}_2) \tag{7.3}$$

where $\hat{\pi}_2$ is the household's anticipated probability that the rationing agent will admit that household to submarket 2. To simplify notation, we may rewrite $\hat{U}_2$ as

$$\hat{U}_2 = \hat{U}(R_2, \overline{X}_2, \hat{\pi}_2, U_o) \qquad (7.4)$$

This may be a more general function than the above risk-neutral formulation. It can include an aversion for risk.

7.3.2 Rationing decisions

The government agency or landlords who do the rationing can be viewed as operating a double queue. On one side is a queue of households desiring a dwelling at the fixed price R_2. On the other hand is a queue of dwellings which are vacant desiring an occupant. The rationing process determines the probability (and thus proportion on the average) that a household in the demand queue will be accepted. This is the probability π_2. At the same time, it also determines q_2 which is the probability that a vacancy will be offered for rent. We assume that

$$\pi_2 = \pi(\lambda_2, R_2) \text{ and } q_2 = q(\lambda_2, R_2) \qquad (7.5)$$

Here λ_2 is the "congestion level" in the queue. It may be, for example, a function of the expected waiting time of the households. It is reasonable to assume that $\partial\pi/\partial\lambda_2 < 0$, the higher the congestion level the lower the acceptance probability that a vacancy will be offered for rent: $\partial q/\partial\lambda_2 > 0$. The signs with respect to R_2 are not important because R_2 is fixed and thus exogenous. They might be as follows, however: $\partial\pi/\partial R_2 < 0$ and $\partial q/\partial R_2 > 0$. These should be the signs if the agency (even though not profit maximizing) shows a tendency towards rent maximization.

The congestion factor λ_2 is endogenous and will be determined in the temporary equilibrium formulation each year.

7.3.3 Temporary equilibrium

The endogenous variables R_1^* and λ_2^* are determined by solving the following temporary equilibrium problem for time t.

$$N^t P_1 [U(R_1^t, \overline{X}_1^t), \hat{U}(R_2^t, \overline{X}_2^t, \pi_2^{t-1}, U_o)]$$

$$+ N^t P_2 [U(R_1^t, \overline{X}_1^t), \hat{U}(R_2^t, \overline{X}_2^t, \pi_2^{t-1}, U_o)][1 - \pi(\lambda_2^t, R_2^t)]$$

$$- S_1^t Q_1(R_1^t, \overline{Y}_1^t) = 0 \tag{7.6}$$

$$N^t P_2 [U(R_1^t, \overline{X}_1^t), \hat{U}(R_2^t, \overline{X}_2^t, \pi_2^{t-1}, U_o)] \pi(\lambda_2^t, R_2^t)$$

$$- S_2^t q(\lambda_2^t, R_2^t) = 0 \tag{7.7}$$

Note that the household's anticipated probability that it will be accepted into submarket 2 is assumed to be determined with a one year lag. The household cannot know the current probability. Thus, it may be assumed that it sets its anticipation equal to the previous probability, or more generally an anticipation function may have the form

$$\hat{\pi}_2^t = \alpha \pi_2^{t-1} + (1 - \alpha) \pi_2^{t-2}$$

where $0 < \alpha < 1$.

The first equilibrium equation for the free submarket, (7.6), states that the demand on the left hand side consists of two parts: those who chose submarket one and those who applied to the controlled queue but were rejected and thus spilled over to the free submarket. In this submarket R_1^t adjusts to equate demand and supply as the landlords make free offer decisions. In submarket 2, (7.7), the effective demand consists of those who applied to the queue and were accepted. Here, rent R_2^t is fixed but the congestion factor

λ_2^t adjusts to equate demand and supply.

The above formulation assumes that households rejected from the queue all spill over to the free submarket. Another possible assumption is that households return to their place of origin. Then, let N^F be the households who, in the beginning of the period, are in the free market and let N^C be those who in the beginning are in the controlled market. Then, the demand supply equations are:

$$N^{Ft}P_1^F[U(R_1^t, \overline{X}_1^t), \hat{U}(R_2^t, \overline{X}_2^t, \hat{\pi}_2^t, U(R_1^t, \overline{X}_1^t))]$$

(those who wish to stay in the free submarket)

$$+ N^{ct}P_1^C[U(R_1^t, \overline{X}_1^t), U(R_2^t, \overline{X}_2^t)]$$

(those in the controlled market who wish to move to the free market)

$$N^{Ft}P_2^F[U(R_1^t, \overline{X}_1^t), \hat{U}(R_2^t, \overline{X}_2^t, \hat{\pi}_2^t, U(R_1^t, \overline{X}_1^t))][1 - \pi(\lambda_2^t, R_2^t)]$$

(those in the free market who applied to the controlled market but were rejected)

$$- S_1^t Q_1(R_1^t, \overline{Y}_1^t) = 0 \qquad (7.8)$$

(part of rental stock in free market offered for rent by landlords)

$$N^{ct}P_2^C[U(R_1^t, \overline{X}_1^t), U(R_2^t, \overline{X}_2^t)]$$

(those in the controlled market who wish to stay)

$$+ N^{Ft}P_2^F[U(R_1^t, \overline{X}_1^t), \hat{U}(R_2^t, \overline{X}_2^t, \pi_2^{t-1}, U(R_1^t, \overline{X}_1^t))] \times \pi(\lambda_2^t, R_2^t)$$

(those in the free market who applied to the controlled market and were accepted)

$$- (S_2^t - N^{dt}P_2^c[U(R_t^t, \overline{X}_1^t), U(R_2^t, \overline{X}_2^t)])q_2(\lambda_2^t, R_2^t)$$

(part of vacant and vacated stock in the controlled market offered to those who enter this market)

$$- N^{ct}P_2^c[U(R_1^t, \overline{X}_1^t), U(R_2^t, \overline{X}_2^t)] = 0 \tag{7.9}$$

(those in the controlled market who wish to stay)
(this last term simply cancels the first)

7.3.4 Recursive relations and updating

Since the model is recursive, many variables need to be updated from t to t + 1. One which we already saw is the household's anticipated probability of being accepted or rejected from the controlled market.

There are other equations. For example the households can grow over time. The number of households which occur at the beginning of time t + 1 will depend on the number of households at the beginning of time t, natural demographic events such as births and deaths, exogenous factors such as unemployment and the changes in marriage-related taxes as well as some feedback from the housing market. If, for example, the queue's congestion factor is low then we can expect more households to be formed. Also, if rents are low, again more households may be formed.

These and other relationships can be used to update $\overline{X}^t$, $\overline{Y}^t$, N^t and R_2^t for time t + 1.

7.3.5 Complete equation structure of the Swedish prototype

The Appendix contains all of the equations of the Swedish prototype model and an explanation of all the variables and equations. Since this Appendix is self-explanatory there is no need to go into the details here. It is important, however, to discuss the transaction options which exist in the Swedish housing market, since it is these transaction options which are chiefly responsible for the model's complexity.

(1) Free buy and sell: owners of cooperative dwellings and single family dwellings less than three years in age can freely buy and sell these dwellings.

(2) Black market: tenants of apartments can illegally let these to others who legally can seek to rent them in exchange for key money.

(3) Swapping: tenants of apartments can legally swap their units with the apartment or owned residence of another household exchanging side payments in the process.

(4) Semi-regulated submarket: non-profit companies let their rental apartments to applicant-tenants at fixed rents by means of a rationing procedure which is blind to the tenant's social characteristics.

(5) Fully-regulated submarket: a government agency rations tenant-applicants to part of the rental housing stock by means of a procedure based on socioeconomic need.

For the complete equation structure see the Appendix.

7.4 Supply Side

The supply side operates with a one period lag. Given the variables at time t, construction and conversion during time t occurs to create the supply available at the beginning of time t + 1. The conversion of existing dwellings can include demolition as well.

Let S_o^t be the potential number of new dwellings that can be built on vacant land at time t. In CATLAS this is obtained for every zone by dividing the available land with the allowable zoning lot size. Let S_1^t, S_2^t, ..., S_j^t be the number of existing dwellings of each type at time t. Then the supply side will find S_o^{t+1}, S_1^{t+1}, S_2^{t+1}, S_3^{t+1}, ..., S_j^{t+1}.

Thus we let P_{ij}^t be the probability that a dwelling of current type i, (i = 0, 1, 2, ..., J), will change into a dwelling of type j, (j = 1, 2, ..., J, J+1), where the last, J+1, denotes demolition. Then

$$S_j^{t+1} = \sum_{i=1}^{J} S_i^t P_{ij}^t, \text{ for } j = 1, 2, \ldots, J$$

$$S_{J+1}^{t+1} = \sum_{i=1}^{J} S_i^t P_{iJ+1}^t$$

$$S_o^{t+1} = S_o^t - \sum_{j=1}^{J} S_o^t P_{oj}^t + gS_{J+1}^{t+1} \qquad (7.10)$$

where g is the potential number of new dwellings created per dwelling demolished.

The conversion/construction/demolition probabilities can be defined as a discrete choice process driven by the profitability in terms of discounted present value of each state. Thus,

π_o^t: discounted expected profit of keeping land vacant at time t.

π_{oj}^t: discounted expected profit of building a type j dwelling on vacant land at time t.

π_{ij}^t: discounted expected profit of transforming a type i dwelling into a type j dwelling at time t. Case J + 1 corresponds to creating vacant land at time t, and j = i corresponds to keeping dwelling as it is.

The transition probabilities can then be of the form

$$P_{oj}^t = F_{oj}[\pi_o^t,\ \pi_{o1}^t,\ \ldots,\ \pi_{oJ}^t],\ j = 1,\ \ldots,\ J \qquad (7.11)$$

$$P_{ij}^t = F_{ij}[\pi_{i1}^t,\ \pi_{i2}^t,\ \ldots,\ \pi_{iJ}^t,\ \pi_{iJ+1}^t],\ i = 1,\ \ldots,\ J,$$

$$j = 1,\ \ldots,\ J+1 \qquad (7.12)$$

7.5 Concluding Comment

This report has briefly identified the basic mathematical
structure of a model that can be constructed for the generalized regulated housing market. As an example, the equations
of the Swedish prototype are presented in the Appendix. Since
cities all over Europe differ vastly in institutional structure,
the basic sketch presented here needs to be adjusted from case
to case.

Appendix to Chapter Seven

MATHEMATICAL FORMULATION OF THE PROTOTYPE MARKET CLEARING
MODEL

Specification of Households' Utility Function, and Demand and
Supply Side Model

1. Household Utility Function:

U^h_{ijk} = Utility of households in group h, who move from
the submarket i to the submarket j using transaction option k between time t and t+1. This is
a function of expected wealth, annual gross
income, federal income tax, municipal tax, interest
payment or annual rent, size of housing allowance,
down-payment, black market premium, swapping price,
expected household acceptance probability, moving
cost, maintenance cost of occupied dwellings,
maintenance cost of vacant dwellings, household
characteristics, locational attributes, etc.

$\dot{U}^h_i$ = Utility of households in group h, who do not move
between time t and t+1. This is a function of
expected wealth, annual gross income, federal
income tax, municipal tax, interest payment or
annual rent, size of housing allowance, household
characteristics, locational attributes etc.

2. Demand Side Model:

$$P^h_{ijk} = \text{Prob} \left| \begin{array}{l} \text{A randomly drawn household in group h will} \\ \text{move from submarket i to submarket j using} \\ \text{transaction option k between time t and t+1} \end{array} \right|$$

$$= \frac{\text{Exp}[U^h_{ijk}]}{\text{Exp}[\overset{\bullet}{U}{}^h_i] + \overset{J}{\underset{j=1}{\Sigma}} \overset{K_{ij}}{\underset{k=1}{\Sigma}} \text{Exp}[U^h_{ijk}]}$$

$$\overset{\bullet}{P}{}^h_i = \text{Prob} \left| \begin{array}{l} \text{A randomly drawn household in group h will} \\ \text{not move between time t and t+1} \end{array} \right|$$

$$= \frac{\text{Exp}[\overset{\bullet}{U}{}^h_i]}{\text{Exp}[\overset{\bullet}{U}{}^h_j] + \overset{J}{\underset{j=1}{\Sigma}} \overset{K_{ij}}{\underset{k=1}{\Sigma}} \text{Exp}[U^h_{ijk}]}$$

where K_{ij} = Number of available transaction options to move
from i to j;

J = Total number of submarkets.

3. Supply Side Model:

(1) Free submarket supply side model: 0^F_i

$$0^F_i = \text{Prob} \left| \begin{array}{l} \text{A randomly drawn initial vacancy in free} \\ \text{submarket i will be offered for sale} \end{array} \right|$$

$$= \frac{\text{Exp}[^F\Pi^0_i]}{\text{Exp}[^F\Pi^0_i] + \text{Exp}[^F\Pi^V_i]}$$

where $^F\Pi_i^O$ = Profit of selling a dwelling in free submarket i

$^F\Pi_i^V$ = Loss of not selling a dwelling in free submarket i

(2) Black market supply side model: Q_i^B

Q_i^B = Prob $\begin{vmatrix} \text{A randomly drawn initial vacancy in black} \\ \text{market i will be rented (or sold)} \end{vmatrix}$

$$= \frac{\text{Exp}[^R\Pi_i^O]}{\text{Exp}[^B\Pi_i^O] + \text{Exp}[^B\Pi_i^V]}$$

where $^B\Pi_i^O$ = Profit of selling (or renting) a dwelling in black market i. This is a function of black market premium and down-payment

$^B\Pi_i^V$ = Loss of not selling (or not renting) a dwelling in black market i.

This is a function of interest payment (or annual rent) and maintenance cost of vacancies.

(3) Semi-regulated and fully-regulated queue-acceptance and queue-assignment probabilities:

A_j = Prob $\begin{vmatrix} \text{A randomly drawn applicant to the semi-} \\ \text{regulated submarket j will be accepted} \end{vmatrix}$

$$= \frac{\text{Exp}[\alpha_1(-\lambda_j)]}{\text{Exp}[\alpha_1(-\lambda_j)] + \text{Exp}[-\beta_1(R_j - C_{oj})]}$$

G_j = Prob $\left|$ A randomly drawn vacancy in the semi-regulated submarket j will be assigned to a household $\right|$

$$= \frac{Exp[\alpha_1 \lambda_j]}{Exp[\alpha_1 \lambda_j] + Exp[-\beta_1 C_{vj}]}$$

A_{hj} = Prob $\left|$ A randomly drawn applicant (in group h) to the fully-regulated submarket j will be accepted $\right|$

$$= \frac{Exp[\alpha_2(-\lambda_{hj}) + \theta_{hj}]}{Exp[\alpha_2(-\lambda_{hj}) + \theta_{hj}] + Exp[-\beta_2(R_j - C_{ohj})]}$$

G_{hj} = Prob $\left|$ A randomly drawn vacancy in the fully-regulated submarket (public queue) j will be assigned to a household in group h $\right|$

$$= \frac{Exp[\alpha_2 \lambda_{hj} + \mu_{hj}]}{\sum\limits_h Exp[\alpha_2 \lambda_{hj} + \mu_{hj}] + Exp[-\beta_2 C_{vj}]}$$

where α_1, α_2, β_1 and β_2 are coefficients, and λ_j, λ_{hj}, θ_{hj}, μ_{hj}, C_{oj}, C_{ohj}, C_{vj} and R_j are defined as before.

177

SYSTEM OF EQUATIONS*

1. Equation associated with free submarket j:

$$\sum_{h=1}^{H} \{ \sum_{i \epsilon F} N_i^h [\sum_{K=1}^{2} P_{ijk}^h] \quad + \quad \sum_{i \epsilon R_o} N_i^h [\sum_{K=2}^{3} P_{ijK}^h] \}$$

$\underbrace{\qquad\qquad\qquad\qquad}$

$$\begin{bmatrix} \text{Number of households} \\ \text{who live in free sub-} \\ \text{market i and buy a} \\ \text{dwelling in free sub-} \\ \text{market j between time} \\ \text{t and t+1} \end{bmatrix} \quad \begin{bmatrix} \text{Number of households} \\ \text{who live in regulated} \\ \text{submarket i and buy a} \\ \text{dwelling in free sub-} \\ \text{market j between time} \\ \text{t and t+1} \end{bmatrix}$$

$$= \sum_{h=1}^{H} N_j^h \{ \sum_{i \epsilon F} P_{ji1}^h \quad + \quad \sum_{i \epsilon SR} [P_{ji2}^h + A_j P_{ji4}^h]$$

$$\begin{bmatrix} \text{Number of households} \\ \text{who sell a dwelling} \\ \text{in free submarket j} \\ \text{and move to free sub-} \\ \text{market i} \end{bmatrix} \quad \begin{bmatrix} \text{Number of households who} \\ \text{sell a dwelling in free} \\ \text{submarket j and move to} \\ \text{semi-regulated sub-} \\ \text{market i} \end{bmatrix}$$

$$+ \quad \sum_{i \epsilon FR} [P_{ji2}^h + A_{hj} P_{ji4}^h] \} \quad + \quad V_j^t O_j^F$$

$$\begin{bmatrix} \text{Number of households} \\ \text{who sell a dwelling} \\ \text{in free submarket j} \\ \text{and move to fully-} \\ \text{regulated submarket} \\ \text{i} \end{bmatrix} \quad \begin{bmatrix} \text{Number of initial} \\ \text{vacancies which} \\ \text{are offered to} \\ \text{sell} \end{bmatrix}$$

---

* See page 183 for the explanation of some notations

Housing - Dynamic Economic Model

where F = {SF(AGE $\geq$ 3), COOP (AGE $\geq$ 1)
SR = {SF(AGE < 3), COOP (AGE < 1), MF in semi-regulated submarket}
R_o = {SF(AGE < 3), MF}
FR = {MF in fully-regulated submarket}

2. Equations associated with semi-regulated submarket j:

(1) For less than three-year-old single family housing:

$$\sum_{j=1}^{H} \{ \sum_{i\epsilon F} N_i^h [\sum_{K=4}^{5} P_{ijK}^h] + \sum_{i\epsilon R_o} N_i^h P_{ij5}^h \} \quad \cdot \quad A_j$$

$\underbrace{\qquad\qquad\qquad\qquad\qquad\qquad\qquad}$ $\underbrace{\qquad}$

$\begin{bmatrix}\text{Total number of households who}\\ \text{choose a less than three-year-}\\ \text{old single family dwelling}\\ \text{time t and t+1}\end{bmatrix}$ $\begin{bmatrix}\text{Proportion}\\ \text{accepted}\end{bmatrix}$

$$= \{ \sum_{h=1}^{H} [\sum_{i\epsilon F} N_j^h P_{ji3}^h + \sum_{i\epsilon R_d} N_j^h P_{ji4}^h] \quad + \quad NS_j \quad + \quad V_j^t \} \quad \cdot \quad G_j$$

$\underbrace{\qquad\qquad\qquad\qquad\qquad}$ $\underbrace{\qquad}$ $\underbrace{\quad}$ $\underbrace{\quad}$

$\begin{bmatrix}\text{Total number of newly}\\ \text{created vacancies}\end{bmatrix}$ $\begin{bmatrix}\text{Total number}\\ \text{of newly}\\ \text{built single}\\ \text{family}\\ \text{dwellings}\end{bmatrix}$ $\begin{bmatrix}\text{Initial}\\ \text{vacan-}\\ \text{cies}\end{bmatrix}$ $\begin{bmatrix}\text{Propor-}\\ \text{tion}\\ \text{sold}\end{bmatrix}$

where F = {SF(AGE $\geq$ 3), COOP(AGE $\geq$ 1)}
R_o = {SF(AGE < 3), MF}
R_d = {SF(AGE < 3), COOP(AGE < 1, MF}

179

(2) For newly built cooperative housing:

$$\sum_{h=1}^{H} \{ \sum_{i \in F} N_i^h [\sum_{K=4}^{5} P_{ijK}^h + \sum_{i \in R_o} N_i^h P_{ij5}^h \} \cdot A_j$$

$$\underbrace{\qquad\qquad\qquad\qquad\qquad\qquad}$$

$$\begin{bmatrix} \text{Total number of households who} \\ \text{choose a newly built cooperative} \\ \text{dwelling between time t and t+1} \end{bmatrix} \quad \begin{bmatrix} \text{Proportion} \\ \text{accepted} \end{bmatrix}$$

$$= NS_j \cdot G_j$$

$$\begin{bmatrix} \text{Total number} \\ \text{of newly} \\ \text{built coop-} \\ \text{erative} \\ \text{dwellings} \end{bmatrix} \quad \begin{bmatrix} \text{Proportion} \\ \text{sold} \end{bmatrix}$$

where $F = \{ SF(AGE \geq 3), COOP(AGE \geq 1) \}$

$R_o = \{ SF(AGE < 3), MF \}$

(3) For multi-family housing in semi-regulated submarket (Landlord's Queue):

$$\sum_{h=1}^{H} \{ \sum_{i \in F} N_i^h [\sum_{K=4}^{5} P_{ijK}^h] + \sum_{i \in R_o} N_i^h P_{ij5}^h \} \cdot A_j$$

$$\underbrace{\qquad\qquad\qquad\qquad\qquad\qquad}$$

$$\begin{bmatrix} \text{Total number of households who} \\ \text{choose a multi-family dwelling} \\ \text{in landlord's queue between} \\ \text{time t and t+1} \end{bmatrix} \quad \begin{bmatrix} \text{Proportion} \\ \text{accepted} \end{bmatrix}$$

$$= \{ NS_j^t + V_j^t + \sum_{h=1}^{H} \sum_{K \in B} [\sum_{i \in F} N_K^h P_{Ki3}^h + \sum_{i \in R_d} N_K^h P_{Ki4}^h] \}$$

$$\begin{bmatrix} \text{Total} \\ \text{number of} \\ \text{newly built} \\ \text{multi-} \\ \text{family} \\ \text{dwellings} \end{bmatrix} \begin{bmatrix} \text{Initial} \\ \text{vacancies} \\ \text{of multi-} \\ \text{family} \\ \text{dwellings} \end{bmatrix} \begin{bmatrix} \text{Total number of newly created} \\ \text{vacancies} \end{bmatrix}$$

$$E_{SR} \qquad \cdot \qquad G_j$$

$$\underbrace{\qquad}_{\begin{bmatrix}\text{Proportion} \\ \text{assigned} \\ \text{to semi-} \\ \text{regulated} \\ \text{submarket:} \\ \text{landlords'} \\ \text{queue}\end{bmatrix}} \quad \underbrace{\qquad}_{\begin{bmatrix}\text{Proportion} \\ \text{rented}\end{bmatrix}}$$

where $F = \{SF(AGE \geq 3), COOP(AGE \geq 1)\}$

$R_o = \{SF(AGE < 3), MF\}$

$B = \{ALL\ MFs\}$

3. Equations associated with fully-regulated submarket:

$$\{ \sum_{i \in F} N_i^h [\sum_{K=4}^{5} P_{ijK}^h] + \sum_{i \in R_o} N_i^h P_{ij5}^h \} \qquad \cdot \qquad A_{hj}$$

$$\underbrace{\hspace{7cm}}_{\begin{bmatrix}\text{Total number of households who} \\ \text{belong to group h and choose a} \\ \text{multi-family dwelling in fully-} \\ \text{regulated submarket } j\end{bmatrix}} \quad \underbrace{\hspace{1cm}}_{\begin{bmatrix}\text{Proportion} \\ \text{accepted}\end{bmatrix}}$$

$$= \{NS_j^t \quad + \quad V_j^t \quad + \quad \sum_{h=1}^{H} \sum_{j \in B} [\sum_{i \in F} N_j^h P_{ji3}^h + \sum_{i \in R_d} N_k^h P_{Ki4}^h] \}$$

$$\underbrace{\qquad}_{\begin{bmatrix}\text{Number of} \\ \text{newly built} \\ \text{multi-} \\ \text{family} \\ \text{dwellings}\end{bmatrix}} \quad \underbrace{\qquad}_{\begin{bmatrix}\text{Initial} \\ \text{vacancies}\end{bmatrix}} \quad \underbrace{\hspace{4cm}}_{\begin{bmatrix}\text{Total number of newly created} \\ \text{vacancies}\end{bmatrix}}$$

$$(1 - E_{SR}) \qquad \cdot \qquad G_{hj}$$

$$\underbrace{\qquad}_{\begin{bmatrix}\text{Proportion assigned} \\ \text{to fully-regulated} \\ \text{submarket: public} \\ \text{queue}\end{bmatrix}} \quad \underbrace{\qquad}_{\begin{bmatrix}\text{Proportion} \\ \text{rented}\end{bmatrix}}$$

181

where F $= \{SF(AGE \geq 3), COOP(AGE \geq 1)\}$

$\quad R_o = \{SF(AGE < 3), MF\}$

$\quad B = \{All\ MFs\}$

4. Equations associated with black market j:

$$\sum_{h=1}^{H} \{ \sum_{i\epsilon F} N_i^h [\sum_{K=2}^{3} P_{ijK}^h] \quad + \quad \sum_{i\epsilon R_o} N_i^h [\sum_{k=2}^{4} P_{ijK}^h]\}$$

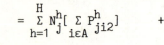
$$\left[\begin{array}{l}\text{Number of households who} \\ \text{enter a black market j} \\ \text{from free submarket in} \\ \text{demand side}\end{array}\right]$$

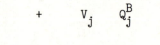
$$\left[\begin{array}{l}\text{Number of households who} \\ \text{enter a black market j} \\ \text{from regulated submarket} \\ \text{in demand side}\end{array}\right]$$

$$= \sum_{h=1}^{H} N_j^h [\sum_{i\epsilon A} P_{ji2}^h] \quad + \quad V_j \quad Q_j^B$$

$$\left[\begin{array}{l}\text{Total number of} \\ \text{households who} \\ \text{enter a black} \\ \text{market in supply} \\ \text{side}\end{array}\right] \quad \left[\begin{array}{l}\text{Initial} \\ \text{vacancies} \\ \text{in black} \\ \text{market j}\end{array}\right] \quad \left[\begin{array}{l}\text{Proportion} \\ \text{traded}\end{array}\right]$$

where F $= \{SF(AGE \geq 3), COOP(AGE \geq 1)\}$

$\quad R_o = \{SF(AGE < 3), MF\}$

$\quad A = FUR_o$

Note: $j\epsilon\{SF(AGE < 3), MF\}$

5. Equations associated with swapping:

$$\sum_{h=1}^{H} N_i^h P_{ij1}^h = \sum_{h=1}^{H} N_j^h P_{ji1}^h$$

where

i	j
SF(AGE < 3)	SF(AGE ≥ 3)
SF(AGE < 3)	COOP(AGE > 1)
SF(AGE < 3)	MF
MF	SF(AGE ≥ 3)
MF	COOP(AGE > 1)

---

* Explanation of Notation

AGE : Housing age

SF : Single family dwellings

COOP : Cooperative dwellings

MF : Multi-family rental dwellings

F : Set of free submarkets

R_o : Set of semi-regulated or fully-regulated submarkets in which households currently live

R_d : Set of semi-regulated or fully-regulated submarkets to which households want to move

SR : Set of semi-regulated submarkets

FR : Set of fully-regulated submarkets

A : Set of all submarkets excluding newly built cooperative dwellings

Chapter 8

HOUSING 2: A MASTER EQUATION APPROACH

G. Haag

8.1 Introduction

The evolution of society consists of a complex network of
interacting processes on political, educational, social,
economic and other levels (Weidlich and Haag, 1983). The main
dynamic processes of the housing subsystem such as household
mobility, housing dynamics, and price adjustment are results
of certain socio-economic decision processes of members of
the society.

The observed and measured macroeconomic set of data is
the result of a certain aggregation of microeconomic variables.
On the microeconomic scale the decision process of actors
(households, landlords, firms, entrepreneurs ...) is related
to the concepts of utilities and utility maximizing principles.
Since the expected utility gain influences the decision
behaviour, the functional dependence of the utility on certain
socio-economic variables is an important task of research. Of
course, we are not able to describe the individual decisions
on a fully deterministic level, but a probabilistic treatment
is possible and adequate. As a consequence, the resulting
theory is stochastic. This means we expect as a main result
the evolution of a probability distribution over the possible
configurations arising in the decision process. From such a
moving distribution it will then be possible to derive deter-

184

ministic equations of motion for the mean values and variances.

The individual actors of society contribute through their cultural and economic activities to the generation of a general "field" of civilisation with cultural, political, religious, social and economic components. This collective field determines the sociopolitical atmosphere and the cultural and economic standard of the society and may be considered as an order parameter of the system characterizing the phase in which the society exists. And vice versa: the collective field strongly influences the individuals in the society by orientating their activities and by influencing their utilities. One of the features of this sort of cyclic coupling of causes and effects is that self-accelerating as well as self-saturating processes result. In the "normal case" the feedback between individuals and the collective field leads to a sustained quasi-stable or evolutionary phase. In this case there exists a certain predictability of further development because the space of mutually influencing relevant macrovariables is known and these macrovariables obey a quasi-closed subdynamics.

If, however, the control parameters governing the dynamic behaviour of the system attain certain critical values due to internal or external interactions, the macrovariables may move into a critical domain out of which highly divergent alternative paths are possible. In this situation small unpredictable fluctuations of the microeconomic atmosphere may determine which of the diverging paths the behaviour of the society - and in this case the household and housing subsystem - will follow. The investigation of the transition from one phase to another demonstrates that there may exist several stable or unstable collective states even under the same external conditions. The aim of this chapter is to use these ideas to provide a unified framework for the modelling of the housing subsystem based on a choice-theoretical approach.

We assume in a simplified manner that the housing subsystem of the economy consists of three parts:

(i)   The residential mobility subsystem

The number of relocations per unit of time of members of a population (in this case, households) between a set of regions depends on a variety of criteria which influence the decision process to move to a new dwelling or not. These include criteria like the household stock situation, a natural preference for certain regions (in relation to landscape or place of birth), the rent or price situation, accessibility to shops, services and other urban facilities, commuting costs, number of job opportunities and so on. Some of the factors in this choice process are treated as endogenous variables, like the housing stock and price level; others are exogenously introduced, such as accessibility to shops and the number of job opportunities.

(ii)   Housing stock dynamics

The vacant stock situation is dependent on the popula-tion flows and may create a demand pressure which together with other important factors influences the decision behaviour of landlords or more generally of investors to build up a new housing unit or to demolish an old one. The decision process is assumed to depend on the land available, the distribution of vacant dwellings, the rent (price) and cost per m^2 of a dwelling, the necessary investment, a risk factor which takes into account the propensity of people to invest in the housing stock and the rate of interest. We assume further, that the cost per m^2 of a housing unit (cost for both land and dwelling unit) depends on the land still available in region i. The amount of total land available is exogenously introduced.

(iii)   Price formation mechanism

On the supply side, the willingness of a landlord to change the asking rents depends on the excess demand in both regions. Net excess demand occurs in region i when the excess demand in i is greater than the excess demand in j, or when the

supplied housing stock in region j is large enough. Since
increases or decreases of asking rents in a region are caused
in single steps by individual land suppliers, we treat the
rental payment variable (price-level) as a stochastic variable
also.

All these subsystems are interlinked to each other as
shown in Figure 8.1 (which also introduces the main algebraic
variables).

The underlying decision processes which generate migration flows of households, dynamic price adjustment processes
and new construction, renewals or demolitions of housing units,
makes necessary a probabilistic description. The dynamic
change of the probability distribution of households (population), housing stock and price distribution over the different
geographical regions is the task of the master equation
approach and will be outlined in the next section. We are
interested in obtaining information about the most probable
spatial distributions and their change with time, of households,
housing stock and prices with respect to certain constraints
(such as budget constraints). Because the different decision
processes are not independent of each other, the probability
distribution does not factorize and we must set up the master
equation involving all variables simultaneously.

From the master equation a set of self-contained and, in
general, nonlinear equations for the mean values and variances
can be obtained. Since the mean values by definition are
averages over paths with fluctuating deviations, their evolution is described by deterministic equations. It must be
expected, however, that the empiric values show stochastic
fluctuations around these mean values, even if the theory is
correct. The mean value equations are the starting point of
all empiric evaluations of the theory.

The theory only becomes operative when the main internal
elements, the transition probabilities of the different deci-

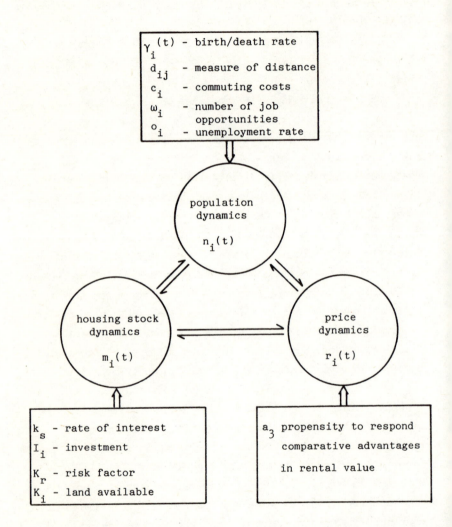

Figure 8.1: A simplified structure of the housing subsystem

sion processes are specified. Since the transition probabilities are functions of utilities and these utilities are
determined by a set of exogenous and endogenous variables,
we must determine the values of the coefficients of these
variables which we call trend parameters. This can be done
by taking empirically measured quantities like population
flows, birth and death rates and matching these quantities
to the corresponding theoretical expressions by appropriate
choice of the trend parameters.

8.2 The Master Equation for the General Model

First, we assume as mentioned in the introductory section and
spelled out in Figure 8.1, that the dynamics of the housing subsystem is mainly based on household mobility (migration of
households), housing stock dynamics and the price (rent)
adjustment process.

We define a total of M housing units. The spatial
distribution of the housing stock is described by the vector

$$\underset{\sim}{m} = (m_1, m_2, \ldots, m_L) \qquad (8.1)$$

with all m_is positive and

$$\sum_{i=1}^{L} m_i = M \qquad (8.2)$$

The housing stock may change with time due to decisions of
investors, for example, to expand, to reduce it or to renovate
it. The underlying decision process is therefore of a birth/
death structure and yields transitions from one initial configuration $\underset{\sim}{m} = (m_1, m_2, \ldots, m_L)$ into one of the neighbouring
configurations $\underset{\sim}{m} + \underset{\sim}{k_1} = (m_1 + k_{11}, m_2 + k_{12}, \ldots, m_L + k_{1L})$
where k_{1i} are positive or negative integers.

We next define a population of N households which can

189

migrate between L regions (or areas). The vector of positive elements:

$$\underset{\sim}{n} = (n_1, n_2, \ldots, n_L) \qquad (8.3)$$

with

$$\sum_{i=1}^{L} n_i = N \qquad (8.4)$$

then characterizes the spatial distribution of households, where the integer n_i is the number of households in region i. In the course of time, transitions due to migration- or birth/ death-processes can occur from any initial configuration $\underset{\sim}{n} = (n_1, n_2, \ldots, n_L)$ into one of the neighbouring configurations $\underset{\sim}{n} + \underset{\sim}{k_2} = (n_1 + k_{21}, n_2 + k_{22}, \ldots, n_L + k_{2L})$ where k_{2i} are again positive or negative integers.

The behaviour and decisions of households, landlords and investors are assumed to be influenced by a price signal $\underset{\sim}{r}$. We sometimes call this price signal rent. The spatial distri- bution of rents

$$\underset{\sim}{r} = (r_1, r_2, \ldots, r_L) \qquad (8.5)$$

changes into another price configuration $\underset{\sim}{r} + \underset{\sim}{k_3} = (r_1 + k_{31}, r_2 + k_{32}, \ldots, r_L + k_{3L})$. Since equal rental values do not affect the decisions, only differences in the rental value or price distribution are important. We assume that rents are positive and

$$\sum_{i=1}^{L} r_i = R \qquad (8.6)$$

Before going into the details of modelling the different socio-economic decision processes, we first introduce the probability distribution function

$$P(\underset{\sim}{m}, \underset{\sim}{n}, \underset{\sim}{r}; t) = P(m_1, \ldots, m_L, n_1, \ldots, n_L, r_1, \ldots, r_L; t)$$

$$(8.7)$$

which is the probability that the configuration $\underset{\sim}{c} = (\underset{\sim}{m}, \underset{\sim}{n}, \underset{\sim}{r})$ is realized at time t. The configuration can be represented (in our case) as a point in the 3L-dimension socio-configuration space Γ. The contributions to the transition probability $w(\underset{\sim}{c} + \underset{\sim}{k}; \underset{\sim}{c}) \geq 0$ of change from a configuration $c \epsilon \Gamma$ to a neighbouring configuration $(\underset{\sim}{c} + \underset{\sim}{k}) \epsilon \Gamma$ where $\underset{\sim}{k} = (\underset{\sim}{k}_1, \underset{\sim}{k}_2, \underset{\sim}{k}_3)$ are due to transfer or migration processes and birth/death processes. If the transition probabilities are specified - and this is the crucial problem of modelling of socio-economic systems - the equation of motion for the evolution of the probability distribution can be derived

$$\frac{dP(\underset{\sim}{m},\underset{\sim}{n},\underset{\sim}{r};t)}{dt} = \sum_{\underset{\sim}{k}} w(\underset{\sim}{m},\underset{\sim}{n},\underset{\sim}{r};\underset{\sim}{m}+\underset{\sim}{k}_1,\underset{\sim}{n}+\underset{\sim}{k}_2,\underset{\sim}{r}+\underset{\sim}{k}_3)P(\underset{\sim}{m}+\underset{\sim}{k}_1,\underset{\sim}{n}+\underset{\sim}{k}_2,\underset{\sim}{r}+\underset{\sim}{k}_3;t)$$

$$- \sum_{\underset{\sim}{k}} w(\underset{\sim}{m}+\underset{\sim}{k}_1,\underset{\sim}{n}+\underset{\sim}{k}_2,\underset{\sim}{r}+\underset{\sim}{k}_3;\underset{\sim}{m},\underset{\sim}{n},\underset{\sim}{r})P(\underset{\sim}{m},\underset{\sim}{n},\underset{\sim}{r};t)$$

$$(8.8)$$

where the sums on the right-hand side extend over all $\underset{\sim}{k}$ with non-vanishing transition probabilities (cf Chapter 4 for the derivation of this equation).

The master equation (8.8) can be interpreted as a probability rate equation. The change of the probability of configuration $\underset{\sim}{c} = (\underset{\sim}{m}, \underset{\sim}{n}, \underset{\sim}{r}) \epsilon \Gamma$ (left-hand side of (8.8)) is due to two effects in opposite directions, namely to the probability flux from all neighbouring configurations $(\underset{\sim}{c}+\underset{\sim}{k}) = (\underset{\sim}{m}+\underset{\sim}{k}_1, \underset{\sim}{n}+\underset{\sim}{k}_2, \underset{\sim}{r}+\underset{\sim}{k}_3)$ into $\underset{\sim}{c}$ and to the probability flux from $\underset{\sim}{c}$ to all $(\underset{\sim}{c} + \underset{\sim}{k})$. The probability distribution is normalized

$$\sum_{\underset{\sim}{c}} P(\underset{\sim}{c}; t) = 1 \qquad (8.9)$$

In the 3L-dimensional configuration space Γ the maximum (or the maxima) of $P(\underset{\sim}{m}, \underset{\sim}{n}, \underset{\sim}{r}; t)$ represents the most probable spatial distribution of housing units, households and price levels of the housing subsystem. In Figure 8.2, schematically, one possible spatial distribution of households $\underset{\sim}{n}$, housing units $\underset{\sim}{m}$, price-level $\underset{\sim}{r}$, is represented.

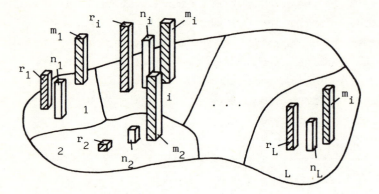

Figure 8.2: Spatial distribution of households $\underset{\sim}{n}$, housing units $\underset{\sim}{m}$ and price-level $\underset{\sim}{r}$ in a system of L regions

Since the master equation (8.8) contains the stochastic information on the system, not only the most probable configuration or the mean values can be obtained but also the variances of the distribution function. Therefore, we are able to make statements of significance. This will be done in detail in Section 8.6 below.

The probability distribution function (8.7) does not factorize in general:

$$P(\underset{\sim}{m}, \underset{\sim}{n}, \underset{\sim}{r}; t) \neq P(\underset{\sim}{m}; t)P(\underset{\sim}{n}; t)P(\underset{\sim}{r}; t) \qquad (8.10)$$

This is because the transition probabilities $w(\underset{\sim}{c} + \underset{\sim}{k}; \underset{\sim}{c})$ are simultaneously dependent on all variables. It can be proved that the condition of detailed balance is not fulfilled for this model of the housing market subsystem. The total transition probabilities are the sum over different contributions due to migration or transfer events between different regions and/or to birth/death processes:

$$w(\underset{\sim}{m}{+}\underset{\sim}{k}_1,\underset{\sim}{n}{+}\underset{\sim}{k}_2,\underset{\sim}{r}{+}\underset{\sim}{k}_3;\underset{\sim}{m},\underset{\sim}{n},\underset{\sim}{r})$$

$$= \sum_{i,j=1}^{L} w_{ij}^{(n)}(\underset{\sim}{m},\underset{\sim}{n}{+}\underset{\sim}{k}_2,\underset{\sim}{r};\underset{\sim}{m},\underset{\sim}{n},\underset{\sim}{r})$$

$$+ \sum_{i=1}^{L} (w_{i+}^{(m)}(\underset{\sim}{m}{+}\underset{\sim}{k}_1,\underset{\sim}{n},\underset{\sim}{r};\underset{\sim}{m},\underset{\sim}{n},\underset{\sim}{r}) + w_{i-}^{(m)}(\underset{\sim}{m}{+}\underset{\sim}{k}_1,\underset{\sim}{n},\underset{\sim}{r};\underset{\sim}{m},\underset{\sim}{n},\underset{\sim}{r}))$$

$$+ \sum_{i=1}^{L} (w_{i+}^{(n)}(\underset{\sim}{m},\underset{\sim}{n}{+}\underset{\sim}{k}_2,\underset{\sim}{r};\underset{\sim}{m},\underset{\sim}{n},\underset{\sim}{r}) + w_{i-}^{(n)}(\underset{\sim}{m},\underset{\sim}{n}{+}\underset{\sim}{k}_2,\underset{\sim}{r};\underset{\sim}{m},\underset{\sim}{n},\underset{\sim}{r}))$$

$$+ \sum_{i=1}^{L} (w_{i+}^{(r)}(\underset{\sim}{m},\underset{\sim}{n},\underset{\sim}{r}{+}\underset{\sim}{k}_3;\underset{\sim}{m},\underset{\sim}{n},\underset{\sim}{r}) + w_{i-}^{(r)}(\underset{\sim}{m},\underset{\sim}{n},\underset{\sim}{r}{+}\underset{\sim}{k}_3;\underset{\sim}{m},\underset{\sim}{n},\underset{\sim}{r}))$$

$$(8.11)$$

where the terms $w_{ij}^{(n)}$ refer to the migration of households and the terms $w_{i+}^{(n)}$ and $w_{i-}^{(n)}$ to birth/death-processes of housing units. The housing stock dynamics $w_{i+}^{(m)}$, $w_{i-}^{(m)}$ and the rent level adjustment process $w_{i+}^{(r)}$, $w_{i-}^{(r)}$ are treated as birth/death-processes, respectively.

In (8.11) we have neglected contributions to the total transition probability of the type present in predator-prey interactions. This means that a transition to a neighbouring state in the configuration space is assumed to be a sequential process of changes in housing stock, migration of households

and rental transfer instead of a simultaneous movement of $\underset{\sim}{m}$, $\underset{\sim}{n}$
and $\underset{\sim}{r}$ (cf Figure 8.3). Since we are interested in obtaining
comparable results for different countries, we later introduce
scaled variables. The transition probabilities then are functions of these scaled variables and predator-prey interactions
would correspond to second order terms in the general Taylor
expansion of the exponent of the individual transition probabilities (see Section 8.4) which, in the first instance can be
neglected. We assume for simplicity single step transitions
from a configuration to a neighbouring one.

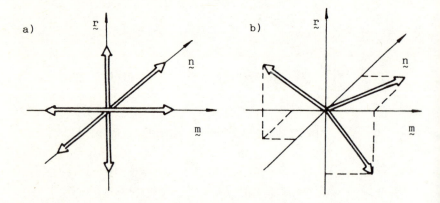

Figure 8.3:   (a) Transitions of the aggregate system to
                       neighbouring states which are taken into
                       account
        (b) A few simultaneous transitions which are
                       neglected

The next step is to introduce specifications of the transition probabilities.

(a) The transition probability $w_{ij}^{(n)}(\underset{\sim}{m},\underset{\sim}{n}+\underset{\sim}{k}_2,\underset{\sim}{r};\underset{\sim}{m},\underset{\sim}{n},\underset{\sim}{r})$ due
to migration of households from region j to region i (i $\neq$ j)
is:

$$w_{ij}^{(n)}(\underset{\sim}{m},\underset{\sim}{n+k_2},\underset{\sim}{r};\underset{\sim}{m},\underset{\sim}{n},\underset{\sim}{r}) = \begin{cases} n_j p_{ij}^{(n)}(\underset{\sim}{m},\underset{\sim}{n},\underset{\sim}{r}) \text{ for} \\ \\ \underset{\sim}{k_2} = (0...1_i...0...(-1)_j...0) \\ \\ 0 \text{ for all other } \underset{\sim}{k_2} \qquad (8.12) \end{cases}$$

where $p_{ij}^{(n)}(m,n,r)$ is the corresponding individual transition probability for a move. This individual transition probability depends in general - among a lot of other socio-economic factors (see Section 8.4.1) which are exogeneously involved - on the spatial distribution of housing units, on the distribution of people and the price distribution. The structure (8.12) of the migration process leads to a conservation law of total population size N.

(b) The price adjustment process is treated as a birth-death process. The transition rates for an increase or a decrease of the asking rent in a region i reflect some profit maximizing principles behind the decision processes of land-lords. This means that the housing situation in each region i is compared with the housing situation in the other regions j, and if there is a net excess demand observable, landlords are motivated to increase their asking rents.

It is reasonable to assume that the transition rates $w_{i+}^{(r)}$, $w_{i-}^{(r)}$ for an increase or a decrease of the payment variable r_i are proportional to the rent level r_i

$$w_{i+}^{(r)}(\underset{\sim}{m},\underset{\sim}{n},\underset{\sim}{r+k_3};\underset{\sim}{m},\underset{\sim}{n},\underset{\sim}{r}) = \begin{cases} \displaystyle\sum_{\substack{j=1 \\ j\neq i}}^{L} r_j p_{ij}^{(r)}(\underset{\sim}{m},\underset{\sim}{n},\underset{\sim}{r}) \text{ for} \\ \\ \underset{\sim}{k_3} = (0...1_i...0) \\ \\ 0 \text{ for all other } \underset{\sim}{k_3} \qquad (8.13) \end{cases}$$

195

and

$$w_{i-}^{(r)}(\underset{\sim}{m},\underset{\sim}{n},\underset{\sim}{r}+k_3;\underset{\sim}{m},\underset{\sim}{n},\underset{\sim}{r}) = \begin{cases} \sum_{\substack{j=1 \\ j \neq i}}^{L} r_i p_{ji}^{(r)}(\underset{\sim}{m},\underset{\sim}{n},\underset{\sim}{r}) \text{ for} \\[12pt] \underset{\sim}{k_3} = (0...(-1)_i...0) \\[12pt] 0 \text{ for all other } \underset{\sim}{k_3} \end{cases} \quad (8.14)$$

where $p_{ij}^{(r)}(\underset{\sim}{m},\underset{\sim}{n},\underset{\sim}{r})$ is the corresponding individual decision probability (the decision-makers are the landlords) for an increase or a decrease or rental value. This $p_{ij}^{(r)} > 0$ is assumed to depend on net excess demand (see Section 8.4.2). The net excess demand is related to the housing stock and household distribution. The p_{ij} describe the comparison of region j with region i and $r_j p_{ij}$, $r_i p_{ji}$ are the rates of increase, decrease in rental values due to this comparison process, respectively.

Since the housing subsystem consists of L regions, we have to sum over all contributions of the different regions j to obtain the birth/death rates of region i. Therefore, the price adjustment process looks similar to a migration process for rental values. Of course, in reality there is no transfer of rental values. It is only a representation of a mechanism for inter-zonal comparison. The process itself is a birth-death process.

(c) The transition probabilities to expand the housing stock $w_{i+}^{(m)}$, or to reduce it, $w_{i-}^{(m)}$, can be treated as birth and death processes, respectively. If new constructions or demolitions are looked at, we want to model the individual investor decision process explicitly. We consider expansion and demolition in turn.

Expansion of the housing stock

It is reasonable to assume that expansions of the housing stock (change of unused land into dwelling units) will occur with a rate proportional to the number of potential new dwelling units $(K_i(t) - m_i(t))$ multiplied by an individual decision probability of investors $p_{i+}^{(m)}$ at time t:

$$
w_{i+}^{(m)}(\underset{\sim}{m}+\underset{\sim}{k_1},\underset{\sim}{n},\underset{\sim}{r},;\underset{\sim}{m},\underset{\sim}{n},\underset{\sim}{r}) =
\begin{cases}
(K_i(t)-m_i(t))p_{i+}^{(m)}(\underset{\sim}{m},\underset{\sim}{n},\underset{\sim}{r}) \text{ for} \\
\underset{\sim}{k_1} = (\ldots 0 \ldots 1_i \ldots 0 \ldots) \\
0 \text{ for all other } \underset{\sim}{k_1} \quad\quad (8.15)
\end{cases}
$$

where $K_i(t)$ is the capacity of total land available in region i (scaled to the same units as m). The $p_{i+}^{(m)}$ depend on such factors as net return, risk factors, rate of interest ... (see Section 8.4.3).

Demolition of housing units

First, we assume for simplicity an age-independent demolition rate for housing units. This restriction can easily be removed if we introduce age groups of housing units and model the corresponding transitions from one age group to another. A location which experiences significant idle capacity for a long time is more likely than others to undergo some demolition activity. Therefore, idle capacity of housing units influences decisions to demolish. We understand demolitions as a removal of housing units from the market. This can be a change (if local circumstances permit this) into a more profitable use. In order to study this case more correctly, explicit interactions with the other land uses and economic activities of the metropolitan areas should be considered.

Assuming that demolitions or removals can only occur for vacant dwellings, the transition probability for reducing the housing stock is proportional to the number of vacant dwellings $(m_i(t) - n_i(t))$ multiplied by an individual decision process $p_{i-}^{(m)}$ to reduce the stock or not:

$$w_{i-}^{(m)}(\underset{\sim}{m}+\underset{\sim}{k}_1,\underset{\sim}{n},\underset{\sim}{r};\underset{\sim}{m},\underset{\sim}{n},\underset{\sim}{r}) = \begin{cases} (m_i(t)-n_i(t))p_{i-}^{(m)}(\underset{\sim}{m},\underset{\sim}{n},\underset{\sim}{r}) \text{ for} \\ \underset{\sim}{k}_1 = (\ldots0\ldots(-1)_i\ldots0\ldots) \\ 0 \text{ for all other } \underset{\sim}{k}_1 \qquad (8.16) \end{cases}$$

The $p_{i-}^{(m)}(\underset{\sim}{m},\underset{\sim}{n},\underset{\sim}{r})$ with their functional form are again specified later (Section 8.4.3).

(d) The transition probabilities $w_{i+}^{(n)}$ and $w_{i-}^{(n)}$ with respect to birth and death, respectively, or members of population of households (people) $\underset{\sim}{n}$ in region i are:

$$w_{i+}^{(n)}(\underset{\sim}{m},\underset{\sim}{n}+\underset{\sim}{k}_2,\underset{\sim}{r};\underset{\sim}{m},\underset{\sim}{n},\underset{\sim}{r}) = \begin{cases} n_i\beta_i^{(n)} \text{ for} \\ \underset{\sim}{k}_2 = (\ldots0\ldots1_i\ldots0\ldots) \\ 0 \text{ for all other } \underset{\sim}{k}_2 \end{cases}$$

$$w_{i-}^{(n)}(\underset{\sim}{m},\underset{\sim}{n}+\underset{\sim}{k}_2,\underset{\sim}{r};\underset{\sim}{m},\underset{\sim}{n},\underset{\sim}{r}) = \begin{cases} n_i\delta_i^{(n)} + n_i^2\gamma_i^{(n)} \text{ for} \\ \underset{\sim}{k}_2 = (\ldots0\ldots(-1)_i\ldots0\ldots) \\ 0 \text{ for all other } \underset{\sim}{k}_2 \qquad (8.17) \end{cases}$$

where $\beta_i^{(n)}$, $\delta_i^{(n)}$ and $\gamma_i^{(n)}$ are the corresponding individual birth, death and saturation rates. The definition (8.17) can, if necessary, be generalized to take into account birth and death rates which are dependent on the existing configuration in a more complicated way.

198

Inserting (8.11) with (8.12) to (8.17) into (8.8) the master equation of the housing market subsystem is obtained in the general form

$$\frac{dP(\underset{\sim}{m},\underset{\sim}{n},\underset{\sim}{r};t)}{dt} = \left(\frac{\partial P}{\partial t}\right)(\underset{\sim}{m},\underset{\sim}{n},\underset{\sim}{r};t) + \left(\frac{\partial P}{\partial t}\right)(\underset{\sim}{m},\underset{\sim}{n},\underset{\sim}{r};t) \qquad (8.18)$$
$$\text{migration} \qquad \text{birth/death}$$

where $P(\underset{\sim}{m},\underset{\sim}{n},\underset{\sim}{r};t)$ is the probability of a given socio-configuration $\underset{\sim}{c} = (\underset{\sim}{m},\underset{\sim}{n},\underset{\sim}{r})$ at time t and the two terms on the right-hand side of (8.18) refer to migration or exchange processes or to birth/death processes respectively, arising from the contributions (8.12) to (8.17) to $w(\underset{\sim}{m}+\underset{\sim}{k}_1,\underset{\sim}{n}+\underset{\sim}{k}_2,\underset{\sim}{r}+\underset{\sim}{k}_3;\underset{\sim}{m},\underset{\sim}{n},\underset{\sim}{r})$ in (8.8).

For the explicit form of these terms it is convenient to introduce "transition operators" $E_{\alpha i}$ (see Weidlich and Haag, 1983) acting on a function of the socio-configuration as follows (with $\alpha = 1$, 2 or 3):

$$E_{\alpha i}^{\pm 1} f(c_{11},\ldots,c_{\alpha i},\ldots,c_{3L}) = f(c_{11},\ldots,c_{\alpha i} \pm 1,\ldots,c_{3L})$$

$$(8.19)$$

Inserting (8.11) with (8.12) to (8.17) into (8.8) and using (8.19) the explicit forms of the right-hand side of the master equation (8.18) are obtained as:

$$\left(\frac{\partial P}{\partial t}\right)(\underset{\sim}{m},\underset{\sim}{n},\underset{\sim}{r};t) = \sum_{\substack{i,j=1 \\ i \neq j}}^{L} (E_{2i}E_{2j}^{-1}-1)[n_i p_{ji}^{(n)}(\underset{\sim}{m},\underset{\sim}{n},\underset{\sim}{r})]P(\underset{\sim}{m},\underset{\sim}{n},\underset{\sim}{r};t)$$
$$\text{migration}$$

$$+ \sum_{\substack{i,j=1 \\ i \neq j}}^{L} (E_{3i}E_{3j}^{-1}-1)[r_i p_{ji}^{(r)}(\underset{\sim}{m},\underset{\sim}{n},\underset{\sim}{r})]P(\underset{\sim}{m},\underset{\sim}{n},\underset{\sim}{r};t)$$

$$(8.20)$$

and

$$(\frac{\partial P}{\partial t})(\underset{\sim}{m},\underset{\sim}{n},\underset{\sim}{r};t) \quad = \quad$$
birth/death

$$\sum_{i=1}^{L} \{(E_{1i}^{-1}-1)[(K_i-m_i)p_{i+}^{(m)}(\underset{\sim}{m},\underset{\sim}{n},\underset{\sim}{r})]+(E_{1i}-1)[(m_i-n_i)p_{i-}^{(m)}(\underset{\sim}{m},\underset{\sim}{n},\underset{\sim}{r})]\}P(\underset{\sim}{m},\underset{\sim}{n}$$

$$+ \sum_{i=1}^{L} \{(E_{2i}^{-1}-1)[n_i\beta_i^{(n)}]+(E_{2i}-1)[n_i\delta_i^{(n)}+n_i\gamma_i^{(n)}]\}P(\underset{\sim}{m},\underset{\sim}{n},\underset{\sim}{r};t)$$

$$(8.21)$$

The master equations can be considered as a set of linear equations for the probabilities $P(\underset{\sim}{m},\underset{\sim}{n},\underset{\sim}{r};t)$. The probability distribution contains the full stochastic information about the system. Not only the interesting mean values of the state variables $\bar{m}_i$, $\bar{n}_i$, $\bar{r}_i$, but also the mean square deviations and correlation functions can be calculated. It is worthwhile emphasizing one important property: an arbitrary initial distribution - for instance, concentrated in a small interval in configuration space - finally develops into a stationary distribution function $P_{st}(\underset{\sim}{m},\underset{\sim}{n},\underset{\sim}{r})$.

8.3 The Mean Value and Variance Equations for the General Model

Directly from the master equation (8.18) with (8.20) and (8.21) it is possible to derive equations of motion for the mean values of the housing stock $\bar{m}_i$, the number of households $\bar{n}_i$ and the price level $\bar{r}_i$. The definitions of these variables are:

$$\bar{m}_i(t) = \sum_{\underset{\sim}{c}} m_i P(\underset{\sim}{c};t) \qquad (8.22)$$

$$\bar{n}_i(t) = \sum_{\underset{\sim}{c}} n_i P(\underset{\sim}{c};t) \qquad (8.23)$$

$$\bar{r}_i(t) = \sum_{\underset{\sim}{c}} r_i P(\underset{\sim}{c};t) \tag{8.24}$$

To achieve this aim (8.18) is multiplied by m_i, n_i and r_i, respectively and the sum over all configurations $\underset{\sim}{c} = (\underset{\sim}{m},\underset{\sim}{n},\underset{\sim}{r})$ is taken. In general the mean value of a function $f(\underset{\sim}{c})$ is defined by

$$\overline{f(\underset{\sim}{c})} = \sum_{\underset{\sim}{c}} f(\underset{\sim}{c}) P(\underset{\sim}{c};t); \quad \underset{\sim}{c} = (\underset{\sim}{m},\underset{\sim}{n},\underset{\sim}{r}) \varepsilon \Gamma \tag{8.25}$$

Making use of the fact that

$$\sum_{\underset{\sim}{c}} E_{\alpha i}^{+1} E_{\alpha j}^{-1} f(\underset{\sim}{c}) P(\underset{\sim}{c};t) = \sum_{c} f(\underset{\sim}{c}) P(\underset{\sim}{c};t) = \overline{f(\underset{\sim}{c})} \tag{8.26}$$

holds for any function $f(\underset{\sim}{c})$, since the sum extends over all configurations $\underset{\sim}{c}$, and because of

$$c_{\gamma k} E_{\alpha i} E_{\alpha j}^{-1} f(\underset{\sim}{c}) \equiv E_{\alpha i} E_{\alpha j}^{-1} (c_{\gamma k} - \delta_{\gamma \alpha} \delta_{ki} + \delta_{\gamma \alpha} \delta_{kj}) f(\underset{\sim}{c}) \tag{8.27}$$

we easily obtain from (8.18) the exact result

$$\frac{d\bar{m}_i}{dt} = \overline{(K_i(t) - m_i) p_{i+}^{(m)}(\underset{\sim}{m},\underset{\sim}{n},\underset{\sim}{r})} - \overline{(m_i - n_i) p_{i-}^{(m)}(\underset{\sim}{m},\underset{\sim}{n},\underset{\sim}{r})};$$

$$\frac{d\bar{n}_i}{dt} = \overline{n_i \beta_i^{(n)}} - \overline{(n_i \delta_i^{(n)} + n_i^2 \gamma_i^{(n)})}$$

$$+ \sum_{j=1}^{L} \overline{n_j p_{ij}^{(n)}(\underset{\sim}{m},\underset{\sim}{n},\underset{\sim}{r})} - \sum_{j=1}^{L} \overline{n_i p_{ji}^{(n)}(\underset{\sim}{m},\underset{\sim}{n},\underset{\sim}{r})};$$

$$\frac{d\bar{r}_i}{dt} = \sum_{j=1}^{L} \overline{r_j p_{ij}^{(r)}(\underset{\sim}{m},\underset{\sim}{n},\underset{\sim}{r})} - \sum_{j=1}^{L} \overline{r_i p_{ji}^{(r)}(\underset{\sim}{m},\underset{\sim}{n},\underset{\sim}{r})} \tag{8.28}$$

Equations (8.28) represent a hierarchy of equations, since for the solution of the mean value equations, the second order

moments are necessary - and for solving the equations of motion
for the second order the third order moments and so on. To
obtain an approximately closed set of equations of motion for
the mean values, assumptions concerning the shape of the
distribution function $p(\underset{\sim}{c};t)$ have to be added.

For distributions with only one sharp peak - which means
that under the given socio-economic conditions the optimal
solution of the housing market subsystem is well known to most
decision makers - the exact equations (8.28) can be substituted
by the approximate closed set of equations for the mean values
as follows.

Housing stock dynamics:

$$\frac{d\overline{m}_i(t)}{dt} = (K_i(t)-\overline{m}_i(t))p_{i+}^{(m)}(\underset{\sim}{\overline{m}},\underset{\sim}{\overline{n}},\underset{\sim}{\overline{r}})-(\overline{m}_i(t)-\overline{n}_i(t))p_{i-}^{(m)}(\underset{\sim}{\overline{m}},\underset{\sim}{\overline{n}},\underset{\sim}{\overline{r}})$$

$$(8.29)$$

Household mobility:

$$\frac{d\overline{n}_i(t)}{dt} = (\beta_i^{(n)}-\delta_i^{(n)})\overline{n}_i(t)-\gamma_i^{(n)}\overline{n}_i^2(t)$$

$$+ \sum_{j=1}^{L} \{\overline{n}_j(t)p_{ij}^{(n)}(\underset{\sim}{\overline{m}},\underset{\sim}{\overline{n}},\underset{\sim}{\overline{r}})-\overline{n}_i(t)p_{ji}^{(n)}(\underset{\sim}{\overline{m}},\underset{\sim}{\overline{n}},\underset{\sim}{\overline{r}})\} \quad (8.30)$$

Price signals:

$$\frac{d\overline{r}_i(t)}{dt} = \sum_{j=1}^{L} \{\overline{r}_j(t)p_{ij}^{(r)}(\underset{\sim}{\overline{m}},\underset{\sim}{\overline{n}},\underset{\sim}{\overline{r}})-\overline{r}_i(t)p_{ji}^{(r)}(\underset{\sim}{\overline{m}},\underset{\sim}{\overline{n}},\underset{\sim}{\overline{r}})\} \quad (8.31)$$

Equations for the variances can be derived in the same way.

8.4 Modelling of Individual Decision Processes

8.4.1 Introduction

In order to make the model so far fully explicit and applicable,
the different individual decision processes which are involved
in the configurational transition probabilities $w(\underset{\sim}{c}+\underset{\sim}{k};\underset{\sim}{c})$ and
which govern the dynamics of the housing market subsystem have
to be adequately specified. Each decision maker considers not
only the observable economic variables (such as income, rate of
interest ...) but also a subjective estimation and valuation of
social events demanding a kind of psychological forecasting:
socio-economic processes can only be effectively modelled if
psychological interactions are also taken into account. How
for a wide class of socio-economic processes this can be done
in a tractable manner has been demonstrated by Weidlich and
Haag (1983). In the following subsection we proceed using
these methods and introduce individual transition probabilities
which seem to be flexible in that several possible effects on
the housing market subsystem are included.

8.4.2 Population dynamics of the households

According to (8.12), we consider the individual transition
probabilities $p_{ij}^{(n)}(\underset{\sim}{m},\underset{\sim}{n},\underset{\sim}{r})$ of a household to migrate from
region j to i (i≠j). The decision makers are the households
themselves. The individual transition probabilities are
assumed to be a function of a mobility factor ν_{ji} and of the
utilities u_i and u_j of the origin and destination area i and
j, respectively:

$$p_{ji}^{(n)}(\underset{\sim}{m},\underset{\sim}{n},\underset{\sim}{r}) = \nu_{ji}e^{u_j(\underset{\sim}{m},\underset{\sim}{n},\underset{\sim}{r})-u_i(\underset{\sim}{m},\underset{\sim}{n},\underset{\sim}{r})} \qquad (8.32)$$

with $\nu_{ji} \geq 0$. Equation (8.32) fulfils the following requirements:

(i) p_{ji} is positive semidefinite, for arbitrary values of u_j and u_i, as it should be; (ii) $p_{ji} > p_{ij}$, if the utility u_j of the destination region j exceeds the utility u_i of the origin region i; (iii) $(p_{ji} - p_{ij})$ is a monotone function of $(u_j - u_i)$; and (iv) the difference $(u_j - u_i)$ between the utilities is relevant for the dynamic process but not their absolute values. Thus, without loss of generality, we can put

$$\sum_{i=1}^{L} u_i(\underset{\sim}{m}, \underset{\sim}{n}, \underset{\sim}{r}) = 0 \qquad (8.33)$$

The mobility matrix

For a wide class of migration problems it is reasonable to assume a symmetric mobility matrix:

$$\nu_{ij}(t) = \nu_{ji}(t) \qquad (8.34)$$

The meaning of (8.34) can be seen from considering two regions i, j with equal utilities $u_i = u_j$ and equal population numbers $n_i = n_j$. It follows from (8.32), with (8.34) assumed, that in this case the number of transitions from i to j is equal to that from j to i. This implies symmetric transportation costs.

The mobility matrix ν_{ij} is related to the concept of "distance" between the regions i and j. "Distance" is one of the most important specific variables in spatial analysis and many possibilities for its analytical specification are offered. However, the concept of "distance" must be generalized to include geographical, economic and social aspects. Geographically the length of routes between places i, j can be used as an appropriate measure, d_{ij}. If the same route is used in both directions, $d_{ij} = d_{ji}$. Economic distances are measured in terms of costs that can be evaluated in time or money. Traffic congestion can be important here. In general, then, the transport-cost-distance matrix will be asymmetric $d_{ij} \neq d_{ji}$. Social distance is concerned with the diffusion of information

concerning, for example, the vacant housing stock or the rent
level distribution in the evaluation process. Vacant dwellings
or jobs which are far away are less likely to be known to a
potential mover. It should be stressed that this discounting
effect of distance on the knowledge of the choice set may be
in general much more important than geographical or economic
distance. The transportation costs are negligible compared to
the expected long-run costs and benefits associated with the
new dwelling, at least in a metropolitan area. On the other
hand, even if the spread of information due to advertising is
assumed to be uniform over the region, a householder who also
looks for a new dwelling by direct search is less exposed to
information about alternatives whose locations he is less
likely to visit, because they are far away from his current
neighbourhood. For an asymmetric information exchange process
then, this "distance" matrix is also asymmetric. This argument refers to distance as it is related to the mobility
matrix. Daily home-to-work commuting costs will be dealt
with later.

For constructive specification, we assume the following
reasonable relation between "distance" and mobility $\nu_{ij}(t)$:

$$\nu_{ij}(t) = \nu(t) \cdot e^{-\beta(t)d_{ij}} \qquad (8.35)$$

where in general $d_{ij} \neq d_{ji}$, hence $\nu_{ij} \neq \nu_{ji}$. In order to be
independent of the special units of d_{ij}, the distance matrix
is normalized accordingly

$$d_{ij} = \frac{\Delta_{ij}}{\sum\limits_{\substack{k,l \\ k \neq l}}^{L} \Delta_{ij}}, \quad i \neq j$$

where Δ_{ij} is the measured distance. Then

$$\sum_{\substack{i,j=1 \\ i \neq j}}^{L} d_{ij} = 1, \; 0 \leq d_{ij} \leq 1$$

Inserting (8.35) into (8.32) and (8.12), we obtain

$$w_{ij}^{(n)}(\underset{\sim}{m},\underset{\sim}{n}+k_2,\underset{\sim}{r};\underset{\sim}{m},\underset{\sim}{n},\underset{\sim}{r}) = \nu(t)n_j \exp[-\beta(t)d_{ij}] \cdot \exp[u_i(\underset{\sim}{m},\underset{\sim}{n},\underset{\sim}{r}) - u_j(\underset{\sim}{m},\underset{\sim}{n},\underset{\sim}{r})$$

$$(8.36)$$

The global mobility parameter $\nu(t)$ and the trend parameter $\beta(t)$ which is a measure of the deterrence of the "costs of travel" will be estimated in Section 8.6.2.

Utilities

Before a household decides to change its location, the utility of several regions will be compared, at least including the origin region and the prospective destination region. In general, many factors merge in this comparative estimation of utilities (cf Anas, 1982). Some, like climate, landscape and the desire to remain in one's birthplace, are independent of the population density of the region considered. Other factors, like the offers for occupations and employment, the availability of schools, the cultural opportunities and options, agglomeration effects and so on turn out to be roughly proportional to the population density of total of the region. It is therefore reasonable to assume that the utility u_i of region i is a polynomial in the number of households n_i, the housing stock situation m_i, the rents r_i and other socio-economic variables. The coefficients of this polynomial which explicitly define the functional behaviour of the utilities will also be called trend parameters.

Since it is our aim to create the housing submarket model in such a way that we are able to compare the housing situation

of different countries, it is useful to introduce normalized
variables which we do later. Further, from the very beginning
the constraint (8.33) should be fulfilled. The utility
involved in the choice process for the residential location
of a household is assumed as:

$$u_i(\underset{\sim}{m},\underset{\sim}{n},\underset{\sim}{r}) = \delta_i + a_1(m_i-\overline{m}) + a_2(n_i-\overline{n}) - a_3(r_i-\overline{r}) \quad (8.37)$$

with the constraint

$$\sum_{i=1}^{L} \delta_i = 0 \qquad (8.38)$$

and the following abbreviations

$$\overline{m} = \frac{1}{L} \sum_{i=1}^{L} m_i = \frac{M}{L}$$

$$\overline{n} = \frac{1}{L} \sum_{i=1}^{L} n_i = \frac{N}{L}$$

$$\overline{r} = \frac{1}{L} \sum_{i=1}^{L} r_i = \frac{R}{L} \qquad (8.39)$$

where

$$0 \leq m_i \leq M$$

$$0 \leq n_i \leq N$$

$$0 \leq r_i \leq R \qquad (8.40)$$

In (8.37) we have neglected all processes of order 2 or higher.
It is one of the main issues of this Chapter to determine the
values of the utilities u_i, and/or the associated trend parameters. We can help to interpret the assumption in (8.37) by

207

discussing the roles of each different term, and this we
proceed to do, taking each coefficient in turn.

Preference parameter δ_i

Clearly, a positive preference parameter δ_i increases the
utility of region i. As already mentioned, social factors like
climate, landscape or the desire to remain in one's birthplace
merge into δ_i but also the number of job opportunities and the
unemployment rate.

In this first step, the number of job opportunities w_i and
the unemployment rate o_i are assumed to be exogenously given
(we drop this assumption later).

$$\delta_i \sim + w_i(t) \tag{8.41}$$

$$\delta_i \sim + o_i(t) \tag{8.42}$$

Of course these two economic parameters are functions of the
population flows and also of the economic situation. The
economic situation must be considered with respect to the
phase and amplitude of any cyclical changes in the economy
(Schumpeter cycles, Kondratieff cycles). A theory of long
waves and political decisions merge here into the housing market
subsystem. The service sector, labour market and effects of
the travel network are treated in more detail in Chapters 11
and 14.

Housing stock influence parameter a_1

The influence of the housing stock dynamics in region i
on the utility in i is described by a_1. We expect $a_1 > 0$.

Agglomeration parameter a_2

The agglomeration or cooperation parameter a_2 contains
all those contributions to the utility u_i which can be

considered as proportional to the population numbers. Positive agglomeration effects, for example intragroup attraction and preference for high-density living are associated with $a_2 > 0$. The value and the sign of the trend parameter a_2 are determined in Section 8.6.

Rental advantage parameter a_3

The parameter $a_3 > 0$ designates the propensity to respond to comparative advantages in rental value (price level) on the demand side.

8.4.3 The rent adjustment process

At the micro level, the decision behaviour of a resident to change his or her location depends in part on a price-type signal - the rent level r_i. This price signal will be measured by the spatial distribution of prices. We assume that each region i has just one average price. The suppliers of housing units (landlords) quote, at any time period, an asking rent in each region. These rents are the result of some profit-maximizing functions of expected net returns, discounted to the present. The adjustment of rents is treated as a decision process of the landlords. The rental payment variable, r_i, is treated as a stochastic variable. The units can be adjusted so that the typical single rent transfer steps from i to j or from j to i lead to transitions (r_i-1) or (r_i+1). Here we will focus on the supply-side dynamic adjustments of rents as they respond to changes in residential population n_i and the housing stock dynamics m_i. Presumably, suppliers are motivated to increase the asking rent at each time period t when net excess demand is observed, defined as

$$[(m_i - n_i) - (m_j - n_j)] = E_{ij} \qquad (8.43)$$

Net excess demand occurs in region i relative to j, when the excess demand in i, $(m_i - n_i) > 0$ is greater than the excess demand in j, $(m_j - n_j) > 0$. It is worth emphasizing that $[(m_i - n_i) - (m_j - n_j)]$ is not really net excess demand but rather the difference in the vacant stock. Since in our model the condition $m_i > n_i$ always holds, "excess demand" does not mean that $m_i > n_i$. Therefore we expect an increase of the rent level in a region i, if $[(m_i - n_i) - (m_j - n_j)] > 0$ for some j: the vacant stock in i is less than the vacant stock in j.

As mentioned in Section 8.2, the rates of increase or decrease (birth/death rates) of rental values depend on the individual decision probability $p_{ij}^{(r)} > 0$

$$p_{ij}^{(r)}(\underset{\sim}{m},\underset{\sim}{n},\underset{\sim}{r}) = \varepsilon e^{-\beta^{(r)}d_{ij}^{(r)}} \cdot e^{u_{ij}(\underset{\sim}{m},\underset{\sim}{n},\underset{\sim}{r})}, \quad \varepsilon > 0 \qquad (8.44)$$

with

$$u_{ij}(\underset{\sim}{m},\underset{\sim}{n},\underset{\sim}{r}) = -u_{ji}(\underset{\sim}{m},\underset{\sim}{n},\underset{\sim}{r}) \qquad (8.45)$$

where $u_{ij}(\underset{\sim}{m},\underset{\sim}{n},\underset{\sim}{r})$ describes utility differences (for the land-lords) between the regions i, j. These u_{ij} are assumed to depend on the excess demand of both regions (see Haag and Dendrinos, 1983, Dendrinos and Haag, 1984)

$$u_{ij}(\underset{\sim}{m},\underset{\sim}{n},\underset{\sim}{r}) = a_4[(m_i - n_i) - (m_j - n_j)] \qquad (8.46)$$

The parameter a_4 describes the influence of net excess demand on the decision behaviour of landlords. The parameter ε is associated with the speed of adjustment (time scale) of the rents. The deterrence parameter $\beta^{(r)}$ takes into account that prices of adjacent regions j are more likely to influence the price dynamics of region i. The distance matrix $d_{ij}^{(r)}$ has the same meaning as already described in Section 8.4.2. It is reasonable to assume in the following sections that the deterrence parameter $\beta^{(r)}$ and the distance matrix $d_{ij}^{(r)}$ of the rent level adjustment process coincide with the corresponding parameters describing household mobility,

$$\beta^{(r)} = \beta; \ d_{ij}^{(r)} = d_{ij}$$

The rent market behaviour of the housing subsystem of certain nations is treated more restrictively by the government. Then, the adjustment process cannot be described by single decision processes of individual landlords. Since these government restrictions and/or the corresponding laws are kept constant for a relatively long period of time (for example the rent policy of Vienna), the exogenous treatment of the rental payment variable $r_{ij}(t)$ seems to be appropriate. Therefore, in our housing subsystem model in this case the equations which describe the dynamics of the rent level adjustment process must be cancelled and the exogenously given values $r_i(t)$ inserted into the other dynamic equations.

8.4.4 Housing stock dynamics

In Section 8.2 the rate of expansion of the housing stock was assumed to be proportional to the number of potential dwelling units $(K_i(t) - m_i(t))$ multiplied by an individual decision probability of investors $p_{i+}^{(m)}(\underset{\sim}{m},\underset{\sim}{n},\underset{\sim}{r})$ at time t. Many different actors are included under the heading of "landlords" and "investors", such as private entrepreneurs, public agencies and households themselves investing in real estate.

It is assumed that $p_{i+}^{(m)}(\underset{\sim}{m},\underset{\sim}{n},\underset{\sim}{r})$ depends on the net return, risk factors and the rate of interest

$$p_{i+}^{(m)}(\underset{\sim}{m},\underset{\sim}{n},\underset{\sim}{r}) = \lambda_i(t)\exp[V_I - (V_S + V_d)] \qquad (8.47)$$

where V_I represents the expected utility gained by the

investment process, V_S the utility if the capital is saved and V_d the utility gained by taking the housing unit out of the market. We further assume:

$$V_I = a_5 [(\frac{r_i - c_i}{I_i}) + k_r]$$ (8.48)

$$V_S = a_5 k_S$$ (8.49)

and

$$V_d = a_6 (m_i - n_i)$$ (8.50)

The utility gained by building up a new dwelling is a function of the return on investment, $(r_i - c_i)/I_i$, where r_i is the expected rent per housing unit, c_i the current cost per housing unit and I_i the investment needed for the creation of a housing unit. The risk factor k_r takes into account that there exists a preference for material things like a dwelling instead of depositing the money in a bank.

The investment per housing unit in region i, I_i mainly depends on two factors: firstly, the cost of the land and secondly the mean investment for building a new dwelling. Since in general the investment for land depends on the land still available, $(K_i - m_i)$, there exists a relation between total investment I_i and housing stock m_i

$$I_i = I_i(m_i)$$ (8.51)

It seems to be reasonable to assume the following relation

$$I_i = \frac{I_{io}}{K_i - m_i}$$ (8.52)

with $n_i(t) \leq m_i(t) \leq K_i(t)$. The I_{io} represents the total costs for a dwelling if the prices for a unit of land are

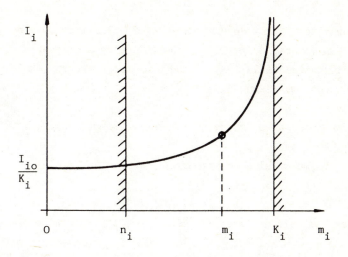

<u>Figure 8.4</u>: Representation of equation (8.52)

still not affected by the housing stock (see Figure 8.4). In
the following we assume $I_{io} = I_o$, i = 1 ... L. The utility
for saving capital, V_S, is a function of the rate of interest.
The utility for demolition of a housing unit, V_d, is assumed
to be a function of the number of vacant dwellings. The
influence of $(m_i - n_i)$ on the decision process is described
by the parameter a_6. The time-scale of the process is fixed
by $\lambda_i(t)$.

  In Section 8.2 we assumed that demolitions or removals
of housing units can only occur for vacant dwellings. The
configurational transition probability for reducing the
housing stock then is proportional to the number of vacant
dwellings $(m_i - n_i)$ multiplied by the individual transition
probability $p_{i-}^{(m)}(m,n,r)$ of a landlord to reduce the stock or
not:

$$p_{i-}^{(m)}(m,n,r) = \mu_i(t)\exp[-(V_I - (V_S + V_d))] \qquad (8.53)$$

The parameter $\mu_i(t)$ determines the mean life-time of a housing unit. In general $\mu_i \neq \lambda_i$. In the following sections we neglect spatial variations of the scaling parameters or, in other words, we assume $\lambda_i = \lambda$; $\mu_i = \mu$.

8.5 The Mean Value Equations for the Housing Subsystem

8.5.1 The mean value equations

Inserting (8.36), (8.44), (8.47) in (8.29) to (8.31) we obtain the mean value equations (ME) of the housing subsystem. We drop the bar on $\overline{m}_i$, $\overline{n}_i$, $\overline{r}_i$ in the following subsections to avoid an over-loaded notation.

ME for housing stock dynamics:

$$\frac{dm_i}{dt} = (K_i(t) - m_i(t))\lambda(t)\exp[V_I - (V_S + V_d)]$$

$$- (m_i(t) - n_i(t))\mu(t)\exp[-(V_I - (V_S + V_d))],$$

$$i = 1, \ldots, L \qquad (8.54)$$

ME for the household migration process:

$$\frac{dn_i}{dt} = (\beta_i^{(n)} - \delta_i^{(n)})n_i - \gamma_i^{(n)}n_i^2$$

$$+ \sum_{j=1}^{L} \nu(t)n_j e^{-\beta(t)d_{ij}} {}_{.e}^{u_i(m_i,n_i,r_i) - u_j(m_j,n_j,r_j)}$$

$$- \sum_{j=1}^{L} \nu(t)n_i e^{-\beta(t)d_{ji}} {}_{.e}^{u_j(m_j,n_j,r_j) - u_i(m_i,n_i,r_i)}$$

$$\qquad (8.55)$$

ME for the rent adjustment process:

$$\frac{dr_i}{dt} = \sum_{j=1}^{L} \varepsilon(t) r_j e^{-\beta(t)d_{ij}} u_{ij}(\underset{\sim}{m},\underset{\sim}{n},\underset{\sim}{r})$$

$$- \sum_{j=1}^{L} \varepsilon(t) r_i e^{-\beta(t)d_{ji}} u_{ji}(\underset{\sim}{m},\underset{\sim}{n},\underset{\sim}{r}) \tag{8.56}$$

with the special utility functions as introduced in Section 8.4.

Residential utility of a household:

$$u_i(m_i,n_i,r_i) = \delta_i + a_1(m_i - \bar{m}) + a_2(n_i - \bar{n}) - a_3(r_i - \bar{r})$$

$$\tag{8.57}$$

with

$$\sum_{i=1}^{L} \delta_i = 0.$$

Transfer utility for rental advantages:

$$u_{ij}(\underset{\sim}{m},\underset{\sim}{n},\underset{\sim}{r}) = -u_{ji}(\underset{\sim}{m},\underset{\sim}{n},\underset{\sim}{r})$$

$$= a_4[(m_i - n_i) - (m_j - n_j)] \tag{8.58}$$

Utility for expansion of the housing stock:

$$V_I = a_5[(\frac{r_i - c_i}{I_i(m_i)}) + k_r] \tag{8.59}$$

Utility for saving of the money:

$$V_S = a_5 k_S \tag{8.60}$$

Utility for demolition of a housing unit:

$$V_d = a_6(m_i - n_i) \tag{8.61}$$

In order to be able to compare the housing subsystems of different countries, it is convenient to introduce scaled variables

$$x_i = \frac{m_i}{M}; \quad \sum_{i=1}^{L} x_i = 1; \quad \bar{x} = \frac{1}{L}\sum_{i=1}^{L} x_i = \frac{1}{L}$$

$$y_i = \frac{n_i}{N}; \quad \sum_{i=1}^{L} y_i = 1; \quad \bar{y} = \frac{1}{L}\sum_{i=1}^{L} y_i = \frac{1}{L}$$

$$z_i = \frac{r_i}{R}; \quad \sum_{i=1}^{L} z_i = 1; \quad \bar{z} = \frac{1}{L}\sum_{i=1}^{L} z_i = \frac{1}{L}$$

where

$$0 \le x_i, y_i, z_i \le 1 \tag{8.62}$$

Since the total number of households $N(t)$, the housing stock $M(t)$, and the total amount of rent $R(t)$ are changing with time, the scaling procedure has to be carried out again for each period of time t (year by year).

Equation (8.62) in (8.54 - 8.62) yields the mean value equations in scaled variables.

ME for the housing stock dynamics:

$$\frac{dx_i}{dt} = (x_i(t)-x_i)\lambda(t)e^{[V_I(x_i,y_i,z_i)-(V_S(x_i,y_i,z_i)+V_d(x_i,y_i,z}$$

$$- (x_i-sy_i)\mu(t)e^{-[V_I(x_i,y_i,z_i)-(V_S(x_i,y_i,z_i)+V_d(x_i,y_i,}$$

$$\tag{8.63}$$

where s is the saturation parameter of the housing market

$$s = N/M \leq 1 \tag{8.64}$$

and x_i the scaled capacity of the housing stock in region i

$$x_i = k_i/M \geq x_i \tag{8.65}$$

ME for the household mobility process:

$$\frac{dy_i}{dt} = \sum_{j=1}^{L} \nu(t) y_j e^{-\beta(t)d_{ij}} e^{u_i(x_i,y_i,z_i)-u_j(x_j,y_j,z_j)}$$

$$- \sum_{j=1}^{L} \nu(t) y_i e^{-\beta(t)d_{ji}} e^{u_j(x_j,y_j,z_j)-u_i(x_i,y_i,z_i)} \tag{8.66}$$

The total population size $N(t)$ does not remain constant with time. It is a growing function for most countries. In the following we assume that the birth/death and saturation rates $\beta_i^{(b)}$, $\delta_i^{(n)}$, $\gamma_i^{(n)}$ do not vary over the different regions i. Then it can easily be shown that the solution $n_i(t)$ of (8.55) including $\beta^{(n)}$, $\delta^{(n)}$, $\gamma^{(n)}$ is related to the solution of (8.66) without birth/death processes by

$$n_i(t) = y_i(t) \cdot N(t)/N(0) \tag{8.67}$$

where $N(0)$ means the total population size at the beginning of the integration procedure, and $N(t)$ the total population size after time period t. Both $N(0)$ and $N(t)$ can be empirically obtained. The same argument holds for the rent adjustment process, too.

217

ME for the rent adjustment process:

$$\frac{dz_i}{dt} = \sum_{j=1}^{L} \varepsilon(t) z_j e^{-\beta(t)d_{ij}} u_{ij}(\underset{\sim}{x},\underset{\sim}{y},\underset{\sim}{z})$$

$$- \sum_{j=1}^{L} \varepsilon(t) z_i e^{-\beta(t)d_{ji}} u_{ji}(\underset{\sim}{x},\underset{\sim}{y},\underset{\sim}{z})$$

$$i = 1, 2, \ldots, L \qquad (8.68)$$

with the scaled utility functions.

Residential utility of a household:

$$u_i(x_i,y_i,z_i) = \delta_i + b_i(x_i-\overline{x}) + b_2(y_i-\overline{y}) - b_3(z_1-\overline{z}) \qquad (8.69)$$

with

$$b_1 = a_1 N; \qquad b_2 = a_2 M; \qquad b_3 = a_3 R$$

Transfer utility for residential advantages:

$$u_{ij}(\underset{\sim}{x},\underset{\sim}{y},\underset{\sim}{z}) = -u_{ji}(\underset{\sim}{x},\underset{\sim}{y},\underset{\sim}{z})$$

$$= b_4[(x_i-sy_i) - (x_j-sy_j)] \qquad (8.70)$$

with

$$b_4 = a_4 N; \qquad s = N/M \leq 1$$

Utility for expansion of the housing stock:

$$V_I(x_i,y_i,z_i) = b_5(z_i-\zeta_i)(\chi_i-x_i) + a_5 \cdot k_r \qquad (8.71)$$

with

$$b_5 = a_5\frac{MR}{I_o}; \qquad \zeta_i = \frac{C_i}{R}$$

Utility for saving of money:

$$V_S(x_i, y_i, z_i) = a_5 k_S \qquad (8.72)$$

Utility for demolition of a housing unit:

$$V_d(x_i, y_i, z_i) = b_6(x_i - sy_i) \qquad (8.73)$$

with

$$b_6 = a_6 M$$

Note that the dynamics of this model of the housing subsystem is based on decision processes of different actors (decision on both the demand and the supply side). Therefore it is natural in this kind of theory that no negative values for the housing stock $x_i(t)$, the household distribution $y_i(t)$ and the rental values $z_i(t)$ can occur.

8.5.2 Some remarks about the time scales

The dynamical subsystem of the housing market exhibits a lot of different time scales. For example, the time scale for shopping trips is really quite different from that of residential mobility and housing stock dynamics. Customers have no long-term commitments with the shops, and can easily change their choices every day. This very fast process can therefore be reasonably described by its steady state. This may lead to analytical simplifications of the model and is called adiabatic elimination procedure (see Haken, 1983). This summarised information is contained in the preference parameter δ_i, describing among others the accessibility to shops in each region i. In the literature (Harris and Wilson, 1978, Allen and Sanglier, 1979, Wilson, 1983-B), the housing stock changes are very often treated as very slow processes compared with the time-scale of the population migration system because of the following argument: a residential building usually has a very long life, while a household typically moves every few years. From the point of analysis this might suggest that the household distribution can be replaced by its steady state and inserted into the equations for the housing stock. However, as Leonardi (1983-B) mentioned, a warning is needed. Changes in the housing stock might cause the household mobility process to reach no steady state at all, or to undergo undamped waves, or even bifurcate to another equilibrium if the fast process depends on the state variable of the slow process. Even stronger, the application of a stochastic migration model to Canadian data (Haag and Weidlich, 1984) demonstrates that this inter-regional system is not at all in a stationary state. The global mobility is about $\nu(t) \simeq 10^{-3}$. This means that the relaxation time of the migration system is of the order of a few hundred years.

Assume that the residential system is in its stationary state with respect to its socioeconomic atmosphere. Now, for example, due to a political decision, the infrastructure or the total available capacity of land $X_i(t)$ is changed. Assume further that the new set of socioeconomic parameters is kept constant. Then the migration system would relax toward the new equilibrium and approaches this equilibrium after a few hundred years. But, since politicians are restless people, this will never happen. For various reasons, there will be slow and fast variations in the socioeconomic atmosphere, and the migration system will always lag behind. These variations drive the migration system abruptly out - and towards its momentary (virtual) equilibrium. This results only because of the fact that, with respect to its population distribution, the virtual equilibrium corresponding to the momentary set of parameters changes rapidly. From this point of view it seems even more reasonable to treat the housing market as a "fast" process compared to the residential mobility system.

If the trend parameters themselves are time-dependent, the transition probabilities become time-dependent too, via their relation to trend parameters. The master equation (8.18) is still valid in this case, but in general, as mentioned earlier, its solution will not reach a stationary state at all. Even in this case we can define for the momentary set of trend parameters a "virtual equilibrium solution". It is the solution $(\hat{x},\hat{y},\hat{z})$ into which the system would relax if from now on the trend parameters would be kept constant.

8.5.3 The virtual equilibrium solution of the housing sub-system

Let us first consider the case of constant trend parameters. It can be proved that under this condition any time-dependent solution of the master equation must approach the unique stationary solution for $t \to \infty$. However, the stationary probability distribution can be shaped like a mountain (in configuration space) with a lot of peaks. The critical points (or stationary points) of the mean value equations correspond to these maxima and minima of the probability distribution. Stable critical points are related to the maxima, unstable critical points to the minima, of the distribution. This means that any time-dependent solution in the vicinity of a stable stationary point (which is a focus) will approach this focus, whereas in the vicinity of an unstable point it will diverge from this focus. The nature of the critical points and their number are determined by the trend parameters of the system and can be found by solving the stationary version of (8.63), (8.66) and (8.68). In Section 8.6 we estimate the trend parameters and the utility functions. Using these estimated trend parameters, we are able to determine the

221

accompanying virtual stationary solution. These describe the
equilibrium situation into which the system would evolve if
the trend parameters remained constant from this point of time.
In particular, the actual development of the housing subsystem would evolve into the maxima of the stationary distri-
bution, which we denote as $\hat{\underset{\sim}{c}} \varepsilon \Gamma$ (virtual equilibrium solution).
We therefore obtain a measure for the momentary deviation of
the housing system from its virtual equilibrium state belonging to the momentary (estimated) set of trend parameters. The
most compact formulation of the "distance from equilibrium" of
the actual configuration $\underset{\sim}{c} \varepsilon \Gamma$ and its virtual equilibrium configuration $\hat{\underset{\sim}{c}} \varepsilon \Gamma$ is given by the correlation coefficient

$$r_c = \text{corr}(\underset{\sim}{c}; \hat{\underset{\sim}{c}}) \tag{8.74}$$

Obviously we have $|r_c| \le 1$ and $r_c \to 1$ for $\underset{\sim}{c} \to \hat{\underset{\sim}{c}}$. This is the
reason why it is still interesting to investigate the (virtual)
equilibrium solution of the housing subsystem, even if it
never reaches a stationary state. The virtual equilibrium
state of the housing stock is determined by setting the left-
hand side of (8.63), (8.66) and (8.68) equal to zero, and we
now proceed to investigate this.

The stationary housing stock, $\hat{x}$
    Using (8.63) we easily obtain the transcendental equation
for the stationary housing stock

$$\frac{\lambda(t)}{\mu(t)} \left(\frac{x_i - \hat{x}_i}{\hat{x}_i - s\hat{y}_i} \right) = \exp[-2(\hat{V}_I - (\hat{V}_S + \hat{V}_d))] \tag{8.75}$$

with

$$(\hat{V}_I - (\hat{V}_S + \hat{V}_d) = b_5(\hat{z}_i - \varsigma_i)(\hat{X}_i - \hat{x}_i) - b_6(\hat{x}_i - s\hat{y}_i) + b_7$$

$$\tag{8.76}$$

and the abbreviation

$$b_7 = a_5(k_r - k_7) \tag{8.77}$$

In Figure 8.5 a qualitative view of the stationary housing stock for given household $\hat{\underset{\sim}{y}}$ and rent distribution $\hat{\underset{\sim}{r}}$ is shown.

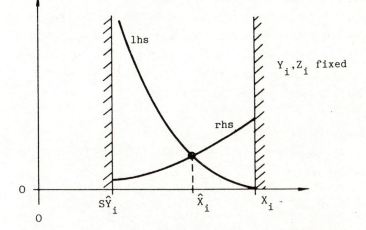

Figure 8.5: Graphic solution of equations (8.75) with (8.76)

The stationary household distribution $\hat{\underset{\sim}{y}}$

Assuming first a symmetric "distance" matrix $d_{ij} = d_{ji}$, we obtain from (8.66) and (8.68) for the stationary household distribution

$$\hat{y}_i = \frac{e^{2\hat{u}_i(\hat{\underset{\sim}{x}},\hat{\underset{\sim}{y}},\hat{\underset{\sim}{z}})}}{\sum\limits_{j=1}^{L} e^{2\hat{u}_j(\hat{\underset{\sim}{x}},\hat{\underset{\sim}{y}},\hat{\underset{\sim}{z}})}} \qquad i = 1, 2, \ldots, L \tag{8.78}$$

223

with

$$\hat{u}_i(\hat{\underset{\sim}{x}},\hat{\underset{\sim}{y}},\hat{\underset{\sim}{z}}) = \delta_i + b_1(\hat{x}_i - \bar{x}) + b_2(\hat{y}_i - \bar{y}) - b_3(\hat{z}_i - z) \quad (8.79)$$

Equation (8.78) can be seen as a spatial interaction model. But, because of the time scales of the migration process, this kind of model can only be used as a very weak approximation. In our case, (8.78) together with the corresponding equations for the stationary housing stock and the stationary price level, the virtual equilibrium situation $\hat{\underset{\sim}{c}} = (\hat{\underset{\sim}{x}},\hat{\underset{\sim}{y}},\hat{\underset{\sim}{z}})$ is determined. Using (8.74) the distance from the virtual equilibrium can be determined and only near the equilibrium state - or in other words if $r_c \simeq 1$, the application of a spatial interaction model is justified.

The stationary rent level $\hat{z}$

From (8.68) and (8.70) we obtain for the stationary rent distribution

$$\hat{z}_i = \frac{e^{2b_4(\hat{x}_i - s\hat{y}_i)}}{\sum\limits_{j=1}^{L} e^{2b_4(\hat{x}_j - s\hat{y}_j)}} \quad i = 1, 2, \ldots, L \quad (8.80)$$

Given our special assumption concerning the utilities for rental advantages, the stationary value $\hat{z}_i$ is completely determined by the household and housing stock distribution. The positivity of the rents $\hat{z}_i$ for the whole range of the parameters and variables $\hat{x}_i$, $\hat{y}_i$ is always guaranteed.

8.6 Estimation of Trend Parameters

8.6.1 Introduction

In the housing subsystem with L regions the empirical quantities
listed in Table 8.1 can be observed year by year. Furthermore
there exists information about the transportation cost or
distance matrix, $d_{ij}(t)$, the capacity of total land available,
$k_i(t)$, and other socio-economic variables like unemployment
rates and so on.

The theoretical expressions for the birth/death rates of
the housing stock, the migration matrix for the households and
the utilities for rental advantages are functions of these
empirical quantities. The unknown trend parameters as well
can be obtained by matching the theoretical expressions in an
optimal way to the empirical data. In general, the number of
observations is much greater than the number of trend parameters
to be determined and the estimation procedure yields significant
results.

8.6.2 Estimation of trend parameters of the housing stock

The theoretical transition probabilities (8.14), (8.15) with
(8.47), (8.53) which reappear in the mean value equations and
can be expressed in the scaled variables x_i, y_i, z_i as

$$w_{i+}^{(m)}(t) \equiv Mw_{i+}^{(m)}[\underset{\sim}{m}+\underset{\sim}{k},\underset{\sim}{n},\underset{\sim}{r};\underset{\sim}{m},\underset{\sim}{n},\underset{\sim}{r}]$$

$$= \lambda(X_i-x_i)e^{b_5(z_i-\zeta_i)(X_i-x_i)-b_6(x_i-sy_i)+b_7}$$

$$(8.81)$$

region i	number of households	housing stock	rent distribution	new houses created	demolished houses	number of transitions from i to j (n) household
1	$n_1^e(t)$	$m_1^e(t)$	$r_1^e(t)$	$w_{1+}^{(m)}(t)$	$w_{1-}^{(m)}(t)$	$0,\ w_{12}^e(t),\ \ldots\ldots\ldots\ w_{1L}^e(t)$
2	$n_2^e(t)$	$m_2^e(t)$	$r_2^e(t)$	$w_{2+}^{(m)}(t)$	$w_{2-}^{(m)}(t)$	$w_{21}^e(t), 0,\ \ldots\ldots\ldots\ w_{2L}^e(t)$
$\cdots$ i	$n_i^e(t)$	$m_i^e(t)$	$r_i^e(t)$	$w_{i+}^{(m)}(t)$	$w_{i-}^{(m)}(t)$	$w_{i1}^e(t), w_{i2}^e(t),\ \ldots\ w_{iL}^e(t)$
$\cdots$ L	$n_L^e(t)$	$m_L^e(t)$	$r_L^e(t)$	$w_{L+}^{(m)}(t)$	$w_{L-}^{(m)}(t)$	$w_{L1}^e(t), w_{L2}^e(t),\ \ldots\ 0$
	$N(t)$	$M(t)$	$R(t)$			

Table 8.1: Observed quantities per year

$$w_{i-}^{(m)}(t) \equiv Mw_{i-}^{(m)}[\underset{\sim}{m+k},\underset{\sim}{n},\underset{\sim}{r};\underset{\sim}{m},\underset{\sim}{n},\underset{\sim}{r}]$$

$$= \mu(x_i-sy_i)e^{-[b_5(z_i-\zeta_i)(\chi_i-x_i)-b_6(x_i-sy_i)+b_7]}$$

$$(8.82)$$

They can now be compared with the corresponding empirical
quantities, $w_{i+}^e(t)$ and $w_{i-}^e(t)$, if such data are available.
For simplicity we have assumed that in the different regions
i, the time scales of the housing market are equal: $\lambda_i = \lambda$
and $\mu_i = \mu$. We assumed further that the necessary investment
I_{io} is not spatially dependent. The estimation of the parameters proceeds in the framework developed in Haag and
Weidlich (1984). The optimization of the trend parameters
amounts to the determination of the least square deviations
between theoretical and empirical expressions. This optimization can be reduced to a linear regression analysis. For this
purpose we introduce (for each year with the time index t
omitted) the empirical quantities

$$r_i^e \equiv \ln\frac{w_{i+}^e(t)}{\chi_i(t)-x_i(t)} \overset{!}{=} \ln\lambda+b_7+b_5(z_i^e-\zeta_i)(\chi_i-x_i^e)-b_6(x_i^e-sy_i^e)$$

$$(8.83)$$

$$s_i^e \quad \ln\frac{w_{i-}^e(t)}{x_i^e(t)-sy_i^e(t)} \overset{!}{=} \ln\mu-b_7-b_5(z_u^e-\zeta_i)(\chi_i-x_i^e)+b_6(x_i^e-sy_i^e)$$

$$i = 1, 2, \ldots, L \qquad (8.84)$$

There are 2L empirical known quantities r_i^e, s_i^e, $i = 1, \ldots L$,
to be matched to the 5 unknown trend parameters $(\mu,\lambda,b_5,b_6,b_7)$.
We require that the sum of square deviations

$$F(e_1,e_2,b_5,b_6) = \frac{1}{L}\sum_{i=1}^{L} [r_i^e-(e_1+b_5(z_i^e-\zeta_i)(\chi_i-x_i^e)-b_6(x_i^e-sy_i^e)]^2$$

$$+ \frac{1}{L}\sum_{i=1}^{L} [s_i^e-(e_2-b_5(z_i^e-\zeta_i)(\chi_i-x_i^e)+b_6(x_i^e-sy_i^e)]^2$$

$$(8.85)$$

with

$$e_1 = \ln\lambda + b_7; \quad e_2 = \ln\mu - b_7 \qquad (8.86)$$

be minimized by an appropriate choice of the parameter set
$\{e_1,e_2,b_5,b_6\}$. Since the parameter b_7 is additional to $\ln\lambda$
and $\ln\mu$ it is only possible to determine two of the three
unknown parameters λ, μ, b_7. We therefore proceed in a different way and determine as a first step the optimal values
of e_1 and e_2. In a second step the parameter b_7 is obtained
by solving dynamically the mean value equations (8.63), (8.66)
and (8.68) for a well-known sequence of years and by fixing
the ratio λ/μ by the requirement that the dynamic simulation
yields an optimal result. Then all parameters of the housing
stock are determined. Let us now consider in more detail the
first step. The requirement of finding the minimum of
$F(e_1,e_2,b_5,b_6)$ leads to

$$\frac{\partial F}{\partial e_1} = -\frac{2}{L}\sum_{i=1}^{L} [r_i^e-(e_1+b_5(z_i^e-\zeta_i)(\chi_i-x_i^e)-b_6(x_i^e-sy_i^e))] \overset{!}{=} 0$$

$$\frac{\partial F}{\partial e_2} = -\frac{2}{L}\sum_{i=1}^{L} [s_i^e-(e_2-b_5(z_i^e-\zeta_i)(\chi_i-x_i^e)+b_6(x_i^e-sy_i^e))] \overset{!}{=} 0$$

$$\cdot \; \frac{\partial F}{\partial b_5} = -\frac{2}{L}\sum_{i=1}^{L}[r_i^e-(e_1+b_5(z_i^e-\zeta_i)(\chi_i-x_i^e)-b_6(x_i^e-sy_i^e))](z_i^e-\zeta_i)(\chi_i-$$

$$+\frac{2}{L}\sum_{i=1}^{L}[s_i^e-(e_2-b_5(z_i^e-\zeta_i)(\chi_i-x_i^e)+b_6(x_i^e-sy_i^e))](z_i^e-\zeta_i)(\chi_i-x_i^e) \overset{!}{=} ($$

$$\frac{\partial F}{\partial b_6} = \frac{2}{L}\sum_{i=1}^{L}[r_i^e-(e_1+b_5(z_i^e-\zeta_i)(\chi_i-x_i^e)-b_6(x_i^e-sy_i^e))](x_i^e-sy_i^e)$$

$$-\frac{2}{L}\sum_{i=1}^{L}[s_i^e-(e_2-b_5(z_i^e-\zeta_i)(\chi_i-x_i^e)+b_6(x_i^e-sy_i^e))](x_i^e-sy_i^e) \overset{!}{=} 0$$

$$(8.87)$$

It is convenient to introduce abbreviations for the following
empirical quantities:

$$p_i = (z_i^e-\zeta_i)(\chi_i-x_i^e) \geq 0$$

$$q_i = (x_i^e-sy_i^e) \geq 0 \qquad\qquad (8.88)$$

Spatial mean values are designated by

$$<A> = \frac{1}{L}\sum_{i=1}^{L}A_i \qquad\qquad (9.89)$$

Using (8.88) and (8.89) in (8.87) yields the non-homogeneous
linear system of equations for $\{e_1,e_2,b_5,b_6\}$

$$\begin{pmatrix} 1 & 0 & <p> & -<q> \\ 0 & 1 & -<p> & <q> \\ <p> & -<p> & 2<p^2> & -2<pq> \\ -<q> & <q> & -2<pq> & 2<q^2> \end{pmatrix} \begin{pmatrix} e_1 \\ e_2 \\ b_5 \\ b_6 \end{pmatrix} = \begin{pmatrix} <r> \\ <s> \\ <rp> - <sp> \\ <sq> - <rq> \end{pmatrix}$$

$$(8.90)$$

with solution

$$b_5 = \frac{1}{2} \frac{(b_{sp} - b_{rp})b_{qq} + (b_{sq} - b_{rq})b_{pq}}{(b_{pp}b_{qq} - b_{pq}^2)} \tag{8.91}$$

$$b_6 = \frac{1}{2} \frac{(b_{sq} - b_{rq})b_{pp} + (b_{sp} - b_{rp})b_{pq}}{(b_{pp}b_{qq} - b_{pq}^2)} \tag{8.92}$$

$$e_1 = <r> - b_5<p> + b_6<q> \tag{8.93}$$

$$e_2 = <s> + b_5<p> - b_6<q> \tag{8.94}$$

with the variances introduced:

$$b_{ab} = <ab> - <a><b> \tag{8.95}$$

From the definition (8.86) the scaling parameters λ, μ are simply given by

$$\lambda = \exp(e_1 - b_7)$$

$$\mu = \exp(e_2 + b_7) \tag{8.96}$$

If we are fixing the ratio

$$\Lambda = \lambda/\mu \tag{8.97}$$

the parameter b_7 is

$$b_7 = \frac{1}{2}[(e_1 - e_2) - \ln\Lambda] \tag{8.98}$$

8.6.3 Estimation of the trend parameters of the household distribution

The theoretical migration matrix (8.36)

$$w_{ji}^e(t) = \nu(t)n_i^e(t)e^{-\beta(t)d_{ji}}e^{u_j(x_j^e,y_j^e,z_j^e)-u_i(x_i^e,y_i^e,z_i^e)}$$

(8.99)

with

$$u_i(x_i^e,y_i^e,z_i^e) = \delta_i(t)+b_1(x_i^e-\overline{x})+b_2(y_i^e-\overline{y})-b_3(z_i^e-\overline{z})$$ (8.100)

is a function of the global mobility parameter $\nu(t)$, the deterrence parameter $\beta(t)$ and the utilities u_i, u_j. The $(L^2 - L)$ empirical observations of the $w_{ij}^e(t)$ now have to be matched to the theoretical migration matrix by an optimal estimation of the $(L + 5)$ trend parameters. We assume an arbitrary distance matrix d_{ij} and consider the product $w_{ij} * w_{ji}$. Using (8.99) we obtain a result independent of u_i:

$$w_{ij}^e(t)w_{ji}^e(t) = \nu^2(t)n_i^e(t)n_j^e(t)\exp[-\beta(t)(d_{ij}+d_{ji})]$$

Therefore, after taking the logarithm,

$$s_{ij}(t) = \mu(t) - \beta(t)(d_{ij}+d_{ji})/2$$

(8.101)

where we have introduced

$$s_{ij}(t) = s_{ji}(t) = \frac{1}{2}\ln\frac{w_{ij}^e(t)w_{ji}^e(t)}{n_i^e(t)n_j^e(t)} < 0$$

(8.102)

and

$$\mu(t) = \ln\nu(t)$$

(8.103)

We now estimate the parameters μ, β by minimizing the functional

$$G_t[\mu,\beta] = \sum_{\substack{i,j=1 \\ i \neq j}}^{L} [s_{ij}(t) - (\mu-\beta(d_{ij}+d_{ji})/2)]^2 \qquad (8.104)$$

according to

$$\frac{\partial G_t[\mu,\beta]}{\partial \mu} = 0, \qquad \frac{\partial G_t[\mu,\beta]}{\partial \beta} = 0 \qquad (8.105)$$

and obtain the result for the deterrence parameter:

$$\beta(t) = \frac{\overline{s(t).d(t)} - \overline{sd}}{\overline{d^2(t)} - \overline{d(t)}^2} \qquad (8.106)$$

and the global mobility parameter of the households:

$$\nu(t) = \exp[\overline{s}(t) + \beta(t)\overline{d}(t)] \qquad (8.107)$$

We have used the following abbreviations:

$$\overline{s}(t) = \frac{1}{L(L-1)} \sum_{\substack{i,j=1 \\ i \neq j}}^{L} s_{ij}(t)$$

$$\overline{d(t)} = \frac{1}{L(L-1)} \sum_{\substack{i,j=1 \\ i \neq j}}^{L} \frac{(d_{ij}(t)+D_{ji}(t))}{2}$$

$$\overline{sd} = \frac{1}{L(L-1)} \sum_{\substack{i,j=1 \\ i \neq j}}^{L} s_{ij}(t).\frac{(d_{ij}(t)+d_{ji}(t))}{2}$$

$$\overline{d^2} = \frac{1}{L(L-1)} \sum_{\substack{i,j=1 \\ i \neq j}}^{L} (\frac{d_{ij}(t)+d_{ji}(t)}{2})^2 \qquad (8.108)$$

The estimation procedure for the parameters $\nu(t)$ and $\beta(t)$ is independent of the estimation of the utilities.

Second, we consider the quotient w_{ij}/w_{ji} and obtain with (8.99)

$$\frac{w_{ij}^e(t)}{w_{ji}^e(t)} = \frac{n_j^e(t)}{n_i^e(t)} \exp\,[-\beta(d_{ij}-d_{ji})].\exp[2(u_i-u_j)]$$

or after taking the logarithm

$$\tilde{c}_{ij}(t) = u_i(t) - u_j(t); \quad i,\,j = 1,\,2,\,\ldots,\,L \qquad (8.109)$$

with

$$\tilde{c}_{ij}(t) = c_{ij}(t) + \frac{\beta(t)}{2}\,(d_{ij}-d_{ji}) = -\tilde{c}_{ji}(t) \qquad (8.110)$$

$$c_{ij}(t) = \frac{1}{2}\,\ln\frac{w_{ij}^e(t).n_i^e(t)}{w_{ji}^e(t).n_j^e(t)} = -\,c_{ji}(t) \qquad (8.111)$$

The equations (8.109) are linear in the utilities to be determined. Since we have $(L^2 - L)$ equations but only L unknown utilities, the utilities in general cannot be chosen to satisfy (8.109) exactly. We can, however, choose an optimal set of utilities, by minimizing the least square deviations:

$$F_t[\underset{\sim}{u}] = \sum_{i,j}^{L} [\tilde{c}_{ij}(t) - (u_i(t) - u_j(t))]^2 \qquad (8.112)$$

This yields the optimal utilities (estimated)

$$u_i(t) = \frac{1}{L} \sum_{\substack{j=1 \\ j\neq i}}^{L} \tilde{c}_{ij}(t) \qquad (8.113)$$

These L.T estimated utilities should fit to the theoretical expression (8.100) in an optimal way by fixing the L + 3 unknown trend parameters δ_i, $i = 1 \ldots L$, b_1, b_2, b_3. (The preference parameter, δ_i, is assumed to be time-independent for simplicity.) This can be done by minimizing the functional

$$F[\delta_k, b_1, b_2, b_3] = \frac{1}{L} \sum_{j=1}^{L} \frac{1}{T} \sum_{t=1}^{T} [u_j(t) - [\delta_j + b_1(x_j^e \frac{1}{L}) + b_2(y_j^e \frac{1}{L}) - b_3(z_j^e \frac{1}{L}$$

(8.114)

with

$$\frac{\partial F}{\partial \delta_k} = 0; \quad \frac{\partial F}{\partial b_1} = 0; \quad \frac{\partial F}{\partial b_2} = 0; \quad \frac{\partial F}{\partial b_3} = 0 \qquad (8.115)$$

or explicitly

$$\frac{\partial F}{\partial \delta_k} = -\frac{2}{LT} \sum_{t=1}^{T} [u_k(t) - [\delta_k + b_1(x_k^e \frac{1}{L}) + b_2(y_k^e \frac{1}{L}) - b_3(z_k^e \frac{1}{L})]] \overset{!}{=} 0$$

(8.116)

$$\frac{\partial F}{\partial b_1} = -\frac{2}{L} \sum_{j=1}^{L} \frac{1}{T} \sum_{t=1}^{T} [u_j - [\delta_j + b_1(x_j^e \frac{1}{L}) + \ldots]](x_j^e \frac{1}{L}) \overset{!}{=} 0$$

$$\frac{\partial F}{\partial b_2} = -\frac{2}{L} \sum_{j=1}^{L} \frac{1}{T} \sum_{t=1}^{T} [u_j - [\delta_j + \ldots + b_2(y_j^e \frac{1}{L}) + \ldots]](y_j^e \frac{1}{L}) \overset{!}{=} 0$$

$$\frac{\partial F}{\partial b_3} = \frac{2}{L} \sum_{j=1}^{L} \frac{1}{T} \sum_{t=1}^{T} [u_j - [\delta_j + \ldots - b_3(z_j^e \frac{1}{L})]](z_j^e \frac{1}{L}) \overset{!}{=} 0$$

(8.117)

Equation (8.116) leads to the determination of the optimal preference parameter δ_k, if the other parameters b_1, b_2, b_3 are to be known

$$\delta_k = \overline{u}_k - b_1(\overline{x}_k - \frac{1}{L}) - b_2(\overline{y}_k - \frac{1}{L}) + b_3(\overline{z}_k - \frac{1}{L}) \qquad (8.118)$$

with the mean values introduced

$$\bar{A}_k = \frac{1}{T} \sum_{t=1}^{T} A_k(t) \tag{8.119}$$

We insert now the result (8.118) into (8.117) and obtain a closed system of equations for b_1, b_2, b_3:

$$\begin{pmatrix} <b_{xx}> & <b_{xy}> & <b_{xz}> \\ <b_{yx}> & <b_{yy}> & <b_{yz}> \\ <b_{zx}> & <b_{zy}> & <b_{zz}> \end{pmatrix} \begin{pmatrix} b_1 \\ b_2 \\ b_3 \end{pmatrix} = \begin{pmatrix} <b_{ux}> \\ <b_{uy}> \\ <b_{uz}> \end{pmatrix} \tag{8.120}$$

with the abbreviations

$$<b_{ab}> = \overline{<ab>} - <\bar{a}><\bar{b}> \tag{8.121}$$

8.6.4 Dynamic estimation of the remaining trend parameters

As mentioned in subsection 8.6.1, the ratio of the time scale parameters λ, μ remains undetermined by the applied least square estimation procedure. The lack of data concerning the rent adjustment process **generates** the parameter ε which is associated with the time scale of the rent adjustment process and b_4 which describes the influence of net excess demand on the decision behaviour of landlords are also undetermined so far. Assume that

$$\underset{\sim}{c}^s(t) = (\underset{\sim}{x}(t), \underset{\sim}{y}(t), \underset{\sim}{z}(t))$$

is the solution of the mean value equations (8.63) to (8.73) solved for the known initial conditions

$$\underset{\sim}{c}^e(t_o) = (\underset{\sim}{x}^e(t_o), \underset{\sim}{y}^e(t_o), \underset{\sim}{z}^e(t_o)).$$

We have inserted the estimated trend parameters

$$\{\nu(t), \beta(t), b_1, b_2, b_3, \delta_i(t)\}, \{b_5, b_6, \mu, \lambda\}$$

into the mean value equations according to the subsections
8.6.2 and 8.6.3. We have also to insert definitive values of
$\{\varepsilon, b_4, b_7\}$. For this purpose we first assign definite but
arbitrary values to the parameters $\{\varepsilon, b_4, b_7\}$ and by comparison
of the computer simulation $\underset{\sim}{c}^S(t)$, $t\varepsilon[1,T]$ with the empirical
known value of $\underset{\sim}{c}^e(t)$, the optimal set of the parameters
$\{\varepsilon, b_4, b_7\}$ is obtained. As a measure for the quality of the
simulation procedure and as a selection principle we use the
well-known correlation coefficient

$$r_{t,t_o}(\varepsilon, b_4, b_7) = \operatorname{corr}(\underset{\sim}{c}^e(t),\ \underset{\sim}{c}^S(t)) \qquad (8.122)$$

The dynamic selection principle for ε, b_4, b_7 then reads

$$(\varepsilon, b_4, b_7) = \max_{\varepsilon, b_4, b_7} r_{T1}(\varepsilon, b_4, b_7) \qquad (8.123)$$

Chapter 9

HOUSING 3: A STOCHASTIC ASSIGNMENT APPROACH

G. Leonardi

9.1 Introduction

In this chapter we shall outline the analysis of the housing
market by means of the theory of stochastic extremal processes
developed in Chapter Five, and in particular by using the
stochastic dynamic assignment model developed in Section 5.7.
The task will be easy, since most of the theory has been built
with the housing market in mind as the main applied example,
and indeed examples based on housing market problems have been
widely used to illustrate theoretical concepts through Chapter
Five.

The main contribution which the theory of stochastic
extremal processes can provide is the description of the
dynamics of market signals, in particular prices. This chapter
will be focussed on the subject of price distributions and
price dynamics, while other aspects of the housing market,
like household mobility, will not be developed here. Although
it is possible to build a household mobility model based on the
theory of stochastic extremal processes, it is also possible
to use the price dynamics as obtained by stochastic extremal
processes in combination with other approaches already developed
to treat population mobility, like the one proposed by Haag in
this book (Chapters Four and Eight), or the one proposed by
Leonardi (1987). The latter is the point of view adopted here,

as it has been outlined in Chapter Six. The subject of
integration of different approaches for different tasks will
be further developed for the housing market as well as for
other subsystems in Chapter Seventeen.

9.2 The Housing Market as a Dynamic Assignment Process

The housing market considered here is simplified relative to
reality. Both for the households and for the dwellings we
will neglect disaggregations other than the geographic ones.
This, for instance, means households and dwellings are assumed
to be uniform in size. Moreover, a household is assumed to
have a single householder working. All the above assumptions
can be easily relaxed with little change in the basic structure
of the model, the only complication to be introduced being
cumbersome notation. Due to the mainly illustrative nature of
this chapter, all the structurally non-essential features of
demand and supply have been ignored.

Other simplifying assumptions are more severe. It is
assumed, for instance, that the market has no regulation;
therefore the price dynamics obtained pertain to a purely free
housing market. The effects of partial public regulation on
prices are not treated here, but the reader is referred to
Chapter Seven, by Anas, for a detailed account of the subject.
On the other hand, one should say that the simplifying assumptions used here are no more severe than the ones used in
classic urban economics - see Alonso (1964), Muth (1969) and
Beckmann (1969, 1973, 1974) for example. Indeed, the model
proposed here is closely related to the housing market model
of Herbert and Stevens (1960), which is basically a discrete-
space version of a classic urban economics housing market model.
We keep the discrete-space setting, as well as other main
classic concepts (like that of bid prices), but we add two
important features which the classic theory neglects: stochastic

heterogeneity of demand preferences and dynamics. The former is not wholly new in the recent literature on housing demand analysis. Its treatment by means of random utility theory has been proposed by McFadden (1978) for instance. The simultaneous use of random utility models to describe both demand and supply behaviour in a market setting is developed in Anas (1976, 1982). What is new here is the treatment of heterogeneity by means of stochastic extremal processes and asymptotic approximations, which provide a more general basis for those which in previous works look like ad hoc assumptions.

Dynamics in the sense considered here, that is, the time unfolding of market signals, is quite new. Most previous work has dealt with market signals at equilibrium, and although aggregate equations for price dynamics (like Walras-type equations) are considered in economic literature, their microeconomic derivation is not usual.

Let us now introduce the basic definitions. We shall assume the urban area under consideration is divided into n zones, and use the subscripts i, j = 1, ..., n for a generic zone. To be consistent with the notation developed in Chapter Five, we will use the label i to denote households in relation to their (single) workplace, because this is the site of demand for dwellings, which we then consider to be in zone j. The only disadvantage of this procedure is that it reverses the i-j conventions of many residential location models and so care should be exercised in reading what follows. The households, as identified by their working householder, are disaggregated by place of work, so that Γ_i is the set of households having their place of work in zone i; $\Gamma = \bigcup_{i=1}^{n} \Gamma_i$ is the total set of households in the area; $P_i = |\Gamma_i|$ is the number of households having workplace in zone i; $P = |\Gamma| = \sum_{i=1}^{n} P_i$ is the

total number of households. The dwellings are disaggregated
by location, and it is assumed each dwelling can be assigned
at most to one household. Thus Ω_j is the set of dwellings

located in zone j; $\Omega = \bigcup\limits_{j=1}^{n} \Omega_j$ is the total set of dwellings in

the area; $Q_j = |\Omega_j|$ is the number of dwellings in zone j;

$Q = |\Omega| = \sum\limits_{j=1}^{n} Q_j$ is the total number of dwellings. It will be

assumed that $Q > P$.

The utility each household attaches to each dwelling is
typically a function of the dwelling's physical attributes
(such as size), price, the zone attributes (eg distance from
place of work, accessibility to services). To these we add a
random term, in order to take heterogeneity of preferences into
account. Since we are neglecting the physical attributes of
the dwellings by assuming they are the same for all, a typical
utility of a household $h\epsilon\Gamma_i$ for a dwelling $z\epsilon\Omega_j$ at time t is:

$$u_{hz}(t) = \varepsilon_{hz} - [\pi_z(t) + c_{ij} + s_j], \quad h\epsilon\Gamma_i, \ z\epsilon\Omega_j$$

$$i,j = 1, \ldots, n \tag{9.1}$$

where ε_{hz} is the random utility term; $\pi_z(t)$ is the market price
of dwelling z at time t; c_{ij} is the commuting cost between
zones i and j; s_j is the average expenditure in services
(including transportation cost) from zone j. As usual, the
variables ε_{hz} will be assumed to be i.i.d. with distribution
$F(x) = Pr\{\varepsilon_{hz} \leq x\}$ for all $(h,z)\epsilon\Gamma x\Omega$. The prices $\pi_z(t)$ can be
further split in two parts, a maintenance cost h_j and an extra
price $\tilde{r}_j(t)$, the result of the bidding process, which is a
random variable whose distribution will be endogenously determined later. The commuting cost, service expenditure and
maintenance cost can be considered as deterministic variables,

240

common to all $(h,z)\varepsilon\Gamma_i \times \Omega_j$ for each (i,j) pair. We can define for short:

$$v_{ij} = - (c_{ij} + s_j + h_j), \quad i,j = 1, \ldots, n$$

and rewrite (9.1) as:

$$u_{hz}(t) = v_{ij} + [\varepsilon_{hz} - \tilde{r}_z(t)], \quad h\varepsilon\Gamma_i, \ z\varepsilon\Omega_j$$

$$i,j = 1, \ldots, n \quad (9.2)$$

In a similar fashion, the bid price* (assuming a rental housing market, the bid rent) of a dwelling $z\varepsilon\Omega_j$ from a household $h\varepsilon\Gamma_i$ at time t is:

$$r_{hz}(t) = v_{ij} + [\varepsilon_{hz} - \tilde{u}_h(t)], \quad h\varepsilon\Gamma_i, \ z\varepsilon\Omega_j$$

$$i,j = 1, \ldots, n \quad (9.3)$$

where $\tilde{u}_h(t)$ is the maximum utility for a household h at time t.

The diffusion of information between demand and supply is assumed to occur randomly in time with intensity λ. This means that each landlord receives information about the bid price offered by any household according to a Poisson process with intensity λ. It also means that each household receives information about the market price of any dwelling (and is therefore able to compute its utility) according to a Poisson process with intensity λ.

---

* We recall that the bid price as defined here is not the whole bid price. It is just its random part. In order to get the total bid price, one should add to it the maintenance cost h_j.

Therefore the total number of items of information a household receives about dwellings in zone j is a Poisson process with intensity

$$\lambda Q_j, \quad j = 1, \ldots, n \qquad (9.4)$$

Similarly, the total number of items of information a landlord receives about households (ie about offered bid prices) in zone i is a Poisson process with intensity

$$\lambda P_i, \quad i = 1, \ldots, n \qquad (9.5)$$

Both demand and supply are assumed not to keep these items of information in memory forever. Each item received at time τ is assumed to have a random lifetime η_τ, with given survival function $F(x) = P_r\{\eta_\tau > x\}$ for all τ. This means that if a household has received information about the price of a dwelling at time t-x, he will keep it in his memory at least until time t with probability $F(x)$, and of course he will have dropped it from his list at time t with probability $1-F(x)$. In the same way a landlord who has received information about the bid price of a household at time t-x still remembers about it at time t with probability $F(x)$, while he has forgotten about it with probability $1-F(x)$. The mean lifetime of an item of information, μ, is assumed to be finite. In terms of the survival function $F(x)$, it is given by:

$$\mu = \int_0^\infty F(\tau)d\tau$$

Both demand and supply are assumed to be related to maximizing behaviour. Demand aims at maximizing utility; therefore a household keeps track of the maximum in the sequence of utility values (9.2) still held in memory at time t. By definition, this maximum is $\tilde{u}_h(t)$. Supply aims at maximizing revenues,

that is to sell at the highest possible price; therefore each
landlord keeps track of the maximum in the sequence of bid
price values (9.3) he still has in memory at time t. If this
maximum is non-negative, he sets the extra market price of his
dwelling, $\tilde{r}_z(t)$, equal to it, so that the total market price
will be equal to the maximum bid plus the maintenance cost, ie
$\tilde{r}_z(t) + h_j$; otherwise, the market price will be set equal to
the pure maintenance cost h_j, without any extra bid component.

The assumptions introduced so far define a dynamic assignment process of the type considered in section 5.7. The household and landlord behaviours are both stochastic extremal
processes, of the type studied in Sections 5.4 and 5.6. In the
next section we shall determine the distributions of utilities
$\tilde{u}_h(t)$ and price $\tilde{r}_z(t)$, and work out some other useful results.

9.3 Price Distributions and Dynamic Equations

In addition to the assumptions introduced in Section 9.2, it
will be further assumed that the condition (5.96) or theorem
5.7.1 in Chapter Five holds. The theorem can thus be applied
to the housing market model, provided the market is large
enough to justify the use of asymptotic approximations.

In order to do so, we know from the theory in Chapter Five
that the constant a_Q, defined as the root of equation

$$1 - F(a_Q) = \frac{1}{\lambda \mu Q}$$

must be subtracted from the random utility terms ε_{hz}. This is
just a change in the origin of the utility scale, which is
arbitrary.

Define $H_i(x,t)$ as the distribution of the maximum utility
at time t for a household $h\varepsilon\Gamma_i$, $i = 1, \ldots, n$, as $Q \to \infty$;
$R(x,t)$, the distribution of the market price at time t for a
dwelling $z\varepsilon\Omega_j$, $j = 1, \ldots, n$, as $Q \to \infty$. Then one has from

theorem 5.7.1 that

$$H_i(x,t) = \exp[-\phi_i(t)e^{-\beta x}], \quad i = 1, \ldots, n \qquad (9.6)$$

$$R_j(x,t) = \begin{cases} \exp[-\psi_j(t)e^{-\beta x}] & x \geq 0, \\ \\ 0 & x < 0, \end{cases} \quad j = 1, \ldots, \qquad (9.7)$$

where

$$\phi_i(t) = \sum_{j=1}^{n} \omega_j e^{\beta[v_{ij}-r_j(t)]} \qquad (9.8)$$

$$\psi_j(t) = \sum_{i=1}^{n} \theta_i e^{\beta[v_{ij}-u_i(t)]} \qquad (9.9)$$

$$\omega_j = Q_j/Q \qquad (9.10)$$

$$\theta_i = P_i/Q \qquad (9.11)$$

and the quantities $r_j(t)$ and $u_i(t)$ are solutions of the integral equations:

$$e^{-\beta u_i(t)} = \int_0^\infty \frac{F(\tau)}{\mu} \frac{1}{\phi_i(t-\tau)} \, d\tau \qquad (9.12)$$

$$e^{-\beta r_j(t)} = \int_0^\infty \frac{F(\tau)}{\mu} \frac{1-e^{-\psi_j(t-\tau)}}{\psi_j(t-\tau)} \, d\tau,$$

$$i,j = 1, \ldots, n \qquad (9.13)$$

From equation (5.113), Section 5.7, one has

$$e^{-\beta \bar{r}_j(t)} = \frac{1-e^{-\psi_j(t)}}{\psi_j(t)} \qquad (9.14)$$

244

where

$$\bar{r}_j(t) = -\frac{1}{\beta} \log \int_{-\infty}^{\infty} e^{-\beta x} dR_j(x,t), \quad j = 1, \ldots, n \quad (9.15)$$

is the exponential average of prices in zone j. The average, (9.15), is different from the expected value, which would be given by the integral

$$\int_{-\infty}^{\infty} x dR_j(x,t)$$

which is not computable in closed form. Therefore, replacing (9.14) in (9.13) one has:

$$r_j(t) = -\frac{1}{\beta} \int_0^{\infty} \frac{F(\tau)}{\mu} e^{-\beta \bar{r}_j(t-\tau)} d\tau \quad (9.16)$$

That is, $r_j(t)$ is the weighted exponential time average of prices in zone j, the weighting factor being $F(\tau)/\mu$. A similar interpretation can be given for $u_i(t)$, which is the weighted exponential time average of maximum utilities for households working in zone i. In the dynamic housing market model considered here time averages become therefore the main aggregate signals. From the application of corollary 5.7.2, Chapter Five, one obtains the demand function. That is: the probability $p_{ij}(t)$ that the best dwelling known up to time t by a household working in zone i is in zone j ($i,j = 1, \ldots, n$) given by a logit model:

$$p_{ij}(t) = \frac{Q_j e^{\beta[v_{ij} - r_j(t)]}}{\sum_{j=1}^{n} Q_j e^{\beta[v_{ij} - r_j(t)]}} \quad (9.17)$$

The supply function is the probability $S_j(t)$ that a dwelling in zone j is offered at a price higher than the pure maintenance cost at time t, that is, it has received at least one non-negative bid $(j = 1, \ldots, n)$ given by

$$S_j(t) = [1 - e^{-\psi_j(t)}] \tag{9.18}$$

In Section 5.7 it is also shown that one can interpret the quantity $\psi_j(t)$ as a time average of potential demand for a dwelling in zone j:

$$\psi_j(t) = \int_0^\infty \frac{F(\tau)}{\mu} T_j(t-\tau)d\tau \tag{9.19}$$

where

$$T_j(t) = \sum_{i=1}^{n} P_i \frac{e^{\beta v_{ij}}}{\sum_{j=1}^{n} Q_j e^{\beta[v_{ij}-r_j(t)]}}$$

is the potential demand for a dwelling in j at time t, defined as the expected number of households who have placed their highest bid on that dwelling up to time t. Replacing from (9.18) and keeping interpretation (9.19) in mind, equation (9.13) can also be written as

$$r_j(t) = \frac{1}{\beta} \log \int_0^\infty \frac{F(\tau)}{\mu} \frac{S_j(t-\tau)}{\psi_j(t-\tau)} d\tau \tag{9.20}$$

Equation (9.20) states that $r_j(t)$ is a weighted exponential time average of supply-demand ratios. We now have two alternative, but equivalent, interpretations of equations (9.13), namely (9.16) and (9.20).

If it is assumed that $F(x) = e^{-\alpha x}$ and $\mu = \int_0^\infty F(x)dx = 1/\alpha$, then, in Section 5.7, it is shown that the integral equations (9.12) and (9.13) are equivalent to the differential equations

$$\dot{X}_i(t) = \alpha/\phi_i(t) - \alpha X_i(t) \tag{9.21}$$

Housing - Stochastic Assignment

$$\dot{Y}_j(t) = \alpha[1-e^{-\psi_j(t)}]/\psi_j(t) - \alpha Y_j(t), \quad i,j = 1, \ldots, n$$

$$(9.22)$$

where the transformed variables $X_i(t)$ and $Y_j(t)$ are defined as

$$X_i(t) = e^{-\beta u_i(t)}$$

$$Y_j(t) = e^{-\beta r_j(t)}, \quad i,j = 1, \ldots, n$$

In analogy with equations (9.16) and (9.20), equation (9.22) can be given two alternative interpretations. It is shown in 5.7 that equation (9.22) is equivalent to either of the equations:

$$\dot{r}_j(t) = \frac{\alpha}{\beta} \{1 - e^{-\beta[\bar{r}_j(t) - r_j(t)]}\}$$

$$(9.23)$$

$$\dot{r}_j(t) = \frac{\alpha}{\beta} \frac{D_j(t) - S_j(t)}{D_j(t)}$$

$$(9.24)$$

where

$D_j(t) = T_j(t)e^{-\beta r_j(t)}$ is the demand forecast for a dwelling in zone j offered at price $r_j(t)$ at time t, $j = 1, \ldots, n$, and $\bar{r}_j(t)$ is the average price at time t, defined by (9.15). Equation (9.23) relates the rate of change of the price time average, $r_j(t)$, to the difference $\bar{r}_j(t) - r_j(t)$: when the average price at time t is greater than the corresponding time average, $r_j(t) > 0$, otherwise $r_j(t) < 0$. Equation (9.24) is of a Walrasian type, since it relates the rate of changes of $r_j(t)$ to the difference between demand and supply.

9.4 The Equilibrium Solution

We shall now investigate the behaviour of the system described in section 9.3 as $t \to \infty$, that is, in the long run. Due to the assumptions introduced so far, we can resort to corollary 5.7.2 of Chapter Five. This basically means that the equilibrium assignment satisfies theorem 5.3.2. That is, the quantities

$$p_{ij} = \lim_{t \to \infty} p_{ij}(t), \quad i,j = 1, \ldots, n$$

are the unique solution to the concave program

$$\max_{\{p_{ij}\}} \sum_{i=1}^{n} P_i \sum_{j=1}^{n} p_{ij} \left(v_{ij} - \frac{1}{\beta} \log \frac{p_{ij}}{Q_j} - \frac{1}{\beta} \sum_{j=1}^{n} Q_j \int_0^{A_j(p)/Q_j} \right.$$

$$\left. \log\left[\frac{-\log(1-x)}{x}\right] dx \right. \tag{9.25}$$

subject to

$$\sum_{j=1}^{n} p_{ij} = 1 \tag{9.26}$$

where

$$A_j(p) = \sum_{i=1}^{n} P_i p_{ij} \tag{9.27}$$

It is shown in Section 5.3 that a mathematical program like (9.25) - (9.27) has a precise economic interpretation. Namely, the objective function (9.25) is the total benefit, the sum of consumers' and producers' surplus, since

$$\sum_{i=1}^{n} P_i \sum_{j=1}^{n} p_{ij} \left(v_{ij} - \frac{1}{\beta} \log \frac{p_{ij}}{Q_j} \right) - \sum_{j=1}^{n} A_j(p) r_j$$

is the consumers' surplus aggregated over all households and

$$\sum_{j=1}^{n} A_j(p)r_j - \frac{1}{\beta} \sum_{j=1}^{n} Q_j \int_0^{A_j(p)/Q_j} \log \left[\frac{-\log(1-x)}{x}\right]dx$$

is the producers' surplus aggregated over all dwellings. The function

$$r(x) = \frac{1}{\beta} \log \left[\frac{-\log(1-x)}{x}\right], \quad 0 < x \leq 1 \tag{9.28}$$

is the supply price function induced by the stochastic housing market described in Section 9.2, x being the quantity supplied for each dwelling (namely, the probability that a dwelling is sold or rented). (9.28) is indeed a well-behaved supply function, since it can be easily checked it is convex non-decreasing and $r(0) = 0$ and $\lim_{x \to 1} r(x) = \infty$.

The fact that at equilibrium corollary 5.7.2 (ie theorem 5.3.2) holds means that the equilibrium average prices can be computed as the unique solution to the set of market clearing equations:

$$\sum_{i=1}^{n} P_i \frac{Q_j e^{\beta(v_{ij}-r_j)}}{\sum_{j=1}^{n} Q_j e^{\beta(v_{ij}-r_j)}} = Q_j(1 - e^{-\psi_j}), \quad j = 1, \ldots, n \tag{9.29}$$

which simply state equality between demand and supply for each zone.

Equations (9.29) justify a closing comment to this chapter. From the way they are written, it looks as if the quantities r_j, $j = 1, \ldots, n$ are the equilibrating signals in our market. This is of course true, provided one remembers that equations like (9.29) relate to expected values: they equate expected demand to expected supply. The r_j themselves

are therefore average prices, not to be confused with any
uniform-price assumption. Even at equilibrium, prices are
still random variables, with distributions given by equation
(9.7), and the r_j just happen to be the parameters one needs
to compute in order to determine such distributions. Stated
in other terms, if equations like (9.29) are interpreted as
deterministic approximations to a stochastic process, then the
r_j are a deterministic approximation to the price signals
exchanged in the market. They actually happen to be the
sufficient statistic in the process, ie the parameters which
convey and summarize all the information needed in the demand-
supply bargaining. One should not forget, however, that in
any realization of the process prices are random variables,
distributed according to a double-exponential distribution of
type (9.7).

Chapter 10

SERVICES 1: A SPATIAL-INTERACTION-DYNAMIC APPROACH

A.G. Wilson

10.1 Introduction

One useful approach to model design (Wilson, 1984-B) is to
consider the following six issues:

* entitation
* level of resolution
* partialness/comprehensiveness
* spatial representation
* theory
* method

It is particularly valuable to start in this first-principles
way in relation to the service sector. There is a tendency
to think of it as a large amorphous "non-industrial" category;
or more narrowly as "retailing". In fact, of course, it is
many sectors. It is particularly important, therefore, to
establish the level of resolution, the basic entities in each
system thus defined (and the units of measurement) and the
partialness/comprehensiveness of the approach to be adopted.
Between them, these three decisions constitute "system definition". Spatial representation is easy, as can be seen in the
argument of the rest of the book so far: we use discrete zone
systems. There are some practical difficulties, however.
How fine a spatial level of resolution should be adopted? Is
a different spatial system needed for population zones and

Services - Spatial Interaction

facility zones? If the equilibrium model is being used, are
many extra currently-empty facility zones needed to enable the
model to predict alternative spatial patterns? In one application, for example, a 30 x 900 (residence x facility) zone
system was used (Clarke and Wilson, 1983-A). We also laid the
ground of theory and methods in Chapter 3, arguing there that
it was appropriate to use dynamical-system models with spatial
interaction model underpinnings. The framework could be used
either to generate equilibrium patterns or to model dynamics
(with the system of interest subject to constant perturbations).

We will return to the argument of Chapter 3 and its
implications for modelling retail systems in Section 10.2
below. However, it is already clear how there can be an interplay between system definition and theory specification. The
Chapter 3 discussion, for example, involved the detailed
specification of cost functions; such specifications would
only be directly meaningful at relatively fine levels of
resolution, since the costs would relate to the kind of service
being provided. This all supports the argument for adopting a
fine sectoral level of resolution. However, limitations on
data and computer storage capacity obviously work in the other
direction when the main objective is to build a comprehensive
model. The partial-comprehensive issue is added to all this:
essentially, it is concerned with whether the model should
represent the units of a single firm in a given sector; or
should represent the whole sector and properly deal with
competition between units. The usual practice in urban and
regional modelling has been to attempt to build a comprehensive
model, but almost inevitably, at a coarse scale. Lowry (1964),
for example, distinguished three service sectors: local, sub-
regional and regional. This involves more resolution than some
other attempts, but is still too coarse to give the most
credible interpretations to cost and attractiveness functions.

In the light of these difficulties, we proceed in the rest

252

of that chapter as though either a coarse or fine sectoral
level of resolution could be adopted. Most of the discussion
is general and could be applied at either scale, but we present
as an example a retail model which demands a finer scale than
that usually adopted. In our choice of examples more broadly,
for instance, there is also a sense in which we imply the
adoption of a fine scale so that we can illustrate the different model building techniques which are applicable for
different sub-sectors.

The rest of the chapter thus has the following structure.
In Section 10.2, we extract from Chapter 3 the main principles
which underpin service-sector modelling. In Section 10.3, we
present three examples: (i) a conventional model which is
suitable for broad-scale systems or for certain kinds of
sectors; (ii) a fine-scale retail model, which distinguishes
different types of shops as well as different kinds of goods;
(iii) a mathematical programming model which is appropriate
for certain kinds of public sectors, such as education. We
conclude this section with a discussion of alternative
approaches. In Section 10.4, we make some concluding comments,
distinguishing different kinds of uses of these different kinds
of models in planning.

10.2 Principles for Building Service-Sector Models

It is useful to summarise the principles implicit in Chapter 3,
using a modified notation to indicate that we will have to
shift to finer scales and ultimately be more specific about
the form of the model.

Let the superscript g denote a service sector, with
$g = 1, 2, 3, \ldots$; let $\underline{m}$ be a vector of population characteristics (age, sex, social class, $\ldots$) defined in such a way
that $e^{\underline{m}g}$ is the per capita demand for g, in suitable units,
from the $\underline{m}$ group, so $\sum_{\underline{m}} e^{\underline{m}g} P_i^{\underline{m}}$ is the total demand in i. Let W_j^g

represent the attractiveness of g-facilities in j and let C_j^g be the cost of supplying these facilities; where appropriate, let D_j^g be the g-revenue attracted to j. Let p_i^g be the price of g as perceived at i; p_j^g the market price at j. Let c_{ij} be a measure of the cost of travel from i to j.

To specify a suitable model for a particular sector g, we then proceed in the following steps

(i) Design of flow model which estimates S_{ij}^g in terms of $E_i^g = \sum_m e^{mg} P_i^m$, W_j^g and c_{ij}:

$$S_{ij}^g = S_{ij}^g(E_i^g, W_j^g, c_{ij}) \qquad (10.1)$$

This model will, of course, involve, for example, W_j^g's for $j' \neq j$, in order to deal effectively with competition.

(ii) Estimate e^{mg} and P_i^m.

(iii) Specify the attractiveness function, W_j^g. (This may involve $W_j^{g'}$'s, for $g' \neq g$, in order to represent consumer scale economies from being able to make several service trips to one site.) The different possible components of W_j^g include the following:

(a) j-elements: total scale of facilities at j, $W_j^* = \sum_g W_j^g$, say; parking costs and facilities at j; measures of environmental quality at j;

(b) (j, g) elements: W_j^g, p_j^g.

We will see in relation to the disaggregated retail example in subsection 10.3.2 below that further detail can be added.

(iv) Ideally, a good measure of generalised costs, c_{ij}, is needed;

(v) Identify the components of facility supply and their costs as a function of the overall scale of supply. This enables C_j^g to be estimated. Let x_{jk}^g be the kth supply component for the g-service at j. Let γ_{jk}^g be associated unit costs. Then the elements might include:

(a) x_{j1}^g : land;

(b) x_{j2}^g : building, measured as floorspace;

(c) x_{j3}^g : labour;

(d) x_{j4}^g : capital;

(e) x_{j5}^g : costs of inputs.

Then the unit costs would be functions of scale:

$$\gamma_{jk}^g = \gamma_{jk}^g(x_{jk}^g, \ldots) \tag{10.2}$$

and total costs would be

$$c_j^g = \sum_k \gamma_{jk}^g(x_{jk}^g) \cdot x_{jk}^g \tag{10.3}$$

It will often be useful to have the levels of inputs determined by a single "activity" variable, say y_j^g. This may be an independently defined variable; or one of the inputs, say floorspace. Then

$$x_{jk}^g = x_{jk}^g(y_j^g) \tag{10.4}$$

and

$$c_j^g(y_j^g) = \sum_k \gamma_{jk}^g(x_{jk}^g(y_j^g))x_{jk}^g(y_j^g) \tag{10.5}$$

specifies total (j, g) cost in terms of activity level.

(vi) A mechanism then has to be specified for either

(a) the determination of the equilibrium pattern $\{y_j^g\}$, say by

$$D_j^g = c_j^g \tag{10.6}$$

or

(b) to determine the change in y_j^g (and other relevant prices and rents), say

$$\Delta y_j^{g(t, \ t+1)} = \varepsilon_1 (D_j^y - c_j^y) y_j^g \tag{10.7}$$

$$y_j^{gt+1} = y_j^{gt} + \Delta y_j^{g(t, \ t+1)} \tag{10.8}$$

Here we have used the Chapter 3 mechanisms for illustration. As we will see with some of the examples below, alternatives are possible.

These steps, (i) - (vi), add flesh to the bones of the model presented in Chapter 3. We can see that much more detail has to be added to specify a model effectively; and we can see that the nature of that detail will be different at different levels of resolution. The best way to proceed now is by example, and we do this in Section 10.3.

10.3 Examples of Service Sector Models

10.3.1 A basic disaggregated model

The first obvious example to develop is an extension of the model presented as an illustration in Chapter 3. Here we add service sector g label as a superscript and pursue in more depth the specification of the various functions in the model, working through steps (i) - (vi) of Section 10.2 above. We work in two stages presenting first an equilibrium model and then an "economic" dynamic model.

A suitable interaction model will be

$$S_{ij}^g = A_i^g E_i^g W_j^g e^{-\beta^g c_{ij}} \tag{10.9}$$

where

$$A_i^g = 1/\sum_k W_k^g e^{-\beta^g c_{ik}} \qquad (10.10)$$

to ensure that

$$\sum_j S_{ij}^g = E_i^g \qquad (10.11)$$

Steps (ii) - (iv) provide the individual elements of the right
hand side of (10.9):

$$E_i^g = \sum_m e^{mg} P_i^m \qquad (10.12)$$

P_i^m has to be estimated from a demographic model and e^{mg} probably simply empirically. There is a potential complication
here that e^{mg} may also be a function of i-variables. For
later convenience, the e-variables should be measured in
suitable quantity units. Any demand elasticities should be
built in at this point - but we will see this when we offer
the form of the dynamic model with prices shortly. Even for
this equilibrium model, e^{mg} could be written e_i^{mg} and be a
function of accessibility. Then (10.12) would be replaced by

$$E_i^g = \sum_m e_i^{mg} P_i^m \qquad (10.13)$$

with

$$e_i^{mg} = e_i^{mg}(0)(\sum_j W_j^g e^{-\beta^g c_{ij}})^{\gamma_1^g} \qquad (10.14)$$

say. The particular functional form would be a matter of
much empirical testing. Another alternative, for instance,
would be

$$e_i^{mg} = e_i^{mg}(\min) + e_i^{mg}(0)(\sum_j W_j^g e^{-\beta^g c_{ij}})^{\gamma_1^g} \qquad (10.15)$$

257

In effect, this specifies a minimum level of per capita demand
plus a term dependent on accessibility.

The next step involves the specification of the attractiveness function and we saw that there may be j-elements and (j, g)
elements. Let A_j^g be floorspace provision for g at j, and

$$Z_j^* = \sum_g Z_j^g \tag{10.16}$$

(or, alternatively,

$$Z_j^* = \sum_{g \in G^g} Z_j^g \tag{10.17}$$

where G^g is the set of goods of the same or higher order than
g). Let π_j be an index of parking availability and charges at
j and Q_j an index of environmental quality. p_j^g is a (given
and fixed for this model) index of prices. Then

$$W_j^g = (Z_j^*)^{\alpha_1} \pi_j^{\alpha_2} Q_j^{\alpha_3} (Z_j^g)^{\alpha_4^g} (p_j^g)^{\alpha_5^g} \tag{10.18}$$

is the most general form of attractiveness function implied by
the earlier discussion. Again, the precise determination and
estimation of this function is a matter of empirical research.
In practice fewer terms are likely.

The generalised travel cost could be taken as

$$c_{ij} = t_{ij} + ad_{ij} \tag{10.19}$$

that is, as being made up of elements proportional to travel
time and to distance. Ideally, of course, the model formulation should distinguish modal choice. This is a further complication which we avoid for the present, but it could be
added straightforwardly if appropriate.

We specified a costs model in some detail in equations
(10.2) - (10.5) above and introduced the idea of one variable

as an activity level to which all other inputs can be related. For practical and illustrative purposes, it is most helpful at this point to present a more specific version of that model. Let us take Z_j^g as the activity level. Let ℓ_j^g be the amount of land implied by this per unit of floorspace, at rent r_j; let p^{Gg} be the input price of goods, v^g the volume of goods per unit of floorspace; and let λ^g be the unit cost of all other inputs. Then the equivalent of (10.5), which relates costs C_j^g to the activity level – in this case Z_j^g – is

$$C_j^g = (\lambda^g v^g + p^{Gg} v^g + r_j \ell_j^g + k_j) Z_j^g \qquad (10.20)$$

where k_j is the unit cost of floorspace at j. The terms in brackets can be recombined by redefining λ and k_j, say, as

$$C_j^g = (\lambda^g + k_j^g) Z_j^g \qquad (10.21)$$

These are usually taken as constants. However, it should be emphasised that any of the coefficients in (10.20) could be taken as functions of Z_j^g (or some other related scale variable) so that the model could incorporate economies or diseconomies of scale. Thus, formally, we might then write (10.21) as

$$C_j^g = [\lambda^g(Z_j^g) + k_j^g(Z_j^g)] Z_j^g \qquad (10.22)$$

The revenue attracted to j for g is simply

$$D_j^g = p_j^g \sum_i S_{ij}^g \qquad (10.23)$$

and $\{Z_j^g\}$ is determined by solving the following simultaneous equations:

$$D_j^g = C_j^g \qquad (10.24)$$

These can be written out in full as:

$$p_j^g \sum_i \frac{(\sum_i e_i^{mg} P_i^m)(Z_j^*)^{\alpha_1} \pi_j^{\alpha_2} Q_j^{\alpha_3} (Z_j^g)^{\alpha_4^g} (p_j^g)^{\alpha_5^g} e^{-\beta^g c_{ij}}}{\sum_k (Z_k^*)^{\alpha_1} \pi_k^{\alpha_2} Q_k^{\alpha_3} (Z_k^g)^{\alpha_4^g} (p_k^g)^{\alpha_5^g} e^{-\beta^g c_{ik}}}$$

$$= [\lambda(Z_j^g + k_j(Z_j^g)]Z_j^g \qquad (10.25)$$

if all the appropriate substitutions are made. This shows the full complexity of the system.

A lot of experience has been gained with this kind of model for relatively simple attractiveness and cost functions (cf, for example, Wilson and Clarke, 1979, Clarke and Wilson, 1983, Lombardo and Rabino, 1983, Pumain, Saint-Julien and Sanders, 1984). What is now needed is more empirical experience with a potentially more realistic model; and some indication from this experience as to which elements in the attractiveness and cost functions - for instance we have almost no experience of the effects of scale economies in the latter - contribute most to the determination of patterns.

It is relatively straightforward now to extend the equilibrium model presented above to a dynamic form. We have to replace the equilibrium mechanism by something like the form of (10.8) in the previous section; or, which is equivalent, disaggregate the model, from equation (3.11) onwards, which was used as an example in Chapter 3. Since the principles have been established, we proceed relatively rapidly in this task, without much commentary, combining the presentation of Chapter 3 with the principles of disaggregation established above.

We can take perceived prices at i as (cf equation (3.11))

$$\hat{p}_i^g = \frac{\sum\limits_j p_j^g e^{-\beta^g c_{ij}}}{\sum\limits_j e^{-\beta^g c_{ij}}} \tag{10.26}$$

and then modify (10.13) and (10.14) to show price elasticity explicitly:

$$E_i^g = \sum_m e_{\bar{i}}^{mg} P_{\bar{i}}^m \tag{10.27}$$

with

$$e_{\bar{i}}^{mg} = e_{\bar{i}}^{mg(0)} (\hat{p}_i^g)^{-\gamma_1^g} \tag{10.28}$$

(where we now assume that $\hat{p}_i^g$ will reflect accessibility through (10.26)).

Equations (10.16) - (10.19), specifying the attractiveness and travel cost functions, remain unchanged, as does the interaction model itself in (10.9) and (10.10). We can add the mechanism which determines p^{Gg} - cf equations (3.13) - (3.16) in Chapter 3:

$$\sum_i e_{\bar{i}}^{mg(0)} (\hat{p}_i^g)^{-\gamma_1^g} P_{\bar{i}}^m = E_0^S (p^{Gg})^{\gamma_2^g} \tag{10.29}$$

for suitable γ_2^g. The rest of the model equations, (10.20) - (10.23), then hold as before, but we replace (10.24) (or (10.25)) by a new mechanism:

$$\Delta Z_j^{g(t, t+1)} = \varepsilon_1^g (D_j^{gt} - C_j^{gt}) \tag{10.30}$$

$$\Delta p_j^{g(t, t+1)} = \pm \varepsilon_2^g (D_j^{gt} - C_j^{gt}) p_j^{gt} \tag{10.31}$$

$$\Delta r_j^{(t, t+1)} = \varepsilon_3^g \sum_g (D_j^{gt} - C_j^{gt}) r_j^t \tag{10.32}$$

where we follow and develop (3.24) - (3.26). The last of the

261

equations needs the most modification to represent the fact
that the market should produce a land rent at j which does not
vary with g. Then

$$Z_j^{gt+1} = Z_j^{gt} + \Delta Z_j^{g}(t, t+1) \tag{10.33}$$

$$p_j^{gt+1} = p_j^{gt} + \Delta p_j^{g}(t, t+1) \tag{10.34}$$

$$r_j^{t+1} = r_j^{t} + \Delta r_j^{(t, t+1)} \tag{10.35}$$

The model would now be run to build on given (and actual)
initial values of the main arrays $\{Z_j^{g}\}$, $\{p_j^{g}\}$ and $\{r_j\}$ and
would be incremented through time with (10.30) – (10.35) with
D_j^{g} and C_j^{g} being specified as in the earlier model equations.

10.3.2 A model with shop-type disaggregation

In this section we present a model which is potentially suitable for the retail sectors within the service model (though
possibly for some other services as well – cf Wilson, 1983-A),
The possibility of using such a model obviously only exists
if it has been decided to work at a fine level of resolution.

The problem to be dealt with is this: the model of
Section 10.3.2, when applied at a fine level of resolution,
runs into difficulties because of an implicit assumption that
a type of good can be identified with a type of shop. In
fact, some shop types – supermarkets, superstores, department
stores, for example – sell a number of types of good. It is
important to reflect this in the model, partly simply to try
to improve realism, but also because much of the interest is
in the modes of development of different types of shop, like
the out-of-town superstore.

To fix ideas, consider the simple and idealised example
shown in Table 10.1, where we relate types of good to types

of shop.

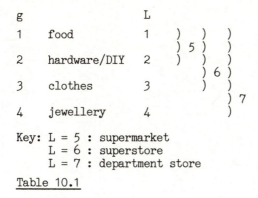

g		L			
1	food	1	)	)	)
			) 5	)	)
2	hardware/DIY	2	)	)	)
				) 6	)
3	clothes	3	)	)	)
					) 7
4	jewellery	4			)

Key: L = 5 : supermarket
     L = 6 : superstore
     L = 7 : department store

Table 10.1

The implied shift to a finer level of resolution also reminds
us of another problem in this kind of modelling: how to relate
information about individual stores to the more usual and
broader concepts of "shops in a zone". We will continue to
use zonal aggregates most of the time, but at the end of the
subsection, we will investigate how to shift to an even finer
scale.

In effect, we have now added something rather like modal
choice in a transport model; but in this context, shop-type
choice. To a large extent, we can add h-superscripts to the
previous model, but there will be differences which allow a
shop-type choice mechanism to be developed. With obvious
definitions - relating to g in shop-type h - the main modified
variables now become S_{ij}^{gh}, W_j^{gh}, z_j^{gh}, p_j^{gh} and the coefficient β^g
becomes β^{gh}. In principle, there could be elements of W_j^{gh}
which related to j, g, h, (j, g, h) or any two selected from
(j, g, h). However, we work with an amended version of (10.18)
allowing the "quality" index, Q_j, to vary with h and so become
Q_j^h. Thus, in effect, Q_j^h, z_j^{gh} and p_j^{gh} will determine the h-type
split. Note that the E_i^g variables are not subdivided by h
because the split should be determined within the interaction

263

model:

$$S_{ij}^{gh} = A_i^g E_i^g W_j^{gh} e^{-\beta^{gh} c_{ij}} \tag{10.36}$$

with

$$A_i^g = 1/\sum_k W_k^{gh} e^{-\beta^{gh} c_{ik}} \tag{10.37}$$

to ensure that

$$\sum_{jh} S_{ij}^{gh} = E_i^g \tag{10.38}$$

E_i^g is as in the subsection 10.3.1. model, W_j^{gh} can be taken as (cf, for example, equation (10.18)):

$$W_j^{gh} = (Z_j^{**})^{\alpha_1} \pi_j^{\alpha_2} (Q_j^h)^{\alpha_3^h} (Z_j^{gh})^{\alpha_4^{gh}} (p_j^{gh})^{\alpha_5^{gh}} \tag{10.39}$$

and it can then be seen how the interplay of Q_j^h, Z_j^{gh} and p_j^{gh} will determine the h-split through (10.36) and (10.37).

This "split" will, in part, determine the $\{Z_j^{gh}\}$ pattern. The other main contributor to this will be the form of cost function. We can make obvious modifications to equation (10.20):

$$C_j^{gh} = (\lambda^{gh} v^{gh} + p^{Gg} v^{gh} + r_j \ell_j^{gh} + k_j^h) Z_j^{gh} \tag{10.40}$$

Note the different combinations of (j, g, h) indices which appear in the different terms. The terms can be combined, as in (10.22), and Z_j^{gh} again used as a measure of an "activity level":

$$C_j^{gh} = [\lambda^{gh}(Z_j^{gh}) + k_j^{gh}(Z_j^{gh})] Z_j^{gh} \tag{10.41}$$

Revenue will be given by

$$D_j^{gh} = p_j^{gh} \sum_i S_{ij}^{gh} \qquad (10.42)$$

The equilibrium pattern for $\{Z_j^{gh}\}$ can be obtained in the usual way by solving

$$D_j^{gh} = C_j^{gh} \qquad (10.43)$$

and a dynamical version of the model obtained by taking

$$\Delta Z_j^{gh(t, \; t+1)} = \varepsilon_1^{gh} [D_j^{ght} - C_j^{ght}] \qquad (10.44)$$

$$\Delta p_j^{gh(t, \; t+1)} = \pm \varepsilon_2^{gh} [D_j^{ght} - C_j^{ght}] p_j^{ght} \qquad (10.45)$$

$$\Delta r_j^{(t, \; t+1)} = \varepsilon_3 \sum_{gh} [D_j^{ght} - C_j^{ght}] r_j^t \qquad (10.46)$$

$$Z_j^{ght+1} = Z_j^{ght} + \Delta Z_j^{gh(t, \; t+1)} \qquad (10.47)$$

$$p_j^{ght+1} = p_j^{ght} + \Delta p_j^{gh(t, \; t+1)} \qquad (10.48)$$

$$r_j^{t+1} = r_j^t + \Delta r_j^{(t, \; t+1)} \qquad (10.49)$$

The potential advantage of this model relative to that of subsection 10.3.1 is that it can potentially explain a much wider range of spatial patterns and modes of development for services. Consider the following examples:

   (i) The main results from previous work will carry over: high α_4^{gh} and β^{gh} will mean fewer, larger (g, h) facilities; and vice versa.
   (ii) The α_1 term will determine the extent to which con-sumers generate larger agglomerations of (g, h) clusters.
   (iii) There will be much variation in pattern in relation to variation in elements of the cost function, C_j^{gh}, partic-ularly with nonlinearities associated with economies and

diseconomies of scale.

(iv) Of particular interest in this disaggregated version of the model will be the variation in pattern brought about by h-variations in these elements. The model should provide the basis, for example, for explaining the increasing importance of the out-of-town superstore.

It is at this point that it is useful to return briefly to the issue of "shops in a zone" versus the identification of individual shops. Some large stores are now so important that it would be valuable if they could be identified individually, and this could in principle be achieved by suitable h-definitions. An alternative is to work with an array like $\{N_g^h\}$, the number of shops of type h in j or prime variables, and to construct $\{Z_j^{gh}\}$ from those.

10.3.3 An example of a public sector model

The first point to emphasise is that the models developed in subsections 10.3.1 and 10.3.2 - particularly the equilibrium models - are often applicable to public sector problems as well as to private sector ones. Attractiveness factors and cost functions would have to be redefined, of course, but there is no difficulty in principle. Another qualification is that the equilibrium solution may be less relevant than usual. In an application to health or education, for example, there may be institutional constraints which inhibit moves in that direction. In such a case, Z_j's have to be taken as given, possibly as planned, and it is useful then to develop performance indicators among which may be measures of "distance" from equlibrium and others related to stability. So even in such a case, the connection of the spatial interaction models to dynamical systems theory is a useful one.

It can also be useful to apply the h-sector disaggregated

model to public sector problems. For example, to education: g's may represent different kinds of courses, and the h's different kinds of educational institution which supply them. In the rest of this subsection, however, we consider an aggregate case, using education as an example, which enables us to illustrate an alternative method for service sector modelling, still within the same broad theoretical framework: that is, mathematical programming.

Coelho and Wilson (1976, 1977) (and see Coelho, Williams and Wilson, 1978) showed that it was possible to embed spatial interaction models within overall mathematical programming frameworks. Indeed, the models which have been described in this chapter can be formulated in this way. Usually it is less convenient. A nonlinear mathematical programming package has to be used and these consume a lot of computer time. However, there are circumstances where the MP formulation is valuable: in particular, where it is useful to impose additional constraints on the $\{Z_j\}$ or $\{Z_j^g\}$ variables. This is particularly straightforward if these are linear constraints.

In the rest of this subsection, we offer one example - an aggregate problem in educational planning. For more details, and specification of a disaggregated model, see Wilson and Crouchley (1984) and Irwin and Wilson (1985). For an account of the greater variety of service sector models which can be generated in this way, see Wilson et al (1981, Chapters 4, 7 and 8).

To illustrate the argument, we return to the aggregate model of Chapter 3 as an example. The mathematical programming model which underpins that (as we saw with the Lagrangian (3.35)) is

$$\underset{\{T_{ij}, Z_j\}}{\text{Max}} \quad M = -\sum_{ij} T_{ij}(\log T_{ij} - 1) \qquad (10.50)$$

subject to

$$\sum_j T_{ij} = O_i \tag{10.51}$$

$$\sum_i T_{ij} = C_j \tag{10.52}$$

$$\sum_{ij} T_{ij} \log Z_j = H \tag{10.53}$$

$$\sum_{ij} T_{ij} c_{ij} = C \tag{10.54}$$

For education purposes, it seems best to have a simple quasi-doubly constrained model and this can be achieved by replacing (10.52) and (10.53) by

$$\sum_i T_{ij} = Z_j \tag{10.55}$$

We then need to add more information in the form of additional constraints or new terms in the objective function to allow the $\{Z_j\}$ pattern to be determined. First, for this kind of public sector problem we need to replace the $C_j = D_j$ "market" mechanism by a constraint which simply ensures that the total budget, say B, is spent. This also allows any nonlinearities in the cost function to be included: let $h_j(Z_j)$ be the budget needed for running a size Z_j school in j, and then $\sum_j h_j(W_j) = B$. We also need a term which reflects the benefits of school-size - for example, a school needing to be above a minimum size to supply an adequate curriculum. Let $f(Z_j)$ be a measure of benefits per pupil of a school of size Z_j. Then this can be added into the objective function and the modified model becomes

$$\max_{\{T_{ij}, Z_j\}} M = -\sum_{ij} T_{ij}(\log T_{ij} - 1) + \sum_i Z_j f(Z_j) \tag{10.56}$$

subject to

$$\sum_j T_{ij} = O_i \qquad (10.57)$$

which ensures that all pupils find a place somewhere,

$$\sum_i T_{ij} = Z_j \qquad (10.58)$$

which ensures that all pupil places in schools are used,

$$\sum_{ij} T_{ij} c_{ij} = C \qquad (10.59)$$

which determines the β parameter in the spatial interaction model and the amount of "cross-handling", and

$$\sum_j h_j(Z_j) = B \qquad (10.60)$$

which is the budget constraint.

Extensive numerical experiments have been carried out with this model by Wilson and Crouchley (1984) and Irwin and Wilson (1985). It is also worth re-emphasising one of the advantages of this formulation: it is easy to add further constraints. For example, if existing sites owned by the education authority were the only ones which could be used, a set of constraints

$$\sum_j s Z_j \leq L_j$$

could be added, where s is the minimum amount of land needed per pupil and L_j is the land supply at possible sites in j.

10.3.4 Further developments and alternative approaches

The spatial interaction model in its modern form, applied to services, has its origins in the work of Huff (1964) and Lakshmanan and Hansen (1965). There are many applications (cf Batty, 1971, Gibson and Pullen, 1972, Stetzer, 1976, Parkhurst and Roe, 1978, Chudzyńska, 1981) - many of the earlier ones reviewed in NEDO (1970) and Openshaw (1975). Huff (1966) used the model as a basis for location decisions within a simulation framework. The post-Harris and Wilson (1978) equilibrium model developments not already referred to include the work of Phiri (1980), Harris, Choukroun and Wilson (1982), Rijk and Vorst (1983-A, 1983-B), Kaashoek and Vorst (1984) and Chudzyńska and Slodkowski (1984). Different but related approaches can be seen in Tobler (1979) and White (1977) - the latter a simulation connecting iteration of the retail model to central place theory.

It may be useful for at least some sectors to use the alternative interaction model of Fotheringham (1983-A, 1983-B) which he himself has embedded into an equilibrium framework (Fotheringham, 1984).

There are alternative approaches to service sector modelling. For the principles of economic approaches, it is useful to refer back to Teitz (1968). A number of programming models have been developed, initially largely under the umbrella of location-allocation modelling (cf Bigman and ReVelle, 1979 and Hogg, 1968, for examples). Most of these approaches suffer from the implied spatial interaction model singling out only least-cost flows as in the transportation problem of linear programming. These restrictions can be lifted and more general mathematical programming methods developed - an example of which was offered in the preceding subsection. For a range of approaches, see Wilson et al (1981), Leonardi (1981-B), Roy and Brotchie (1984) and Roy and Johansson (1984). A particularly interesting task is to add an elastic demand component into these models as part of an appropriate price-dependence mechanism. This has been explored in different contexts by Wagner and Falkson (1975), Erlenkotter (1977), Sheppard (1981), Curry and Sheppard (1982) and Curry (1984). Empirical evidence on price variations has been presented by Parker (1979) and O'Connor and Parker (1982).

A further alternative basis for service-sector modelling is provided by statistical methods. These range from application of logit models (Miller and Lerman, 1979, 1981, Recker and Kostynuik, 1978, and Koppelmann and Hansen, 1978) to a range of other methods - McCarthy (1980), Beavon and Hay (1977), Hay and Johnston (1979) and Timmermans (1981). Some attention has been paid to problems of cognition of service opportunities (Spencer, 1980). It should be emphasised that the interaction part of any of these models could be replaced - say by a logit model - without substantially affecting the main ideas of the locational analysis.

There are many applications to a range of sectors other than retailing. Examples include health (Morrill and Earickson, 1969, Morrill and Kelley, 1970, Mayhew and Leonardi, 1982, Clarke and Wilson, 1984-C), education (as in 10.3.3 above and Bach, 1980, 1981), and waste disposal (Schultz, 1969, Helms and Clark, 1971).

Excellent reviews of model developments in the whole area are provided by Leonardi (1981-A, 1981-B).

10.4 Summary: alternative models for different kinds of application

In Section 10.3 we presented three examples of service models in some detail. The first two illustrated the application of principles of model design to two different levels of resolution; the third showed how to use a different technique for a different kind of system. By using the principles enunciated in Sections 10.1 and 10.3, it would be possible to lengthen the list of examples considerably. It is hoped that the combination of principles and examples which have been presented will facilitate the building of a model for a wide range of circumstances.

The likely categories of application of the model are largely described by the examples, but we can add some detail and indicate directions towards some easy extensions to different kinds of examples.

(i) The aggregate or g-disaggregated cases

In the aggregate case, the only point to note is that inevitably the treatment of the cost function will be very coarse; this and related functions can only be regarded as "indices" because there is such diversity within the aggregates. However, this is the level of resolution at which we are typically forced to work in building comprehensive models. Many of the same points can usually be made for the g-disaggregated model, since the categories will usually be broad - like the three used by Lowry (1964). However, there is one obvious exception in this case: such a model could be developed for a single fine-scale sector with some realism.

(ii) The (g-h)-disaggregated model

This will usually demand too much detail to be useable in a comprehensive model. Its main use, therefore, will be in cases where a group of finely-defined sectors is to be modelled - a fine subdivision of retailing is an obvious example.

(iii) Mathematical programming

It is useful to know that the stock equilibrium model can be represented as a mathematical programme. This is particularly useful when the sector being modelled demands a mechanism involving constraints which cannot easily

be handled in the conventional iterative scheme. However, as
with case (ii) above, it is more likely to be applicable to
single sector modelling, or to subcategories within a sector.

The extension to be added to all these cases is this: an
alternative mode for running one of these models is to take
"facilities in zone j" not as a composite but as individual
organisational units: shops, hospitals, schools, or whatever.
This is obviously more feasible for a sector like hospitals,
where the numbers are relatively small, than shops. This,
however, leads to a further interesting idea for sectors like
the latter: to model mixed systems of zones and shops where
appropriate. The only difficulty in principle is to scale
one of the two sets of attractiveness factors so that elements
of the two sets are comparable. Such a scaling factor could
become a model parameter.

Chapter 11

SERVICES 2: A MASTER EQUATION APPROACH

G. Haag

11.1 Introduction

In this chapter, we describe a service-sector model on the
basis of a master equation approach. We will here not use
any equilibrium assumption in deriving the fundamental dynamic
equations of motion for the relevant macrovariables of the
system. A discrete zone system consisting of L-zones is used.
We assume that the N members of the population may have their
residence in any one zone and use the service-sector in any
other zone they want to.

   This individual decision process is motivated by optimiz-
ing their utilities. For a given housing location i, optimization is with respect to the services, $\{Z_j\}$, available in the
different zones, j = 1 ... L, and to the cost of travel from
i to j, c_{ij}. The resulting expenditure or population flows
between the different zones generate a revenue attracted to
each zone, $D_j(t)$, j = 1 ... L.

   Changes in the supply side, the facility stock $Z_j(t)$ are
made in response to changes in demand and vice versa. The
speed of adjustment of the facility stock and the mobility of
the individuals in service-sector choice may be quite different. But, because the speeds are finite, the service-
sector system always lags behind equilibrium.

   The demand side and the supply side are highly interdependent on each other. The utility of individuals on the demand side depends on the existing facility stock. The facility stock, on the other hand, depends on decision processes of investors to expand or reduce. There is an underlying profit optimization procedure which is influenced by the demand.

The individual decision processes are stochastic. Thus the service-sector as a whole cannot be fully deterministic. Both the demand and supply sides are therefore described by equations of motion for the evolution of a probability distribution over its possible states. This can again be achieved by using a master equation approach. This will be done in the following sections.

What we gain are dynamic equations of motion for both the demand and supply side and a connection to their microeconomic foundation. This enables us to formulate an estimation procedure for the parameters introduced even if the system is not in equilibrium. Under certain conditions, the theory of Wilson (Chapter 10) can be derived from this more fundamental point of view. This also suggests direction of extension.

The notation used in this chapter is as far as possible the same as those of Wilson in Chapters 3 and 10. To avoid repeating references already cited, the reader is asked to use the bibliography in relation to the citations in Chapters 3 and 10.

11.2 Modelling of Decision Processes on the Demand Side

Let $n_{ij}(t)$ be the number of individuals having residence in zone i, i = 1 ... L, and using facilities in j. Then

$$n_i(t) = \sum_{j=1}^{L} n_{ij}(t) \qquad (11.1)$$

is the number of individuals living in i; and

$$m_j(t) = \sum_{j=1}^{L} n_{ij}(t) \qquad (11.2)$$

is the number of people using the facilities in j. The total number of individuals is

$$N(t) = \sum_{i=1}^{L} n_i(t) = \sum_{j=1}^{L} m_j(t) \qquad (11.3)$$

Then a money (expenditure) flow, $T_{ij}(t)$, can be related to the population flow $n_{ij}(t)$. This flow forms the basis of a service-sector model. The expenditure or population flows may lead to an imbalance between supply and demand of given facilities in each region j. An adjustment process and/or reorientation process of the service-sector then begins.

In many cases it is reasonable to assume

$$T_{ij}(t) = g(t)n_{ij}(t) \qquad (11.4)$$

where the factor g(t) can be determined by a comparison of the total stocks

$$T(t) = \sum_{i,j=1}^{L} T_{ij}(t) = g(t).N(t) \qquad (11.5)$$

g(t) can be interpreted as an average of individual needs. Following the notation of Wilson in Chapter 10, we introduce the demand or "needs" O_i in region i as

$$O_i(t) = \sum_{j=1}^{L} T_{ij}(t) \qquad (11.6)$$

and interpret the $T_{ij}(t)$ as the amount of O_i which is met at j, at time t. Then

$$D_j(t) = \sum_{i=1}^{L} T_{ij}(t) \qquad (11.7)$$

is the amount of revenue attracted to j (assuming O_i is measured in suitable units).

Let $Z_j(t)$ represent service-sector provision at time t in zone j. Then changes in the service-sector, $\dot{Z}_j(t)$, influence the expenditure flow of the system. This feedback leads to highly nonlinear interactions for all kinds of economic decisions. Since these decision processes must be described at a stochastic level, we introduce the socio-configuration $\underset{\sim}{n}(t)$

$$\underset{\sim}{n}(t) = \{n_{11}(t), n_{12}(t), \ldots, n_{1L}(t), n_{21}(t), n_{22}(t), \ldots,$$

$$n_{2L}(t), \ldots, n_{ij}(t), \ldots, n_{LL}(t)\} \qquad (11.8)$$

This socio-configuration describes a possible realization of a flow pattern in an abstract configuration space $\mathcal{L}$, $\underset{\sim}{n}(t)\varepsilon\mathcal{L}$.

Due to decision processes of people changing their residential location or using facilities of another region, the actual socio-configuration changes in the course of time.

The number of transitions (in configuration space $\mathcal{L}$) due to a "decision process" from a state having residence in k using facilities in l to a state of residence in i and using facilities in j is assumed proportional to $n_{kl}(t)$ times an individual "transition probability", $p_{ij,kl}(\underset{\sim}{n})$. This can be written in the usual notation (cf Chapters 4 and 8) as

$$w_{ij,kl}(\underset{\sim}{n} + \underset{\sim}{k}; \underset{\sim}{n}) = \begin{cases} n_{kl}(t)p_{ij,kl}(\underset{\sim}{n}) \\ \quad \text{for } \underset{\sim}{k} = (\ldots 0 \ldots 1_{ij} \ldots 0 \ldots (-1)_{kl} \ldots 0 \ldots \\ 0 \text{ for all other combinations} \end{cases}$$

$$(11.9)$$

This means, of course, that we assume independent decision processes of the individuals. A process such as (11.9) changes the socio-configuration (11.8). It is our aim to derive equations of motion for the behaviour of the most probable socio-configuration.

The equation of motion is the master equation for the probability $P(\underline{n}; t)$ to find the socio-configuration $\underline{n}$ to be realized at time t.

$$\frac{dP(n; t)}{dt} = \sum_{\substack{i,j \\ k,l}}^{L} w_{ij,kl}(\underline{n}; \underline{n} + \underline{k})P(\underline{n} + \underline{k}; t) -$$

$$\sum_{\substack{i,j \\ k,l}}^{L} w_{ij,kl}(\underline{n} + \underline{k}; \underline{n})P(\underline{n}; t) \qquad (11.10)$$

The flow rate (11.9) then has to be inserted into the master equation.

In order to obtain explicit results, the individual decision processes $p_{ij,kl}(\underline{n})$ have to be modelled. A reasonable and flexible assumption for the individual transition probabilities is

$$p_{ij,kl}(\underline{n}) = e^{v_{ij}(\underline{n}) - v_{kl}(\underline{n})} \cdot \delta_{ij,kl} \qquad (11.11)$$

for a change from residence in k using the service sector in l to living in i and using facilities in j. The $v_{ij}(\underline{n})$ can be interpreted as "utilities" for living in i and using the service sector in j. Moreover the utilities $v_{ij}(\underline{n})$ have two subscripts since they relate to competition in both housing and service sectors. The coefficients $\delta_{ij,kl}(> 0)$ describe the corresponding mobilities for this decision process. At each time, two choices are now possible for an individual: changing residence, or using services of a different region. We assume the time interval is sufficiently short to exclude the joint occurrence of both types of events. Then

$$\delta_{ij,kl} = \begin{cases} \nu(t), & \text{for } (k,\,l) \rightarrow (i,\,l) \\ \mu(t), & \text{for } (k,\,l) \rightarrow (k,\,j) \\ 0, & \text{for all other combinations} \end{cases} \qquad (11.12)$$

The parameter $\nu(t)$ describes the housing mobility, the parameter $\mu(t)$ the mobility of the individuals in relation to services of different regions or zones.

To keep at as general a level as possible, assumptions concerning the fundamental structure of the utility function $v_{ij}(\underset{\sim}{n})$ will be introduced later.

11.3 The Mean Value Equations

From the master equation (11.10) the most interesting structure of the mean value equations can be obtained. The mean values are defined as

$$\overline{n}_{ij}(t) = \sum_{\underset{\sim}{n}} n_{ij} P(\underset{\sim}{n};\, t) \qquad (11.13)$$

We multiply the left-hand side and right-hand side of (11.10) with n_{ij} and sum over all possible configurations. This yields - using the unessential assumption $\overline{f}(\overline{n}) \simeq f(\overline{n})$ - with (11.9), (11.11), (11.12) for the approximate mean value equations

$$\dot{\overline{n}}_{ij}(t) = \mu(t)\{ \sum_{k=1}^{L} e^{v_{ij}-v_{ik}} \overline{n}_{ik} - \sum_{k=1}^{L} e^{v_{ik}-v_{ij}} \overline{n}_{ij} \}$$

$$+ \nu(t)\{ \sum_{k=1}^{L} e^{v_{ij}-v_{kj}} \overline{n}_{kj} - \sum_{k=1}^{L} e^{v_{kj}-v_{ij}} \overline{n}_{ij} \};$$

$$i,j = 1 \ldots L \qquad (11.14)$$

The first line describes changes in the behaviour of individuals in the service sector, the second line the dynamics in the housing sector. In general (11.14) will be a system of L^2 coupled nonlinear differential equations. The $(v_{ij} - v_{kl})$ measure the competition between the different "states" (i, j) and (k, l). Using (11.4), it is also possible to transform (11.14) into a system of equations of motion for the expenditure flows in the spatial system.

Using (11.4) in (11.14) and assuming that the factor g is independent of time, we obtain the dynamic equations of motion for the flow matrix $T_{ij}(t)$:

$$\dot{T}_{ij}(t) = \mu(t)\{ \sum_{k=1}^{L} e^{v_{ij}-v_{ik}} T_{ik}(t) - \sum_{k=1}^{L} e^{v_{ik}-v_{ij}} T_{ij}(t)\}$$

$$+ \nu(t)\{ \sum_{k=1}^{L} e^{v_{ij}-v_{kj}} T_{kj}(t) - \sum_{k=1}^{L} e^{v_{kj}-v_{ij}} T_{ij}(t)\};$$

$$j = 1 \ldots L \qquad (11.15)$$

Both the competition in the service sector and in the housing sector enter into the dynamic equations. From (11.15) the dynamic equations for the demand $D_j(t)$ of region j can easily be obtained:

$$\dot{D}_j(t) = \mu(t) \sum_{k,i}^{L} \{e^{v_{ij}} T_{ik} e^{-v_{ik}} - e^{v_{ik}} T_{ij} e^{-v_{ij}}\}$$

$$+ \nu(t) \sum_{k,i} \{e^{v_{ij}} T_{kj} e^{-v_{kj}} - e^{v_{kj}} T_{ij} e^{-v_{ij}}\}$$

$$j = 1 \ldots L \qquad (11.16)$$

11.4 The Exact Stationary Solution of the Mean Value Equations

We consider the stationary version of (11.14) that is, with $\dot{n}_{ij} = 0$.

$$0 = \mu\{ \sum_{k=1}^{L} e^{\hat{v}_{ij}-\hat{v}_{ik}} \hat{n}_{ik} - \sum_{k=1}^{L} e^{\hat{v}_{ik}-\hat{v}_{ij}} \hat{n}_{ij} \} \text{ (service)}$$

$$+ \nu\{ \sum_{k=1}^{L} e^{\hat{v}_{ij}-\hat{v}_{kj}} \hat{n}_{kj} - \sum_{k=1}^{L} e^{\hat{v}_{kj}-\hat{v}_{ij}} \hat{n}_{ij} \} \text{ (housing)}$$

$$(11.17)$$

where $\hat{n}_{ij}$, $\hat{v}_{ij}$ represent the stationary values of the flow matrix and utilities, respectively.

By insertion of

$$\hat{n}_{ij} = C\, e^{2\hat{v}_{ij}(\hat{n})} \tag{11.18}$$

into (11.17) it can easily be proved, that (11.18) is the exact stationary solution. The constant C is determined by (11.3). Then

$$\hat{n}_{ij} = N \frac{e^{2\hat{v}_{ij}(\underset{\sim}{\hat{n}})}}{\sum_{k,l}^{L} e^{2\hat{v}_{kl}(\underset{\sim}{\hat{n}})}} \tag{11.19}$$

Therefore, the stationary flow matrix $\hat{n}_{ij}$ or $\hat{T}_{ij}$ depends on the utility $\hat{v}_{ij}(\underset{\sim}{\hat{n}})$ to live in i and using services in j. Since this result is obtained without making use of any assumption concerning the functional shape and the set of variables introduced, (11.14) and (11.19) are rather general. Equation (11.19) can be seen as a spatial interaction model. But since our model based on the master equation approach ends up with the same structure for the stationary solution as random utility theory did, it seems justified to interpret $v_{ij}(\underset{\sim}{n})$ as a "utility" function even if our system is out of equilibrium.

Equation (11.18) can also be written in the more convenient form by use of (11.1)

$$\hat{n}_{ij} = \hat{n}_i \; \frac{e^{2\hat{v}_{ij}}}{\displaystyle\sum_k e^{2\hat{v}_{ik}}} \tag{11.20}$$

or with (11.4), (11.6)

$$\hat{T}_{ij} = \hat{O}_i \cdot \hat{A}_i \cdot e^{2\hat{v}_{ij}(\underline{\underline{T}})} \tag{11.21}$$

with the abbreviation

$$\hat{A}_i = \frac{1}{\displaystyle\sum_{k=1}^{L} e^{2\hat{v}_{ik}}} \tag{11.22}$$

11.5 Modelling of the Utility Function

In this section we now introduce and test different assumptions concerning the utility function v_{ij}. First, let us note that only utility differences are important as driving motivations in the decision process of individuals. Therefore, without loss of generality, we can scale the utilities as follows:

$$\sum_{i,j=1}^{L} v_{ij}(\underset{\sim}{n}) = 0 \tag{11.23}$$

Different assumptions about the functional shape of the utility functions can now be tested. It follows immediately from (11.21) that for

$$e^{2\hat{v}_{ij}} = \hat{Z}_j^{\alpha} e^{-\beta c_{ij}}$$

or in other words, for

$$v_{ij}^{(w)} = \frac{1}{2} \alpha \ln Z_j + U_i - \frac{1}{2} \beta c_{ij} \tag{11.24}$$

the constrained spatial interaction model of Wilson (Chapter

Services - Master Equations

9), is obtained where Z_j describes the facility stock, U_i the preference for housing in i:

$$\hat{T}_{ij}^{(w)} = \hat{A}_i \hat{O}_i \hat{Z}_j^\alpha e^{-\beta c_{ij}} \tag{11.25}$$

with

$$\hat{A}_i = 1/\sum_k Z_k^\alpha e^{-\beta c_{ik}} \tag{11.26}$$

it is worthwhile remarking that this result is independent of the housing attractivity U_i of the different regions i.

Another reasonable assumption (Haag) is

$$v_{ij}^{(H)} = \frac{1}{2} \alpha Z_j - \frac{1}{2} \gamma Z_j^2 + U_i - \frac{1}{2} \beta c_{ij} \tag{11.27}$$

and this yields the stationary flow relation

$$\hat{T}_{ij}^{(H)} = \hat{A}_i \hat{O}_i e^{\alpha \hat{Z}_j - \gamma \hat{Z}_j^2 - \beta c_{ij}} \tag{11.28}$$

with

$$\hat{A}_i = 1/\sum_k e^{\alpha \hat{Z}_k - \gamma \hat{Z}_k^2 - \beta c_{ik}} \tag{11.29}$$

By insertion of (11.24) or (11.27) in (11.15), respectively, the temporal change of demand due to housing and service competition by consideration of transportation costs is obtained. Therefore the demand side of the service sector is completed.

11.6 The Master Equation for the Facility Stock

On the supply side the stock dynamics of facilities $Z_j(t)$, at each possible location is dependent (among other factors) on the decisions of investors to increase or decrease the scale of facilities. Since the stock variable Z_j is a stochastic variable, too, we again choose a master equation approach to introduce dynamics.

Thus, the facility-configuration

$$\underset{\sim}{Z}(t) = (Z_1(t),\ Z_2(t),\ \ldots,\ Z_j(t),\ \ldots,\ Z_L(t)) \qquad (11.30)$$

is introduced, which describes one possible realization of a facility distribution $P(\underset{\sim}{Z};\ t)$. The stock dynamics is treated as a birth/death process. Hence, the appropriate master equation is:

$$\frac{dP(\underset{\sim}{Z};\ t)}{dt} = \sum_{i=1}^{L} \{(E_i^{-1} - 1)w_{i+}(\underset{\sim}{Z} + \underset{\sim}{k};\ \underset{\sim}{Z})$$

$$+ (E_i - 1)w_{i-}(\underset{\sim}{Z} + \underset{\sim}{k};\ \underset{\sim}{Z})\}P(\underset{\sim}{Z};\ t) \qquad (11.31)$$

with the translation operator

$$E_i^{\pm 1}f(Z_1,\ \ldots,\ Z_i,\ \ldots,\ Z_L) = f(Z_1,\ \ldots,\ (Z_i \pm 1),\ \ldots,\ Z_L)$$

$$(11.32)$$

We are interested in getting information about the behaviour of the most probable spatial distribution of the facilities $Z_j(t)$. The $w_{i+}(\underset{\sim}{Z} + \underset{\sim}{k};\ \underset{\sim}{Z})$, $w_{i-}(\underset{\sim}{Z} + \underset{\sim}{k};\ \underset{\sim}{Z})$ are the birth and death rates, respectively. We now multiply the left-hand side and the right-hand side of (11.31) by Z_j and sum up over all configurations. This yields

$$\dot{\overline{Z}}_j(t) = w_{j+}(\underset{\sim}{\overline{Z}}) - w_{j-}(\underset{\sim}{\overline{Z}}) \qquad (11.33)$$

where we have assumed that the most probable value of Z is comparable to the mean value $\overline{Z}_j(t)$

$$\overline{Z}_j(t) = \sum_{Z} Z_j \cdot P(Z; t) \qquad (11.34)$$

In the following we omit the bar $\overline{Z} \to Z$ to avoid an overloaded notation.

11.7 Birth/Death Rates for the Facility Stock

We assume that the propensity to increase (decrease) the facility stock of a region depends on the demand $D_j(t)$ and cost $C_j(t)$ of providing Z_j at t. Therefore, it seems to be reasonable to assume the following functional relationship for the birth/death rates which is flexible enough to comprise a lot of observable effects

birth-rate

$$w_{j+}(Z + k; Z) = \begin{cases} \frac{1}{2} f_j(Z) \exp \phi_j(Z) \text{ for} \\ k = (0, \ldots, 1_j, 0, \ldots) \\ 0 \text{ otherwise} \end{cases} \qquad (11.35)$$

and

death-rate

$$w_{j-}(Z + k; Z) = \begin{cases} \frac{1}{2} f_j(Z) \exp[-\phi_j(Z)] \text{ for} \\ k = (0, \ldots, (-1)_j, 0, \ldots) \\ 0 \text{ otherwise} \end{cases} \qquad (11.36)$$

with

$$f_j(Z) > 0$$

The first factor $\frac{1}{2} f_j(\underset{\sim}{Z})$ has the meaning of a speed parameter of adjustment. In many cases it is reasonable to treat the speed parameter as a constant

$$\frac{1}{2} f_j(\underset{\sim}{Z}) = \frac{1}{2} \varepsilon \qquad (11.37)$$

independent of the specific region. Another plausible assumption reads

$$\frac{1}{2} f_j(\underset{\sim}{Z}) = \frac{1}{2} \varepsilon \, \underset{\sim}{Z_j} \qquad (11.38)$$

This means that the speed of adjustment depends on the scale of the facilities.

The function $\phi_j(\underset{\sim}{Z})$ takes into account the imbalance between cost of supply and the revenue attracted to facilities in the region under consideration. We assume:

$$\phi_j(\underset{\sim}{Z}) = \chi(D_j(\underset{\sim}{Z}) - C_j(\underset{\sim}{Z})) \qquad (11.39)$$

If there is an economic surplus $D_j > C_j$ it is more likely that the facility stock is expanded; and vice versa (see Figure 11.1).

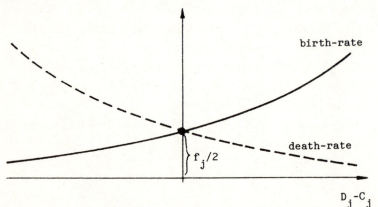

Figure 11.1: Graphical representation of the birth and death rates

Services - Master Equations

11.8 Mean Value Equations for the Facility Stock

We insert (11.35), (11.36) into (11.33) and obtain the mean value equations for the facility stock

$$\dot{Z}_j(t) = f_j(\underset{\sim}{Z}) \sin h\, \phi_j(\underset{\sim}{Z}); \quad j = 1 \ldots L \tag{11.40}$$

The stationary points are obtained from

$$\hat{\phi}_j(\underset{\sim}{Z}) = 0; \quad j = 1 \ldots L \tag{11.41}$$

Near equilibrium $|\phi_j| \ll 1$ the right-hand side of (11.40) can be expanded into a Taylor series yielding the approximate equations

$$\dot{Z}_j(t) \simeq f_j(\underset{\sim}{Z}) \cdot \phi_j(Z); \quad j = 1 \ldots L \tag{11.42}$$

which together with (11.39) yielding the Harris and Wilson (1978) hypothesis

$$\dot{Z}_j(t) \simeq \varepsilon(D_j - C_j)f(Z_j) \tag{11.43}$$

In this sense the Harris and Wilson model (1978) is completely incorporated into this framework. But, on the other hand, the microeconomic foundation of (11.40) and (11.43) enables us to estimate the parameters of the model even if we are out of equilibrium. This estimation procedure will be outlined in Section 11.9.

By substituting (11.37), (11.39) in (11.40) yields

$$\dot{Z}_j(t) = \varepsilon Z_j^{\gamma} \sin h\, [\lambda\, (D_j(\underset{\sim}{Z}) - C_j(\underset{\sim}{Z}))]; \quad j = 1 \ldots L$$
$$\gamma = 0,\, 1 \tag{11.44}$$

The dynamics of the facility stock $Z_j(t)$ (11.44) on the supply side together with dynamic equations for the demand (11.15), (11.16) complete our dynamic system. The stationary solution of (11.44) reads

$$\hat{D}_j(\hat{\underset{\sim}{Z}}) = \hat{C}_j(\hat{\underset{\sim}{Z}}) \tag{11.45}$$

The function $C_j(\underset{\sim}{Z})$ represents the cost of providing Z_j at region j. $C_j(\underset{\sim}{Z})$ has often been taken as the linear function

$$C_j(\underset{\sim}{Z}) = k_j . Z_j \tag{11.46}$$

for a suitable set of constants, k_j (see Chapter 10).

11.9 Estimation of the Parameters

We assume that for a finite time series $t = 1 \ldots T$ the empirical quantities listed below can be observed

$n_{ij}^e(t)$ — population flow between housing and service sector

$\dot{n}_{ij}^e(t) \equiv m_{ij}^e(t)$ — change of population flow

$Z_j^e(t)$ — facility stock

$w_{i+}^e(t)$ — birth rate in the facility stock

$W_{o-}^e(t)$ — death rate in the facility stock

$c_{ij}(t)$ — transport-cost matrix;

$$t = 1 \ldots T \tag{11.47}$$

It is reasonable to assume that the housing mobility ν will be

considerably slower than the shopping mobility μ of the population. Indeed decisions to buy in another shop can be taken
more easily than changing an apartment ($\nu \ll \mu$). Alternatively
we could assume that the system is in "equilibrium" with
respect to the housing market. Then from (11.14) it follows that

$$\dot{n}_{ij}(t) = \mu(t)\{ \sum_{k=1}^{L} e^{v_{ij}-v_{ik}} n_{ik} - \sum_{k=1}^{L} e^{v_{ik}-v_{ij}} n_{ij}\};$$

$$i, j = 1 \ldots L \qquad\qquad (11.48)$$

since the different residential areas are no longer coupled.
It is now our aim to estimate the shopping mobility parameter
$\mu(t)$ and the preference parameters $v_{il}(t)$, $i,l = 1, \ldots, L$.
The time series of the parameters are now to be determined by
the requirement that the approximate mean value equation
(11.48) describes the dynamics of the system as precisely as
possible. Since a discrete set of empirical values (11.47)
is used, the equation of motion yields a difference equation
instead of a differential equation for the estimation
procedure

$$n_{ij}^{e}(t + 1) - n_{ij}^{e}(t) =$$

$$\mu(t) \sum_{k=1}^{L} \{ e^{v_{ij}(t)-v_{ik}(t)} n_{ik}^{e}(t) - e^{v_{ik}(t)-v_{ij}(t)} n_{ij}^{e}(t)\};$$

$$i,j = 1 \ldots L \qquad\qquad (11.49)$$

Assuming that the parameters $\mu(t)$, $v_{ik}(t)$, $i,k = 1, \ldots, L$
are varying with time only slowly, the optimal set of the
parameters can be found by setting the requirement that the
functional

$$F_t(\mu(t), \,_{il}(t)) =$$

$$\frac{1}{L(2\tau+1)} \sum_{t'=t-\tau}^{t+\tau} \sum_{j=1}^{L} [(n_{ij}^e(t' + 1) - n_{ij}^e(t'))$$

$$- \mu(t) \sum_{k=1}^{L} \{e^{v_{ij}(t)-v_{ik}(t)} n_{ik}^e(t') - e^{v_{ik}(t)-v_{ij}(t)} n_{ij}^e(t')\}]^2$$

$$(11.50)$$

be minimized in the interval $t' \varepsilon [t-\tau, \ t+\tau]$.

This procedure yields a set of two nonlinear equations for the set of parameters

$$\frac{\delta F_t[\mu(t), \ v_{il}(t)]}{\delta\mu(t)} = 0$$

$$\frac{\delta F_t[\mu(t), \ v_{il}(t)]}{\delta v_{il}(t)} = 0 \qquad\qquad (11.51)$$

Using an appropriate computer algorithm the unique solution of (11.51) can easily be obtained.

It is now an interesting point to link the estimated "utility" functions $v_{ij}(t)$, $t = 1, \ldots, T$ to the assumptions (11.24) and (11.27) of Wilson and Haag, respectively $(U_i = 0, \ \gamma = 0)$

$$v_{ij}^{(W)}(t) = \frac{1}{2} \alpha \ln Z_j - \frac{1}{2} \beta c_{ij} \qquad\qquad (11.52)$$

$$v_{ij}^{(H)}(t) = \frac{1}{2} \alpha Z_j - \frac{1}{2} \beta c_{ij} \qquad\qquad (11.53)$$

The determination of α, β are explained in the equations (11.52). From (11.52) it is easily obtained that

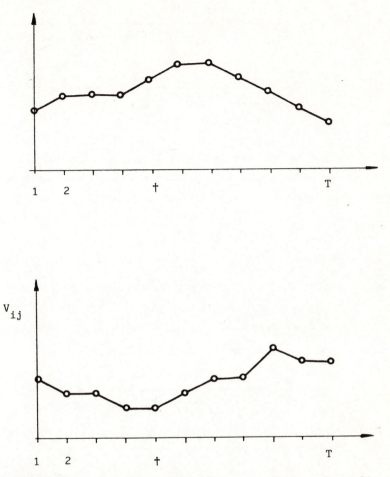

Possible graphical representation of results

$$(v_{ij}^{(w)} + v_{ji}^{(w)}) = \frac{1}{2} \alpha[\ln Z_j + \ln Z_i] - \frac{1}{2} \beta(c_{ij} + c_{ji})$$

$$(v_{ij}^{(w)} - v_{ji}^{(w)}) = \frac{1}{2} \alpha[\ln Z_j - \ln Z_i] - \frac{1}{2} \beta(c_{ij} - c_{ji})$$

Then we obtain for $\alpha^{(w)}$, $\beta^{(w)}$ by insertion of empirical values. This leads to

$$\alpha_{ij}^{(w)}(t) = 2\frac{(v_{ij}-v_{ji})(c_{ij}+c_{ji}) - (v_{ij}+v_{ji})(c_{ij}-c_{ji})}{(\ln Z_j^{(e)}-\ln Z_i^{(e)})(c_{ij}+c_{ji})-(\ln Z_j^{(e)}+\ln Z_i^{(e)})(c_{ij}-c_{ji})}$$

$$\beta_{ij}^{(w)}(t) = 2\frac{(v_{ij}-v_{ji})(\ln Z_j^{(e)}+\ln Z_i^{(e)})-(v_{ij}+v_{ji})(\ln Z_j^{(e)}-\ln Z_i^{(e)})}{(c_{ij}+c_{ji})(\ln Z_j^{(e)}-\ln Z_i^{(e)})-(c_{ij}-c_{ji})(\ln Z_j^{(e)}+\ln Z_i^{(e)})}$$

$$(11.54)$$

Then we assume that α, β are global and time-independent parameters and we have to choose their spatial and temporal mean value instead of (11.54)

$$\alpha^{(w)} = \frac{1}{L^2 T} \sum_{t=1}^{T} \sum_{i,j}^{L} \alpha_{ij}^{(w)}(t)$$

$$(11.55)$$

$$\beta^{(w)} = \frac{1}{L^2 T} \sum_{t=1}^{T} \sum_{i,j}^{L} \beta_{ij}^{(w)}(t)$$

In an analogous manner we obtain from (11.53)

$$\alpha_{ij}^{(H)}(t) = 2\frac{(v_{ij}-v_{ji})(c_{ij}+c_{ji}) - (v_{ij}+v_{ji})(c_{ij}-c_{ji})}{(Z_j^{(e)}-Z_i^{(e)})(c_{ij}+c_{ji}) - (Z_j^{(e)}+Z_i^{(e)})(c_{ij}-c_{ji})}$$

$$\beta_{ij}^{(H)}(t) = 2\frac{(v_{ij}-v_{ji})(Z_j^{(e)}+Z_i^{(e)}) - (v_{ij}+v_{ji})(Z_j^{(e)}-Z_i^{(e)})}{(c_{ij}+C_{ji})(Z_j^{(e)}-Z_i^{(e)}) - (c_{ij}-c_{ji})(Z_j^{(e)}+Z_i^{(e)})}$$

$$(11.56)$$

and

$$\alpha^{(H)} = \frac{1}{L^2 T} \sum_{t} \sum_{i,j} \alpha_{ij}^{(H)}(t)$$

$$(11.57)$$

$$\beta^{(H)} = \frac{1}{L^2 T} \sum_{t} \sum_{i,j} \beta_{ij}^{(H)}(t)$$

It is worthwhile emphasizing that for a symmetric transport-cost matrix $c_{ij} = c_{ij}$, the relevant parameter $\alpha^{(w)}$, $\alpha^{(H)}$ does

not depend on the matrix c_{ij}. Therefore the important parameter α can be estimated without being influenced by the
inherent uncertainties of the c_{ij}. By insertion of the
estimated parameters (11.55), (11.57) in (11.52), (11.53),
respectively and comparison with estimated values of $v_{ij}(t)$,
for example by computation of the correlation coefficient,
one should be able to answer the question whether the assumption (11.52) or (11.53) is better justified. The variance of
the parameters α, β can also be determined. We can also
decide whether $\alpha > 1$ or $\alpha < 1$ without using stationarity
assumptions.

11.10 Estimation of Parameters on the Supply side

On the supply side, the relevant parameters to be calculated
are the k_j, ε and λ. We assume that the stock variable
$\underset{\sim}{Z^e}(t)$, $t = 1$, ..., T as well as the birth/death rates of the
facility stock, namely $w^e_{i+}(t)$, $w^e_{i-}(t)$, $t = 1$, ..., T are
empirically known.

$$w^{(e)}_{j+}(t) = \frac{1}{2}\, \varepsilon Z^\gamma_j(t) e^{\lambda(D_j(t) - k_j Z^e_j(t))} \tag{11.58}$$

$$w^{(e)}_{j-}(t) = \frac{1}{2}\, \varepsilon Z^\gamma_j(t) e^{-\lambda(D_j(t) - k_j Z^e_j(t))}\,; \tag{11.59}$$

$$t = 1 \ldots T$$
$$\gamma = 0,\ 1$$

where
$$D_j(t) = g \sum_{i=1}^{L} n^e_{ij}(t) \tag{11.60}$$

To determine the average individual need $g(t)$ according to
(11.5) only the observations (countings) of the total stock
$T(t)$, $N(t)$ are necessary.

It should be emphasised that we have $2L.T$ equations but
only $T+L+1$ unknown parameters (if λ, k_j are assumed to be

time-independent). We determine as a first step the time-scaling parameter $\varepsilon(t)$, by multiplication of (11.58), (11.59)

$$\varepsilon_j(t) = \frac{2}{Z_j^\gamma(t)}\sqrt{w_{j+}^e(t)w_{j-}^e(t)} \, ; \, \gamma = 0, \, 1$$

$$j = 1 \ldots L$$

$$t = 1 \ldots T \qquad (11.61)$$

Since we assume that $\varepsilon(t)$ is a global measure of the population in the system under consideration we are only interested in its spatial mean value

$$\varepsilon(t) = \frac{1}{L}\sum_{j=1}^{L}\varepsilon_j(t) \qquad (11.62)$$

Thus $\varepsilon(t)$ can be estimated without being influenced by the economic surplus function ϕ_j.

In a second step, we consider the quotient of (11.58), (11.59)

$$\frac{w_{j+}^e(t)}{w_{j-}^e(t)} = \exp[2\,\lambda(D_j(t) - k_j Z_j^e(t))]$$

Introducing the abbreviation

$$r_j(t) = \frac{1}{2}\ln\frac{w_{j+}^e(t)}{w_{j-}^e(t)} \, ; \quad j = 1 \ldots L, \, t = 1 \ldots T \quad (11.63)$$

we obtain the linear relation

$$r_j(t) = \lambda(D_j(t) - k_j Z_j^e(t)); \quad j = 1 \ldots L, \, t = 1 \ldots T$$

$$(11.64)$$

The parameters λ, k_j of the excess demand function $\phi_j(t)$ are then estimated using a least square procedure

$$G[\lambda, k_1] = \frac{1}{L.T} \sum_{t=1}^{T} \sum_{j=1}^{L} [r_j(t) - \lambda(D_j(t) - k_j Z_j^e(t))]^2$$

(11.65)

according to

$$\frac{\partial G}{\partial \lambda}[\lambda, k_1] = 0$$

(11.66)

$$\frac{\partial G}{\partial k_1}[\lambda, k_1] = 0; \quad 1 = 1 \ldots L$$

(11.67)

It is interesting that the estimation of the parameters λ, k_1 is independent of the estimation of the time-scaling parameter $\varepsilon(t)$.

If the rates $w_{j+}^e(t)$, $w_{j-}^e(t)$ are not empirically available, but their differences $\dot{Z}_j(t)$, we have obviously only L.T equations but still T+L+1 unknown parameters.

Chapter 12

THE LAND MARKET IN ECONOMIC URBAN MODELS

A. Anas

12.1 Introduction

The treatment of the land market in economic urban models
follows a simple and straightforward logic which can be
briefly examined. First, the land market part of a model
explains the transactions in land between land-owners and
developers who use land as an input in producing structures.
Second, the land market model determines the price of each
type of land in the urban economy. Third, the land market
model addresses the heterogeneity of land parcels within an
urban area by identifying these by location. Consequently
the quantity of land at each location is limited and treated
as a constraint. At the margin, however, the urban land
supply can be extended by introducing additional locations
which represent land claimed from other uses such as
agriculture.

There are two mathematical traditions for the treatment
of land in urban models. One which follows Alonso (1964) and
von Thünen (1826) is to treat land as a continuous "variable".
Another which is more common in the operational models of
Herbert and Stevens (1960) and Mills (1972-A), to cite two
examples, treats land as a discrete variable. The urban area
is divided into a finite number of zones ignoring intrazonal
locational decisions and thus treating each zone as a point

(at its centroid) but allocating to that point the land area
of the zone. In this Chapter we will confine ourselves to the
discrete models to stay within the style followed in this book.

A very basic principle in the treatment of the land market
is that payments to land can be treated as residuals after
taking into account payments to all other factors used in the
production of structures. Generally, it is not true that land
prices (or land rent) computed as such a residual equal the
marginal product of land (see Anas, 1978). This inequality
follows in models which treat structures as durable goods
supplied with less than perfect foresight of the future.

A second basic principle, related to the first, is that
each owner of land is a monopolist since location and other
features uniquely differentiate each parcel. The behavioural
principle assumed is that each landowner attempts to extract
the highest land price possible by selling or renting to the
highest bidder. With many bidders in competition with each
other, landowners succeed in this and thus the price of land
is determined as the upper envelope of bid prices. Thus, let
P_{ih} be the bid price of land use h for parcel i, then the land
price, P_i is given by

$$P_i = \max_h (0, P_{ih}, \forall h) \qquad (12.1)$$

Because of competition, the bid price of each land rises to
absorb all of that land use's profits in present value terms,
or more precisely all expected future profits from the land.
Thus,

$$P_{ih}^t = \int_t^\infty e^{-r(s-t)} [\hat{R}_i(s) - \hat{C}_i(s)] ds \qquad (12.2)$$

where r is the interest rate, $\hat{R}_i(s)$ is the expected revenue
from parcel i at time s and $\hat{C}_i(s)$ the expected cost of parcel
i at time s. The dynamic theory of land use under perfect

foresight has been developed by Fujita (1976).

Another important aspect of the treatment of the land market in economic urban models is whether the land market is "open" or "closed". An "open" land market means that landowners are treated as absentee. Thus the total land price is a benefit of the urban economy which is not remaining within the urban economy. It is important to add this total land price to the consumer surplus or other measure of internal benefit generated for the consumers of land when the economy is open. When the economy is "closed" then landowners are themselves consumers in the economy and receive a share of total land rent according to their ownership pattern. In this case their consumer surplus, which takes into account this rental income, is the full measure of benefits generated by the urban economy. In realistic cases some landowners are absentee. Thus their share of land rent is a "producer's surplus" and should be counted in benefit calculations.

We now develop two general models of the land market. These are compatible with any economic models of the rest of the urban economy and can be interfaced with them appropriately. Those two models will be labelled the "programming model" and the "excess demand model" respectively.

12.2 The Programming Model

Suppose developers receive bids R_{ikh} from type h land users for type k finished structures on land parcel (or zone) i and suppose C_{ik} is the cost of supplying one type k structure on land parcel i. Then the efficient land development pattern is given by

$$\underset{[X_{ikh}]}{\text{Max}} \quad \underset{hik}{\Sigma\Sigma\Sigma}(R_{ikh}-C_{ik})X_{ikh} \qquad (12.3)$$

subject to:

$$\sum_{kh} q_k X_{ikh} \leq L_i, \; \forall i \qquad (12.4)$$

$$X_{ikh} \geq 0, \; \forall i,k,h \qquad (12.5)$$

In this linear program q_k is the lot size of type k structures and L_i is the total land available at i, X_{ikh} is the decision variable: the number of type k structures to be supplied at i and occupied by type h land users. A very large gradation of lot sizes can be defined for each physical structure type, thus making q_k essentially continuous. The linear program maximizes total development profits. The dual is

$$\underset{[V_i]}{\text{Minimize}} \; \sum_i V_i L_i \qquad (12.6)$$

subject to

$$q_k V_i \geq R_{ikh} - C_{ik}, \; \forall i,k,h \qquad (12.7)$$

$$V_i \geq 0 \qquad (12.8)$$

where V_i is the shadow price of land at location i. The dual minimizes the total cost of land subject to the constraint that the marginal land cost of each unit of development (i,k) is not less than its marginal benefit. From complementary slackness we know that the optimal solution (*) satisfies the following:

$$(\sum_{kh} q_k X_{ikh}^* - L_i) V_i^* = 0 \qquad (12.9)$$

$$[q_k V_i^* - (R_{ikh} - C_{ik})] X_{ikh}^* = 0 \qquad (12.10)$$

$$\sum_{hik} (R_{ikh} - C_{ik}) X_{ikh}^* - \sum_i V_i^* L_i = 0 \qquad (12.11)$$

Condition (12.9) implies that if all the land is not developed, (.) < 0, then $V_i^* = 0$ in i. On the other hand, if (.) = 0 then $V_i^* \geq 0$. This means that land at a location must be fully utilized to be valuable. Condition (12.10) implies that if the marginal cost of a unit development is larger than its marginal benefit, (.) > 0, then this unit development will not occur and thus $X_{ikh}^* = 0$. On the other hand, if the marginal cost equals the marginal benefit then the unit development breaks even and is possible, $X_{ikh}^* \geq 0$. Condition (12.11) states that total land rent absorbs total development profits which is the definition of land rent in a competitive market. From (12.7) we know that

$$q_k V_i^* = \max_h \{R_{ikh} - C_{ik}\} \qquad (12.12)$$

If the highest bidding use is m, then

$$q_k V_i^* = R_{ikm} - C_{ik}$$

and

$$V_i^* = R_{ikm}/q_k - C_{ik}/q_k \qquad (12.13)$$

12.3 The Excess Demand Model

Models have been developed which do not identify bidders but, instead, set up equations which measure the excess demand for the number of unit developments (or floor space) at each location. An example of such a model is CATLAS (see Anas and Duann, 1984).

Suppose $D_i(\bar{p})$ is the demand by consumers for the quantity of floor space they wish to rent at location i given the price vector $\bar{p}$ of floor space prices at all locations. Let $S_i(p_i)$

be the quantity of floor space the developers will supply at location i given price p_i. Then the excess demand equilibrium conditions are

$$E_i(\overline{p}) = D_i(\overline{p}) - S_i(p_i) = 0, \forall i \qquad (12.14)$$

and equilibrium is obtained by solving the above equations for $\overline{p}^*$.

The above model implicitly determines land rent (or price) at i. This can be calculated as the producer surplus or area between the supply function and the price line, and equals the profit from development before rent is paid. Thus

$$(\text{Rent at } i) = \int_0^{P_i^*} S_i(u)du \qquad (12.15)$$

To give a specific example of this we consider the CATLAS model. In this model S_i is the number of dwellings in zone i and $Q_i(R_i)$ is the proportion of these dwellings that will be rented at rent R_i. This proportion is given by

$$Q_i(R_i) = \frac{\exp[\pi_i(R_i)]}{\exp[\pi_i(R_i)]+\exp[\pi_{io}]}$$

or

$$Q_i(R_i) = \frac{1}{1+\exp[\pi_{io}-\pi_i(R_i)]} \qquad (12.16)$$

Here $\pi_i(R_i)$ is the average profit from an occupied dwelling in zone i if it is rented for R_i and π_{io} is the average loss if that dwelling is kept vacant. Assuming $\pi_i(R_i)$ is linear in rent and integrating we get that the average (expected) land rent in zone i is,

$$(\text{Rent at } i) = \ell n\{1+\exp[\pi_{io}-\pi_i(R_i)]\} \qquad (12.17)$$

The relationship between consumer and producer surplus at equilibrium can be seen in Figure 12.1.

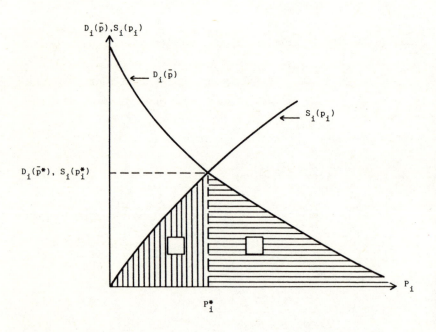

Figure 12.1: Relationship between CS (consumer surplus) and land rent (or producer surplus, PS) at equilibrium at a given location i

12.4 Conclusions

This brief chapter provided two models of the land market and land rent determination following the appropriate economic principles. Land was treated as a residual payment factor in production and the appropriate computations for land rent determination were presented.

Chapter 13

LABOUR MARKET 1: AN ECONOMIC MODEL

A. Anas

13.1 Introduction

This chapter develops a labour market model which follows
economic principles such as those discussed in Chapter Two.
Since the approach is economic, a key aspect of the model is
the explanation of market clearing by means of the action of
wages. Another feature is that institutional aspects such as
unions or wage controls are ignored. The proposed model is
intended as a "pure" labour market prototype.

The model takes into account both the discrete and continuous aspects of labour market choices. Individuals in the
labour market choose the region and occupation in which they
want to supply their labour and also how much (hours per year)
labour they wish to supply. They may also choose to remain
unemployed and receive government benefits. Firms in each
region choose the amount of labour (hours per year) they need
to hire from each occupation. Neither households nor firms are
assumed capable of influencing wages and markets are cleared
by balancing demand and supply by region (and occupation) and
in each time period of the labour market.

In the dynamic model individuals who are employed or
unemployed can move from one region to another incurring a
mobility cost. Markets are still assumed to clear without
lags but mobility costs introduce further diversification of

the labour pool in any given region or occupation.

The discrete choice technique is used to develop the
labour supply equations, the continuous aspect of labour supply
being determined simultaneously. This "pure" labour market
model is easily extendable to include complex institutional
aspects by following the approach of the housing market prototype model developed for Stockholm (see Chapter Seven).

13.2 The Static Model

13.2.1 The supply of labour: a mixed discrete and continuous
        choice problem

Each individual of a given total population, N, must decide in
which region and in which occupation to become employed. Thus
the choice set consists of discrete combinations of region-
occupations labelled j = 1, ..., J. We will assume that each
individual has all regional-occupations available; it is easy
to follow the example of mode choice models and define arbitrary
choice sets.

The individual's utility maximization problem for each
alternative j is as follows:

$$\text{Maximize}_{Z_j, L_j} U_j = \alpha \ln Z_j + \beta \ln L_j \qquad (13.1)$$

subject to:

$$y_j + w_j H = Z_j + w_j L_j \qquad (13.2)$$

The utility U_j is log linear in leisure hours, L_j, and "all
other consumption expenditures", Z_j, with coefficients α,
$\beta > 0$. The budget "income" consists of y_j, unearned income
(or non-wage income) and potential earnings which are obtained
by taking the total hours, H, available for work and leisure

and multiplying by the wage rate, w_j. This total income endowment is allocated between leisure ("purchased" at the wage rate) and consumption. Work hours, q_j, and leisure hours, L_j, sum up to H, so we have

$$H = q_j + L_j \tag{13.3}$$

Thus, the budget constraint (13.2) can also be written as

$$y_j + w_j q_j = Z_j \tag{13.4}$$

where $q_j = H - L_j$.

Using Lagrangian maximization of (13.1) subject to (13.2) we get

$$L_j = \frac{\beta}{\alpha+\beta} (y_j + w_j H) w_j^{-1} \tag{13.5}$$

$$Z_j = \frac{\alpha}{\alpha+\beta} (y_j + w_j H) \tag{13.6}$$

These are the demand functions for leisure hours and for consumption (a composite commodity purchased at some price P_j so that $Z_j = P_j Q_j$, Q_j being the quantity of the composite commodity). Subtracting (13.5) from H we get work hours as

$$q_j = \frac{\alpha}{\alpha+\beta} H - \frac{\beta}{\alpha+\beta} \frac{y_j}{w_j} \tag{13.7}$$

The solution L_j, Z_j (and q_j) given by (13.5) - (13.7) maximizes the individual's utility if the individual chooses region-occupation j. To evaluate this maximum utility we substitute (13.5) and (13.6) into (13.1) and we get U_j^*:

$$U_j^* = (\text{constant}) + (\alpha+\beta)\ln(y_j + H w_j) - \beta \ln w_j \tag{13.8}$$

the constant being invariant with region. We see from (13.8)

that the work-leisure trade-off makes the utility function
nonmonotonic in the wage rate.   Thus

$$\frac{\partial U^{*}_{j}}{\partial w_{j}} = \frac{(\alpha+\beta)H}{y_{j}+Hw_{j}} - \frac{\beta}{w_{j}} \gtreqless 0 \tag{13.9}$$

The special case of zero non-wage income is of interest.
Suppose $y_{j} = 0$, then $q_{j} = \frac{\alpha}{\alpha+\beta} H$ and $\partial U^{*}_{j}/\partial w_{j} = \alpha/w_{j}$, namely
utility increases monotonically with the wage rate.   But as
non-wage income increases then utility can decrease with wage
when wages are low and reaches a low point subsequently rising
with wage.

Equation (13.9) is the indirect utility function because
it expresses utility (maximized) in terms of wages and income.

Having found $U^{*}_{j}(H, y_{j}, w_{j})$ for each region j the household can now choose among the regions by means of a discrete
choice process.   One of the options is unemployment in each
region denoted as U_{jo}.   In this case $L_{jo} = H$ and the household receives as consumption the government benefit B_{jo}.
Thus, the utility of unemployment is

$$U_{jo} = \alpha \ell n \ B_{jo} + \beta \ell n \ H \tag{13.10}$$

We can now introduce the random utility terms ε_{j} and ε_{jo}
which are uncorrelated with the choice of Z_{j} and L_{j}.   We add
ε_{j} to U^{*}_{j} and ε_{jo} to U_{jo}.   Then we can make appropriate assumptions about the distribution of errors deriving a specific
discrete choice model.   The multinomial logit model, for
example, is

$$P_{j} = \frac{\exp\{U^{*}_{j}(H, y_{j}, w_{j})\}}{\sum\limits_{k} \exp\{U^{*}_{k}(H, y_{k}, w_{k})\} + \sum\limits_{k}\exp\{U_{ko}\}} \tag{13.11}$$

and

$$P_{jo} = \frac{\exp\{U_{jo}\}}{\sum_k \exp\{U_k^*(H, y_k, w_k)\} + \sum_k \exp\{U_{ko}\}} \qquad (13.12)$$

The choice probabilities add up to one as follows: $\sum_j P_j + \sum_j P_{jo} = 1$.

13.2.2 The demand for labour

Firms' demand for labour can be derived under various assumptions about production technology. The most realistic is that each firm has an S-shaped production function which exhibits a phase of increasing returns with respect to labour followed by decreasing returns.

Under these assumptions the firm's problem can be stated as the following profit maximization problem:

$$\underset{p,N}{\text{Maximize}} \; p \, \frac{D(p)}{n} - wN \qquad (13.13)$$

subject to

$$\frac{D(p)}{n} \geq F(N) \qquad (13.14)$$

Here p is the price of the firm's output, $D(p)$ is the demand for the firm's output as a decreasing function of the price, n is the number of firms sharing the market, w is the wage rate and N is the labour hired by the firm, $F(N)$ being the production function. In this production function other inputs are treated as constant since we are focussing on the labour market.

Solving the above problem the firm will obtain its demand function for labour (as a function of the wage, w). We will assume that this function expressed as $Q(w) = Q(n^*, p^*, w)$ is a decreasing function of w given n^* and p^*. The number of firms n^* is determined in such a way that each firm actually

maximizes profit at zero. This occurs because of free entry
and exit in each industry. Thus the total j^{th} industry
(occupation)-region demand for labour can be expressed as
$n_j^* N_j^*$ or

$$H_j(w_j) \equiv n_j^* Q_j(n_j^*, p_j^*, w_j) \qquad (13.15)$$

13.2.3 Market clearing

We can now set up the labour market equilibrium model for the
static case as follows. Suppose there are $h = 1, \ldots, H$
socioeconomic individual types with utility coefficients α_h,
β_h and with labour market choices $q_{jh}(w_j)$ and $P_j^h(\overline{w})$ and
$P_{jo}^h(\overline{w})$. Then the equilibrium problem can be expressed as the
following excess demand problem for each $j = 1, \ldots, J$:

$$E_j(\overline{w}) = \sum_h N^h P_j^h(\overline{w}) q_{jh}(w_j) - H_j(w_j) = 0; \; \forall j \qquad (13.16)$$

This is a system of simultaneous equations in $\overline{w}$ given y_j, and
all other constants which are treated as exogenous. The
existence, uniqueness and stability of an equilibrium solution
can be determined by referring to appropriate theorems in the
literature discussed briefly in Chapter Two.

13.3 The Dynamic Model

To make the model dynamic we need a few simple adjustments.
We let N_{ih}^t denote the number of type h individuals employed
in region i at time t and N_{ioh}^t the number of type h individuals
unemployed in region i at time t. We represent unearned
income as y_{ijh}^{t+1}, the unearned income at time t+1 of an individual moving from i to j during t. This includes a moving cost
adjustment. Labour hours supplied are now q_{ijh}^{t+1} and q_{ijoh}^{t+1}

respectively and probabilities are P_{ijh}^{t+1} and P_{ijoh}^{t+1}. Finally, the demand for labour is $H_j^t(w_j)$. The excess demand for t can now be set up as follows:

$$E_j^t(\overline{w}) = \underset{hi}{\Sigma\Sigma} N_{ih}^{t-1} P_{ijh}^t(\overline{w}_t) q_{ijh}^t(w_{jt})$$

$$+ \underset{hi}{\Sigma\Sigma} N_{ioh}^{t-1} P_{ijoh}^t(\overline{w}_t) q_{ijoh}^t(w_{jt}) - H_j^t(w_{jt}) = 0$$

$$(13.17)$$

for each j. This system can be solved for the wage vector $\overline{w}_t$ at each time t. The exogenous variables shift the system to a new equilibrium at each time.

13.4 Possible Extensions

There are a number of extensions of the model developed here. First, it is possible to treat region-occupation classifications more precisely and distinguish the choice between the two by means of a nested logit model. Second, wage rigidities can be introduced in a manner which is analogous to the treatment of rent control in the regulated housing market prototype (see Chapter Seven). Third, firms may be allowed to choose a mix of labour occupations simultaneously treating different occupations as substitutes. Fourth, the model can be embedded into a mathematical programming formulation in which government unemployment benefits are treated as decision variables.

Chapter 14

LABOUR MARKET 2: A MASTER EQUATION APPROACH

G. Haag

14.1 Introduction

Regional labour market conditions depend in a complex manner
on the decisions of individuals on the supply side and firms
on the demand side of the market. The individuals must decide
whether to quit or retain the present jobs, to search for new
employment, perhaps in another region, and/or to search for a
new residential location which increases their utility. Firms
must set desired employment levels and determine the number of
job opportunities in the different regions, taking into
account the market conditions. The highly complex interactions between the labour market and the housing market
require an adequate explanation of the nature of the decisions
made by the different decision-makers.

The theory of job search (Rogerson, 1983, Lippman and
McCall, 1976) and residential search (Clark, 1983, Clark and
Smith, 1982) is concerned with optimal behaviour of individuals
who want to maximize their utility. Optimal policy for firms
is concerned with maximizing profits (Eaton and Watts, 1977).

Innovations can be seen as the mainspring of economic
growth (Mensch, 1979). According to the business cycle theory
of Schumpeter and its dynamical modelling (Mensch, Weidlich
and Haag, 1986) an innovative input is generated in the socio-
economic system via a dynamic feedback. Innovations influence

the productivity and demand for labour and change the investment shares of firms (expansionary or rationalizing investment)
and bias the decision behaviour of investors at all socio-
economic levels. Therefore there is a strong interaction
between regional growth or decline and the embedding of
appropriate innovations into the production process.

Since the spatial aspects of the residential and labour
mobility processes are crucial for a better understanding of
regional growth or decline, a spatial structure is introduced.
It is risky to assume equilibrium conditions for the market,
so a dynamic description is preferred. The inherent fluctuations of the decision process in this Chapter are again
treated via a master equation approach (compare Chapters Four,
Eight and Eleven).

14.2 The Individual Transition Probabilities for the Search Process

We subdivide the system into L nonoverlapping regions as in
Chapters Eight and Eleven. Moreover, the whole population is
supposed to be made up of workers, unemployed people and a kind
of background population. Being pedagogical, we start with a
more simplified version and drop more and more assumptions
later on. Changes in both residence and workplace are taken
into account, and commuting costs are introduced explicitly.
The housing stock and workplaces are differentiated by zones
or regions only, with no further sectoral disaggregation. A
further simplification will be introduced by dropping moving
costs from the model (and they are in any case negligible
compared with other costs and benefits, cf Leonardi, 1987).

The basic definitions are: $n_{ij}(t)$ is the number of people
living in region i and working in region j, at time t. Therefore, the number of people living in i and working somewhere
is

$$n_i(t) = \sum_{j=1}^{L} n_{ij}(t) \tag{14.1}$$

and the number of people working in zone j, at time t is

$$w_j(t) = \sum_{i=1}^{L} n_{ij}(t) \tag{14.2}$$

The total number of working people is

$$n(T) = \sum_{i=1}^{L} n_i(t) = \sum_{j=1}^{L} w_j(t) \tag{14.3}$$

The following variables are then exogenous: $N_i(t)$ is the number of people living in i and wanting to work (fraction of the total population in i); $M_i(t)$ is the number of housing units in i (scaled on $N_i(t)$) or in other words, the housing stock in i; $W_i(t)$ is the number of job opportunities in i; $R_i(t)$ is rent or price-level in i; $Y_i(t)$ is income in zone i. Then, by definition, we have $(N_i(t) - n_i(t))$ as number of unemployed people in i; $(W_i(t) - w_i(t)) = O_i(t)$ as number of open positions in i; $(M_i(t) - n_i(t))$ as number of vacant dwellings in i. We can proceed to build a model using the principles introduced in Weidlich and Haag (1983) and in Chapter Four and already illustrated in Chapters Eight and Eleven.

The number of transitions (in configuration space) due to a "migration process" from a state living in k, working in l to a state living in i, working in j is proportional to $n_{kl}(t)$ times an individual transition probability (rate) $p_{ij,kl}(\underset{\sim}{n})$ for a transition $(k,l) \to (i,j)$. Thus

$$w_{ij,kl}(\underset{\sim}{n}+\underset{\sim}{k};\underset{\sim}{n}) = \begin{cases} n_{kl}(t)\, p_{ij,kl}(\underset{\sim}{n}) \\ \quad \text{for } \underset{\sim}{k} = (\ldots 0 \ldots 1_{ij} \ldots 0 \ldots (-1)_{kl} \ldots 0 \ldots) \\ 0 \text{ for all other combinations} \end{cases}$$

$$\tag{14.4}$$

This flow rate (14.4) has to be inserted into the master equation

$$\frac{dP(\underset{\sim}{n};t)}{dt} = \sum_{\substack{i,j \\ k,l}}^{L} w_{ij,kl}(\underset{\sim}{n};\underset{\sim}{n}+\underset{\sim}{k})P(\underset{\sim}{n}+\underset{\sim}{k};t)$$

$$- \sum_{\substack{i,j \\ k,l}}^{L} w_{ij,kl}(\underset{\sim}{n}+\underset{\sim}{k};\underset{\sim}{n})P(\underset{\sim}{n};t) \qquad (14.5)$$

In order to obtain explicit results, the individual transition probabilities describing residential and labour mobility have to be modelled.

We consider in this contribution the residential and labour market on a more spatially disaggregated level. The utility of an individual depends on commuting costs and also on conditions in both the residential zone and the employment zone. It seems to be reasonable to introduce the following individual transition probability

$$p_{ij,kl}(\underset{\sim}{n}) = e^{v_{ij}(\underset{\sim}{n})-v_{kl}(\underset{\sim}{n})}\delta_{ij,kl} \qquad (14.6)$$

for a change from living in k and working in l to living in i and working in j; where $v_{ij}(\underset{\sim}{n})$ is the utility of an individual for living in i and working in j. Moreover the utilities $v_{ij}(\underset{\sim}{n})$ have two subscripts (for place of residence and place of work) since they measure the competition for housing and for labour in different zones. The $\delta_{ij,kl} > 0$ are coefficients which describe the corresponding mobilities for this migration process.

To obtain further insights, it is useful to split the utilities v_{ij} into two parts

$$v_{ij}(\underset{\sim}{n}) = u_{ij}(\underset{\sim}{n}) - \beta c_{ij}, \; i,j = 1, \ldots, L \qquad (14.7)$$

where $c_{ij} > 0$ are the commuting costs per unit time between
zone i and zone j. The intra-zonal c_{ii} refer to the mean
commuting costs for living and working in the same region or
zone. On a daily basis, it can be assumed that

$$c_{ij} = c_{ji} \tag{14.8}$$

The deterrence parameter $\beta > 0$ describes the influence of the
commuting costs on the utility as judged by an individual.
It should be mentioned that in this section we do not distinguish between different routes of travel from the zone of
residence to the zone of work or between different travel
modes. These restrictions will be dropped in Section 14.8.

The $u_{ij}(n)$ is that part of the utility for an individual
living in i and working in j at time t which is independent
of commuting costs. Therefore, it is reasonable to assume
that $u_{ij}(n)$ depends on two parts

$$u_{ij}(\underset{\sim}{n}) = U_i(\underset{\sim}{n}) + V_j(\underset{\sim}{n}) \tag{14.9}$$

where $U_i(n)$ is the utility of living in zone i, and $V_j(n)$ the
utility of working in j. Without loss of generality we can
scale the utilities u_{ij} so that

$$\sum_{i,j=1}^{L} u_{ij}(\underset{\sim}{n}) = 0 \tag{14.10}$$

At each time, two types of choice are now possible for an
individual: changing residence or changing job (and it is also
possible to change nothing, of course). We assume the time
interval is sufficiently short to exclude the joint occurrence
of both types of events.

Then the coefficients $\delta_{ij,kl}$ can be defined as

$$\delta_{ij,kl} = \begin{vmatrix} \nu, & \text{for } (k,l) \rightarrow (i,l) \\ \nu, & \text{for } (k,l) \rightarrow (l,l) \\ \rho, & \text{for } (k,l) \rightarrow (k,j) \\ \rho, & \text{for } (k,l) \rightarrow (k,j) \\ 0, & \text{for all other combinations} \end{vmatrix} \qquad (14.11)$$

The parameter ν describes the housing mobility, the parameter ρ the labour mobility. In general these mobilities will be different $\rho \neq \nu$. Figure 14.1 depicts the basic events taken into account in this joint model.

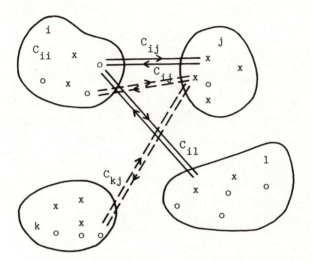

<u>Figure 14.1</u>: The basic events taken into account in the joint model. The O,x correspond to places of living and working respectively

14.3 The Mean Value Equations

Insertion of (14.4), (14.6) in (14.5) yields the explicit form of the master equation for the joint model for residential and labour mobility. The corresponding exact mean value equations can be obtained straightforwardly (as described in Chapters Four, Eight and Eleven):

$$\dot{n}_{ij}(t) = \sum_{k,1}^{L} \overline{w_{ij,kl}(\underset{\sim}{n})} - \sum_{k,1}^{L} \overline{w_{kl,ij}(\underset{\sim}{n})} \qquad (14.12)$$

$$i,j = 1, 2, ..., L \qquad (14.12)$$

Using again the (unessential) assumption that $\overline{f(n)} \simeq f(\overline{n})$, the closed set of approximate mean value equations reads

$$\dot{\overline{n}}_{ij}(t) = \sum_{k=1}^{L} p_{ij,ik}(\underset{\sim}{\overline{n}}) \, \overline{n}_{ik} - \sum_{k=1}^{L} p_{ik,ij}(\underset{\sim}{\overline{n}}) \, \overline{n}_{ij}$$

$$+ \sum_{k=1}^{L} p_{ij,kj}(\underset{\sim}{\overline{n}}) \, \overline{n}_{kj} - \sum_{k=1}^{L} p_{kj,ij}(\underset{\sim}{\overline{n}}) \, \overline{n}_{ij},$$

$$i,j = 1, ..., L \qquad (14.13)$$

where the first line describes labour mobility and the second line housing mobility. In general (14.13) will be a nonlinear system of L^2 coupled differential equations. With (14.6) substituted in (14.13), the more detailed version of the mean value equations is obtained:

$$\dot{\overline{n}}_{ij}(t) = \rho(t)\{ \sum_{k=1}^{L} e^{v_{ij}-v_{ik}} \, \overline{n}_{ik} - \sum_{k=1}^{L} e^{v_{ik}-v_{ij}} \, \overline{n}_{ij}\}$$

$$+ \nu(t)\{ \sum_{k=1}^{L} e^{v_{ij}-v_{kj}} \, \overline{n}_{kj} - \sum_{k=1}^{L} e^{v_{kj}-v_{ij}} \, \overline{n}_{ij}\}$$

$$(14.14)$$

It is worthwhile to emphasize that the utility of an individual for living in one zone and working in another zone explicitly appears in (14.14). Since, according to (14.7), commuting costs c_{ij} and the evaluation of housing and working conditions

u_{ij} appear in v_{ij}, the structure of (14.14) is still very general. We insert (14.7), (14.9) in (14.14)

$$\dot{\overline{n}}_{ij}(t) = \rho(t) \sum_{k=1}^{L} e^{-\beta(c_{ij}-c_{ik})} e^{V_j(\underline{\overline{n}})-V_k(\underline{\overline{n}})} \overline{n}_{ik}$$

$$- \rho(t) \sum_{k=1}^{L} e^{-\beta(c_{ik}-c_{ij})} e^{V_k(\underline{\overline{n}})-V_j(\underline{\overline{n}})} \overline{n}_{ij}$$

$$\left. \begin{array}{l} \\ \\ \\ \\ \end{array} \right\} \text{labour mobility}$$

$$+ \nu(t) \sum_{k=1}^{L} e^{-\beta(c_{ij}-c_{kj})} e^{U_i(\underline{\overline{n}})-U_k(\underline{\overline{n}})} \overline{n}_{kj}$$

$$- \nu(t) \sum_{k=1}^{L} e^{-\beta(c_{kj}-c_{ij})} e^{U_k(\underline{\overline{n}})-U_i(\underline{\overline{n}})} \overline{n}_{ij}$$

$$\left. \begin{array}{l} \\ \\ \\ \\ \end{array} \right\} \text{housing mobility}$$

$$i,j = 1, 2, \ldots, L \tag{14.15}$$

In (14.15) the commuting costs appear explicitly, thus introducing a relationship among housing, workplaces and transport in a dynamic framework. Moreover, accessibilities have two subscripts (for place of residence and place of work) while potential utilities $U_i(n)$, $V_j(n)$ each have one subscript (for the place of work in the case of the labour market). $(U_i(n) - U_k(n))$ measure the competition for housing and $(V_j(n) - V_k(n))$ the competition for workplaces in specific zones. The potential utilities U_i, V_j characterize the attraction of each zone with respect to socioeconomic preferences of the individuals.

14.4 The Dependence of Utilities on Key Factors

So far we have been rather general and we were not concerned with the (exogenous and endogenous) variables which determine the functional shape of the potential utilities $U_i(n)$, $V_j(n)$. We will demonstrate later (Section 14.7) how exogenous

variables introduced as a first step can be made endogenous
in a second step.

We assume that the utility u_{ij} is a function of the
(endogenous) state variables n_{ij} and a set of other relevant
(exogenous) socioeconomic variables. Then we can expand
$u_{ij}(\underset{\sim}{n})$ into a Taylor series and take into account terms up to
first order. This procedure yields (cf the equivalent step
in Chapter Eight):

$$u_{ij}(\underset{\sim}{n}) = \delta_i - \alpha_1(N_i - n_i) + \alpha_2(M_i - n_i) - \alpha_3 P_i + \alpha_4(W_j - w_j)$$

$$+ \alpha_5 Y_j + C \qquad (14.16)$$

The first term, δ_i, describes the basic preference for zone i.
Social factors like the desire to remain in one's birthplace
are part of δ_i, but also factors like accessibility to shops
(in the first step), schools and retail activities. It is
further assumed that unemployment $(N_i - n_i)$ in the residential
area reduces the attractivity of that zone. The residential
attractivity U_i is assumed to depend also on the number of
vacant dwellings in i and the price-level (rents) in zone i.
On the other hand, we expect that income Y_j and the number
of open positions $(W_j - w_j)$ are crucial components of the
attractivity, V_j, of the place of work. Since the amounts and
signs of the trend parameters $\{\alpha_i, \delta_i\}$ are determined explicitly
by the estimation procedure, the weights of the different
variables can be tested. The constant C is fixed by (14.10).
In addition it is convenient to scale the preference parameter
according to

$$\sum_{i=1}^{L} \delta_i = 0 \qquad (14.17)$$

Then

$$U_{ij}(\underset{\sim}{n}) = U_i(\underset{\sim}{n}) + V_j(\underset{\sim}{n}) \tag{14.18}$$

with

$$U_i(\underset{\sim}{n}) = \delta_i - \alpha_1[(N_i - n_i) - \frac{1}{L}(N-n)] + \alpha_2[(M_i - n_i) - \frac{1}{L}(M-n)]$$

$$- \alpha_3(P_i - \overline{P}),$$

$$V_j(\underset{\sim}{n}) = \alpha_4[(W_j - w_j) - \frac{1}{L}(W-w)] + \alpha_5(Y_j - \overline{Y}) \tag{14.19}$$

where

$$\overline{P} = \frac{1}{L} \sum_{i=1}^{L} P_i, \; \overline{Y} = \frac{1}{L} \sum_{i=1}^{L} Y_i \tag{14.20}$$

Therefore the following relations hold:

$$\sum_{i,j}^{L} u_{ij}(\underset{\sim}{n}) = 0; \; \sum_{i=1}^{L} U_i(\underset{\sim}{n}) = 0; \; \sum_{j=1}^{L} V_j(\underset{\sim}{n}) = 0 \tag{14.21}$$

The equations (14.19) with (14.15) complete our construction of a joint dynamic model for residential and labour mobility. Since we are dealing with a highly nonlinear system we can expect phase transitions in a synergetic sense (Nijkamp and Schubert, 1985, Weidlich and Haag, 1987). Therefore a variety of stationary points (attractors) may occur. Our model describes the dynamics of commuting trips in a spatial system and a natural question to be asked is to what extent the steady state solution is related to the known static trip distribution models.

14.5 The Exact Stationary Solution

In order to explore this problem, let us consider the static version ($\dot{\overline{n}}_{ij} = 0$) of (14.14)

$$0 = \rho \left| \sum_{k=1}^{L} e^{\hat{v}_{ij}-\hat{v}_{ik}}\hat{n}_{ik} - \sum_{k=1}^{L} e^{\hat{v}_{ik}-\hat{v}_{ij}}\hat{n}_{ij} \right|$$

$$+ \nu \left| \sum_{k=1}^{L} e^{\hat{v}_{ij}-\hat{v}_{kj}}\hat{n}_{kj} - \sum_{k=1}^{L} e^{\hat{v}_{kj}-\hat{v}_{ij}}\hat{n}_{ij} \right|$$

for $i,j = 1, \ldots, L$ (14.22)

where $\hat{\underline{n}}$, $\hat{\underline{v}}$ denote the stationary values of $\underline{n}$, $\underline{v}$, respectively. Of course, the residential mobility parameter and the labour mobility parameter ρ are not zero.

From (14.22) it can easily be seen, by insertion of (14.23) in (14.22), that the exact stationary trip distribution fulfils the nonlinear system of transcendental equations

$$\hat{n}_{ij} = Ce^{2\hat{v}_{ij}(\hat{\underline{n}})}, \quad i,j = 1, \ldots, L \tag{14.23}$$

where C is determined by (14.3). This yields the very general and interesting result

$$\hat{n}_{ij} = \hat{n} \frac{e^{2\hat{v}_{ij}(\hat{n})}}{\sum_{k,l}^{L} e^{2\hat{v}_{kl}(\hat{n})}}, \quad i,j = 1, \ldots, L \tag{14.24}$$

with

$$\hat{n} = \sum_{i,j}^{L} \hat{n}_{ij}$$

Therefore the stationary trip distribution $\hat{n}_{ij}$, (14.24), depends on the utility of an individual $\hat{v}_{ij}$ to live in i and to work in j. Since this result is obtained without making use of any assumption concerning the functional shape and the set of variables introduced, (14.24) is rather general.

The commuting costs c_{ij} appear via (14.7) explicitly in the stationary solution

$$\hat{n}_{ij} = \hat{n}\,\frac{e^{2(\hat{u}_{ij}(\hat{\underset{\sim}{n}})-\beta c_{ij})}}{\underset{k,l}{\overset{L}{\Sigma}}e^{2(\hat{u}_{kl}(\hat{\underset{\sim}{n}})-\beta c_{kl})}},\quad i,j = 1,\ \ldots,\ L \qquad (14.25)$$

thus introducing a relationship between housing, work-places and transport. The residential mobility ν and the labour mobility ρ do not enter the stationary solution.

In our more specific model $\hat{u}_{ij}$ has to be replaced by (14.18), (14.19). The result (14.25) is different from a standard demand model. The interaction between housing and work-place is mediated by the utility $\hat{u}_{ij}(\hat{\underset{\sim}{n}})$ for the pair of origin-destination zones and the commuting costs. (14.25) is a nontrivial system of L^2 coupled transcendental equations for the L^2 stationary values of $\hat{n}_{ij}$. From the mathematical point of view a variety of critical points is possible if the utilities $\hat{u}_{ij}(\hat{\underset{\sim}{n}})$ are functions of the state variable n. The basins of the attractors determine which solution will finally be realized as $(t \to \infty)$.

14.6 Estimation of the Parameters

The theoretical transition probabilities (14.4), (14.6) can be compared with the corresponding empiric quantities $w^{(e)}_{ij,ik}(t)$, $w^{(e)}_{ij,kj}(t)$ using regression analysis

$$w^{(e)}_{ij,ik}(t) = \rho n^{(e)}_{ik}e^{v_{ij}-v_{ik}};\ w^{(e)}_{ik,ij}(t) = \rho n^{(e)}_{ij}e^{v_{ik}-v_{ij}}$$

$$(14.26)$$

and

$$w^{(e)}_{ij,kj}(t) = \nu n^{(e)}_{kj}e^{v_{ij}-v_{kj}};\ w^{(e)}_{kj,ij}(t) = \nu n^{(e)}_{ij}e^{v_{kj}-v_{ij}}$$

$$(14.27)$$

In Haag and Weidlich (1984) and Chapters Eight and Eleven above, we discussed in detail the regression analysis of this kind of model, and so we describe the estimation procedure here only briefly. Consider the product of (14.26) and (14.27) and then we obtain for the labour mobility $\rho(t)$

$$\rho(t) = \frac{1}{L^2(L-1)} \sum_{\substack{i,j,k \\ k \neq j}}^{L} \sqrt{\frac{w_{ij,ik}^{(e)}(t) \; w_{ik,ij}^{(e)}(t)}{n_{ik}^{(e)} \; n_{ij}^{(e)}}} \qquad (14.28)$$

and similarly for the housing mobility $\nu(t)$

$$\nu(t) = \frac{1}{L^2(L-1)} \sum_{\substack{i,j,k \\ i \neq k}}^{L} \sqrt{\frac{w_{ij,kj}^{(e)}(t) \; w_{kj,ij}^{(e)}(t)}{n_{kj}^{(e)} \; n_{ij}^{(e)}}} \qquad (14.29)$$

These results are independent of the v_{ij}. By considering the quotient of (14.26) and (14.27) we obtain the over-determined set of equations

$$r_{ij,ik} = v_{ij} - v_{ik}, \quad i,j,k = 1, \ldots, L, \; j \neq k$$

$$r_{ij,kj} = v_{ij} - v_{kj}, \quad i,j,k = 1, \ldots, L, \; i \neq k \qquad (14.30)$$

where

$$r_{ij,ik} = \frac{1}{2} \ln \frac{w_{ij,ik}^{(e)}(t) \; n_{ij}^{(e)}}{w_{ik,ij}^{(e)}(t) \; n_{ik}^{(e)}}$$

$$r_{ij,kj} = \frac{1}{2} \ln \frac{w_{ij,kj}^{(e)}(t) \; n_{ij}^{(e)}}{w_{kj,ij}^{(e)}(t) \; n_{kj}^{(e)}} \qquad (14.31)$$

and

$$v_{ij} = -\beta c_{ij} + U_i + V_j \qquad (14.32)$$

We can, however, choose an optimal set of attractivities for residence U_i and work-place V_j by minimizing the least square deviations of the functional

$$F_t[\underset{\sim}{U},\underset{\sim}{V}] = \frac{1}{L^2(L-1)} \sum_{\substack{i,j,k \\ j \neq k}}^{L} \{[r_{ij,ik}-(-\beta(c_{ij}-c_{ik})+(V_j-V_k))]^2$$

$$+ [r_{ji,ki}-(-\beta(c_{ji}-c_{ki})+(U_j-U_k))]^2\} \qquad (14.33)$$

We introduce the abbreviations

$$R_{jk} = \frac{1}{L} \sum_{i=1}^{L} r_{ij,ik}; \quad S_{jk} = \frac{1}{L} \sum_{i=1}^{L} v_{ji,ki} \text{ and } C_j = \frac{1}{L} \sum_{i=1}^{L} c_{ij}$$

$$(14.34)$$

and obtain

$$F_t[\underset{\sim}{U},\underset{\sim}{V}] = \frac{1}{L(L-1)} \sum_{\substack{j,k=1 \\ j \neq k}}^{L} \{[R_{jk}-(-\beta(C_j-C_k)+(V_j-V_k))]^2$$

$$+ [S_{jk}-(-\beta(C_j-C_k)+(U_j-U_k))]^2\} \qquad (14.35)$$

The optimal set of attractivities $\{\underset{\sim}{U},\underset{\sim}{V}\}$ is found by setting the derivatives of (14.35) to zero

$$\frac{\partial F_t}{\partial U_i} = 0; \quad \frac{\partial F_t}{\partial V_i} = 0; \quad i = 1, 2, \ldots, L \qquad (14.36)$$

This yields the attractivity of the place of residence (potential utility)

$$U_i(t) = \frac{1}{L} \sum_{j \neq i}^{L} S_{ij} - \beta(\overline{C}-C_i) \qquad (14.37)$$

and for the attractivity of the place of work (potential utility)

$$V_i(t) = \frac{1}{L} \sum_{j \neq i}^{L} R_{ij} - \beta(\overline{C} - C_i) \qquad (14.38)$$

where

$$\overline{C} = \frac{1}{L} \sum_{i=1}^{L} C_i \qquad (14.39)$$

This yields a very robust estimation of the utilities for living in i and working in j, or in other words for U_i, V_j, i, j = 1, 2, ..., L. The trend parameters in the origin-destination utility v_{ij}, namely β, α_1, ..., α_5, can be determined by an optimal spatial correlation. We therefore drop this part because of its simplicity.

This model does not lose its validity or applicability if instead of (14.16), (14.18) the utility functions $v_{ij}(n)$ are modelled in a different manner. This is one of the fundamental points of this kind of model building. Different input factors to $v_{ij}(n)$ can therefore be tested and the key factors of the joint model for residential and labour mobility can be determined. By insertion of the estimated parameters into the dynamic system of equations (14.15), the model can be used for forecasting purposes. The equilibrium solution can also be obtained by (14.24), (14.25).

14.7 How Exogenous Variables Become Endogenous Variables

Although the model outlined here so far is still lacking some realistic features, the method is quite general and the model can easily be generalized in several respects. For example we introduced a set of exogenous variables and the problem to be solved is, in effect, how to make them endogenous. It is an advantage of this method that the fundamental structure of the equations [(14.4)-(14.6), (14.12)-(14.14), (14.24)] remain unchanged even if we change the character of the variables. We have to add to the dynamic equations (14.12)-(14.14) the more general version of the utilities $v_{ij}(\underset{\sim}{n})$, together with the additional dynamic equations for the new endogenously treated variables.

For demonstrational purposes, we show how the exogenous variable M_i, which describes the housing stock in region or zone i, can be made endogenous, or in our notational convention

$$M_i \rightarrow m_i(t) \qquad\qquad\qquad (14.40)$$

We consider the dynamic system (14.15) with (14.18). In (14.19) we replace according to (14.40) the exogenous housing stock variable M_i by the endogenous variable $m_i(t)$. Then we add the mean value equations of the housing stock to the dynamic system. By comparing computer simulations of the model with observed data we can decide whether this is an improvement or not. Other exogenous variables such as prices or number of job opportunities can be transformed into endogenous variables in the same way.

14.8 Dynamic Theory of Travel Networks and Residential Location Markets and Labour Mobility

In treating the problem of the travel network, it is normally assumed that the travel networks and the residential location market are in equilibrium (Anas, 1984-B, Wilson, 1983-B). In the framework of the dynamic master equation approach we derived a joint model for residential and labour mobility. The output of our model yields as one main result predictions of the mean number of trips (or flows) between residence in zone i and workplace in zone j, namely $\overline{n}_{ij}(t)$. The number of trips may also be split into different routes and/or modes.

Then $\overline{n}_{ij}^{(\gamma)}(t)$ is the mean number of trips of people living in zone i and working in zone j, at time t using route and/or travel mode γ. Of course, each of the available routes between an origin-destination pair will carry some traffic, even though these route costs can vary greatly among them. Since the mean number of trips between i and j is the sum over all contributions from different routes (see Figure 14.2).

$$\overline{n}_{ij}(t) = \sum_{\gamma} \overline{n}_{ij}^{(\gamma)}(t) \tag{14.41}$$

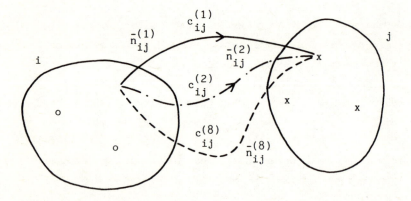

Figure 14.2:   Several different routes between zone i and zone j, distinguished by aggregate travel costs $c_{ij}^{(\gamma)}$

The utilities of the commuters $v_{ij}^{(\gamma)}(n)$ are functions of travel time, travel costs, the rent of housing, income at work-place in j, and other attributes of the route of travel, the zone of residence and the zone of work-place. All the attributes of the route of travel γ are assumed to merge into the aggregate travel costs $c_{ij}^{(\gamma)}$:

$$c_{ij}^{(\gamma)} = f \text{ (travel time, travel costs, travel risk)} \quad (14.42)$$

A possible decomposition of $c_{ij}^{(\gamma)}$ is described in Anas (1984-B). Then for each mode under consideration we can derive the corresponding set of mean value equations:

$$\dot{\bar{n}}_{ij}^{\gamma}(t) = \rho(t) \sum_{\gamma'} \sum_{\substack{k=1 \\ k \neq j}}^{L} \{e^{v_{ij}^{(\gamma)} - v_{ik}^{(\gamma')}} . \bar{n}_{ik}^{(\gamma')} - e^{v_{ik}^{(\gamma')} - v_{ij}^{(\gamma)}} . \bar{n}_{ij}^{(\gamma)}\}$$

$$+ \nu(t) \sum_{\gamma'} \sum_{\substack{k=1 \\ k \neq j}}^{L} \{e^{v_{ij}^{(\gamma)} - v_{kj}^{(\gamma')}} . \bar{n}_{kj}^{(\gamma')} - e^{v_{kj}^{(\gamma')} - v_{ij}^{(\gamma)}} . \bar{n}_{ij}^{(\gamma)}\}$$

$$i,j = 1, 2, \ldots, L \qquad \gamma\gamma'\epsilon\Omega_{ij} \qquad\qquad (14.43)$$

with

$$v_{ij}^{(\gamma)} = -\beta c_{ij}^{(\gamma)} + U_{ij}(\underset{\sim}{n}) \qquad\qquad (14.44)$$

and these must be solved simultaneously. This kind of generalization of our model does not create any difficulties in principle. The flows are distributed among the routes available for travel between each origin-destination pair. The positivity of all variables is always guaranteed.

14.9 The Stationary Solution of Travel Networks, Residential Location and Labour Markets

By insertion of the generalization of (14.23)

$$\hat{n}_{ij}^{(\gamma)} = Ce^{2\hat{v}_{ij}^{(\gamma)}(\underset{\sim}{\hat{n}})} \qquad\qquad (14.45)$$

into (14.43), it can be proved that (14.45) is the exact

stationary solution. The constant C is determined by normalization. This finally yields:

$$\hat{n}_{ij}^{(\gamma)} = \hat{n} \frac{e^{2[\hat{u}_{ij}(\hat{\underset{\sim}{n}})-\beta c_{ij}^{(\gamma)}]}}{\underset{\gamma'}{\Sigma} \underset{k,l}{\overset{L}{\Sigma}} e^{2[\hat{u}_{kl}(\hat{\underset{\sim}{n}})-\beta c_{kl}^{(\gamma')}]}} \qquad (14.46)$$

where

$$\hat{n} = \underset{\gamma}{\Sigma} \underset{i,j}{\overset{L}{\Sigma}} \hat{n}_{ij}^{(\gamma)} \qquad (14.47)$$

The stationary trip distribution $\hat{n}_{ij}^{(\gamma)}$ (14.46) of mode γ,
depends on the utility $\hat{u}_{ij}(\hat{\underset{\sim}{n}})$, to live in i and work in j and
on the aggregate travel costs $c_{ij}^{(\gamma)}$. Equation (14.46) can be
seen as a logit model. But, it is worthwhile to emphasize
that the result of (14.46) coincides with the stationary
points of the mean value equations (14.43) and with the
extremal values of the stationary probability distribution as
well.

Therefore, assumptions concerning the distribution function of the random utility part, as used in random utility
theory (Leonardi, 1987), are not needed. But since our model
based on the master equation approach ends up with the same
structure of the stationary solution as random utility theory,
it seems to be justified to interpret $v_{ij}(\underset{\sim}{n})$ as a utility
function even if our system is out of equilibrium. In this
sense, random utility theory is embedded.

This model can be used in regional planning to answer
several questions: for example: what will happen if a new mode
is introduced between i and j assuming that the "travel costs"
are about 30% less than the alternative connections? The new
route leads to an additional choice possibility in the travel
network. By a simulation of this travel network the optimal
path of the new route as well as its "capacity" can be obtained
with respect to several strategies.

Chapter 15

LABOUR MARKET 3: A STOCHASTIC ASSIGNMENT APPROACH

G. Leonardi

15.1 Introduction

In this chapter we shall outline the analysis of an urban
labour market by means of the theory of stochastic extremal
processes developed in Chapter Five, and in particular by
using the stochastic dynamic assignment model developed in
Section 5.7. The lines along which this chapter will be
developed closely parallel those used for Chapter Nine, on the
housing market. Indeed it can be said that, "mutatis mutandis",
we are basically using the same model in both cases, in the
sense that a one-to-one mapping can be established between the
actors and variables used in the housing market and those used
in the labour market. A warning is needed, however: the existence
of this mapping should not be misinterpreted as identical definition of terms and symbols whenever they appear to be the same.
One should not forget that in the labour market the roles of
households (or, more precisely, working householders) and
entrepreneurs is interchanged relative to the housing market.
In terms of modelling style, this means that we attribute to
households a utility maximizing behaviour, while we attribute
to entrepreneurs a revenue maximizing behaviour and a price
(rent) setting option. Moreover, we insist on all demand units
being satisfied (ie everybody must be somewhere), while some
supply units might remain vacant (ie some dwellings might remain

empty). In a labour market the working householders (both employed and unemployed) are the supply, while the entrepreneurs (ie the firms) are the demand. In terms of modelling style, this means that we attribute to householders an income maximizing behaviour (a close analogue of revenue maximizing) and a wage setting option (a close analogue of price setting), while we attribute to entrepreneurs a utility maximizing behaviour (utility in this case being often interpreted as productivity, or profit). We still insist on all demand units being satisfied (which now means all jobs must be filled), while some supply units might remain vacant (which now means some householders might remain unemployed).

As for the housing market, the main contribution which the theory of stochastic extremal processes can provide is the description of the dynamics of the signals regulating the interactions between demand and supply in the labour market, in particular wages and incomes. This chapter will be focussed on the subject of income distributions and income dynamics, while other aspects of the labour market, like labour mobility, will not be developed here. Although it is possible to build a labour mobility model based on the theory of stochastic extremal processes, it is also possible to use the income (or wage) dynamics as obtained by stochastic extremal processes in combination with other approaches already developed to treat labour mobility, like the one proposed by Haag in this book (Chapter Fourteen), which closely parallels the one developed by Leonardi (1987). The latter is the point of view adopted here, as outlined in Chapter Six. The subject of integration of different approaches for different tasks will be further developed, for the labour market as well as for other subsystems, in Chapter Seventeen.

15.2 The Labour Market as a Dynamic Assignment Process

The labour market considered here is simplified as with the housing market in Chapter Nine. Many simplifying assumptions are common to both cases (the level of disaggregation used for instance) and they will not be repeated here. Other assumptions introduced are more specific to the labour market and, while some of them are common to most classic models, some others are peculiar to our approach.

First, it is assumed that the labour market is "pure", ie public control on wages and the effect of trade unions are ignored, and wages, freely negotiated at the individual level, are the only regulating signal. In this respect, our model is similar to the one considered by Anas in this book (Chapter Thirteen). The distinctive feature of our model, as compared to the one by Anas, is that both firms and households influence wages through an explicit bidding process, and the equivalent market clearing conditions at equilibrium are derived as a by-product, rather than used as a starting assumption.

Secondly, the total demand for labour is fixed, that is, there is a given list of job positions available in each zone. This amounts to ignoring problems of production technology and production functions. Although this assumption can be relaxed in more complex versions (see Chapter Thirteen in this book, by Anas) here, for illustration, each job will be considered as given and performed by some worker, and the only type of decision the firm can take is to choose among a list of applicants to the job the one yielding the highest utility to the firm.

Thirdly, households are assumed to have no other sources of income besides their wages[*], which therefore become the main

---

[*] This assumption can be easily extended to include a public subsidy for unemployed. This point will be discussed again later.

component in their budget constraint. For a different treatment of the household budget constraint the reader is referred again to Chapter Thirteen in this book.

Let us now introduce the basic definitions. As usual, the urban area under consideration is divided into n zones, and the subscripts i,j = 1, ..., n denote a generic zone. A list of available jobs is specified for each zone so that Γ_i is the set of jobs located in zone i. Note that, since at equilibrium each job will be occupied, that is, performed by some worker, Γ_i will also coincide with the set of households having their job in zone i, as it was defined in Chapter Nine. The difference in emphasis used here is justified by the fact that now we look at the sets Γ_i as lists of jobs (that is, from the firms' point of view), rather than lists of workers (that is, from the household point of view). We shall define

also $\Gamma = \bigcup\limits_{i=1}^{n} \Gamma_i$ as the total set of jobs in the area;

$P_i = |\Gamma_i|$, the number of jobs available in zone i; and

$P = |\Gamma| = \sum\limits_{i=1}^{n} P_i$, the total number of jobs. The households, as

identified by their working householder, are disaggregated by place of residence and it is assumed each worker can have at most one job. Thus, Ω_j is the set of households living in zone j. Note that the definition of Ω_j is different from that used in Chapter Nine. Here Ω_j coincides with the set of occupied dwellings, while in Chapter Nine it includes also the vacant dwellings.

We shall define also $\Omega = \bigcup\limits_{j=1}^{n} \Omega_j$ as the total set of house-

holds; $Q_j = |\Omega_j|$ as the number of households (workers) living

in zone j; $Q = |\Omega| = \sum\limits_{j=1}^{n} Q_j$ as the total number of households

(workers) in the area. It will be assumed that Q > P. This

implies that all jobs P will be filled, while Q-P workers will
be unemployed. The utility each firm or entrepreneur responsible for a job attaches to each worker is typically a measure
of the profit each worker can produce, that is, the difference
between the revenue and the wage to be paid for him. We shall
for simplicity assume the revenues have no systematic relationship with workers of different groups: workers are basically
homogeneous in skill and productivity on average. However, we
allow for heterogeneity of skills and productivity in a
stochastic fashion by adding a random term. The treatment of
productivity as a random variable and its analysis by means of
extreme value theory was first proposed by Beckmann, whose
work inspired the approach used in this chapter.

A typical utility for a job $h\epsilon\Gamma_i$ of worker $z\epsilon\Omega_j$ at time t
is:

$$u_{hz}(t) = \epsilon_{hz} - w_{hz}(t), \quad h\epsilon\Gamma_i, \ z\epsilon\Omega_j, \quad i,j = 1, \ldots, n$$

$$(15.1)$$

where ϵ_{hz} is the random utility term, and $w_{hz}(t)$ is the market
wage to be paid for a worker living in zone z and working in
zone h, at time t. The variables ϵ_{hz} will be assumed as usual
to be i.i.d. with distribution $F(x) = Pr\{\epsilon_{hz} \leq x\}$ for all
$(h,z)\epsilon\Gamma \times \Omega$.

We assume each household has a budget constraint; that is,
expenses for the consumption of transportation, housing and
services must be less than the wage. This means that for each
$(h,z)\epsilon\Gamma_i \times \Omega_j$ the following inequality must hold:

$$c_{ij} + s_j + r_j \leq w_{hz}(t) \quad\quad\quad (15.2)$$

where c_{ij} is the commuting cost between zones i and j; s_j is
the average expenditure in services (including transportation

cost) from zone j; and r_j is the average housing expenditure for a household living in j^*. If we define the variables $\tilde{y}_z(t)$ as disposable income for a household $z\epsilon\Omega_j$ at time t, $y_z(t) \geq 0$, then inequality (15.2) can be rewritten as the equality

$$w_{hz}(t) = c_{ij} + s_j + r_j + \tilde{y}_z(t), \quad h\epsilon\Gamma_i, \ z\epsilon\Omega_j,$$

$$i,j = 1, \ldots, n \qquad\qquad (15.3)$$

The commuting cost, service expenditure and housing expenses can be considered as deterministic variables, common to all $(h,z)\epsilon\Gamma_i \times \Omega_j$ for each (i,j) pair, while the disposable income is in general a random variable, whose distribution will be determined later. We can define for short:

$$v_{ij} = - (c_{ij} + s_j + r_j) \qquad\qquad (15.4)$$

and substitution of (15.3) and (15.4) into (15.1) yields

$$u_{hz}(t) = v_{ij} + [\epsilon_{hz} - \tilde{y}_z(t)], \quad h\epsilon\Gamma_i, \ z\epsilon\Omega_j,$$

$$i,j = 1, \ldots, n \qquad\qquad (15.5)$$

Some comments to clarify equation (15.3) are useful. The fact that the wage is expressed as a sum of different consumptions and a disposable income does not mean that the firm offering the job $h\epsilon\Gamma_i$ is aware of the detailed consumption list of the

---

*   In Chapter Nine the housing prices are shown to be time-dependent random variables. Here for simplicity we consider only a time-independent average. A fully stochastic formulation combining the housing and labour market could be developed, but this will not be pursued here.

worker $z\epsilon\Omega_j$. The only information exchanged in the bidding
process between firm and worker is the whole wage w_{hz}. However, the worker knows the composition of his budget constraint
and he negotiates his wage with the firms in such a way as to
get the highest possible value for $\tilde{y}_z(t)$, the disposable income.
The variable $\tilde{y}_z(t)$ should therefore be interpreted as the
highest disposable income a worker $z\epsilon\Omega_j$ can get from the market.
This is the result of a maximization the worker carries out
over the whole list of jobs he has information about up to time
t, and does not depend on a specific job. This is why it is
labelled by the subscript z only. There is a close analogy
between the disposable income $\tilde{y}_z(t)$ in the labour market and
the dwelling price $\tilde{r}_z(t)$ in the housing market. Both are
obtained through a process of bid maximization. In the housing
market, the landlord receives bids from households, that is,
the highest prices they are willing to pay, and sets the price
of his dwelling equal to the maximum of such bids. In the
labour market, the worker receives bids from firms, that is,
the highest wage they are willing to pay for a job, and through
the budget constraint the corresponding disposable incomes are
computed and the "price" is set equal to the maximum among
such incomes. Let us call for short the disposable income a
worker would get from the offer of a specific wage the "bid
income" and define $y_{hz}(t)$ as the bid income of a worker $z\epsilon\Omega_j$
from a job $h\epsilon\Gamma_i$ at time t. Then using the theory developed in
Chapter Five

$$y_{hz}(t) = v_{ij} + [\epsilon_{hz} - \tilde{u}_h(t)], \quad h\epsilon\Gamma_i, \ z\epsilon\Omega_j,$$

$$i,j = 1, \ldots, n \tag{15.6}$$

where $\tilde{u}_h(t)$ is the maximum utility for a job h at time t.
Equation (15.6) specifies the bid income a worker $z\epsilon\Omega_i$
receives from a firm offering a job $h\epsilon\Gamma_i$ as the income the

firm could offer to the worker without decreasing its utility[*].
As in the housing market, a bid is considered by the supply
only if it is non-negative. In the labour market, the non-
negativity of acceptable bid incomes derives from the budget
constraint (15.2); we insist that a worker would not accept a
job whose wage is not enough to cover his basic consumption and
the associated commuting costs. If the worker fails to find a
job which is satisfactory in this sense, he will remain
unemployed and his disposable income will be zero. In fact,
since no other source of income has been assumed for households,
his whole income will be zero, and this leads to an inconsistency in the model (or at least to hard times for the
unemployed!), since even the unemployed household consumes
housing and services. This inconsistency could be partly over-
come by assuming a simple scheme of unemployment subsidies,
according to which the unemployed receive public subsidies to
cover their living costs. If this assumption is made, then the
sum $s_j + r_j$ plays in the labour market a role somewhat similar
to that of the maintenance cost of housing in Chapter Nine.

The diffusion of information between demand and supply is
assumed to occur randomly in time with intensity λ. This means
each household receives information about the wage (and corresponding bid income) offered by any job according to a Poisson
process with intensity λ. It also means that firms receive
information about the cost of labour, that is about the wage
asked by any household according to a Poisson process with
intensity λ. Then the total number of units of information a
firm receives (for a specific single job) about workers living
in zone j is a Poisson process with intensity

---

[*] Remember that the firm actually offers the maximum wage
which can be paid without decreasing its utility, and the
worker computes the corresponding bid income from it.

$$\lambda Q_j \qquad j = 1, \ldots, n \qquad\qquad (15.7)$$

Similarly, the total number of units of information a worker receives about jobs in zone i is a Poisson process with intensity:

$$\lambda P_i \qquad i = 1, \ldots, n \qquad\qquad (15.8)$$

Both firms and workers are assumed not to keep information in memories forever. Each unit of information received at time τ is assumed to have a random lifetime η_τ, with given survival function $F(x) = \Pr\{\eta_\tau > x\}$ for all τ. This means that if a firm has received information about the cost of a worker at time $t - x$, it will be kept in memory at least until time t with probability $F(x)$, while it will be forgotten before time t with probability $1-F(x)$.

In the same way a worker who has received information about the wage (and bid income) offered by a job at time $t - x$ still remembers it at time t with probability $F(x)$, while it is forgotten with probability $1-F(x)$. The mean lifetime of a unit of information is given by

$$\mu = \int_0^\infty F(\tau)d\tau$$

and we assume μ is finite.

As we mentioned already, both demand and supply are assumed to have a maximizing behaviour. Demand (ie the firms) aims at maximizing utility (profit); therefore for each job, firms keep track of the maximum in the sequence of utility values (15.5) which are still in memory at time t. By definition this maximum is $\tilde{u}_h(t)$. Supply (ie the workers) aims at maximizing the disposable income; therefore each worker keeps track of the maximum in the sequence of bid income values (15.6) he has still in memory at time t. If this maximum is non-negative, he sets his "price" equal to it, ie he is not willing to accept a job offering a disposable income less than $\tilde{y}_z(t)$. Otherwise, the worker will accept a zero disposable income.

The assumptions introduced so far define a dynamic assignment process of the type considered in Section 5.7. Both firm and worker behaviour are stochastic extremal processes of the type studied in Section 5.4 to 5.6. In the next section, we shall determine the distributions of utilities $\tilde{u}_h(t)$ and disposable incomes $\tilde{y}_z(t)$, and work out some other useful results.

15.3 Income Distributions and Dynamic Equations

In addition to the assumptions introduced in Section 15.2, it will be further assumed that the condition (5.96) of theorem 5.7.1 in Chapter Five holds. The theorem can thus be applied to the labour market model, provided the market is large enough to justify the use of asymptotic approximations. In order to do so, we know from the theory in Chapter Five that the constant a_Q, defined as the root of equation:

$$1 - F(a_Q) = \frac{1}{\lambda \mu Q}$$

must be subtracted from the random utility terms ε_{hz}. This is just a change in the origin of the utility scale, which is arbitrary.

Define $H_i(x,t)$ as the distribution of the maximum utility at time t for a job $h\varepsilon\Gamma_i$ as $Q \to \infty$; $R_j(x,t)$, the distribution of the required disposable income at time t for a worker $z\varepsilon\Omega_j$ as $Q \to \infty$. Then one has from theorem 5.7.1 that

$$H_i(x,t) = \exp[-\phi_i(t)e^{-\beta x}], \quad i = 1, \ldots, n \qquad (15.9)$$

$$R_j(x,t) = \begin{cases} \exp[-\psi_j(t)e^{-\beta x}] & x > 0 \\ \\ 0 & x < 0 \end{cases} \qquad j = 1, \ldots, n \quad (15.10)$$

where

$$\phi_i(t) = \sum_{j=1}^{n} \omega_j e^{\beta[v_{ij} - y_j(t)]} \qquad (15.11)$$

$$\psi_j(t) = \sum_{i=1}^{n} \theta_i e^{\beta[v_{ij} - u_i(t)]} \qquad (15.12)$$

$$w_j = Q_j/Q \qquad (15.13)$$

$$\theta_i = P_i/Q \qquad (15.14)$$

The quantities $y_j(t)$ and $u_i(t)$ are solutions of the integral equations:

$$e^{-\beta u_i(t)} = \int_0^\infty \frac{F(\tau)}{\mu} \frac{1}{\phi_i(t-\tau)} \, d\tau \qquad (15.15)$$

$$e^{-\beta y_j(t)} = \int_0^\infty \frac{F(\tau)}{\mu} \frac{1-e^{-\psi_j(t-\tau)}}{\psi_j(t-\tau)} \, d\tau \qquad (15.16)$$

From equation (5.113), section 5.7, one has

$$e^{-\beta \bar{y}_j(t)} = \frac{1-e^{-\psi_j(t)}}{\psi_j(t)} \qquad (15.17)$$

where

$$\bar{y}_j(t) = -\frac{1}{\beta} \log \int_{-\infty}^{\infty} e^{-\beta x} dR_j(x,t), \qquad j = 1, \ldots, n \quad (15.18)$$

is the exponential average of disposable incomes in zone j.

The average (15.18) is different from the expected value, which would be given by the integral

$$\int_{-\infty}^{\infty} x \, dR_j(x,t)$$

which is not computable in closed form.

Replacing (15.17) in (15.16) one has:

$$y_j(t) = -\frac{1}{\beta} \int_0^{\infty} \frac{F(\tau)}{\mu} e^{-\beta y_j(t-\tau)} d\tau \tag{15.19}$$

That is, $y(t)$ is the weighted exponential time average of disposable incomes required by households living in zone j, the weighting factor being $F(\tau)/\mu$.

A similar interpretation can be given for $u_i(t)$, which is the weighted exponential time average of maximum utilities for jobs (firms) located in zone i. In the dynamic labour market model considered here time averages therefore become the main aggregate signals.

From the application of corollary 5.7.1, Chapter Five, one obtains the demand function, ie the probability $p_{ij}(t)$ that the best worker (ie the one yielding the highest utility) known up to time t by a firm offering a job in zone i lives in zone j as given by a logit model

$$p_{ij}(t) = \frac{Q_j e^{\beta[v_{ij}-y_j(t)]}}{\sum_{j=1}^{n} Q_j e^{\beta[v_{ij}-y_j(t)]}} \tag{15.20}$$

The supply function, the probability $S_j(t)$ that a worker living in zone j is potentially employed at time t, ie that he has received at least one non-negative bid, is given by

$$S_j(t) = [1-e^{-\psi_j(t)}] \tag{15.21}$$

In section 5.7 it is also shown that one can interpret the quantity $\psi_j(t)$ as a time average of potential demand for a worker living in zone j:

$$\psi_j(t) = \int_0^\infty \frac{F(\tau)}{\mu} \, \Gamma_j(t-\tau) d\tau \qquad (15.22)$$

where

$$T_j(t) = \sum_{i=1}^n P_i \frac{e^{\beta v_{ij}}}{\sum_{j=1}^n Q_j e^{\beta[v_{ij}-y_j(t)]}}$$

is the potential demand for a worker living in j at time t, defined as the expected number of jobs (firms) who have placed their highest bid on that worker up to time t.

Replacing from (15.21) and keeping interpretation (15.22) in mind, equation (15.16) can also be written as:

$$y_j(t) = -\frac{1}{\beta} \log \int_0^\infty \frac{F(\tau)}{\mu} \frac{S_j(t-\tau)}{\psi_j(t-\tau)} \, d\tau \qquad (15.23)$$

Equation (15.23) states that $y_j(t)$ is a weighted exponential time average of supply-demand ratios. We now have two alternative, but equivalent interpretations of equations (15.16), namely (15.19) and (15.23).

If it is assumed that $F(x) = e^{-\alpha x}$ and $\mu = \int_0^\infty F(x)dx = 1/\alpha$ then in Section 5.7 it is shown that the integral equations (15.15) and (15.16) are equivalent to the differential equations:

$$\dot{X}_i(t) = \alpha/\phi_i(t) - \alpha X_i(t) \qquad (15.24)$$

$$\dot{Y}_j(t) = \alpha[1-e^{-\psi_j(t)}]/\psi_j(t) - \alpha Y_j(t) \qquad (15.25)$$

where the transformed variables $X_i(t)$ and $Y_j(t)$ are defined as

341

$$X_i(t) = e^{-\beta u_i(t)}$$

$$Y_j(t) = e^{-\beta y_j(t)}$$

In analogy with equations (15.19) and (15.23), equation (15.25) can be given two alternative interpretations. It is shown in section 5.7 that equation (15.25) is equivalent to either of the equations:

$$\dot{Y}_j(t) = \frac{\alpha}{\beta} \{1 - e^{-\beta[\overline{y}_j(t) - y_j(t)]}\} \qquad (15.26)$$

$$\dot{Y}_j(t) = \frac{\alpha}{\beta} \frac{D_j(t) - S_j(t)}{D_j(t)} \qquad (15.27)$$

where $D_j(t) = T_j(t)e^{-\beta y_j(t)}$ is the demand forecast for a worker living in zone j and asking for a disposable income $y_j(t)$ at time t and $\overline{y}_j(t)$ is the average disposable income asked at time t by a worker living in j, as defined by (15.18). Equation (15.26) relates the rate of change of the time average, $y_j(t)$, to the difference $\overline{y}_j(t) - y_j(t)$: when the average disposable income at time t is greater than the corresponding time average, $\dot{Y}_j(t) > 0$, otherwise $\dot{Y}_j(t) < 0$. Equation (15.27) is of a Walrasian type, since it relates the rate of change of $y(t)$ to the difference between demand and supply.

15.4 The Equilibrium Solution

We shall now investigate the behaviour of the system described in section 15.3 as $t \to \infty$, that is, in the long run. Given the assumptions introduced so far, we can resort to corollary 5.7.2, Chapter Five. This basically means that the equilibrium assignment satisfies theorem 5.3.2, ie the quantities $P_{ij} = \lim_{t \to \infty} P_{ij}(t)$ are the unique solution to the concave programming problem

$$\max_{\{p_{ij}\}} \sum_{i=1}^{n} P_i \sum_{j=1}^{n} p_{ij}(v_{ij} - \frac{1}{\beta}\log\frac{p_{ij}}{Q_j}) - \frac{1}{\beta}\sum_{j=1}^{n} Q_j \int_0^{A_j(p)/Q_j} \log[\frac{-\log(1-x)}{x}]dx$$

$$(15.28)$$

subject to

$$\sum_{j=1}^{n} p_{ij} = 1 \qquad\qquad (15.29)$$

where

$$A_j(p) = \sum_{i=1}^{n} P_i p_{ij} \qquad\qquad (15.30)$$

It is shown in section 5.3 that a mathematical program like (15.28) - (15.30) has a precise economic interpretation. Namely, the objective function (15.28) is the total benefit, ie the sum of demand and supply surplus[*], since

$$\sum_{i=1}^{n} P_i \sum_{j=1}^{n} p_{ij}(v_{ij} - \frac{1}{\beta} \log \frac{p_{ij}}{Q_j}) - \sum_{j=1}^{n} A_j(p)y_j$$

is the demand (ie firms) surplus aggregated over all jobs offered and

$$\sum_{j=1}^{n} A_j(p)y_j - \frac{1}{\beta}\sum_{j=1}^{n} Q_j \int_0^{A_j(p)/Q_j} \log[\frac{-\log(1-x)}{x}]dx$$

is the supply (ie households) surplus aggregated over all

---

[*] A more standard terminology would be "consumers' and producers' surplus", but in this case it sounds rather odd to call the firms "consumers" and the households "producers" of labour.

households. The function

$$y(x) = \frac{1}{\beta} \log \left[\frac{-\log(1-x)}{x} \right], \quad 0 < x \le 1 \qquad (15.31)$$

is the supply price function induced by the stochastic labour market described in Section 15.2. Here the price of labour is disposable income $y(x)$ requested. Of course the whole price paid by the firm is the total wage, as defined by equation (15.3), but we know from the previous discussion that only the disposable income is subject to the worker's evaluation, the other components in the budget constraints being fixed costs x is the expected quantity of labour supplied by each worker; more precisely, x is the probability that a worker will be employed. Equation (15.31) defines a well-behaved supply function, which is convex, non-decreasing and such that

$$y(0) = 0$$

$$\lim_{x \to 1} y(x) = \infty$$

The fact that at equilibrium, corollary 5.7.2 (ie theorem 5.3.2) holds, means that the equilibrium average incomes can be computed as the unique solution to the set of market-clearing equations:

$$\sum_{i=1}^{n} P_i \frac{Q_j e^{\beta(v_{ij}-y_j)}}{\sum_{j=1}^{n} Q_j e^{\beta(v_{ij}-y_j)}} = Q_j(1-e^{-\psi_j}) \qquad (15.32)$$

which state equality between demand and supply for each zone.

The final comment on prices made at the end of Section 9.4, for the housing market, applies here as well for incomes. Although the quantities y_j act as equilibrating signals, they should not be confused with uniform incomes in each zone. Actual incomes are random variables, whose distributions are

given by equation (15.10). Equations (15.32) are therefore
deterministic approximations, ie market clearing conditions
based on expected demand and supply and on average incomes.

Chapter 16

TRANSPORT

A.G. Wilson

16.1 Introduction

At first sight it may be argued that transport models are
redundant within a comprehensive model since all trips would
be calculated in some form in other submodels: journey to
work, trips to shops, and so on. However, there is one crucial
theoretical reason why this argument will not hold for a complete comprehensive model: it is through the transport model
that trips for different purposes are combined and loaded onto
transport networks; and it is this which facilitates the
computation of a congestion-sensitive generalised inter-zonal
cost measure which can be used in other submodels. There are
also practical reasons why a transport model will usually be
necessary. The comprehensive model will not typically be so
comprehensive that all trips will be enumerated; nor will they
always be categorised in such a way that they match the
purposes usually employed in a transport model. A further
practical consideration is that for transport modelling and
generalised cost calculations, we are not interested in total
trips, but in numbers split by time-of-day: at least a subdivision into peak and off-peak trips.

There are a number of good reasons, therefore, theoretical
and pragmatic, why it is usually necessary to build a transport
submodel. In the rest of this introduction, we outline the main

issues which arise in the specification of an appropriate
model. There are four kinds of sets of issues: first, concerned with the conventional model itself; second, with the
representation and modelling of the supply side; third, with
the fitting of the transport model into a comprehensive model;
and fourth, issues concerned with the use of the models, particularly evaluation measures. We discuss each of these areas
in turn.

The basic transport model is usually considered to have
four main submodels: trip generation, trip distribution, modal
choice and network assignment. They can be combined in different ways - and, recently, Boyce (1984) has argued that most
of the elements are best combined, certainly the last three.
We will return to that issue later. Meanwhile, it is convenient to keep the four areas separate as the basis for discussing the main issues which arise in model design.

The trip generation submodel typically employs regression
or category analysis methods and has had remarkably little
research devoted to it relative to the other three submodels.
Usually it is inelastic. Attempts have been made to relate
trip production, at least, to, say, accessibility to some
power; and we pursue this idea below. This also has a bearing
on whether to use singly- or doubly-constrained distribution
(spatial interaction) models.

The distribution and modal choice models are often
combined - though in the example we present below, they are
separated to allow for greater freedom to investigate parameter variation between the two submodels. Beyond that, the
basic issue is the assumption about the underpinning theory.
The most common methods used are entropy-maximizing (Wilson,
1967, 1970) or some form of disaggregate model, such as the
logit model (cf for example, Williams, 1977; McFadden, 1974).
For the convenience of this particular author, the entropy-
maximizing method will be used in the example below; but it

would be easy to substitute an alternative without affecting
the bulk of the argument.

In the case of the assignment submodel, there are a number
of issues. They range from the theoretical: how do people
choose routes? - to the practical: how detailed should the
representation of the network be? In relation to the first
(theoretical) set of issues, it is known that here, or in
other submodels, there is some dispersion of behaviour around
the apparent optimum - the "least cost" route. This can occur
for all sorts of reasons: imperfect information, different
choice mechanisms not captured in the least-cost model, and so
on. This problem can be easily handled (with an entropy term
or the logit random error term) in the distribution case, but
not in the assignment case for a technical reason: while it is
(now) straightforward to compute the best (least-cost) route,
it is not easy to define, let alone compute, sensible second,
third, fourth routes and so on. So commonly, heuristic algorithms
are used: for example, to load a fraction of the trips into the
least-cost routes in the network, to adjust travel times for
congestion effects; then to assign another fraction to recal-
culated least-cost routes; and so on. There are obviously
many possible variants of this.

There is an implicit and difficult theoretical issue
which relates all the submodels: how to define a generalised
cost for each level, and how to relate the costs so defined.
Williams (1977) showed that for most models, there is only one
consistent way to do this and in many transport models mis-
takes are made in this respect (cf also Williams and Senior,
1977). It is worth sketching the nature of the issue in a
little more detail. We work backwards. At the assignment
level, we would seek costs γ_{ij}^{kr} on route r within mode k between
i and j. At the modal split level, we need $\hat{c}_{ij}^{k}$; at the distribution level, C_{ij}; even at the generation level, a measure
dependent on i only which is a measure of average trip length

(as accessibility). The problem is: there will be several r's
to a (k,i,j) set; several k's to an (i,j) set; many (i,j)'s to
an i. How is γ_{ij}^{kr} to be averaged over r to generate $\hat{c}_{ij}^{k}$, $\hat{c}_{ij}^{k}$
over k to obtain C_{ij}?

The second set of issues was concerned with the supply
side of the transport model. Essentially these are the elements of the generalised cost term, as we will see when we
model this explicitly below. The travel time component of
this will depend strongly on the (multimodal) transport network itself. An interesting question is the extent
to which it is possible to model the equilibrium structures
of such networks - and explore the stability both of the whole
system and individual links - in much the same way as we
investigated $\{W_j\}$ structures in Chapters Three and Eight. It
turns out that this is an interesting question to pursue, but
one which is intrinsically more difficult to handle than the
service case because of the higher degree of connectivity of
the links of a network. It is also potentially useful to
explore other ways of analysing network structure, ranging
from the Nystuen and Dacey (1961) method to Q-analysis (cf
Atkin, 1974).

The third set of issues involves the interconnection of the
transport submodel to the other submodels of a comprehensive
model. The main connections are through the generalised costs,
$\{c_{ij}\}$, which figure in all the submodels; and the production
and attraction quantities in the trip generation submodel which
are directly functions of the distribution of activities.
There is a mutual relationship between transport flows and
urban structure, the nature of which is difficult to tease out.
But we will pursue this in the context of examples below.

Finally, there are issues concerned with the use of the
transport model. Traditionally, the main use has been in the
appraisal of transport investment schemes within the framework
of something like cost-benefit analysis. This remains important

but there is also the broader issue of the influence of transport investment on urban development and the way in which this
can be measured. We need to connect all submodels to a performance indicator package, and the influence of the $\{c_{ij}\}$
matrix will be important for many of these indicators.

The rest of the chapter is structured in relation to these
sets of issues. In Section 16.2 we present an example of a
transport model and then proceed to discuss in turn the supply
side (16.3), the connections with the comprehensive model
(16.4) and the uses of the model in investment appraisal and
planning more broadly (16.5). Some concluding comments are
offered in Section 16.6.

16.2 An Example of a Transport Model

It is important to capture quite a fine level of detail in
principle in building a transport model and to show this
explicitly. This involves working with trips by person type,
n, mode k and purpose p from origins, i, to destination, j.
So the main trip matrix will be T_{ij}^{knp} with production and
attraction terms O_i^{np} and D_j^p. Note that both generation terms
are independent of mode, k (though modal provision will have
an implicit influence through any travel cost matrix), and that
the attraction term is independent of person-type. However, we
will distinguish the average perceived generalised cost of
travel from i to j by person type, n - and this shows that the
person type definition will have to distinguish, for example,
car availability and no-car availability. The main generalised
cost arrays will then be this one, C_{ij}^n, modal costs, c_{ij}^k,
modal link costs $\gamma_{\ell m}^k$ for the (ℓ,m) link on the k-model network,
and route costs c_{ij}^{kr} for route r between i and j on mode k.
For convenience, we allow the number of superscripts (one or
two) to distinguish c_{ij}^k and c_{ij}^{kr} rather than introduce another
(unfamiliar) letter for the route-cost array.

Since this model is being developed in the context of a dynamic comprehensive model, we also distinguish time, t, on each of the relevant variables. We then proceed by writing down the appropriate model equations, and follow each subset by discussing the underlying rationale for them. The model is largely a conventional one, but more detail is made explicit than is customary and, in the first submodel, an attempt is made to construct "elastic" generation terms through accessibility variables.

Let

$$U_i^{np}(t) = \sum_{jq} b^{npq(1)}(t) X_j^q(t) e^{-\beta^{np} C_{ij}^n(t)} \tag{16.1}$$

$$V_j^p(t) = \sum_{iq} b^{pq(2)}(t) X_i^q(t) e^{-\hat{\beta}^{np} \hat{C}_{ij}^n(t)} \tag{16.2}$$

$X_j^q(t)$ is the amount of activity (or a measure of land use) of type q in zone j at time t; $b^{npq(1)}$ is the relative importance of this for producing trips by type n people for purpose p and $b^{pq(2)}$ its relative importance for attracting trips to j. Then $U_i^{np}(t)$ and $V_j^p(t)$ are measures of accessibility. β^{np} is the appropriate parameter from the distribution model - so we are already building in feedback from later submodels. The coefficient $\hat{\beta}^{np}$ (and indeed the array $\hat{C}_{ij}$) in (16.2), however, shows the difficulties involved in attempting to be consistent in this kind of modal specification. The "natural" units, as in (16.1), are β^{np} and C_{ij}^n. However, we wish $V_j^p(t)$, and hence $D_j(t)$, to be independent of n. Thus $\hat{\beta}^p$ and $\hat{C}_{ij}$ need to be some kind of "average" of β^n and C_{ij}^n respectively. A development of the argument in Williams (1977) suggests that C_{ij} should be calculated from

$$e^{-\hat{\beta}^p(t) C_{ij}} = \sum_n e^{-\hat{\beta}^{np}(t) \hat{C}_{ij}^n} \tag{16.3}$$

with $\hat{\beta}^p(t)$ calculated to ensure that

$$\sum_n T_{ij}^{**p} C_{ij}^n = C^p \tag{16.4}$$

where C^p is some observed quantity. Again we have a potential feedback to the distribution model and it may be simpler to take a weighted average.

Consider now the following hypotheses for $O_i^{np}(t)$ and $D_j^p(t)$

$$O_i^{np}(t) = \sum_q a^{npq(1)}(t)\{1 + \hat{a}^{nq(1)}(t) \left[\frac{U_i^{np}(t) - U_i^{np}(0)}{U_i^{np}(0)} \right]^{\phi_1^{np}(t)} \} X_i^q(t) \tag{16.5}$$

$$D_j^p(t) = \sum_q a^{pq(2)}(t)\{1 + \hat{a}^{pq(2)}(t) \left[\frac{V_j^p(t) - V_j^p(0)}{V_j^p(0)} \right]^{\phi_2^p(t)} \} X_j^q(t) \tag{16.6}$$

This is an extension of a conventional category analysis model (cf Wootton and Pick, 1967). The coefficients $a^{npq(1)}(t)$ and $a^{pq(2)}(t)$ give the number of trips produced and attracted respectively by activity (or land use) $X_i^q(t)$ or $X_j^q(t)$. These totals are modified through the coefficients $\hat{a}^{npq(1)}(t)$ and $\hat{a}^{pq(2)}(t)$ to take account of any changes in accessibility (in either direction). The coefficients $\phi_1^{np}(t)$ and $\phi_2^p(t)$ also contribute to a description of the strength of this effect.

As noted at an earlier point in the argument, we propose to separate trip distribution and modal split. We therefore first seek T_{ij}^{*np} (with an asterisk replacing an index denoting summation or, where appropriate, averaging) and then M_{ij}^{knp} such that

$$T_{ij}^{knp} = M_{ij}^{knp} T_{ij}^{*np} \tag{16.7}$$

An appropriate distribution model, based on entropy-maximizing methods, is

$$T_{ij}^{*np}(t) = A_i^{np}(t)B_j^{p}(t)O_i^{np}(t)D_j^{p}(t)e^{-\beta^{np}(t)C_{ij}^{n}(t)} \qquad (16.8)$$

with

$$A_i^{np}(t) = 1/\sum_j B_j^{p}(t)D_j^{p}(t)e^{-\beta^{np}(t)C_{ij}^{n}(t)} \qquad (16.9)$$

and

$$B_j^{p}(t) = 1/\sum_{in} A_i^{np}(t)O_i^{n}(t)e^{-\beta^{np}(t)C_{ij}^{n}(t)} \qquad (16.10)$$

to ensure that

$$\sum_j T_{ij}^{*np} = O_i^{np} \qquad (16.11)$$

and

$$\sum_{in} T_{ij}^{*np} = D_j^{p} \qquad (16.12)$$

Again following Williams (1977), it can be argued that $C_{ij}^{n}(t)$ can be obtained from

$$e^{-\lambda^{np}(t)C_{ij}^{n}(t)} = \sum_{k\in M(n)} e^{-\lambda^{np}(t)c_{ij}^{k}(t)} \qquad (16.13)$$

where $M(n)$ is the set of modes, k, available to type-n people and $\lambda^{np}(t)$ is the set of parameters from the modal choice model which we will present explicitly shortly.

The parameter $\beta^{np}(t)$ should be estimated by maximum likelihood which in effect means solving the equations

$$\sum_{ij} T_{ij}^{*np}C_{ij}^{n}(t) = C^{np}(t) \qquad (16.14)$$

where $C^{np}(t)$ is the expenditure at time t by type-n people for trips of purpose p.

An alternative, which may be particularly important when the transport model is a component of a comprehensive model and the focus is on urban development, is to solve

$$\sum_j T_{ij}^{*np}(t)C_{ij}^n(t) = C_i^{np}(t) \qquad (16.15)$$

for a set of parameters $\beta_i^{np}(t)$, and to model $C_i^{np}(t)$ in terms of the incomes of the residents of i, the accessibility of i, and so on. Provided a model for C_i^{np} can be built involving a small number of parameters, then the large number of β_i^{bp}'s should be considered as intermediate variables rather than as independent parameters. Southworth (1979) has developed distribution models of this kind with origin-disaggregated β-parameters.

Whether we proceed by entropy-maximizing or disaggregate route, the modal choice model will take the form

$$M_{ij}^{knp}(t) = \frac{e^{-\lambda^{np}(t)c_{ij}^k(t)}}{\sum_{k\epsilon M(n)} e^{-\lambda^{np}(t)c_{ij}^k(t)}} \qquad (16.16)$$

The parameters $\lambda^{np}(t)$ are obtained within the entropy-maximizing framework by solving

$$\sum T_{ij}^{knp}(t)\left[c_{ij}^k(t) - c_{ij}^{kmin}(t)\right] = \hat{C}^{np}(t) \qquad (16.17)$$

where $C_{ij}^{kmin}(t)$ is the generalised cost on the minimum cost route and $\hat{C}^{np}(t)$ is observed. There may also be the possibility at this stage of estimating other coefficients within the generalised cost term, an issue which we pursue further below. Southworth (1978) has also calibrated models of this type with origin-specific parameters.

This is also a convenient place to note that if T_{ij}^{knp} was modelled directly - that is, the distribution and modal choice submodels were combined - then implicit in such a model would be an assumption that the parameters $\lambda^{np}(t)$ in (16.16) were replaced by $\beta^{np}(t)$. Thus, the β-parameters would have to do two jobs: relate trips to observed mean trip length, and determine the sensitivity of travellers to the differences in the elements of generalised cost which determine modal split. Common sense seems to demand that two sets of parameters are needed for these different roles.

A possible variant on the modal split model presented here involves building in lag effects. Let $x_{\ell}^{np}(t)$ be the proportion of the type-n population who operate with a lag of length ℓ when considering modal choice for trips of purpose p. Then

$$M_{ij}^{knp}(t) = \sum_{\ell} \frac{x_{\ell}^{np}(t)e^{-\lambda^{np}(t-\ell)c_{ij}^{k}(t-\ell)}}{\sum_{k \in M(n)} e^{-\lambda^{np}(t-\ell)c_{ij}^{k}(t-\ell)}} \tag{16.18}$$

It can be seen that this includes hysteresis as well as lag effects: if a price rise loses passengers from a model, a corresponding price decrease would not immediately get them all back again. Needless to say, this kind of potentially very attractive model would be much more difficult to calibrate than the conventional one.

The assignment model lies at the heart of any linkage between the transport submodel and the remaining submodels in a comprehensive system. There is also a crucial feedback between the assignment submodel and the other three elements of the transport model. Both kinds of linkages turn on the travel time component of the generalised cost function and whether this is an adequate representation of congestion in the system. In many comprehensive models, there is no transport model: the other submodels are relied upon to generate flows; even when there is a transport model, there is a tendency for this to be of a rudimentary kind without an assignment submodel. The reason for this lies in the difficulty of coding the underlying networks in a realistic way. Typically, this process alone takes a lot of effort; and then more labour has to be devoted to the "cleaning-up" of the network to obtain realistic results from the model.

It probably remains the case that it is best to develop a complete transport model which includes a detailed network representation and an assignment submodel. However, in order to suggest a way of coping with the difficulties referred to above, and also to facilitate further insights when we come to discuss the supply side, we explore an alternative intermediate position: to build a notional "spider" network. This involves connecting nearby zone centroids with notional links and then making some judgement about the time-flow relationships for each link in relation to the underlying real network. Higher capacities could be given, for example, to links which paralleled main radial arterials; or motorways in whatever direction.

To make further progress, we need to specify the generalised cost function more formally. Its elements are, typically:

(i)   the money cost of travel from i to j by mode k, m_{ij}^k;

(ii)   the travel time, t_{ij}^k;

(iii) the so-called "excess" time: waiting time, and so on, e_{ij}^k;

(iv)   a term associated with the origin, $p_i^{(1)k}$ - this might be high in relation to public transport for a low density residential area for instance;

(v)   a term associated with destination, $p_j^{(2)k}$ - which might include parking charges for example.

Then, defining appropriate coefficients for the time terms:

$$c_{ij}^{k}(t) = m_{ij}^{k}(t) + a_1^{k}(t)t_{ij}^{k}(t) + a_2^{k}(t)e_{ij}^{k}(t) + p_i^{(1)k}(t) + p_j^{(2)k}(t)$$

$$(16.19)$$

We will also on occasion add a further superscript r when it is necessary to distinguish routes within a model:

$$c_{ij}^{kr}(t) = m_{ij}^{kr}(t) + a_1^{k}(t)t_{ij}^{kr}(t) + a_2^{k}(t)e_{ij}^{kr}(t) + p_i^{(1)k}(t) + p_j^{(2)k}(t)$$

$$(16.20)$$

Here we assume that the coefficients which represent the values of different kinds of time are independent of r, and that the origin and destination costs are independent of r.

We can now focus on the travel time components, $t_{ij}^{k}(t)$, mainly at first in relation to the car mode which we will take to be given by k = 1. We first need to define some variables which will characterise the network. Let ℓ and m denote nodes of the network. When there is a link, we have already defined $\gamma_{\ell m}^{k}(t)$ to be the travel time on that link. Given a set of such times, it is possible to use a standard algorithm to find $R_{ij}^{i}(t)$ as the set of nodes which form the best path between i and j by mode k. We will also extend this notation in two obvious ways, first by taking $R_{ij}^{kr}(t)$ as the set of nodes on alternative routes r between i and j by mode k; and second, in the case of spider networks, to emphasise the fact that the nodes are zone centroids, to replace (ℓ,m) by (i',j'), so $\gamma_{i'j'}^{k}(t)$ becomes the "link" cost in that case.

We can then assume that a standard algorithm is used to find the sets $R_{ij}^{k}(t)$; and another to find alternative routes and the sets $R_{ij}^{kr}(t)$ - possibly by incremental loading as noted earlier. Let $q_{\ell m}^{i}(t)$ be a set of variables which characterise the "capacity" of the links (ℓ,m) and let $Q_{\ell m}^{k}(t)$ be the flow on link (ℓ,m) of the mode-k network. Assume a set of initial link times, $\gamma^k_{\ell m}(t)$, are known. Then in the case of assignment to the best (least-cost) path, we can set up the following iterative scheme:

$$t^k_{ij}(t) = \sum_{(\ell,m)\epsilon R^k_{ij}} \gamma^k_{\ell m}(t) \qquad (16.21)$$

$$Q^k_{\ell m}(t) = \sum_{p(i,j)\epsilon \hat{R}^k_m(t)} T^{knp}_{ij}(t) \qquad (16.22)$$

(where $\hat{R}^k_{\ell m}(t)$ is the set of origin-destination nodes (i,j) for which (ℓ,m) is on the best path); and third, the readjustment of $\gamma^k_{\ell m}(t)$:

$$\gamma^k_{\ell m}(t) = \gamma^k_{\ell m}\left[t,Q^k_{\ell m}(t),q^k_{\ell m}(t)\right] \qquad (16.23)$$

This last equation is assumed to be one of the standard time-flow relationships in terms of a capacity parameter $q^k_{\ell m}(t)$.

The same equations hold for least-cost assignment in a spider network, but with (i',j') replacing (ℓ,m) in the notation.

The situation is slightly more complicated in the multiple-route case. Let Γ^{kr}_{ij} be the proportion taking route r. An obvious model is then:

$$\Gamma^{kr}_{ij} = \frac{e^{-\nu^k(t)c^{kr}_{ij}(t)}}{\sum_r e^{-\nu^k(t)c^{kr}_{ij}(t)}} \qquad (16.24)$$

and then, using an **obvious extension of notation**

$$\Gamma_{ij}^{knpr} = \Gamma_{ij}^{knp*} \Gamma_{ij}^{kr} \qquad\qquad (16.25)$$

For any of these possibilities, the whole transport model has to be solved iteratively. To illustrate this point, we return to equations (16.21) - (16.23): the argument can be demonstrated for the simplest case and can then be applied straightforwardly to the others. $t_{ij}^{k}(t)$ in (16.21) is part of the generalised cost and this will affect $\Gamma_{ij}^{knp}(t)$ through the other transport submodels. This is the main input on the right-hand side of (16.22), producing link flows which are then used to adjust the travel times through (16.23). This leads to new t_{ij}^{k}'s in (16.21), and then new $\Gamma_{ij}^{knp}(t)$'s; however, as with all these iterative schemes it is a matter of experimentation to decide whether it is better to iterate to convergence in the assignment programme before recycling through the other submodels, or whether the whole cycle should form one stage in the iteration.

Conventional pre-mathematical programming models are reviewed by van Vliet (1976-A, 1976-B, 1976-C). A multi-mode example of a programming version is presented by Florian (1977). The broader principles are reviewed by Boyce (1984), and we return to the issues raised there below.

There are various reviews available of the conventional transport model and the way it is assembled and used. A useful recent book in this respect is that by Black (1981). A thorough testing and exploration of the conventional model is offered in Bonsall et al (1977).

Boyce (1984), however, would argue that it was now appropriate to develop combined distribution - modal split - assignment models based on mathematical programming algorithms. The main advantage of these formulations is that the algorithms can be shown to converge to an appropriate solution. Boyce argues that, typically, the more conventional iterative scheme sketched earlier is oscillatory.

The combined model is based on the work of Evans (1976) who produced a mathematical programming version of a combined distribution-modal split model. It was shown that the Frank and Wolf (1956) algorithm could be used to solve the problem. Early applications were by Florian (1977), Boyce and Southworth (1979), Erlander, Nguyen and Stewart (1979) and the calibration properties of the algorithm were explored by Hearn and Ribera (1981). The history of this development is reviewed by Boyce (1984) using mathematical frameworks presented by Kuhn (1982).

It is useful to give a flavour of the combined model, and the new notation which has facilitated its development, by presenting one of the models from Boyce (1984). The notational trick is to allow a single index, i, to range over origin-destination pairs and to label these through membership of sets I_j and I_k which determine whether j or k is an origin or destination respectively of i (out of a total set I). Similarly $r \varepsilon P_i$ is the set of routes which make up the i interchange. h_r is the number of trips on route r, T_i the number of trips on O-D interaction, i. $a_{\ell r}$ is 1 if link ℓ (εL) is included in r or 0 if not. All the difficulties are absorbed into the set definitions. $c_\ell(f_\ell)$ is the user cost of using link ℓ at flow level f_ℓ. The model is then

$$\underset{\{h_r, T_i\}}{\text{Min}} \ \underset{\ell \varepsilon L}{\Sigma} \ \int_0^{f_\ell} c_\ell(x)dx + \frac{1}{\beta} \underset{i \varepsilon I}{\Sigma} T_i \log T_i \qquad (16.26)$$

such that

$$f_\ell \equiv \underset{r \varepsilon P}{\Sigma} h_r a_{\ell r} < b', \ \ell \varepsilon L \qquad (16.27)$$

$$\underset{r \varepsilon P_i}{\Sigma} h_r = T_i \qquad (16.28)$$

360

$$\sum_{i\epsilon I_j} T_i = O_j, \quad j\epsilon J \qquad\qquad (16.29)$$

$$\sum_{i\epsilon I_k} T_i = D_k, \quad k\epsilon K \qquad\qquad (16.30)$$

$$h_r \geq 0, \quad r\epsilon P \qquad\qquad (16.31)$$

16.3 The Supply Side

The variables which represent the supply side of the transport
system are largely exogenous as yet: the link capacities,
$q_{\ell m}^k(t)$ and some of the parameters (particularly for public
transport) which describe route frequency and spacing and
which determine elements of the generalised cost function like
the excess times and the terminal components. Any changes in
these variables are usually taken to constitute a plan and the
model is used to calculate the impact of the plan (cf Section
16.5 below). This is likely to remain the main use of the
model. Formal treatments of the supply side are presented in
Manheim (1980) and various other papers in a special issue of
Transportation Research (Florian and Gaudry, 1980). The
editors of that issue updated their own contribution later
(Florian and Gaudry, 1983). However, it is also useful to ask
the question as to whether the methods of dynamical systems
theory can be used to model changes in supply-side variables
on the basis of some criterion like the maximisation of consumer benefits relative to costs. It would be necessary to be
careful in the interpretation of the results of such an
analysis, but they may have a relevance to developing good
"designs" for networks for example.

The only way in which this analysis could proceed for a
transport model which included a full network would involve a

specification of cost and benefit functions for developments of
any scale for any link – and including notional links not yet
built. This is obviously an impossible task, but that lay
behind the earlier suggestion that a spider network should be
used. Consider, therefore, explicit versions of equations
(16.21) – (16.23) for the links of a spider network:

$$t_{ij}^k(t) = \sum_{(i',j') \in R_{ij}^k(t)} \gamma_{i'j'}^k(t) \tag{16.32}$$

$$Q_{i'j'}^k(t) = \sum_{p(i,j) \in \hat{R}_{i'j'}^k(t)} T_{ij}^{knp}(t) \tag{16.33}$$

$$\gamma_{i'j'}^k(t) = \gamma_{i'j'}^k \left| t, Q_{i'j'}^k(t), q_{i'j'}^k(t) \right| \tag{16.34}$$

The crucial step is now the specification of the functions
$\gamma_{i'j'}^k$. If there are N zones and, say, an average of 3 links of
the spider network connected to each centroid, then there will
be 3N such functions. While this can be a large number, it is
much less than the number of actual and possible links of a
real network.

We can now proceed to explore $\Delta q_{i'j'}^k(t,t+1)$ – the change
in capacity in the notional (i',j') spider network link for
mode k – using the ideas applied to locational variables in
Chapter Three. Let $\Delta B_{i'j'}^k(t,t+1)$, $\Delta q_{i'j'}^k(t,t+1)$, be the
increment in consumers' benefits resulting from this change,
let $K_{i'j'}^k$ ($q_{i'j'}^k$) be the capital cost and r a suitable rate of
interest. Then the arguments of Chapter Three would suggest
a mechanism of the following form:

$$\Delta q_{i'j'}^k(t,t+1) = \varepsilon(\Delta B_{i'j'}^k - rK_{i'j'}^k) \tag{16.35}$$

The remaining step involves the measurement of benefits. We
can now deduce from Williams (1977) that a suitable measure is

$$\Delta B(t,t+1) = \sum_{\substack{np \\ k\varepsilon M(n)}} \frac{1}{\beta^{np}} \log \frac{\sum_{ij} e^{-\beta^{np}(t+1)c_{ij}^k(t+1)}}{\sum_{ij} e^{-\beta^{np}(t)c_{ij}^k(t)}} \qquad (16.36)$$

for a change in the generalised cost matrix from $\{c_{ij}^k(t)\}$ to $\{c_{ij}^k(t+1)\}$ (see also Jara-Dias and Friesz, 1982). However, this relates to the whole system: we need to find a way of breaking it down to extract the (i',j') contribution. However, there is no obvious way of doing this. We can try

$$\Delta B_{i'j'}^k(t,t+1) = \Delta B(t,t+1,\Delta q_{i'j'}^k, |\Delta q_{ij}^k = 0, i \neq i', j \neq j')$$

$$(16.37)$$

That is, we use (16.35) to calculate the system wide impacts of an (i',j') change. This is how it will be necessary to proceed. However, that does leave us with a version of the "backcloth" problem outlined in Wilson and Clarke (1979): for any (i',j') in (16.37) it will be necessary to assume the q_{ij}^k's for all other (i,j) links.

It would be useful to attempt to run a dynamic supply-side model of this kind, if only as a design aid – to see where the pressures to increase notional link capacities are. It would then be possible to relate these to the real under-lying networks.

These ideas can be compared to more conventional mathematical-programming-based ideas on network design (cf Steenbrink, 1974, Boyce, ed., 1979, Boyce, 1984).

16.4 Connections to the Comprehensive Model

The formal connections can be specified rather simply: they
are through the land use-activity variables X_j^q in equations
(16.1) and (16.2), and equations (16.5) and (16.6) - in other
words mainly through the trip generation submodel; and through
the generalised cost terms, usually written as c_{ij}, which play
a role in almost all other submodels. The details of the connection are likely to be more troublesome. The q-categories
in X_j^q will have to be defined to be compatible with the submodels which generate X_j^q's and sensible in the transport context for when coefficients are applied to turn X_j^q's into trips.
It is also clear that there is no "natural" c_{ij} to take from
the transport model and use elsewhere. We generate C_{ij}^n or
c_{ij}^k; but the other submodels will require person-type categories
which differ from the n-groups used in the transport model, and
usually they will not be able to carry the detail involved in
making transport modes explicit. A $\{c_{ij}\}$ matrix will typically
have to be constructed, therefore, as some kind of average of
$\{C_{ij}^n\}$ or $\{c_{ij}^k\}$.

Not many attempts have been made to incorporate a full
transport model into a comprehensive model. One such is
offered by Bonsall et al (1977) in the Models of Cities and
Regions book.

It remains to consider the extent to which a dynamic
transport model could be more fully integrated into a comprehensive urban model. This issue has been explored fully
in Wilson (1984-A) and we will present only the main issues
here. The first point to note is that for some trip purposes,
say service trips, it may be better to revert to a singly-
constrained rather than a doubly-constrained distribution
model. This then leaves open the possibility of a fuller
integration: since a $\{D_j^g\}$ array could be calculated from the
transport model and used in the dynamic services model - cf

Chapters Ten and Eleven.

Two further issues can be usefully noted as topics for further research. First, we have implicitly assumed in the transport model that if there is a supply-side change, then there is an instant shift to a new equilibrium. Some lags probably should be incorporated. More broadly, the speed of adjustment in the transport model should be related to the different speeds in other submodels. But this is a difficult area of empirical research.

Secondly, no effective models have yet been developed for the prediction of β-values over time. Indeed, there are two different theoretical positions on this, neither of which has been investigated empirically. The entropy-maximiser would shift the problem to modelling aggregate expenditure terms, like $C^{np}(t)$ in equation (16.14) or C_i^{np} in (16.15). The disaggregate modeller would probably argue that β-parameters, once estimated, should be kept constant. If the first of these views is taken, then the $C^{np}(t)$ or $C_i^{np}(t)$ terms need to be modelled in terms of urban structure variables among others; and so this provides a further connection between the transport model and the rest of the urban model.

16.5 The Use of the Model

We have already given the equation for benefits generated from investment in the system - see equation (16.36) above - and this can be used as the basis for transport investment appraisal. More generally, c_{ij} elements will play an important role in other performance indicators - see Wilson (1984-A, 1984-C) for a more detailed explanation. We have also, in relation to the topic of the supply side, noted how the transport model can be used as the basis of various approaches to network design. Indeed this argument can be extended to any controllable component of the generalised cost formula: for example, parking charges, public transport route frequency or whatever.

Thus the model provides the outputs which can be used to evaluate the impacts of plans and to suggest alternative designs and policies, either narrowly within the context of the transport model itself, or more broadly in the field of urban structure.

A final point: it should also be borne in mind that for certain planning uses, a completely different approach might help: focussed on transport in relation to the total activity packages of households. This has been most extensively explored in Sweden (see Hagerstrand, 1970); an economic approach was initiated by Becker (1965) and attempts made to integrate this into geographical analysis by Wilson (1972).

Chapter 17

A FIRST EXAMPLE OF AN INTEGRATED OPERATIONAL MODEL

C.S. Bertuglia, G. Leonardi, S. Occelli, G. Rabino and
R. Tadei

17.1 Introduction

In Chapter Six we introduced the main three dimensions underpinning the design of an integrated model as state variables
(or components), subsystems, and approaches. The relationships among the three dimensions were summarized in Figure 6.1.
This is used as a starting point here to develop a specific
example of an integrated model fulfilling the requirements of
Chapter Six. We emphasize again that in Figure 6.1 several
alternative paths are offered and several options are available
at each branching point. The specific choice made here has no
claim to be better than others: it simply illustrates how the
framework can be put to work as a guideline for model design.
If our specific choice has a comparative advantage, this lies
in maintaining a balance between the three main approaches
presented in the theoretical chapters: the master equations
approach has been used as a general accounting framework for
population mobility; the stock dynamics approach for economic
structures (although a slight revision in order to achieve
consistency with the population accounting framework was
required); and both economic theory and stochastic extremal
processes have been used to derive specifications for the
behavioural models and the price formation mechanisms. The
joint use of the two behavioural approaches is not surprising

since they lead largely to the same conclusions: behavioural demand and supply models of the logit type are proposed by Anas in Chapters Two and Seven, and similar models are derived from the theory of stochastic extremal processes by Leonardi in Chapters Five and Nine. There are alternative ways of handling market clearing in the behavioural models and we explore these in the appropriate sections below.

17.2 A Simplified Model Structure

Although five subsystems are listed in Figure 6.1, only three of them will be explicitly considered here: the housing market; services; and the labour market. Explicit treatments of the land market and the transport system are excluded. While this can be justified for the land market if only because such modelling is not yet operational, it might seem a serious shortcoming for the transport system. It should·be recalled, however, that many transport variables are embedded in the other subsystems: for example O-D matrices for home-to-work and home-to-service trips. What is missing is the dynamics of stocks and prices in the transport sector, which have to be neglected or taken as exogenously given. In any event, the choice of subsystems made here is "classic", in the sense that the interaction between housing, services and labour has been the main feature of urban activity and structure models since the work of Lowry (1964).

The medium-term time scale is emphasized. That is, we neglect the dynamics of very fast processes, which reach a steady state in a matter of a few days (like service demand choices) or even of a few hours (like route choice in a transport network). We focus instead on processes which undergo changes over longer periods, typically years, like housing mobility, labour mobility and locational changes in services. The focus on the medium-term can be partly used to justify treating as constants some very slowly-varying quantities, like the total population or the housing stock. We are aware of this being more a provisional simplification rather than an assumption of general validity, and we shall return to it in the concluding section.

In terms of actual computation, either discrete or con-tinuous time can be used. Discrete time has, of course, some computational advantages, and most of this chapter will be based on it. Continuous time is more convenient in some respects for theoretical investigation, but is computationally more difficult and is only briefly outlined here.

17.3 The Discrete-time Model

17.3.1 Accounting framework

The accounting framework for population mobility is made con-sistent with the master equations approach. This will be more obvious in the section on the continuous time version, where the master equations for the mean values appear in their standard form. Here, we develop a discrete-time version of the equations for the means. These are difference equations which will be shown to tend to the standard differential (master) equations in the limit. The equations proposed here have the same structure as those of a discrete-time Markov chain, a model widely used in multistate demography (Rogers, 1975). However, unlike the assumption in conventional multi-state population models, the process here is non-homogeneous; that is, the transition probabilities are not constant over time - indeed they are endogenously determined as a function of the state variables. A distinctive feature of the frame-work is that the trajectory of the whole origin-destination matrix for journeys-to-work is computed, rather than the residence and job counts separately.

The main notation and accounting framework can now be
introduced. Let i, j, k be subscripts (or superscripts)
labelling zones convenient for the urban area under study;
i,j,k = 1, ..., n as usual. Then the main state variable in
our accounting equations is $P_{ij}(t)$ the population living in
zone i and working in zone j at time t, i,j = 1, ..., n,
t = 0, Δ, 2Δ, ... Here Δ is a small time interval (such as
one year). Although no generality would be lost by conventionally setting Δ = 1, we prefer to keep the more general
notation, in order to make the passage to the limit easier to
generate the continuous-time version. $P_{ij}(t)$ conveys all the
information needed both for the population counts and for
employment measures of economic activities. The matrix,
$\{P_{ij}(t)\}$, is augmented by an additional column accounting for
unemployment: $P_{i0}(t)$ is the number of unemployed, living in
zone i at time t.

The dynamics of the process are specified by assuming the
existence of suitable transition probabilities. To facilitate
this, the additional assumption is made that the time interval
Δ is small enough for multiple events to be neglected: in an
interval (t, t+Δ) an individual can undergo only one change
(if any), but not more. For instance, a resident might change
house or lose a job (if he or she is employed), but not both.
(It would be possible to use the methods of Rees and Wilson
(1977) to avoid this assumption.) This assumption is, of
course, only approximately true in discrete time, but it will
become exactly true in continuous time, as Δ shrinks to 0.

We therefore define for zones i,j,k = 1, 2, ..., n and
for the period (t, t+Δ): $q_{ij}^k(t,\Delta)$ as the probability that
people living in zone i and working in zone j at time t move
to a dwelling in zone k; $q_{i0}^k(t,\Delta)$, the probability that an
unemployed person living in zone i at time t moves to a dwelling in zone k; $p_{ij}^k(t,\Delta)$, the probability that a workplace in
zone j occupied by a worker living in i at time t is occupied

by a worker living in k at time t + Δ - ie the worker living
in i is replaced by an unemployed person living in k; $p_{ij}^{0}(t+\Delta)$,
the probability that a workplace in zone j occupied by a worker
living in zone i at time t is closed down; $\rho_{ij}(t,\Delta)$, the probability that a new workplace is opened in zone j and occupied
by a worker living in i - this probability being applied to a
stock of potential workplaces which can be opened in zone j,
which is assumed to be exogenously given from land-use constraints. (In this notation in this chapter, a superscript
always refers to the new residential location (unless it is
zero when it indicates a shift to unemployment).)

In the version outlined here, the model uses some
simplifying assumptions, which can be easily relaxed in future
versions: (a) the total population is assumed to be exogenously
given, that is no births, deaths or migrations to and from the
rest of the world occur in the area; (b) the total housing
stock is also exogenous for each zone in the area - that is,
no new construction or demolition takes place; (c) levels of
economic activity are assumed to be endogenous; (d) a land-
use constraint is exogenously given for the development of
economic activities in each zone, expressed in terms of the
maximum number of workplaces which can be opened. This is
likely to be a crucial planning variable in applications of
the model. Thus, the following variables are given exogenously:
P, total population in the area; Q_i, total housing stock (both
vacant and occupied dwellings) in zone i; S_j, the maximum
number of possible workplaces in zone j. We need in addition
to define

$$T_j(t) = S_j(t) - \sum_{i=1}^{n} P_{ij}(t)$$

as the number of new workplaces which can be opened in zone j
at time t.

The state variables, transition probabilities and

exogenous variables defined above can be combined in relation
to all possible changes of state which can occur in the interval $(t, t+\Delta)$. We then obtain the following difference equations for the employed and unemployed populations respectively:

$$P_{ij}(t+\Delta) = \sum_{k=1}^{n} P_{kj}(t)[q_{kj}^{i}(t,\Delta) + p_{kj}^{i}(t,\Delta)]$$

$$+ P_{ij}(t)[1 - \sum_{k=1}^{n} q_{ij}^{k}(t,\Delta) - \sum_{k=0}^{n} p_{ij}^{k}(t,\Delta)]$$

$$+ T_{j}(t)\rho_{ij}(t,\Delta) \tag{17.1}$$

$$P_{i0}(t+\Delta) = \sum_{k=1}^{n} P_{k0}(t)q_{k0}^{i}(t,\Delta) + P_{i0}(t)[1 - \sum_{k=1}^{n} q_{i0}^{k}(t,\Delta)]$$

$$+ \sum_{j=1}^{n} P_{ij}(t) \sum_{k=0}^{n} p_{ij}^{k}(t,\Delta) - \sum_{k=1}^{n} \sum_{j=1}^{n} P_{kj}(t)p_{kj}^{i}(t,\Delta)$$

$$- \sum_{j=1}^{n} T_{j}(t)\rho_{ij}(t,\Delta) + \delta_{1} \frac{L_{i}(t,\Delta)}{P_{i0}(t)} W_{i}(t)q_{i}^{0}(t,\Delta)$$

$$- \delta_{2}[P_{i0}(t) - L_{i}(t,\Delta)] \tag{17.2}$$

where δ_{1}, $\delta_{2} > 0$ are parameters and

$$q_{i}^{0}(t,\Delta) = \frac{W_{i}(t)e^{\beta_{1}u_{i0}(t)}}{\sum_{k=1}^{n} W_{k}(t)e^{\beta_{1}u_{k0}(t)}}$$

In equation (17.2) W_i is the number of vacant dwellings in
zone i and L_i is the total demand for workers living in zone
i. These are discussed in more detail in Section 17.3.2 and
17.3.4 respectively. β is a parameter. It is easy to check
that equations (17.1) and (17.2) imply the conservation of
the total population, by summing them over all zones. That
is, if one defines

$$P(t) = \sum_{i=1}^{n} \sum_{j=0}^{n} P_{ij}(t)$$

as the total population in the whole area at time t, then
summation of equations (17.1) and (17.2) yields (with some
rearrangement):

$$P(t+\Delta) = P(t)$$

for all t. This provides an accounting basis for the model.
The transition probabilities will be specified in relation
to various behavioural hypotheses below.

17.3.2 Behaviour models: preliminaries

It is a distinctive feature of this illustrative model that
the transition probabilities have a structure derived from
micro-economic justifications. More precisely, they are
assumed to be given by logit models. Such models are by now
well established and accepted in urban economic applications
due to their combination of theoretical rigour and ease of
computation. The derivation of such models from classic
random utility theory can be found in Domencich and McFadden
(1975). Their extensive use in urban economics has been
thoroughly explored in Anas (1982 and Chapter Seven in this
volume). Their derivation in a dynamic setting, using the
asymptotic properties of stochastic extremal processes, is

developed by Leonardi (Chapter Five in this volume), who
proposes their use for modelling both residential and labour
mobility (Chapters Nine and Fifteen in this volume). The
models for the transition probabilities given in this section
are mostly based on the latter references, although of course
they are similar in some respects to the approach of Anas.

Let us define the following additional variables, all for
time t: c_{ij} is the cost of a return trip between zones i and
j; $\bar{c}_i(t)$, the average per-capita expenditure on services for
people living in zone i; $r_i(t)$, the average dwelling price in
zone i; $y_i(t)$, the average disposable income for people living
in zone i; $d_j(t)$, the average revenue per unit of employment
at a workplace in zone j,

$$W_i(t) = Q_i(t) - \sum_{j=0}^{n} P_{ij}(t)$$

is the number of vacant dwellings in zone i. For one version
of the model, it will also be useful to define $w_j(t)$ as the
wage rate in zone j. With the exception of transport costs
c_{ij}, it can be emphasised that all the variables defined
above are time-varying and indeed are endogenously determined
within the model.

We can now begin to specify the transition probabilities.
There are two alternative ways of proceeding according to
whether market-clearing is focussed on zones of residence or
zones of employment. In the former case, wage rates are
derived by place of employment which depend on the place of
residence of the worker. This is at first sight an odd result
but can be interpreted in this aggregate model as a way of
generating jobs of different wage levels within employment
zones. We develop transition probabilities for the two
alternative approaches explicitly. In subsection 17.3.3, we
present Model A based on residence-focussed market clearing
and in subsection 17.3.4, Model B, based on workplace market
clearing.

17.3.3 Model A: transition probabilities

In order to derive the transition probabilities for people in state (i,j) we will proceed in steps, first considering housing and labour mobility separately and then combining them. For housing choice, we assume demand is related to minimisation of total cost, that is the sum of transport, service and housing expenditures (and thus, in effect, to maximise disposable income). The utility function of a dwelling in zone i for people working in zone j is therefore

$$u_{ij}(t) = -[c_{ij} + \overline{c}_i(t) + r_i(t)]$$

and a standard logit specification for the rate of change based on choice probability, without considering labour changes, would be:

$$q_{ij}^k(t,\Delta) = \frac{\lambda \Delta W_k(t) e^{\beta_1 u_{kj}(t)}}{\lambda \Delta \sum\limits_{k'=1}^{n} W_{k'}(t) e^{\beta_1 u_{k'j}(t)} + e^{\beta_1 u_{ij}(t)}} \qquad (17.3)$$

where λ and β_1 are non-negative parameters - the latter having already been introduced in the definition of q_i^Δ following equation (17.2). The term $\lambda \Delta W_i(t)$ is the number of vacant dwellings in zone i known to each demand unit in a time interval (t, t+Δ). Equation (17.3) therefore implies the assumption that moves can be made only to vacant dwellings; moreover, it implies that not all the choice set is known, but only a fraction of it $\lambda \Delta$, and that the smaller the interval length Δ, the smaller this fraction. The parameter λ is therefore a rate of diffusion of information about vacant dwellings available.

Similarly, assume that in choosing workers, firms tend to maximize total profit, which, neglecting other costs, is

given by the difference between revenue gained from, and wage
paid to, the worker. We assume that each worker is subject
to a budget constraint related to the place of residence, so
that he would not be willing to accept a wage which does not
cover his expenditure. The part of the wage which is left
after expenditure is, by definition, the disposable income.
Therefore, the wage a firm in zone j pays for a worker living
in zone i is:

$$w_{ij}(t) = (c_{ij} + \overline{c}_i(t) + r_i(t)) + y_i(t)$$

The utility function for a firm in j hiring a worker from zone
i (that is the profit) is:

$$v_{ij}(t) = d_j(t) - w_{ij}(t)$$

Again a standard logit specification, without considering
housing changes, would lead to the following rates of change:

$$\tilde{p}_{ij}^k(t,\Delta) = \frac{\mu\Delta P_{k0}(t)e^{\beta_2 v_{kj}(t)}}{\mu\Delta[\sum_{k'=1}^{n} P_{k'0}(t)e^{\beta_2 v_{k'j}(t)}+1] + e^{\beta_2 v_{ij}(t)}}$$

(17.4)

The parameter μ is a rate measuring the intensity of hiring
and firing decisions. β_2 is a non-negative parameter. The
assumption implicit in equation (17.4) is that only unemployed
persons can be hired, and for an already occupied workplace,
the previous worker becomes unemployed. Replacement can also
occur without any turnover, and with no profit for the firm,
when the workplace is closed down. This is reflected in the
additional unit term appearing in the denominator of (17.4).
More specifically, the probability that a worker in j with
residence in i is replaced because the workplace is closed

down would be:

$$\tilde{p}_{ij}^{0}(t,\Delta) = \frac{\mu\Delta}{\mu\Delta[\sum\limits_{i=1}^{n} P_{i0}(t)e^{\beta_2 v_{ij}(t)} + 1] + e^{\beta_2 v_{ij}(t)}} \quad (17.5)$$

We shall also need the probabilities of making no change, which for residential and labour mobility are given respectively by the following equations, easily derived from equations (17.3) and (17.4):

$$\tilde{q}_{i}^{j}(t,\Delta) = 1 - \sum\limits_{k=1}^{n} \tilde{q}_{ij}^{k}(t,\Delta) = \frac{e^{\beta_1 u_{ij}}}{\lambda\Delta \sum\limits_{i=1}^{n} W_i(t)e^{\beta_1 u_{ij}(t)} + e^{\beta_1 u_{ij}(t)}}$$

$$(17.6)$$

$$\tilde{p}_{j}^{i}(t,\Delta) = 1 - \sum\limits_{k=0}^{n} \tilde{p}_{ij}^{k}(t,\Delta)$$

$$= \frac{e^{\beta_2 v_{ij}(t)}}{\lambda\Delta[\sum\limits_{k'=1}^{n} P_{k'0}(t)e^{\beta_2 v_{k'j}(t)} + 1] + e^{\beta_2 v_{ij}(t)}} (17.7)$$

We can now combine the two processes. Given the assumption that each individual can undergo at most one change in the period (t, t+Δ), the simultaneous occurrence of housing and job changes is excluded. Therefore the probability of moving given by (17.3) can be applied only to those who kept their workplace in (t, t+Δ). Similarly the probability of being fired (or of hiring a new worker, from the firm's point of view) given by (17.4) can only be applied to those who kept their residence in (t, t+Δ). Under the above assumptions, the actual transition probabilities to be used in the difference equations (17.1) and (17.2) are given by:

$$q_{ij}^{k}(t,\Delta) = \tilde{p}_{j}^{i}(t,\Delta)\tilde{q}_{ij}^{k}(t,\Delta) \quad (17.8)$$

Integrated Operational Model

$$p_{ij}^k(t,\Delta) = \tilde{p}_{ij}^k(t,\Delta)\tilde{q}_i^j(t,\Delta) \tag{17.9}$$

Substituting from equations (17.3) – (17.7) and neglecting the terms of order Δ^2, equations (17.8) and (17.9) finally yield:

$$q_{ij}^k(t,\Delta) = \frac{\lambda\Delta W_k(t)e^{[\beta_1 u_{kj}(t)+\beta_2 v_{ij}(t)]}}{D_j^i(t,\Delta)} \tag{17.10}$$

$$p_{ij}^k(t,\Delta) = \frac{\mu\Delta P_{k0}(t)e^{[\beta_1 u_{ij}(t)+\beta_2 v_{kj}(t)]}}{D_j^i(t,\Delta)} \tag{17.11}$$

$$p_{ij}^0(t,\Delta) = \frac{\eta\Delta e^{\beta_1 u_{ij}(t)}}{D_j^i(t,\Delta)} \tag{17.12}$$

where the denominator is given by:

$$D_j^i(t,\Delta) = \lambda\Delta e^{\beta_2 v_{ij}(t)}\sum_{k'=1}^{n} W_{k'}(t)e^{\beta_1 u_{k'j}(t)}$$

$$+ \Delta e^{\beta_1 u_{ij}(t)}[\mu\sum_{k'=1}^{n} P_{k'0}(t)e^{\beta_2 v_{k'j}}+\eta]$$

$$+ e^{[\beta_1 u_{ij}(t)+\beta_2 v_{ij}(t)]} \tag{17.13}$$

The transition probabilities for the unemployed and for the new jobs are somewhat simpler than the ones above, since they refer to a single-actor rather than a two-actor decision – that is, the unemployed have no firm associated with them and therefore they can only make residential changes. Similarly, the new jobs have no worker associated with them, and they can only be opened with consequent recruitment. The unemployed

have no commuting cost and so the utility function for their
residential choice is

$$u_{i0}(t) = -[\overline{c}_i(t) + r_i(t)]$$

The probability that an unemployed person moves from zone i to
zone k is given by the following logit model:

$$q_{i0}^k(t,\Delta) = \frac{\lambda\Delta W_k(t)e^{\beta_1 u_{k0}(t)}}{\lambda\Delta \sum_{k=1}^{n} W_k(t)e^{\beta_1 u_{k0}(t)} + e^{\beta_1 u_{i0}(t)}} \qquad (17.14)$$

The firm opening a new workplace has the same expected profit
as that associated with already existing jobs, therefore the
probability that a potential workplace in zone j is open and
occupied by a worker living in zone i is given by the following
logit model:

$$\rho_{ij}(t,\Delta) = \frac{\mu\Delta P_{i0}(t)e^{\beta_2 v_{ij}(t)}}{\mu\Delta \sum_{i=1}^{n} P_{i0}e^{\beta_2 v_{ij}(t)} + 1} \qquad (17.15)$$

Equations (17.10) to (17.15) specify all the transition probabilities required in the difference equations (17.1) and
(17.2). It can easily be checked from their definitions that
they are consistent probabilities. That is

$$q_{ij}^k(t,\Delta) < 1$$

$$p_{ij}^k(t,\Delta) < 1$$

$$q_{ij}^k(t,\Delta) + p_{ij}^k(t,\Delta) < 1$$

$$p_{ij}^0(t,\Delta) < 1$$

$$q_{i0}^k(t,\Delta) < 1$$

$$\rho_{ij}(t,\Delta) < 1$$

and moreover:

$$\sum_{k=1}^{n} [q_{ij}^k(t,\Delta) + p_{ij}^k(t,\Delta)] + p_{ij}^0(t,\Delta) < 1 \qquad (17.16)$$

$$\sum_{k=1}^{n} q_{i0}^k(t,\Delta) < 1 \qquad (17.17)$$

$$\sum_{k=1}^{n} \rho_{ij}(t,\Delta) < 1 \qquad (17.18)$$

Equations (17.16) to (17.18) state the conservation properties of the system. The total probability of a change of state in $(t,\ t+\Delta)$, for any initial state, is less than 1. Its complement to unity is of course the probability of making no change, that is, of remaining in the initial state.

17.3.4 Model A: prices, incomes and revenues

In sections 17.3.2 and 17.3.3 several endogenous time-varying signals which enter in the definition of the utility functions used in the transition probabilities were introduced. They are dwelling prices, disposable incomes, unit revenues per employee for firms and the average per-capita expenditures on services. In this section, models are provided to compute these variables. In the discrete-time version of the model, it is assumed that all the markets under consideration (housing, labour, services) are cleared within one period. That is, the prices at the end of each period (say at time $t+\Delta$) are computed in such a way as to balance demand and supply as

determined by the conditions at the beginning of the period
(say at time t). During the time interval (t, t+Δ) demand-
supply interactions take place; however, Δ is assumed to be
large enough for the interactions to settle down to partial
equilibrium at the end of the period.

The underlying assumption behind this approach is that
the price adjustment process is fast enough compared with
changes in quantities (population, economic activity levels
and stocks) for its dynamics to be very short term. This
assumption might not be fully justified in some cases, and
indeed it will be abandoned in the continuous-time version
which does not require it. However, in discrete time this is
the most practical way of maintaining consistency in the
accounting framework and ensuring feasible trajectories for
the quantities. The period market clearing approach is
extensively used by Anas (1982 and Chapter Seven in this volume)
and Anas and Duann (1984), under the assumption that both demand
and supply behave according to a logit model. Here a slightly
different approach will be used, based on the models of Chapters
Nine and Fifteen. While the demand behaviour is still described
by logit models (the transition probabilities in **subsection**
17.3.3), the supply behaviour is assumed to be bid-price maximizing, as described in the general theory of stochastic
extremal processes (Chapter Five).

For the housing market, the results of Chapter Nine will
be used. Let $H_i(t,\Delta)$ be the total demand for housing in zone
i in (t, t+Δ), that is the number of households looking for a
dwelling in zone i in (t, t+Δ). Using equations (17.10) and
(17.14) this is given by:

$$H_i(t,\Delta) = \sum_{k=1}^{n} \sum_{j=0}^{n} P_{kj}(t)q_{kj}^i(t,\Delta) \qquad (17.19)$$

According to the bid-price maximizing assumption, a landlord owning a vacant dwelling is willing to sell it if he has received at least one non-negative bid. From the theory in Chapter Nine the probability that this event occurs in the period $(t, t+\Delta)$ is:

$$1 - e^{-\phi_i(t,\Delta)}$$

where $\phi_i(t,\Delta)$ is defined as:

$$\phi_i(t,\Delta) = e^{\beta_1 r_i(t)} H_i(t,\Delta)/\Delta W_i(t)$$

Hence the total supply of housing in zone i in $(t, t+\Delta)$ is given by:

$$W_i(t)[1 - e^{-\phi_i(t,\Delta)}] \tag{17.20}$$

and the market-clearing equations for the housing prices $r_i(t)$ are:

$$H_i(t,\Delta) = W_i(t)[1 - e^{-\phi_i(t,\Delta)}] \tag{17.21}$$

Similar arguments applied to the labour market (using the results of Chapter Fifteen) lead to the following market-clearing equations for the disposable incomes $y_i(t)$:

$$L_i(t,\Delta) = P_{i0}(t)[1 - e^{-\psi_i(t,\Delta)}] \tag{17.22}$$

where $L_i(t,\Delta)$ is the total demand for workers living in zone i in $(t, t+\Delta)$ and using equations (17.11) and (17.15) this is given by:

$$L_i(t,\Delta) = \sum_{j=1}^{n} \sum_{k=1}^{n} P_{kj}(t)p_{kj}^i(t,\Delta) + \sum_{j=1}^{n} T_j(t)\rho_{ij}(t,\Delta)$$

$$\tag{17.23}$$

where

$$P_{i0}(t)[1 - e^{-\psi_i(t,\Delta)}] \qquad\qquad (17.24)$$

is the total supply of labour from the unemployed living in
zone i and the quantity $\psi_i(t,\Delta)$ is defined as:

$$\psi_i(t,\Delta) = e^{\beta_2 y_i(t)} L_i(t,\Delta)/\Delta\, P_{i0}(t)$$

This is because applicants offered jobs are assumed to be
disposable-income maximizers: they evaluate alternative jobs
according to the disposable income they provide, once fixed
consumptions are deducted, and choose the one providing the
highest disposable income, if it is non-negative (the non-
negativity condition being implied by the assumption of a
budget constraint for the households). If not, they prefer
to remain unemployed and do not contribute to the labour
supply.

Some additional assumptions need to be introduced in
order to derive equations for the revenues of the firms. It
has already been said that only endogenous (ie market-oriented
or non-basic) economic activities are considered in this version of the model. This amounts to focussing our attention
on the service sector, and indeed to assuming that our urban
area has only service activities. This is by far the most
interesting sector from the point of view of the urban structure and dynamics, and in many instances it is also the pre-
dominant one. However, it should not be forgotten that a
basic industrial sector, whose production is not orientated
towards local consumption, is still important in most cities.
We leave this as a subject for future generalizations which
can be introduced without altering the structure of the model.

As a second simplification, we do not disaggregate services
by sector. Such a disaggregation could also be introduced with-

out disrupting the structure of the model, but it would require
a cumbersome notation, which would obscure the basic structure
of the model at this stage.

As a third assumption, demand for services is considered
to be in equilibrium at every instant in time. In other words,
demand adjusts to changes in service location in a time span
which is negligible compared to other changes in the process
(like housing and labour mobility).

For the structure of services, a modified flow model has
been used

$$F_{ij}(t) = G_i(t) \frac{A_j^\alpha(t)e^{-\beta_3[c_{ij}+x_j(t)]}}{\sum_{j=1}^{n} A_j^\alpha(t)e^{-\beta_3[c_{ij}+x_j(t)]}} \qquad (17.25)$$

for a new non-negative parameter, β_3, and where $F_{ij}(t)$ is the
flow of customers from zone i to services in zone j at time t;
$G_i(t)$, the total flow of customers from zone i, it is assumed
to be of the form

$$G_i(t) = \psi_{1i} \sum_{k=0}^{n} P_{ik}(t) + \psi_{2i} \sum_{k=1}^{n} P_{ki}(t)$$

where ψ_{1i} and ψ_{2i} are the frequencies of trips generated from
residences and workplaces, respectively (and could be functions
of incomes in i)

$$A_j(t) = \sum_{k=1}^{n} P_{kj}(t)$$

is the total size of service activities in zone j, measured in
terms of employment; $x_j(t)$ is the average price for an average
unit of service[*] offered in zone j; and α is a non-negative

---

[*] Having just one sector, a unit of service here can only be
interpreted as an average bundle of goods and services consumed per unit time.

parameter.

From equation (17.25) the revenues $d_j(t)$ can be computed

$$d_j(t) = \frac{\sum_{i=1}^{n} F_{ij}(t)x_j(t)}{A_j(t)} + \delta e_j(1 - e^{-\theta_j}) \qquad (17.26)$$

where $\delta > 0$ is a parameter, as well as the average per-capita expenditure in service consumption (including transport costs) for people living in zone i, $\overline{c}_i(t)$

$$\overline{c}_i(t) = -\frac{\delta}{\beta_3} \ln \frac{\sum_{j=1}^{n} A_j^{\alpha}(t)e^{-\beta_3[c_{ij}+x_j(t)]}}{\sum_{j=1}^{n} A_j^{\alpha}(t)} \qquad (17.27)$$

Equation (17.27) is not an arithmetic mean, but an inclusive value, in the sense defined by Domencich and McFadden (1975) and Williams (1977). Its form is rooted in random utility theory, and several examples of how this sort of average arises are provided in Chapter Five. Let us interpret the term $A_j^{\alpha}(t)$ as a production function of services in zone j: a A_j^{α} is the total production of service units in zone j at time t, for some constant a > 0 (a: number of customers in unit time Δ).

Then, if the main equilibrating mechanism is price, arguments similar to those used for the housing and labour markets lead to the following market-clearing equations for the service prices $x_j(t)$

$$F_j(t) = aA_j^{\alpha}(t)[1 - e^{-\theta_j(t)}] \qquad (17.28)$$

where

$$F_j(t) = \sum_{i=1}^{n} F_{ij}(t)$$

is the total demand for services in j at time t and the
quantity $\theta_j(t)$ is defined as

$$\theta_j(t) = e^{\beta_3 x_j(t)} F_j(t)/aA_j^\alpha(t)$$

As an alternative (from among the range of alternatives outlined in Chapter Six) it would also be possible to write an
equilibrium condition in A_j

$$D_j(t) = C_j(t) = k_j A_j(t)$$

where $C_j(t)$ is suppliers' costs (and k_j is a constant).

17.3.5 Model B: an alternative approach to labour market
        clearing

This alternative model is based on the same accounting structure as Model A, and so equations (17.1) and (17.2) and the
definitions of the main variables remain the same. The differences arise in the ways in which some of the transition
rates are calculated and in the behavioural hypotheses which
generate them. We proceed, therefore, by describing the
modifications only. The main difference is in the way in which
the labour market is assumed to operate. We assume that market
clearing is focussed on each employment zone and that this
process generates a set of wage rates, $w_j(t)$. This brings
about a marginal change to the residential model and more
fundamental changes in the labour market model.

The residential model is affected mainly through the
definition of the utility function which precedes equation
(17.3). The wage rate should now obviously be taken as a
component of utility and so $u_{ij}(t)$ becomes

$$u_{ij}(t) = w_j(t) - [c_{ij} + \bar{c}_i(t) + r_i(t)] \qquad (17.29)$$

with $w_j(t)$ replacing $w_{ij}(t)$. This means that $v_{ij}(t)$ is $d_j(t) - w_j(t)$ and thus depends only on j and can be written as $v_j(t)$. Equation (17.3) remains the same, but uses this new definition of utility. (17.3), with this modification, then serves to change the emphasis of the previous hypothesis. Now, people will be discouraged from taking up houses which they cannot afford because u_{ij} is, in effect, disposable income which takes into account both wage and house price (and the transport and service elements of the cost of living at i).

Equation (17.4) is now slightly modified with $v_j(t)$ replacing $v_{ij}(t)$ - and thus hypothesising that more profitable firms will have relatively higher turnover rates.

$$\tilde{p}^k_{ij}(t,\Delta) = \frac{\mu\Delta P_{k0}(t)e^{\beta_2 v_j(t)}}{\mu\Delta[1+e^{\beta_2 v_j(t)} \sum_{k'=1}^{n} P_{k'0}(t)] + e^{\beta_2 v_j(t)}} \qquad (17.30)$$

Note that the r.h.s. of this equation is now independent of i. Similarly, (17.5) becomes

$$\tilde{p}^0_{ij} = \frac{\mu\Delta}{e^{\beta_2 v_j(t)} + \mu\Delta[1+e^{\beta_2 v_j(t)} \sum_{k'=1}^{n} P_{k'0}(t)]} \qquad (17.31)$$

Equations (17.6) are unchanged (again given the new definition of u_{ij}). (17.7) clearly becomes

$$\tilde{p}_{ij}(t,\Delta) = \frac{e^{\beta_2 v_j(t)}}{\mu\Delta[\sum_{k'} P_{k'0}(t)e^{\beta_2 v_{k'}(t)} +1] + e^{\beta_2 v_j(t)}} \qquad (17.32)$$

while (17.8) and (17.9) are unchanged. When we substitute for the p-variables in (17.8) and (17.9) (and the p^k_{ij} equation) we get new versions of (17.10) - (17.12) where the only modification is the replacement of $v_{ij}(t)$ by $v_j(t)$, and using the new definition of $u_{ij}(t)$.

The utility function for the residential choice of unemployed $u_{i0}(t)$ becomes

$$u_{i0}(t) = w_0 - [\overline{c}_i(t) + v_i(t)]$$

where w_0 is the total benefit paid to an unemployed person.

The system of transition rates can be completed as follows: (17.14) remains as before, but with the new definition of $u_{i0}(t)$, equation (17.15) becomes

$$\rho_{ij}(t) = \frac{P_{i0}(t)e^{\beta_4 u_{ij}(t)}}{\sum\limits_k P_{k0}(t)e^{\beta_4 u_{ik}(t)}} \cdot \frac{\tilde{\mu}\Delta e^{\beta_2 v_j(t)}}{\sum\limits_k e^{\beta_2 v_k(t)}} \qquad (17.33)$$

where $\tilde{\mu}$ is a new constant rate relating to the probability of a new workplace being opened, and β_4 is a parameter relating to the workplace choices of newly-hired workers.

We then turn to prices, incomes and revenues as in subsection 17.3.4. Incomes are now determined through labour market clearing. The residential market clearing mechanism remains the same. We now have to specify the alternative Model B for labour market clearing.

Let

$$E_j(t) = \sum\limits_i P_{ij}(t) \qquad (17.34)$$

be the total number of jobs in j at time t. The turnover is $\sum\limits_{ik} \tilde{p}^k_{ij}(t,\Delta)P_{ij}(t)$ and the number of new jobs is $\sum\limits_i T_j(t)\rho_{ij}(t,\Delta)$.

The total number of vacant jobs at t in j is therefore

$$V_j(t,\Delta) = A_j(t) \sum\limits_{k=1}^{n} \tilde{p}^k_{ij}(t,\Delta) + \sum\limits_{i=1}^{n} T_j(t)\rho_{ij}(t,\Delta) \qquad (17.35)$$

(adjusted to take into account the constraint on the maximum number of jobs permitted). The number of vacancies filled by workers resident in i can be hypothesised to be

$$\Pi_{ij}(t) = \frac{P_{i0}(t)V_j(t)e^{\beta_4 u_{ij}(t)}}{\sum_k V_k(t)e^{\beta_4 u_{ik}(t)}} \tag{17.36}$$

Define

$$k = \Sigma_j V_j(t)/\Sigma_j\Sigma_i \frac{P_{i0}(t)V_j(t)e^{\beta_4 u_{ij}(t)}}{\sum_k V_k(t)e^{\beta_4 u_{ik}(t)}} \tag{17.37}$$

as the relation between the total number of vacancies $\Sigma_j V_j(t)$ and the total number of unemployed, the latter being

$$\Sigma_j\Sigma_i \frac{P_{i0}(t)V_j(t)e^{\beta_4 u_{ij}(t)}}{\sum_k V_k(t)e^{\beta_4 u_{ik}(t)}}$$

as can easily be shown. k is the probability that each unemployed person has of finding a job, independently of where he lives (i) and where the job is (j).

From the theory exposed in Chapter Fifteen we have the following labour-market clearing equation

$$V_j(t) = \Sigma_i\Pi_{ij}(t)(1 - e^{-\psi_j(t)}) \tag{17.38}$$

where

$$\psi_j(t) = e^{\beta_2 w_j(t)} \frac{V_j(t)}{\Sigma_i\Pi_{ij}(t)} \tag{17.39}$$

is the time average of potential demand for a worker in i;
$(1 - e^{-\psi_j(t)})$ represents the probability that a workplace in

j is taken by any worker, independently of his residence i.

This market equation is similar in form to those for the houses and services markets, if we take w_j, defined on the work area j, as playing the same role as x_i and t_i defined on the residence area i. The difference with Model A is that now the independent variable is the state function w_j, the wage in j, not y_i, the disposable income in i.

It is easy to derive in the limit $\beta \to 0$, with w_j finite, a form of (17.38) where the probability $(1 - e^{-\psi}j)$ is approximated by k

$$V_j(t) \simeq k\Sigma_i \Pi_{ij}(t) \tag{17.40}$$

This approximation ceases to be valid, in the sense of yielding a w_j agreed between employer and employee, if $\beta_2 w_j(t)$ is big. In this case, it can be shown that equation (17.40) degenerates into an identity with respect to w_j.

17.4 Outline of a Continuous-time Model

In order to build a continuous-time version of the accounting (difference) equations (17.1) and (17.2) we simply take their limit as $\Delta \to 0$. We first use Model A hypotheses for illustration. Assume the following limiting transition rates exist

$$q_{ij}^k(t) = \lim_{\Delta \to 0} q_{ij}^k(t,\Delta)/\Delta$$

$$q_{i0}^k(t) = \lim_{\Delta \to 0} q_{i0}^k(t,\Delta)/\Delta$$

$$p_{ij}^k(t) = \lim_{\Delta \to 0} p_{kj}^i(t,\Delta)/\Delta$$

$$p_{ij}^0(t) = \lim_{\Delta \to 0} p_{k0}^i(t,\Delta)/\Delta$$

$$\rho_{ij}(t) = \lim_{\Delta \to 0} \rho_{ij}(t,\Delta)/\Delta$$

Then equations (17.1) and (17.2) tend to the following differential equations

$$\dot{P}_{ij}(t) = \sum_{k=1}^{n} P_{kj}(t)[q_{ij}^{k}(t)+p_{ij}^{k}(t)] - P_{ij}(t)[\sum_{k=1}^{n} q_{ij}^{k}(t)+ \sum_{k=0}^{n} p_{ji}^{k}(t)]$$

$$+ T_{j}(t)\rho_{ij}(t) \tag{17.41}$$

$$\dot{P}_{i0}(t) = \sum_{k=1}^{n} P_{k0}(t)q_{i0}^{k}(t) - P_{i0}(t)\sum_{k=1}^{n} q_{k0}^{i}(t) + \sum_{i=1}^{n} P_{ij}(t)\sum_{k=0}^{n} p_{ij}^{k}(t)$$

$$- \sum_{i=1}^{n} \sum_{k=1}^{n} P_{ik}(t)p_{kj}^{i} - \sum_{i=1}^{n} T_{j}(t)\rho_{ij}(t) \tag{17.42}$$

The limiting transition rates do actually exist, and from equations (17.10) to (17.15) they are given by

$$q_{ij}^{k}(t) = \lambda W_{k}(t)e^{\beta_1[u_{kj}(t)-u_{ij}(t)]} \tag{17.43}$$

$$q_{i0}^{k}(t) = \lambda W_{k}(t)e^{\beta_1[u_{k0}(t)-u_{i0}(t)]} \tag{17.44}$$

$$p_{ij}^{k}(t) = \mu P_{i0}(t)e^{\beta_2[v_{kj}(t)-v_{ij}(t)]} \tag{17.45}$$

$$p_{ij}^{0}(t) = \mu e^{-\beta_2 v_{ij}(t)} \tag{17.46}$$

$$\rho_{ij}(t) = \mu P_{i0}(t)e^{\beta_2 v_{ij}(t)} \tag{17.47}$$

Equations (17.43) to (17.47) deserve a remark. Although the
functional form of the transition probabilities in the discrete-
time model looks quite different, the corresponding transition

rates in the continuous-time model have a form which is identical to the one proposed in the master equations approach by Weidlich and Haag (1983) and Haag (Chapters Four, Six, Eleven and Fourteen in this volume), although they have been derived from different assumptions. It seems therefore that full unification of the different approaches discussed in this book has been reached.

In order to find dynamic equations for prices and incomes, define the following limits

$$\phi_i(t) = \lim_{\Delta \to 0} \phi_i(t,\Delta)$$

$$\psi_i(T) = \lim_{\Delta \to 0} \psi_i(t,\Delta)$$

Then from the theory developed in Chapters Five, Nine and Fifteen, one has the following differential equations for the housing prices and disposable incomes

$$\dot{r}_i(t) = \frac{\gamma}{\beta} \left[1 - \frac{1-e^{-\phi_i(t)}}{\phi_i(t)e^{-\beta_1 r_i(t)}} \right] \tag{17.48}$$

$$\dot{y}_i(t) = \frac{\gamma}{\beta} \left[1 - \frac{1-e^{-\psi_i(t)}}{\psi_i(t)e^{-\beta_2 y_i(t)}} \right] \tag{17.49}$$

A similar equation holds for the service prices

$$\dot{x}_j(t) = \frac{\gamma}{\beta} \left[1 - \frac{1-e^{-\theta_j(t)}}{\theta_j(t)e^{-\beta_3 x_j(t)}} \right] \tag{17.50}$$

where γ is a non-negative parameter. It is shown in Chapters Nine and Fifteen that equations of the form (17.48) to (17.50) can be interpreted in Walrasian terms, relating the rate of change in prices to the difference between demand and supply.

392

We can then proceed to Model B. We can derive from (17.38) the disequilibrium equation for this model

$$\frac{d}{dt} (\dot{w}_j) = \frac{\gamma}{\beta} [1 - \frac{1-e^{\psi_j}}{e^{\beta w_j}\psi_j}] \tag{17.51}$$

Similarly, if we take the approximate version, (17.40), a suitable disequilibrium equation is

$$\dot{w}_j = \lim_{\beta \to 0} \frac{\gamma}{\beta} [1 - \frac{1-e^{\psi_j}}{e^{\beta w_j}\psi_j}]$$

$$= \lim_{\beta \to 0} \frac{\gamma}{\beta} [1 - \frac{1-e^{-k}}{V_j/\sum_i \Pi_{ij}}]$$

$$= \lim_{\beta \to 0} \frac{\gamma}{\beta} [1 - \frac{1-e^{-k}}{k}] \tag{17.52}$$

We can carry out a series expansion

$$\dot{w}_j = \lim_{\beta \to 0} \frac{\gamma}{\beta} [1 - \frac{1 - (1 - k + \frac{k^2}{2!} - \frac{k^3}{3!} + \dots}{k}]$$

$$= \lim_{\beta \to 0} \frac{\gamma}{\beta} [\frac{1}{2!}k - \frac{1}{3!}k^2 + \frac{1}{4!}k^3 \dots] \tag{17.53}$$

This limit is infinite, but we note that the approximation is better for small k. Then

$$\dot{w}_j \simeq \lim_{\beta \to 0} \frac{\gamma}{\beta} [\frac{1}{2}k]$$

If we then take k as being infinitesimally small, and $k \simeq \beta$, then

$$\dot{w}_j \simeq \frac{1}{2} \gamma \qquad\qquad (17.55)$$

That is, in the limit of constant probability of an unemployed person finding a job somewhere, there is a steady increase in wages!

(17.55) can be derived more formally as

$$\dot{w}_j = \lim_{\beta \to 0} [\lim_{k \to 0} \frac{\gamma}{\beta} (1 - \frac{1-e^{-k}}{k})] \qquad\qquad (17.56)$$

and if $k \sim y$ and $\beta \sim y$, this is

$$\dot{w}_j = \lim_{y \to 0} [\frac{\gamma}{\beta} (1 - \frac{1-e^{-y}}{y})] \qquad\qquad (17.57)$$

$$= \frac{\gamma}{2} \qquad\qquad (17.58)$$

BIBLIOGRAPHY AND REFERENCES

Allen, P.M., Sanglier, M. (1979) A Dynamic Model of Growth in
a Central Place System, *Geographical Analysis*, *11*, 256–
272.

Alonso, W. (1964) *Location and Land Use*, Harvard University
Press, Cambridge, Mass.

Anas, A. (1976) Short-run Dynamics in the Spatial Housing
Market, in Papageorgiou, Y.Y. (ed.) *Essays in Mathematical
Land Use Theory*, Lexington Books, Lexington, Mass., 261–
275.

Anas, A. (1978) Dynamics of Urban Residential Growth, *Journal
of Urban Economics*, *5*, 66–87.

Anas, A. (1980) A Probabilistic Approach to the Structure of
Urban Housing Markets, *Journal of Urban Economics*, *7*,
225–247.

Anas, A. (1981) Competitive Nash Equilibrium Analysis
(unpublished).

Anas, A. (1982) *Residential Location Markets and Urban Transportation: economic theory, econometrics and policy
analysis with discrete choice models*, Academic Press,
New York.

Anas, A. (1983) *The Chicago Area Transportation-Land Use
Analysis System*, Northwestern University, Evanston, Ill.

Anas, A. (1984-A) Discrete Choice Theory and the General
Equilibrium of Employment, Housing and Travel Networks
in a Lowry Type Model of the Urban Economy, *Environment
and Planning*, *A*, *16*, 1489–1502.

Anas, A. (1984-B) The Combined Equilibrium of Travel Networks
and Residential Location Markets, CP-84-11, International
Institute for Applied System Analysis, Laxenburg, Austria.

Anas, A. (1987) *Modelling in Urban and Regional Economics*,
Vol. 25, *Fundamentals of Pure and Applied Economics*,
Urban and Regional Economics Section (Arnott, R.J.,
Section Ed.; Lasourne, J., Sonnenschein, H., editors-in-
chief), Harwood, New York.

Anas, A., Cho, J.R. (1985) A Model of the Regulated Housing
Market Dynamics: the case of Sweden, Northwestern University, Evanston, Ill. (in preparation).

Anas, A., Duann, L.S. (1984) Dynamic Forecasting of Travel
Demand, Residential Location and Land Development:
policy simulations with the Chicago Area Transportation-
Land Use Analysis System, *Sistemi Urbani*, *6*, 37–70.

Anas, A., Eum, S.J. (1984) Hedonic Analysis of a Housing
Market in Disequilibrium, *Journal of Urban Economics*, *15*,
87–106.

Anas, A., Eum, S.J. (1986) Disequilibrium Models of Single
Family Prices and Transactions: the case of Chicago,
1972-1976, *Journal of Urban Economics*, *20*, 75–96.

Anas, A., Jirlow, U., Gustafsson, J., Härsman, B., Snickars, F. (1985) The Swedish Housing Market: structure, policy and issues, *Scandinavian Housing and Planning Research, 2,* 169-187.

Arrow, K.J., Block, H.D., Hurwicz, L. (1959) On the Stability of Competitive Equilibrium, II, *Econometrica, 27,* 82-109.

Arrow, K.J., Hahn, F. (1971) *General Competitive Analysis,* Holden Day, San Francisco.

Arrow, K.J., Hurwicz, L. (1958) On the Stability of Competitive Equilibrium, I, *Econometrica, 26,* 522-552.

Atkin, R.H. (1974) *Mathematical Structure in Human Affairs,* Heinemann, London.

Bach, L. (1980) Locational Models for Systems of Private and Public Facilities Based on Concepts of Accessibility and Access Opportunity, *Environment and Planning, A, 12,* 301-320.

Bach, L. (1981) The Problem of Aggregation and Distance for Analyses of Accessibility and Access Opportunity in Location-Allocation Models, *Environment and Planning, A, 13,* 955-978.

Batty, M. (1971) Exploratory Calibration of a Retail Location Model Using Search by Golden Section, *Environment and Planning, 3,* 411-432.

Beavon, K., Hay, A.M. (1977) Consumer Choice of Shopping Centre - A Hypergeometric Model, *Environment and Planning, A, 9,* 1357-1393.

Becker, G.S. (1965) A Theory of the Allocation of Time, *Economic Journal, 75,* 488-517.

Beckmann, M.J. (1969) On the Distribution of Urban Rent and Residential Density, *Journal of Economic Theory, 1,* 60-67.

Beckmann, M.J. (1973) Equilibrium Models of Residential Location, *Regional and Urban Economics, 3,* 361-368.

Beckmann, M.J. (1974) Spatial Equilibrium in the Housing Market, *Journal of Urban Economics, 1,* 99-108.

Benassy, J.P. (1982) *The Economics of Market Disequilibrium,* Academic Press, New York.

Benhabib, J., Day, R. (1981) Rational Choice and Erratic Behaviour, *Review of Economic Studies, 48,* 459-471.

Bertuglia, C.S., Gualco, J., Occelli, S., Rabino, G.A., Salomone, C., Tadei, R. (1986) Residential Location and Dynamic Urban Processes: theoretical aspects and modelling, *Sistemi Urbani, 8,* 197-218.

Bertuglia, C.S., Leonardi, G. (1979) Dynamic Models for Spatial Interaction, *Sistemi Urbani, 1, 2,* 3-25.

Bertuglia, C.S., Leonardi, G. (1980) A Model for the Optimal Location of Multi-level Services, *Sistemi Urbani, 2,* 283-297.

Bertuglia, C.S., Leonardi, G., Occelli, S., Rabino, G.A., Tadei, R. (1987) An Integrated Model for the Dynamic Analysis of Location-transport Interrelations, *European Journal of Operational Research, 31,* 198-208.

Bertuglia, C.S., Leonardi, G., Occelli, S., Rabino, G.A., Tadei, R., Wilson, A.G. (eds.) (1987) *Urban Systems: contemporary approaches to modelling*, Croom Helm, London.

Bertuglia, C.S., Leonardi, G., Tadei, R. (1983) A Nested Random Utility Model for Multi-service Systems: an application to the high school system in Turin, *Sistemi Urbani*, 5, 55-105.

Bertuglia, C.S., Occelli, S., Rabino, G.A., Tadei, R. (1980) A Model of Urban Structure and Development of Turin: theoretical aspects, *Sistemi Urbani*, 2, 59-90.

Bertuglia, C.S., Rabino, G.A. (1975) *Modello per l'Organizzazione di un Comprensorio*, Guida, Napoli.

Bigman, D., ReVelle, C. (1979) An Operational Approach to Welfare Considerations in Applied Public-Facility-Location Models, *Environment and Planning, A*, 11, 83-95.

Biondini, R., Siddiqui, M.M. (1975) Record Values in Markov Sequences, in Puri, A. (ed.) *Statistical Inference and Related Topics, Volume 2*, Academic Press, New York, 291-352.

Birkin, M., Clarke, M., Wilson, A.G. (1984) Interacting Fields: comprehensive models for the dynamical analysis of urban spatial structure, Working Paper 385, School of Geography, University of Leeds, Leeds.

Birkin, M., Wilson, A.G. (1984-A) Industrial Location Models I: a review and an integrated framework, Working Paper 400, School of Geography, University of Leeds, Leeds.

Birkin, M., Wilson, A.G. (1984-B) Industrial Location Models II: Weber, Palander, Hotelling and extensions within a new framework, Working Paper 401, School of Geography, University of Leeds, Leeds.

Black, J. (1981) *Urban Transport Planning*, Croom Helm, London.

Bonsall, P.W., Champernowne, A.F., Cripps, E.L., Goodman, P.R., Hankin, A., Mackett, R.L., Sanderson, I., Senior, M.L., Southworth, F., Spence, R., Williams, H.C.W.L., Wilson, A.G. (1977) Models for Urban Transport Planning, in Wilson, A.G., Rees, P.H., Leigh, C.M. (eds.) *Models of Cities and Regions*, Wiley, Chichester, 457-519.

Bonsall, P.W., Champernowne, A.F., Mason, A.C., Wilson, A.G. (1977) *Transport Modelling: sensitivity analysis and policy testing*, Pergamon, Oxford.

Boyce, D.E. (ed.) (1979) Special Issue on Transportation Network Design, *Transportation Research, B*, 13, 1-90.

Boyce, D.E. (1984) Urban Transportation Network-Equilibrium and Design Models: recent achievements and future prospects, *Environment and Planning, A*, 16, 1445-1474.

Boyce, D.E., Southworth, F. (1979) Quasi-Dynamic Urban-Location Models with Endogenously-Determined Travel Costs, *Environment and Planning, A*, 11, 575-584.

Chudzyńska, I. (1981) Locational Specialisation of Retail Trade Functions in Warsaw, *Environment and Planning, A*, 13, 929-942.

Chudzyńska, I., Slodkowski, Z. (1984) Equilibria of a Gravity
    Demand Model, *Environment and Planning, A, 16,* 185-200.
Clark, W.A. (1983) Structures for Research on the Dynamics of
    Residential Search, in Griffith, D.A., Lea, A.C. (eds.)
    Evolving Geographical Structures, Nijhoff, The Hague,
    372-397.
Clark, W.A., Smith, T.R. (1982) Housing Market Search Behaviour
    and Expected Utility Theorem, *Environment and Planning, A,
    14,* 681-698, 717-737.
Clarke, G.P. (1984) Retail Centre Usage and Structure:
    empirical, theoretical and dynamic explorations, PhD
    Thesis, School of Geography, University of Leeds, Leeds.
Clarke, G.P., Clarke, M. (1984) EQUILIB: a computer program to
    solve the equilibrium version of the production-constrained
    spatial-interaction model, Computer Manual 24, School of
    Geography, University of Leeds, Leeds.
Clarke, G.P., Clarke, M., Wilson, A.G. (1985) Multiple Bifurca-
    tion Effects with a Logistic Attractiveness Function in
    the Supply Side of a Service System, *Sistemi Urbani, 7,*
    43-76.
Clarke, M. (1981-A) A First-principles Approach to Modelling
    Socio-economic Interdependence Using Micro-simulation,
    Computers, Environment and Urban Systems, 6, 211-227.
Clarke, M. (1981-B) A Note on the Stability of Equilibrium
    Solutions of Production-constrained Spatial-interaction
    Models, *Environment and Planning, A, 13,* 601-604.
Clarke, M. (1984) Integrating Dynamical Models of Urban
    Structure and Activities, PhD Thesis, School of Geography,
    University of Leeds, Leeds.
Clarke, M., Wilson, A.G. (1983-A) Exploring the Dynamics of
    Urban Housing Structure: a 56 parameter residential loca-
    tion and housing model, Working Paper 363, School of
    Geography, University of Leeds, Leeds.
Clarke, M., Wilson, A.G. (1983-B) The Dynamics of Urban Spatial
    Structure: progress and problems, *Journal of Regional
    Science, 21,* 1-18.
Clarke, M., Wilson, A.G. (1984-A) A Model-based Approach to
    Planning in the National Health Service, *Environment and
    Planning, B, 12,* 287-302.
Clarke, M., Wilson, A.G. (1984-B) Modelling for Health Service
    Planning: an outline and an example, in Clarke, M. (ed.)
    Planning and Analysis in Health Care Systems, Pion,
    London, 22-56.
Clarke, M., Wilson, A.G. (1984-C) Models for Health Care Plan-
    ning: the case of the Piemonte region, Working Paper 36,
    IRES, Turin, Italy.
Clarke, M., Wilson, A.G. (1984-D) The Analysis of Bifurcation
    Phenomena Associated with the Evolution of Urban Spatial
    Structure, in Hazewinkel, M., Jurkovic, M., Paelink, J.H.P.
    (eds.) *Bifurcation Analysis. Principles, Applications and
    Synthesis,* Reidel, Dordrecht, 67-99.

Coelho, J.D. (1979) A Locational Surplus Maximization Model of
    Land Use Plan Design, in Breheny, M.J. (ed.) *Developments
    in Urban and Regional Analysis*, London Papers in Regional
    Science, *10*, Pion, London, 48-60.
Coelho, J.D., Williams, H.C.W.L. (1978) On the Design of Land
    Use Plans through Locational Surplus Maximization, *Papers*,
    Regional Science Association, *40*, 71-85.
Coelho, J.D., Williams, H.C.W.L., Wilson, A.G. (1978) Entropy
    Maximising Submodels within Overall Mathematical Program-
    ming Frameworks: a correction, *Geographical Analysis*, *10*,
    195-201.
Coelho, J.D., Wilson, A.G. (1976) The Optimum Location and Size
    of Shopping Centres, *Regional Studies*, *10*, 413-421.
Coelho, J.D., Wilson, A.G. (1977) An Equivalence Theorem to
    Integrate Entropy Maximising Submodels within Overall
    Mathematical Programming Frameworks, *Geographical
    Analysis*, *9*, 160-173.
Curry, L. (1984) Inefficiency of Spatial Prices Using the
    Thermodynamic Formulation, *Environment and Planning*, *A*,
    16, 5-16.
Curry, L., Sheppard, E.S. (1982) Spatial Price Equilibria,
    Geographical Analysis, *14*, 279-304.
Daganzo, C.F., Sheffi, Y. (1977) On Stochastic Models of Traffic
    Assignment, *Transportation Science*, *11*, 253-274.
Dantzig, G.B. (1951) Application of the Simplex Method to a
    Transportation Problem, in Koopmans, T.C. (ed.) *Activity
    Analysis of Production and Allocation*, Wiley, New York,
    359-373.
Debreu, G. (1959) *Theory of Value*, Wiley, New York.
De Leeuw, F., Struyk, R.M. (1975) The Web of Urban Housing:
    analyzing policy with a simulation model, The Urban
    Institute, Washington, D.C.
Dendrinos, D., Haag, G. (1984) Toward a Stochastic Dynamical
    Theory of Location. Empirical Evidence, *Geographical
    Analysis*, *15*, 287-300.
Domencich, T., McFadden, D. (1975) *Urban Travel Demand: a
    behavioural analysis*, North Holland, Amsterdam.
Dwass, M. (1964) Extremal Processes, *Annals of Mathematical
    Statistics*, *35*, 1718-1725.
Eaton, B., Watts, M. (1977) Wage Dispersion, Job Vacancies and
    Job Search in Equilibrium, *Econometrica*, *44*, 23-35.
Ellickson, B. (1981) An Alternative Test of the Hedonic Theory
    of Housing Markets, *Journal of Urban Economics*, *9*, 56-79.
Erlander, S., Nguyen, S., Stewart, N.F. (1979) On the Calibra-
    tion of the Combined Distribution-assignment Model,
    Transportation Research, *B*, *13*, 259-267.
Erlenkotter, D. (1977) Facility Location with Price-sensitive
    Demands in Private, Public and Quasi-public, *Management
    Science*, *24*, 378-386.

Evans, S.P. (1973) A Relationship between the Gravity Model for Trip Distribution and the Transportation Problem in Linear Programming, *Transportation Research, 7, 39-61.*

Evans, S.P. (1976) Derivation and Analysis of Some Models for Combining Trip Distribution and Assignment, *Transportation Research, 10, 37-57.*

Fair, R.C., Jaffee, D.M. (1972) Methods of Estimation for Markets in Disequilibrium, *Econometrica, 40, 497-514.*

Feldman, A. (1981) *Applied Welfare Economics and Social Choice Theory,* Prentice Hall, New York.

Florian, M. (1977) A Traffic Equilibrium Model of Travel by Car and Public Transport Modes, *Transportation Science, 11, 166-179.*

Florian, M., Gaudry, M. (1980) Special Issue on Transportation Supply Models, *Transportation Research, B, 14, 1-220.*

Florian, M., Gaudry, M. (1983) Transportation Systems Analysis: illustrations and extensions of a conceptual framework, *Transportation Research, B, 17, 147-153.*

Ford, L.R.Jr., Fulkerson, D.R. (1956) Solving the Transportation Problem, RAND Report RM-1736, RAND Corporation, Santa Monica, Calif.

Forrester, J. (1969) *Urban Dynamics,* MIT Press, Cambridge, Mass.

Fotheringham, A.S. (1983-A) A New Set of Spatial Interaction Models: the theory of competing destinations, *Environment and Planning, A, 15, 15-36.*

Fotheringham, A.S. (1983-B) Some Theoretical Aspects of Destination Choice and their Relevance to Production-constrained Gravity Models, *Environment and Planning, A, 15, 1121-1132.*

Fotheringham, A.S. (1984) Modelling Discontinuous Change in Retail Systems: extensions of the Harris-Wilson framework with results from a simulated urban retailing system. Paper presented at the Annual Conference, Institute of British Geographers, Leeds.

Frank, M., Wolfe, P. (1956) An Algorithm for Quadratic Programming, *Naval Research Logistics Quarterly, 3, 95-110.*

Fujita, M. (1976) Spatial Patterns of Urban Growth: optimum and market, *Journal of Urban Economics, 3, 209-241.*

Galambos, J. (1978) *The Asymptotic Theory of Extreme Order Statistics,* Wiley, New York.

Gale, D., Nikaido, H. (1965) The Jacobian Matrix and the Global Univalence of Mappings, *Mathematische Annalen, 159, 81-93.*

Gass, S.I. (1958) *Linear Programming: methods and applications,* McGraw-Hill, New York.

Gaver, D.P. (1976) Random Record Models, *Journal of Applied Probability, 13, 538-547.*

Gibson, M., Pullen, M. (1972) Retail Turnover in the East Midlands: a regional application of a gravity model, *Regional Studies, 6, 183-196.*

Glickmann, N. (1979) *Econometric Analysis of Regional Systems,* Academic Press, New York.

Haag, G. (1978) Transition Factor Method for Discrete Master
    Equations and Application to Chemical Reactions,
    Zeitschrift für Physik, B, 29, 153-159.
Haag, G., Dendrinos, D. (1983) Toward a Stochastic Dynamical
    Theory of Location. A Non-linear Migration Process,
    Geographical Analysis, 15, 269-286.
Haag, G., Hänggi, P. (1979) Exact Solution of Discrete Master
    Equations in Terms of Continued Fractions, *Zeitschrift
    für Physik, B, 34,* 411-417.
Haag, G., Weidlich, W. (1984) A Stochastic Theory of Inter-
    regional Migration, *Geographical Analysis, 16,* 331-357.
Haag, G., Weidlich, W., Alber, P. (1977) Approximation Methods
    for Stationary Master Equations, *Zeitschrift für Physik,
    B, 26,* 207-215.
Hagerstrand, T. (1970) What About People in Regional Science?
    Papers, Regional Science Association, 24, 7-21.
Hahn, F. (1958) Gross Substitutes and the Dynamic Stability of
    General Equilibrium, *Econometrica, 26,* 169-170.
Haken, H. (1975) Cooperative Phenomena in Systems far from
    Thermal Equilibrium and in Nonphysical Systems, *Review of
    Modern Physics, 47,* 67-168.
Haken, H. (1977) *Synergetics, An Introduction,* 2nd ed.,
    Springer-series in Synergetics, 1, Springer, Berlin.
Haken, H. (1983) *Advanced Synergetics, Instability Hierarchies
    of Self-organizing Systems and Devices, Springer-series
    in Synergetics, 20,* Springer, Berlin.
Hänggi, P., Haag, G. (1980) Continued Fraction Solutions of
    Discrete Master Equations not Obeying Detailed Balance,
    Zeitschrift für Physik, B, 39, 269-279.
Harris, B., Choukroun, J.M., Wilson, A.G. (1982) Economies of
    Scale and the Existence of Supply-side Equilibria in a
    Production-constrained Spatial-interaction model,
    Environment and Planning, A, 14, 813-827.
Harris, B., Wilson, A.G. (1978) Equilibrium Values and Dynamics
    of Attractiveness Terms in Production-constrained Spatial-
    interaction Models, *Environment and Planning, A, 10,* 371-
    388.
Hay, A.M., Johnston, R.J. (1979) Search and the Choice of
    Shopping Centre: two models of variability in destination
    selection, *Environment and Planning, A, 11,* 791-804.
Hearn, D.W., Ribera, J. (1981) Convergence of the Frank-Wolfe
    Method for Certain Bounded Variable Traffic Assignment
    Problems, *Transportation Research, B, 15,* 437-442.
Helms, B.P., Clark, R.M. (1971) Locational Model for Solid
    Waste Management, *American Society of Civil Engineers,
    Journal of the Urban Planning and Development Division,
    97,* 1-13.
Herbert, J.C., Stevens, B.H. (1960) A Model for the Distribu-
    tion of Residential Activity in Urban Areas, *Journal of
    Regional Science, 2,* 21-36.

Hill, D.M. (1965) A Growth Allocation Model for the Boston Region, *Journal of the America Institute of Planners, 31,* 111-120.

Hitchcock, F.L. (1941) Distribution of a Product from Several Sources to Numerous Localities, *Journal of Mathematical Physics, 20.*

Hogg, J.M. (1968) The Siting of Fire Stations, *Operational Research Quarterly, 3,* 275-287.

Huff, D.L. (1964) Defining and Estimating a Trading Area, *Journal of Marketing, 28,* 4-38.

Huff, D.L. (1966) A Programmed Solution for Approximating an Optimal Retail Location, *Land Economics, 42,* 293-303.

Irwin, S., Wilson, A.G. (1985) Modelling School Systems - A Framework for Planning for Falling Rolls, Working Paper 412, School of Geography, University of Leeds, Leeds.

Jara-Diaz, S.R., Friesz, T.L. (1982) Measuring the Benefits Derived from a Transportation Investment, *Transportation Research, B, 16,* 57-77.

Jefferson, T.R., Scott, C.H. (1979) The Analysis of Entropy Models with Equality and Inequality Constraints, *Transportation Research, B, 13,* 123-132.

Kaashoek, J.F., Vorst, A.C.F. (1984) The Cusp Catastrophe in the Urban Retail Model, *Environment and Planning, A, 16,* 851-862.

Kain, J.F., Apgar, W.C.Jr. (1976) Simulation of the Market Effects of Housing Allowances, Vol. I: description of the NBER urban simulation model, Report R77-2, Harvard University, Cambridge, Mass.

Kain, J.F., Apgar, W.C.Jr. (1977) Simulation of the Market Effects of Housing Allowances, Vol. II: baseline and policy simulations for Pittsburgh and Chicago, Report R77-3, Harvard University, Cambridge, Mass.

Koopmans, T.C. (1949) Optimum Utilization of the Transport System, *Econometrica, 17,* 136-149.

Koppelman, F.S., Hansen, J.R. (1978) Destination Choice Behaviour for Non-grocery Shopping Trips, *Transportation Research Record, 673,* 157-165.

Kuhn, H.W. (1982) Complementary Problems: an eclectic view, in Larsson, R., Smeds, P. (eds.) *Nordic Symposium on Linear Complementarity Problems and Related Areas,* Linköping Institute of Technology, Linköping.

Lakshmanan, T.R., Hansen, W.G. (1965) A Retail Market Potential Model, *Journal of the American Institute of Planners, 31,* 134-143.

Lamperti, J. (1964) On Extreme Order Statistics, *Annals of Mathematical Statistics, 35,* 1726-1737.

Leonardi, G. (1978) Optimum Facility Location by Accessibility Maximising, *Environment and Planning, A, 10,* 1287-1305

Leonardi, G. (1981-A) A Unifying Framework for Public Facility Location Problems, Part 1, A Critical Review and Some Unsolved Problems, *Environment and Planning, A, 13,* 1001-1028.

402

Leonardi, G. (1981-B) A Unifying Framework for Public Facility Location Problems, Part 2, Some New Models and Extensions, *Environment and Planning, A, 13,* 1085-1108.

Leonardi, G. (1983-A) The Use of Random-utility Theory in Building Location-allocation Models, in Thisse, J.F., Zoller, H.G. (eds.) *Location Analysis of Public Facilities,* North Holland, Amsterdam, 357-383.

Leonardi, G. (1983-B) Transient and Asymptotic Behaviour of a Random-utility Based Stochastic Search Process in Continuous Space and Time, WP-83-108, International Institute for Applied Systems Analysis, Laxenburg, Austria.

Leonardi, G. (1984) The Structure of Random Utility Models in the Light of the Asymptotic Theory of Extremes, in Florian, M. (ed.) *Transportation Planning Models,* North Holland, Amsterdam, 107-133.

Leonardi, G. (1985-A) Asymptotic Approximations of the Assignment Model with Stochastic Heterogeneity in the Matching Utilities, *Environment and Planning, A, 17,* 1303-1314.

Leonardi, G. (1985-B) Equivalenza asintotica tra la teoria delle utilita casuali e la massimizzazione dell'entropia, in Reggiani, A. (ed.) *Territorio e Trasporti,* Angeli, Milano, 29-66.

Leonardi, G. (1987) The Choice-theoretic Approach: population mobility as an example, in Bertuglia, C.S., Leonardi, G., Occelli, S., Rabino, G.A., Tadei, R., Wilson, A.G. (eds.) *Urban Systems: contemporary approaches to modelling,* Croom Helm, London, 136-188.

Leontief, W. (1957) *The Structure of the American Economy, 1919-1939,* Oxford University Press, New York.

Lerman, S.R., Kern, C.R. (1983) Hedonic Theory, Bid Rents and Willingness to Pay: some extensions of Ellickson's results, *Journal of Urban Economics, 13,* 358-363.

Lippman, S., McCall, J. (1976) The Economics of Job Search: a survey, *Economic Inquiry, 34,* 155-189.

Lombardo, S.R., Rabino, G.A. (1983) Non-linear Dynamic Models for Spatial Interaction: the results of some empirical experiments, Paper presented at the 23rd European Congress of the Regional Science Association, Poitiers, France.

Lowry, I.S. (1964) *A Model of Metropolis,* RM-4035-RC, RAND Corporation, Santa Monica, Calif.

Manheim, M.L. (1980) Understanding "Supply" in Transportation Systems, *Transportation Research, A, 14,* 119-135.

Marsden, J.E., McCracken, M. (1976) The Hopf Bifurcation and its Applications, *Applied Mathematical Science, 19,* Springer, Berlin.

May, R.M. (1976) Simple Mathematical Models with Very Complicated Dynamics, *Nature, 261,* 459-467.

Mayhew, L.D., Leonardi, G. (1982) Equity, Efficiency and Accessibility in Urban and Regional Health-care Systems, *Environment and Planning, A, 14,* 1479-1507.

403

McCarthy, P.S. (1980) A Study of the Importance of Generalized Attributes in Shopping Choice Behaviour, *Environment and Planning, A, 12,* 1269-1286.

McFadden, D. (1974) Conditional Logit Analysis of Qualitative Choice Behaviour, in Zarembka, P. (ed.) *Frontiers in Econometrics,* Academic Press, New York, 105-142.

McFadden, D. (1978) Modelling the Choice of Residential Location, in Karlqvist, A., Lundqvist, L., Snickars, F., Weibull, J.W. (eds.) *Spatial Interaction Theory and Planning Models,* North Holland, Amsterdam, 75-96.

McKenzie, L.W. (1960) Matrices with Dominant Diagonals and Economic Theory, *Proceedings of a Symposium on Mathematical Methods in the Social Sciences,* Stanford University Press, Palo Alto, Calif., 277-292.

Mensch, G. (1979) *Stalemate in Technology,* Ballinger, Cambridge.

Mensch, G., Weidlich, W., Haag, G. (1986) *The Schumpeter Clock,* Ballinger, Cambridge.

Miller, E.J., Lerman, S.R. (1979) A Model of Retail Location, Scale and Intensity, *Environment and Planning, A, 11,* 177-192.

Miller, E.J., Lerman, S.R. (1981) Disaggregate Modelling and Decisions of Retail Firms: a case study of clothing retailers, *Environment and Planning, A, 13,* 729-746.

Mills, E.S. (1967) An Aggregative Model of Resource Allocation in a Metropolitan Area, *American Economic Review, 57,* 197-210.

Mills, E.S. (1972-A) Markets and Efficient Resource Allocation in Urban Areas, *Swedish Journal of Economics, 1,* 100-113.

Mills, E.S. (1972-B) *Studies in the Structure of the Urban Economy,* Johns Hopkins Press, Baltimore.

Morrill, R.L., Earickson, R.J. (1969) Locational Efficiency of Chicago Hospitals: an experimental model, *Health Services Research, 4,* 128-141.

Morrill, R.L., Kelley, M.B. (1970) The Simulation of Hospital Use and the Estimation of Locational Efficiency, *Geographical Analysis, 2,* 283-300.

Muth, R.F. (1969) *Cities and Housing,* Chicago University Press, Chicago.

NEDO (1970) *Urban Models in Shopping Studies,* National Economic Development Office, London.

Negishi, T. (1962) The Stability of the Competitive Equilibrium: a survey article, *Econometrica, 30,* 635-669.

Neuburger, H.L.I. (1971) User Benefit in the Evaluation of Transport and Land Use Plans, *Journal of Transport Economics and Policy, 5,* 52-75.

Nijkamp, P., Schubert, U. (1985) Structural Change in Urban Systems, *Sistemi Urbani, 7,* 147-168.

Nystuen, J.D., Dacey, M.F. (1961) A Graph Theory Interpretation of Nodal Regions, *Papers, Regional Science Association, 7,* 29-42.

O'Connor, T., Parker, A.J. (1982) Variations in the Retail
    Price of Chemists' Goods: testing spatial and structural
    hypotheses and the "sample of one", *Environment and Plan-
    ning, A, 11,* 1509-1522.
Openshaw, S. (1975) *Some Theoretical and Applied Aspects of
    Spatial Interaction Shopping Models,* CATMOG 4, Geo-
    Abstracts, Norwich.
Parker, A.J. (1979) A Review and Comparative Analysis of Retail
    Grocery Price Variations, *Environment and Planning, A, 11,*
    1267-1288.
Parkhurst, K.C., Roe, P.G. (1978) An Empirical Study of Two
    Shopping Models, *Regional Studies, 12,* 727-748.
Phiri, P.H. (1980) Calculation of the Equilibrium Configuration
    of Shopping Facility Sizes, *Environment and Planning, A,
    12,* 983-1000.
Poston, T., Wilson, A.G. (1977) Facility Size Versus Distance
    Travelled: urban services and the fold catastrophe,
    Environment and Planning, A, 9, 681-686.
Pumain, D., Saint-Julien, T., Sanders, L. (1984) Dynamics of
    Spatial Structure in French Urban Agglomerations, *Papers,
    Regional Science Association, 55,* 71-82.
Quirk, J., Ruppert, R. (1965) Qualitative Economics and the
    Stability of Equilibrium, *Review of Economic Studies, 32,*
    311-326.
Quirk, J., Saposnik, R. (1960) *General Equilibrium and Welfare
    Economics,* McGraw-Hill, New York.
Recker, W.W., Kostynuik, J. (1978) Factors Influencing Destina-
    tion Choice for the Urban Grocery Shopping Trip, *Trans-
    portation, 7,* 19-33.
Rees, P.H., Wilson, A.G. (1977) *Spatial Population Analysis,*
    Edward Arnold, London; Academic Press, New York.
Rijk, F.J.A., Vorst, A.C.F. (1983-A) Equilibrium Points in an
    Urban Retail Model and their Connection with Dynamical
    Systems, *Regional Science and Urban Economics, 13,* 383-
    399.
Rijk, F.J.A., Vorst, A.C.F. (1983-B) On the Uniqueness and
    Existence of Equilibrium Points in an Urban Retail Model,
    Environment and Planning, A, 15, 475-482.
Rogers, A. (1975) *Introduction to Multiregional Mathematical
    Demography,* Wiley, New York.
Rogerson, P. (1983) The Effects of Job Search and Competition
    on Unemployment and Vacancies in Regional Labour Markets,
    in Griffith, D.A., Lea, A.C. (eds.) *Evolving Geographical
    Structures,* Nijhoff, The Hague, 349-371.
Roy, J.R., Brotchie, J.F. (1984) Some Supply and Demand Con-
    siderations in Urban Spatial Interaction Models, *Environ-
    ment and Planning, A, 16,* 1137-1147.
Roy, J.R., Johansson, B. (1984) On Planning and Forecasting
    the Location of Retail and Service Activity, *Regional
    Science and Urban Economics, 14,* 433-452.

Sattinger, D.H. (1973) *Topics in Stability and Bifurcation Theory, Lecture Notes in Mathematics, 309,* Springer, Berlin.

Scarf, H. (1960) Some Examples of Global Instability of the Competitive Equilibrium, *Econometrica, 1,* 157-72.

Schultz, G.P. (1969) Facility Planning for a Public Service System: domestic solid waste collection, *Journal of Regional Science, 2,* 291-307.

Schweizer, U., Varaiya, P., Hartwick, J. (1976) General Equilibrium and Location Theory, *Journal of Urban Economics, 3,* 285-303.

Senior, M.L., Wilson, A.G. (1974) Exploration and Synthesis of Linear Programming and Spatial Interaction Models of Residential Location, *Geographical Analysis, 7,* 209-38.

Sheppard, E.S. (1981) Public Facility Location with Elastic Demand. Users' Benefits and Redistribution Issues, *Sistemi Urbani, 3,* 435-54.

Southworth, F. (1978) A Highly Disaggregated Modal-split Model - some tests, *Environment and Planning, A, 10,* 795-812.

Southworth, F. (1979) Spatial Structure and Parameter Disaggregation in Trip Distribution Models, *Regional Studies, 13,* 381-94.

Spencer, A.H. (1980) Cognition and Shopping Centre Choice: a multidimension scaling approach, *Environment and Planning, A, 12,* 1,235-51.

Steenbrink, P.A. (1947) *Optimization of Transport Networks,* Wiley, Chichester.

Stetzer, F. (1976) Parameter Estimation for the Constrained Gravity Model: a comparison of six methods, *Environment and Planning, A, 8,* 673-83.

Stratonovich, R.L. (1967) *Topics in the Theory of Random Noise,* Vols. 1 and 2, Gordon and Breach, New York.

Teitz, M.B. (1968) Towards a Theory of Urban Public Facility Location, *Papers, Regional Science Association, 21,* 35-51.

Thünen, von J.H. (1826) *Der Isolierte Staat in Beziehung auf Landwirtschaft und Nationa-Ökonomie,* Hamburg (3rd Vol., and new edn., 1963); English translation (1966) *The Isolated State,* Pergamon Press, New York.

Timmermans, H.J.P. (1981) Multiattribute Shopping Models and Ridge Regression Analysis, *Environment and Planning, A, 13,* 43-56.

Tobler, W.R. (1979) Estimation of Attractivities from Interaction, *Environment and Planning, A, 11,* 121-7.

Uzawa, H. (1961) The Stability of Dynamic Processes, *Econometrica, 29,* 617-31.

Varian, H.R. (1978) *Microeconomic Analysis,* W.W. Norton & Company Inc., New York.

Vliet, van D. (1976-A) Road Assignment I: principles and parameters of model formulation, *Transportation Research, 10,* 137-43.

Vliet, van D. (1976-B) Road Assignment II: the GLTS model, *Transportation Research, 10,* 145-150.

Vliet, van D. (1976-C) Road Assignment III: comparative tests of stochastic methods, *Transportation Research, 10,* 151-157.

Wagner, J.L., Falkson, L.M. (1975) The Optimal Model Location of Public Facilities with Price-sensitive Demand, *Geographical Analysis, 7,* 69-83.

Weidlich, W., Haag, G. (1983) *Concepts and Models of a Quantitative Sociology. The Dynamics of Interacting Population, Springer-series in Synergetics, 14,* Springer, Berlin.

Weidlich, W., Haag, G. (1985) A Dynamic Phase Transition Model for Spatial Agglomeration Processes, *Journal of Regional Science, 27,* 529-569.

White, R.W. (1977) Dynamic Central Place Theory: results of a simulation approach, *Geographical Analysis, 9,* 226-243.

Williams, H.C.W.L. (1977) On the Formation of Travel Demand, Models and Economic Measures of User Benefit, *Environment and Planning, A, 9,* 285-344.

Williams, H.C.W.L., Senior, M.L. (1977) Model Based Transport Assessment 2: removing fundamental inconsistencies from the models, *Traffic Engineering and Control, 18,* 464-469.

Wilson, A.G. (1967) A Statistical Theory of Spatial Distribution Models, *Transportation Research, 1,* 253-269.

Wilson, A.G. (1970) *Entropy in Urban and Regional Modelling,* Pion, London.

Wilson, A.G. (1972) Some Recent Development in Micro-economic Approaches to Modelling Household Behaviour, with Special Reference to Spatio-temporal Organisation, in Wilson, A.G. (ed.) *Papers in Urban and Regional Analysis,* Pion, London, 216-236.

Wilson, A.G. (1974) *Urban and Regional Models in Geography and Planning,* Wiley, Chichester, Sussex.

Wilson, A.G. (1979) Equilibrium and Transport Systems Dynamics, in Hensher, D.A., Stopher, P.R. (eds.) *Behavioural Travel Modelling,* Croom Helm, London, 164-186.

Wilson, A.G. (1981-A) *Catastrophe Theory and Bifurcation: applications to urban and regional systems,* Croom Helm, London.

Wilson, A.G. (1981-B) Some New Sources of Instability and Oscillation in Dynamic Models of Shopping Centres and Other Urban Structures, *Sistemi Urbani, 3,* 391-401.

Wilson, A.G. (1983-A) A Generalised and Unified Approach to the Modelling of Service-supply Structures, Working Paper 352, School of Geography, University of Leeds, Leeds.

Wilson, A.G. (1983-B) Location Theory: a unified approach, Working Paper 355, School of Geography, University of Leeds, Leeds.

Wilson, A.G. (1983-C) Transport and the Evolution of Urban Spatial Structures, in *Atti delle Giornate di Lavoro AIRO 1983,* Guida, Naples, 7-27.

Wilson, A.G. (1984-A) Dynamic Models for Person Transportation and their Relationship to Urban Structure and Change, in Predisposizione di un modello dinamico per il trasporto di persone, Report GEAS n. 3 for CNR, GEAS, Roma.

Wilson, A.G. (1984-B) Making Urban Models More Realistic: some strategies for future research, *Environment and Planning*, *A*, *16*, 1419-1432.

Wilson, A.G. (1984-C) Spatial Dynamics: classical problems, an integrated modelling approach and system performance, Working Paper 402, School of Geography, University of Leeds, Leeds.

Wilson, A.G. (1985) Structural Dynamics and Spatial Analysis: from equilibrium balancing models to extended economic models for both perfect and imperfect markets, Working Paper 431, School of Geography, University of Leeds, Leeds.

Wilson, A.G., Birkin, M. (1983) Industrial Location Theory: explorations of a new approach, Working Paper 361, School of Geography, University of Leeds, Leeds.

Wilson, A.G., Birkin, M. (1985) Dynamic Model of Agricultural Location in a Spatial Interaction Framework, Working Paper 399, School of Geography, University of Leeds, Leeds.

Wilson, A.G., Clarke, M. (1979) Some Illustrations of Catastrophe Theory Applied to Urban Retailing Structures, in Breheny, M. (ed.) *Developments in Urban and Regional Analysis*, *London Papers in Regional Science*, *10*, Pion, London, 5-27.

Wilson, A.G., Coelho, J.D., Macgill, S.M., Williams, H.C.W.L. (1981) *Optimization in Locational and Transport Analysis*, Wiley, Chichester.

Wilson, A.G., Crouchley, R. (1984) The Optimum Sizes and Locations of Schools, Working Paper 369, School of Geography, University of Leeds, Leeds.

Wilson, A.G., Oulton, M.J. (1976) A New Representation of the Urban System for Modelling and for the Study of Micro-level Interdependence, *Area*, *8*, 146-254.

Wilson, A.G., Senior, M.L. (1974) Some Relationships between Entropy Maximising Models, Mathematical Programming Models and their Duals, *Journal of Regional Science*, *14*, 207-215.

Wootton, H.J., Pick, G.W. (1967) A Model for Trips Generated by Households, *Journal of Transport Economics and Policy*, *1*, 137-153.

INDEX

411

416